SIXTH
EDITION

Sheffield Hallam University
Learning and IT Services
Collegiate Learning Centre
Collegiate Crescent Campus
Sheffield   S10 2BP

101 929 541 4

D0809963

Perspectives on Personality

Charles S. Carver
University of Miami

Michael F. Scheier
Carnegie Mellon University

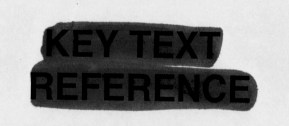

KEY TEXT
REFERENCE

PEARSON

Boston • New York • San Francisco
Mexico City • Montreal • Toronto • London • Madrid • Munich • Paris
Hong Kong • Singapore • Tokyo • Cape Town • Sydney

Sponsoring Editor: Michelle Limoges
Production Supervisor: Karen Mason
Marketing Manager: Karen Natale
Editorial-Production Service: Omegatype Typography, Inc.
Manufacturing Buyer: JoAnne Sweeney
Cover Administrator: Linda Knowles
Text Designer: Joyce Weston
Electronic Composition: Omegatype Typography, Inc.

For related titles and support materials, visit our online catalog at www.ablongman.com.

Copyright © 2008, 2004, 2000, 1996, 1988 Pearson Education, Inc.

All rights reserved. No part of the material protected by this copyright notice may be reproduced or utilized in any form or by any means, electronic or mechanical, including photocopying, recording, or by any information storage and retrieval system, without written permission from the copyright owner.

To obtain permission(s) to use material from this work, please submit a written request to Allyn and Bacon, Permissions Department, 75 Arlington Street, Boston, MA 02116, or fax your request to 617-848-7320.

Between the time website information is gathered and published, some sites may have closed. Also, the transcription of URLs can result in typographical errors. The publisher would appreciate notification of any problem with URLs so that they may be corrected in subsequent editions.

Library of Congress Cataloging-in-Publication Data

Carver, Charles S.
    Perspectives on personality / Charles S. Carver, Michael F. Scheier. — 6th ed.
        p. cm.
    Includes bibliographical references and indexes.
    ISBN-13: 978-0-205-52262-0 (hardcover)
    ISBN-10: 0-205-52262-9 (hardcover)
    1. Personality—Textbook.   I. Scheier, Michael. II. Title.
    BF698.C22 2008
    155.2—dc22

                                                    2007008463

Printed in the United States of America

10 9 8 7 6 5 4 3 2 1   11 10 09 08 07

Photo credits are on page 539, which constitutes a continuation of the copyright page.

SHEFFIELD HALLAM UNIVERSITY
COLLEGIATE LEARNING CENTRE
155.2
CA

To Linda Cahan
For her boundless enthusiasm,
energy, devotion, and courage
CSC

To Karen Matthews
For her wisdom, support, and love
through the good times, and
also the hard times
MFS

Contents

Part Seven: The Phenomenological Perspective: Major Themes and Underlying Assumptions   319

14 HUMANISTIC PSYCHOLOGY: SELF-ACTUALIZATION AND SELF-DETERMINATION   321

Part Nine: Personality in Perspective   423

Preface

PERSPECTIVES ON PERSONALITY, Sixth Edition, examines one of the most engaging and mysterious topics in all of life: human personality. As the book's title implies, there are many perspectives on personality, many ways to think about human nature. This book describes a range of viewpoints that are held by personality psychologists today.

WHAT'S THE SAME IN THIS EDITION?

As in the five earlier editions, the book's content reflects two of our strongly held beliefs. The first is that *ideas* are the most important part of a first course on personality. For this reason, we stress concepts throughout the book. Our first priority has been to present as clearly as we can the ideas that form each theoretical viewpoint.

The second belief is that *research* is important in personality psychology. Ideas and intuitions are valuable, but an idea shouldn't lie around too long before someone checks to see whether it actually works. For this reason, along with each theory, we discuss research that bears on the theory. This emphasis on the role of research stresses the fact that personality psychology is a living, dynamic process of ongoing scientific exploration.

As in previous editions, we present the theories in groups, which we've labeled *perspectives*. Each group of theories depends on a particular sort of orienting viewpoint, an angle from which the theorists proceeded. Within a given perspective, there often are several theories that differ from one another. In each case, however, the theories of a given perspective share fundamental assumptions about human nature.

Each perspective on personality is presented in a pair of chapters that are introduced by a prologue. The prologue provides an overview of that perspective's orienting assumptions and core themes. By starting with these orienting assumptions, you'll be placed right inside the thought processes of the theorists as you go on to read the chapters themselves. Each chapter concludes with a discussion of current problems within that theoretical viewpoint and our own best guess about its future prospects.

The perspectives are presented in an order that makes sense to us, but they can easily be read in other orders. Each theoretical section of the book is intended to stand on its own, with no assumptions about previous exposure to other parts of the book. Thus, instructors can move through the perspectives in whatever order they prefer.

As in the previous editions, the final chapter takes up the question of how the different viewpoints relate to each other. The main goal of this chapter is to tie together ideas from theories discussed separately in earlier chapters. A second goal is to consider the usefulness of blending theoretical viewpoints, treating theories as complementary to each other, rather than competing.

This edition also continues our use of the boxed feature "The Theorist and the Theory." These boxes focus on how the personal experiences of some of the theorists have influenced the forms their theories took. In several cases, theorists almost literally took events from their own lives as models of human events more generally and went on to derive entire theories from those personal experiences. Not all cases are quite this striking, but personal experiences do appear to have played a role in the development of several views of personality.

In this revision, we've continued to try very hard to make the content accessible. We use an informal, conversational style throughout to try to draw you into the ideas. We've also included examples of how the ideas can apply to your own life. We hope these qualities make the book engaging and enjoyable, as well as informative.

WHAT'S DIFFERENT ABOUT THIS EDITION?

This edition retains the prior structure (the same chapters, in the same perspectives). However, the content of this edition differs in several ways from that of the fifth edition. These changes reflect four years of rapid change in the continually evolving research literature of personality psychology. Updates have been made to every substantive chapter. In fact, we used information from over 300 new sources. Although updates have been made everywhere, several areas of change are major enough that we should note them explicitly.

First, work has continued at a rapid rate on the trait structure of personality and the implications of that structure for behavior. Most of this work is taking place within the framework of the five-factor model. This has resulted in considerable change in Chapter 4 (Types, Traits, and Interactionism). It has also resulted in the inclusion of additional material bearing on the five-factor model in several other chapters.

Second, *incredibly* rapid advances continue to be made in work concerning behavioral genetics, molecular genetics, temperament, neurotransmitters, and other biological processes and how they relate to aspects of personality. Theorists have approached these processes and their relations to personality from several directions. As a result, Chapters 6 and 7 have both undergone major updates, and Chapter 7 has been reorganized.

Another area of rapid expansion is work on adult attachment patterns and their implications for personality and social behavior. This explosion of work has resulted in major changes in the chapter dealing with psychosocial theories in the neoanalytic perspective (Chapter 11).

Rapid expansion has also taken place in work on self-actualization and related models. Research deriving from self-determination theory, terror management theory, and related theories has continued to be very active. The information produced by this work has re-invigorated interest in this view of personality, resulting in changes to Chapter 14.

Finally, we've included a good deal of new material in the chapters of the cognitive self-regulation perspective. This new material includes a discussion of connectionist models of cognitive processes and the related idea that cognition takes two somewhat distinct forms. We've also expanded information on contextual models of behavior and the process by which intentions are implemented.

Despite adding a great deal of new information, we've also been able again to shorten several of the book's longer chapters. We did this by simplifying and tightening the writing. We hope the result is more readable but with no loss of clarity.

For more information on *Perspectives on Personality,* Sixth Edition, consult its webpage at www.mypsychkit.com.

Acknowledgments

WE HAVE SEVERAL DIFFERENT KINDS of acknowledgments to make, in recognition of people who have been helpful and important in one way or another. First, we would like to express our thanks to some of those who played roles in the continuing evolution of the book. In particular, we are grateful to Mia Weinberger Biran, Miami University; Amy Corbett, Siena College; M. Brent Donnellan, Michigan State University; and Brian H. Stagner, Texas A&M University, who reviewed the previous edition and offered comments and suggestions.

A second set of acknowledgments is more diffuse in focus. These acknowledgments are not about this book, but rather about how we grew to be academic psychologists who were able to write a book at all. These acknowledgments pertain to the mentors and educators who inspired us, taught us, and opened doors of opportunity to us. These people include (alphabetically) Mark Bickhard, Arnie Buss, Kenneth Craik, David Glass, Lew Goldberg, Al Riley, and Bob Wicklund. We owe them a great debt of gratitude. Without their influence, this book (and, for that matter, our careers in psychology) would have been much less likely.

Each of us also has some individual acknowledgments:

• From Coral Gables, my thanks to those who've been part of my life during the past four years, particularly Linda Cahan, Sheri Johnson, Youngmee Kim, André Perwin, Rod Gillis, Mike Antoni, Jean-Philippe Laurenceau, and Rod Wellens. A special bow to Linda Cahan, whose Herculean efforts are presently being applied to getting well. Major thanks to Danny Garzon, who entered all 300 of the new references in this edition. I am unceasingly grateful to my family: Jeff, Allysen, Alexandra, and Julia; Carol; Nancy Lorey; all the Sherricks; and Mike, Karen, Meredith, and Jeremy. Finally, a very special thank you to my shag terrier, Calvin (www.psy.miami.edu/faculty/ccarver/CCdog.html), who continues to amaze me with his deep insights about life and his ability to sleep upside down.

• From Pittsburgh, thanks go first to my partner in life, Karen Matthews, and to our two children, Jeremy and Meredith. Thanks also to the following group of friends and colleagues: Chuck Carver, Sheldon Cohen, Ed Gerrard, Vicki Helgeson, David Klahr, Ken Kotovsky, Rich Schulz, and Jim Staszewski. I'd also like to express my gratitude to Ginger Placone, my administrative assistant, for her help in keeping my professional life somewhat organized and under control. Finally, I'd like to thank my project director, Suzanne Colvin. Her dedication and effort have made it possible to keep my research program moving forward in the face of many conflicting demands.

About the Authors

Charles S. Carver and **Michael F. Scheier** met in graduate school at the University of Texas at Austin, where they both earned Ph.D. degrees in personality psychology. After graduation, they took jobs at the University of Miami and Carnegie Mellon University, respectively, where they have remained throughout their careers. They've collaborated for over three decades in work that spans personality, social, motivational, clinical, and health psychology. In 1998, they received awards for Outstanding Scientific Contribution (Senior Level) from the Division of Health Psychology of the American Psychological Association. Mike was the 2003–2004 president of the Division of Health Psychology of the American Psychological Association and currently serves as department head at CMU. Chuck is currently editor of the *Journal of Personality and Social Psychology*'s section on *Personality Processes and Individual Differences*. Along with six editions of *Perspectives on Personality,* the authors have published two books on self-regulation (the more recent titled *On the Self-Regulation of Behavior,* in 1998) and over 260 articles and chapters. Mike is an avid outdoorsman, hunter, and fisherman. Chuck keeps intending to take up painting but gets distracted by things that need fixing.

www.psy.miami.edu/faculty/ccarver
www.psy.cmu.edu/faculty/scheier/index.html

PART 1

An Introduction

What Is Personality Psychology?

CHAPTER 1

Sue met Rick in a philosophy class when both were sophomores. They started to date casually, and their relationship gradually deepened. Now, two years later, they're talking seriously of marriage. Sue describes Rick this way: "He's attractive to me in so many ways. He's good looking, and athletic, and smart, and he likes the same music I like. He knows how to do lots of things you don't expect a guy to know, like cooking. But the best part I don't even know how to describe, except to say he has a really wonderful personality."

EVERY NOW and then, someone surveys the qualities people value in a potential husband or wife. Most people want their mate to have a sense of humor, good looks, and a streak of romance. Almost always, though, a high priority is placed on the person's personality. Most people want someone who has a "good personality."

A good personality. What does that mean? If you were to describe a friend of yours who *does* have a good personality, what would you say? "Rick has a really wonderful personality...." But then what?

Describing someone's personality means trying to portray the essence of who the person is. It means crystallizing something from the things you know about the person. It means taking a large pile of information and reducing it to a smaller set of qualities. Personality is reflected partly in what people do and say. Partly, though, it's a matter of *how* they do what they do—the style that puts a unique stamp on their actions.

Defining Personality

Trying to describe someone's personality is an exercise in being a psychologist. Each of us is a psychologist part of the time, because we all spend part of our lives trying to understand what other people are like. When you think about how to describe someone and what reveals those qualities to you, you're doing informally what personality psychologists do more formally.

There's a little difference in focus between what you do in daily life and what personality psychologists do. Use of the word *personality* in everyday speech tends to focus on the *specific* personalities of specific persons (Rick, for instance). Psychologists are more likely to focus on personality as an abstraction. When psychologists use the word *personality,* they usually are referring to a conception of what everyone's personality is like.

What *is* personality, viewed that way? Psychologists have argued for a long time about exactly how to define personality. Many definitions have been offered, but none is universally accepted. Personality is, in fact, something of an elusive concept.

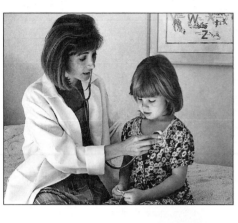

Personality produces consistencies in behavior across different contexts. Although this woman finds herself in different situations, her warm and caring nature comes through in all of them.

WHY USE PERSONALITY AS A CONCEPT?

In trying to define personality as a concept, a good way to start is to think about why the word is used. Understanding why it's used should help us decide what it means. When *you* use the word *personality,* why do you use it? What makes you use that word instead of another one?

One reason people use the word *personality* appears to be the desire to convey a sense of *consistency* or *continuity* about a person. There are several kinds of consistency. All of them evoke the concept of personality. You may see consistency in a person across time (Sue talked a lot when you first met her, and years later she still dominates conversations). You may see consistency across similar situations (André is very polite to waiters in restaurants and has been that way every time you've had dinner with him). You sometimes even see consistency across situations that are quite different from each other (Virginia tends to order people around—in stores, at work, even at *parties*). In each of these, there's the sense that it's undeniably the same person from one instance to another, because the person acts (or talks, or thinks, or feels) in consistent ways from time to time and from setting to setting. One reason for using the word *personality,* then, is to imply this consistency or continuity within the person.

A second reason people use the word *personality* is to convey the sense that whatever the person is doing (or thinking or feeling) *originates from within.* The idea that behavior comes from inside the person may seem so obvious that it hardly deserves mention, but not everyone sees it that way. Nonetheless, using the term *personality* conveys the sense of a causal force *within* the person, influencing how the person acts. There is, in fact, very good reason to assert that personality has very important behavioral consequences (Ozer & Benet-Martínez, 2006).

These two reasons for using the term *personality* come together when you try to predict and understand people's behavior (even your own). It can be important to predict behavior. When you choose a roommate for next year, you're predicting you'll get along well. When you tell a chronically late friend that the movie starts at 8:00 when it really starts at 8:30, you're predicting that this will get her to arrive more or less on time. An important contributor to these predictions is your view of the other person's personality.

The term *personality* is also used for another reason. It often conveys the sense that a few qualities can summarize what a person is like because they're so prominent in that person's behavior. Saying that Karen has a sociable personality implies that sociability stands out in her actions. Saying that Tanya has a hostile personality implies that hostility is a key quality in her. Taking note of the most prominent characteristics of a person brings to mind the concept of personality, because those characteristics seem to capture the person's personality.

This patchwork of reasons for using the term *personality* moves us closer to having a definition for it. That is, the word *personality* conveys a sense of consistency, internal causality, and distinctiveness. As it happens, these elements are in almost all definitions of personality.

A Working Definition

Here's one definition. We're not saying it's the "right" one, but we think it comes close. We've adapted it slightly from one written decades ago by Gordon Allport (1961): ***Personality*** *is a dynamic organization, inside the person, of psychophysical systems that create the person's characteristic patterns of behavior, thoughts, and feelings.*

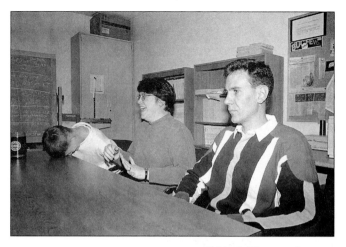

Individual differences in behavior and reactions are an important part of personality.

This definition makes several points:

- Personality isn't just an accumulation of bits and pieces; it has organization.
- Personality doesn't just lie there; it has *processes* of some sort.
- Personality is a *psychological* concept, but it's inextricably tied to the *physical* body.
- Personality is a *causal force* that helps determine how the person relates to the world.
- Personality shows up in individualized *patterns*—recurrences and consistencies.
- Personality is displayed not just in one way but in *many ways*—in behaviors, thoughts, and feelings.

This definition covers a lot. It points to several elements that should be part of any conceptualization of personality. As good as it is, though, it isn't perfect. Even this careful definition seems to let something about the concept slip through your fingers. This elusiveness is something that personality psychologists have struggled with for many years.

Two Fundamental Themes in Personality Psychology

From what we've said so far, two core themes stand out in thinking about personality. One of them is the existence of **individual differences.** Each person who ever lived is different from everyone else. No two personalities are quite alike—not even those of identical twins. Some people are happy, some are sad. Some people are sociable, some are shy and reclusive. As we said earlier, one reason to use the word *personality* in the first place is to capture central features of a person. This couldn't happen if the features didn't differ from one person to another. Thus, the notion of individual differences is key to everyday use of the term *personality*.

Individual differences are also important to the theorist who tries to understand personality. To be useful, any approach to personality has to have something to say about these differences. A really complete account of personality should consider where the differences come from. A complete account should also consider the questions of why the differences matter.

The other theme concerns what we'll call **intrapersonal functioning.** By this phrase, we mean the processes within the person that Allport (1961) referred to as a "dynamic organization" of systems. The idea here is that personality isn't like a rubber stamp that you pound onto each situation you enter. Instead, there are processes that go on inside you, leading you to act the way you do. Such processes create a sense of continuity within the person, even if the person acts differently in different circumstances. That is, the same processes are engaged, even if the results differ in different situations.

Here's an example. Some theorists believe that behavior is a product of motives. Motivational tendencies rise and fall as time passes and situations change. Which motive is strongest at any given time determines what the person does at that time. A person may work in isolation for four hours, then spend a couple of hours socializing, then go eat dinner, followed by some reading. The behaviors differ, but they all stem from motives within the person that vary in strength over the course of the day. This view of personality treats the motives as key variables. The processes by which motives vary in strength are some of the processes of intrapersonal functioning.

This is just one example of an intrapersonal process. It's not the only kind of process that has been argued for. Regardless of what processes are assumed, though, the idea of *process* is important. A complete account of personality should say what kinds of processes underlie personality and how and why they work.

Various approaches to personality place differing emphases on these two themes. Some approaches emphasize process and consist largely of a view of intrapersonal functioning, with little attention to differences among people. Other approaches treat individual uniqueness as the most important aspect of personality and are more vague about the processes underlying the uniqueness. These differing emphases contribute to the diversity among personality theories.

Why have we spent so much effort here describing what personality psychology is about? We've placed you in the role of a theorist in this discussion. Theorists have to keep in mind what aspects of human experience they want to understand. To understand the theories, you'll have to do that too.

Theory in Personality Psychology

Much of this book is a series of statements of theoretical principles. Because theories are so important, let's spend a little time on what they are, what they do, and how to evaluate them.

WHAT DO THEORIES DO?

What *is* a theory? A **theory** is a summary statement, a general principle or set of principles about a class of events. More informally, a theory is a set of ideas about how to think about that class of events. A theory can apply to a very specific class of events, or it can be broader. Some theories in psychology are about processes in a single nerve cell. Others concern complex behaviors, such as maintaining close relationships, playing chess, and living all of life.

Theories are used for two purposes (no matter what the theory is about). The first purpose is to *explain* the phenomena it addresses. A theory always provides a way to explain some things that are known to be true. For example, some biological personality theories hold that heredity influences personality. This idea provides a way to explain why children act like their parents in certain ways (things we know to be true).

Every theory about personality provides an account of at least some phenomena. This first purpose of the theory—explanation—is fundamental. Without giving an explanation for at least some of what's already known, a theory would be useless.

Theories also have a second purpose, though. A theory should suggest possibilities you don't yet know for sure are true. To put it differently, a theory should allow you to *predict new information*. A theory of personality should let you predict things you haven't thought to look for yet—maybe things *nobody* has thought to look for yet. For the psychologist, this is where much of the excitement lies.

Psychologists generally want to make predictions about large numbers of people, but the same principle holds when you make predictions in your own life. It's exciting to take an idea about personality and use it to predict how your roommate will react to a situation you haven't seen her in before. It's particularly exciting when your prediction turns out to be right!

The predictive aspect of theories is more subtle and more difficult than the explanatory aspect. The difficulty lies partly in the fact that most theories have a little ambiguity. This often makes it unclear exactly what the prediction should be. In fact, the broader the theory (the more things it has to account for), the more likely it is to be ambiguous. As you've seen, personality is a very broad concept. This forces theories of personality to be broad and complex. As a result, it's sometimes hard to use them to make predictions.

EVALUATING THEORIES: THE ROLE OF RESEARCH

How do psychologists decide whether a theory is any good? In describing the predictive function of theories, we've revealed a bias held by many personality psychologists: Theories should be *testable*, and they should be *tested*. It's important to find out whether a theory makes predictions that receive support.

We want to be quite clear about what we're saying here. Personality is so important in life that lots of people besides psychologists think about it. Theologians, philosophers, artists, poets, novelists, and songwriters have all written about personality, and many of them have had good insights about it. We don't mean to diminish the value of these insights. But are they enough?

People have different opinions on this question. Some believe that insight stands on its own and requires nothing more. Even some personality theorists have believed this. Sigmund Freud, who's often viewed as the father of personality psychology, wasn't much interested in whether his ideas were supported in research by others. He saw the insights as sufficient in themselves.

The view that dominates today's psychology, however, is that ideas—even brilliant ideas—have to be tested before they can be trusted. Too often, things that *seem* true turn out not to be true after all. Unfortunately, until you test them, you never know which ideas are brilliant and right and which are brilliant but wrong. Because of this, today's personality psychology is a scientific field, in which research counts for a lot. Studies of personality provide information about how accurate or useful a theory is. The studies either confirm or disconfirm predictions and thereby support or undermine the theory.

When theories are used to generate predictions for research, a continuous interplay arises (see Figure 1.1). If a theory makes predictions, the result is research—scientific studies—to test the predictions. Results often support the predictions. Sometimes, however, the result either fails to support the theory or supports it only partly. The outcome may suggest a limit on the theory—perhaps it

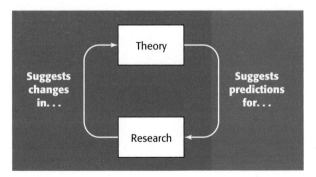

FIGURE 1.1

In a scientific approach to personality psychology, there is a continuous cycling between theory and research. Theory suggests predictions to be tested, and the results of studies suggest the need for new or modified theory.

predicts accurately under some conditions but not others. Such a finding leads to revision of the theory.

Once it's been revised, the theory must be tested again, because it's no longer quite the same theory as before. Its new elements must be examined for other predictions they might make. The cycle of prediction, testing, revision or refinement, and additional prediction and testing can be virtually never ending.

WHAT ELSE MAKES A THEORY GOOD?

An important basis for deciding whether a theory is good is whether it does what a theory's supposed to do: explain and predict. But that's not the only way people evaluate theories. There are several more criteria for why one theory may be preferable to another (Maddi, 1980).

One criterion is the breadth of the information behind the theory. Some theories are criticized because they're based heavily on the theorists' experiences conducting therapy. Other theories are criticized because they're based on studies of laboratory animals in highly artificial situations. Others are criticized because they rest largely on information from long sets of rating scales. None of these sources of information is bad in itself. But to base a theory on just one source of information weakens the theory.

A theory should also have the quality of **parsimony**. That is, it should include as few assumptions (or concepts) as possible. To put it differently, it should be as simple as possible. This criterion is important, but there's a danger in applying it too rigidly to personality theories. Knowledge about personality is far from complete. A theory that looks parsimonious today may not be able to account for something that will be discovered tomorrow. A theory that looks too complex today may be the *only* one that can handle tomorrow's discovery. Nevertheless, excess theoretical "baggage" is a cause for concern.

Another basis for evaluating theories is highly subjective. To put it bluntly, some theories "feel" better than others. Some theories you'll read about will fit your personal worldview better than others. You're not the only one who reacts this way. So do psychologists. There's even evidence that behavioral scientists prefer theories that fit their images of *themselves* (J. A. Johnson, Germer, Efran, & Overton, 1988). William James, an important figure in the early years of psychology, said people will prefer theories that "are most interesting, . . . appeal most urgently to our aesthetic, emotional, and active needs" (James, 1890, p. 312). Which theories feel best to you, then, depends partly on how you see the world. This shouldn't be the only criterion you use, but it can be an important one.

A theory should also be *stimulating* (Maddi, 1980). Being stimulating may mean provoking enthusiasm, interest, or excitement, but a theory can also be stimulating by provoking outrage and efforts to show how wrong it is. Provoking either kind of reaction is good, because it leads to efforts to test the theory. Theories so dull that they provoke no reaction at all are less useful, because no one bothers to study their implications.

Like a good work of art, a good theory should evoke some sort of reaction, either positive or negative, but not indifferent.

Perspectives on Personality

Next let's preview the theories about personality you will be reading about in this book. The theories range considerably in their starting points, which can make matters a little confusing. The starting point, in some sense, is always a vague conception of human nature. How often have you heard someone say "It's just human nature"? That phrase implies a view of what people are like. But what *is* human nature? *In what terms* should we think about people? Different theorists have had very different answers to these questions.

GROUPINGS AMONG THEORIES

Theories bearing on personality tend to form groups. Each group is characterized by a broad viewpoint on human nature. Each group's view of human nature differs (sometimes slightly, sometimes radically) from those of the other groups. Throughout the book we refer to each of these views as a *perspective* on personality.

Another term that means much the same as this is **metatheory.** A metatheory is a set of orienting assumptions *within which* theories are devised. These orienting assumptions are more general than are the assumptions of a particular theory. Metatheories are guides to what kinds of concepts are appropriate to use in theories. For example, the view that life involves competition among energy systems is a metatheory. There are lots of ways to think about energy systems, which could lead to many theories. But all of them would be grounded in the idea that life is about energy systems. Each perspective, or metatheory, thus provides a core metaphor for human nature. The metaphor becomes a guide for developing specific theories.

In this book we discuss seven perspectives on personality, each in a separate part. The perspectives are termed *dispositional, biological, psychoanalytic, neoanalytic, learning, phenomenological, and cognitive self-regulation.* Most of them include several theories. The theories of a given perspective sometimes differ substantially from one another, but they seem to share a set of orienting assumptions.

For each perspective, we start with a brief prologue that describes the basic themes and core assumptions of that section's metatheory. This is the metaphor of human nature that serves as a foundation for that view on personality. This prologue is followed by two content chapters, each covering a theoretical view of personality within that perspective. Each of these chapters ends with a statement on problems that type of theory faces, and our guesses about its prospects for future development. Here are brief overviews of the perspectives you'll be reading about.

The *dispositional perspective* (Part Two) is based on the idea that people have fairly stable qualities (dispositions) that are displayed across diverse settings but are deeply embedded in the person. Theorists of this perspective vary in how they view dispositions. Some emphasize that various dispositions exist, and don't say much about how they go about influencing behavior. Others focus on the idea that dispositions pertain to motive forces, which influence behavior. These two sets of ideas are described in separate chapters in the dispositional section.

Another way of thinking about human nature, the *biological perspective* (Part Three), emphasizes the fact that humans are biological creatures. One biological view resembles dispositional theories, but with a different emphasis. This approach says personality is genetically based: Dispositions are inherited. Indeed, some theorists take this idea a step further to suggest that many qualities of human behavior exist precisely because long ago they had evolutionary benefits. Another part of the biological perspective stems from the idea that personality reflects the workings of the body we inhabit. This kind of biological theory focuses on how the nervous system and hormones influence the kind of person you are.

The *psychoanalytic perspective* (Part Four) is a very different view of the world. It's based on the idea that personality is a set of internal forces that compete and conflict with one another. The focus of this perspective is on the dynamics of these forces (and the way they influence behavior). Human nature, from this viewpoint, involves a set of pressures inside the person that sometimes work with each other and sometimes are at war with each other. This perspective is the most tightly focused of all, in the sense that one theory dominates it—the theory of Sigmund Freud.

We've termed the next perspective *neoanalytic* (Part Five). In a sense, neoanalytic theories aren't really a distinct perspective: they all derive in one way or another from psychoanalytic theory (thus the name *neoanalytic*). One might argue that this makes them all variations on the psychoanalytic perspective. (Indeed, that's what we said in the first edition of this book.) On the other hand, the theories evolved in ways that make them very different from Freud's theory. For this reason, we believe they no longer share the worldview assumed in Freud's theory. The ideas that form the core of the neoanalytic perspective concern the development of the ego (the person's executive functions), and the importance of social relationships in personality.

The next perspective, the *learning perspective* (Part Six) begins with a view of human nature in which *change*, rather than constancy, is paramount. That is, the key quality of human nature, from this perspective, is that behavior changes systematically as a result of experience. Because there are several views of how learning takes place, several theories link learning to personality. Though they differ, they share a single metatheory, holding that a person's personality is the integrated sum of what the person has learned up till now.

Next comes the *phenomenological perspective* (Part Seven). The roots of this perspective trace to two ideas. The first is that everyone's subjective experience is important, valuable, meaningful—and unique. The second is that people tend naturally toward self-perfection and that all people can move themselves in that direction by exercising their free will to do so. The sense of self-determination is central to this view of human nature. A person's personality, in this view, is partly a matter of the uniqueness hidden within, and partly a matter of what the person chooses to make of that uniqueness.

We've labeled the final perspective *cognitive self-regulation* (Part Eight). This view holds that cognitive processes underlie personality. The nervous system is a huge matrix of neurons, sending messages to one another. Somehow the nervous system yields systematic sets of decisions. It uses information in organized, coherent, patterned ways, rather than randomly. In this view, these patterns give rise to personality. Another aspect of this perspective is that people are self-regulating systems, setting goals and progressing toward those goals. Again, there is an assumption of organization, coherence, patterning.

How Distinct Are the Perspectives?

The brief description we just gave makes it clear that different perspectives on personality start with different views of human nature. There are also links among the perspectives, however. For example, phenomenological theories emphasize the concept of *self* and the need for the self to grow and develop naturally. The concept of self isn't too different from the concept of *ego,* which is a focus of neoanalytic theories. Thus, there's a conceptual link between neoanalytic and phenomenological theories. As another example, George Kelly, a phenomenological theorist, developed ideas that were reflected in later cognitive theories. This creates a link between the phenomenological and cognitive self-regulation views.

Is our linking of each theory to particular perspectives arbitrary, then? No, but it's imperfect. Here's an analogy. Think of theories as hot-air balloons (certainly a dangerous metaphor). All are attached by mooring ropes to posts in the ground. Each post represents a metatheory. Each balloon is tied quite firmly to one post, with a boarding ramp for passengers. However, most also have second ropes (and sometimes third and fourth ones) tied to other posts. Some posts have lots of balloons tied to them, others have only one or two. Some of the mooring ropes are strong and heavy, some are lighter. In an analogous way, each theory in this book is placed according to the metatheory it's tied to most firmly, but theories often have secondary ties to other metatheories.

ANOTHER KIND OF PERSPECTIVE

One more thing about our use of the term *perspective*. There was a time when personality psychologists created grand theories aimed at explaining the total complexity of personality. Freud's theory is the clearest example (and some would say the only good example). However, this has become less common. More common today are theories that deal with some *aspect* of personality. Most of these theories weren't really intended to be full models of personality, and it's a little misleading to present them (and judge them) as though they were.

The fact that a theory isn't a grand-scale theory doesn't mean it has nothing important to say about personality. It does mean, though, that such a theory won't say *everything* about personality. It gives us a particular viewing angle on the subject (a more literal meaning of the word *perspective*). This viewing angle may be special and may yield insights you can't find from other angles. But it yields only part of the picture. This limitation is important to keep in mind as you think about the various theories and what each has to say.

The fact that specific theories today tend to focus on smaller pieces of the puzzle also has another implication. Many people who have contributed to today's understanding of personality have made contributions to *several* points of view. Don't be surprised when you see the same name show up in two or three different places. In today's personality psychology, people whose work informs us about psychoanalytic concepts may also have had useful things to say about principles of self-regulation. People who helped us to understand learning may also have contributed to trait psychology.

This is one reason why, in general, we haven't focused the chapters in this book on particular individuals. Rather, in each chapter, we've emphasized *concepts* emphasized by a given theoretical viewpoint.

Organization within Chapters

Each chapter in a given perspective addresses a specific type of theory. Most of the content of each chapter is a description of the basic elements and processes of personality, as viewed from that theoretical view. Each chapter thus tells you something about individual differences and intrapersonal functioning, as seen by that theory.

Each chapter also addresses two more subjects. One is the process of measuring personality, called *assessment*. The other is the potential for problems to arise in human experience, and the processes by which behavior is changed for the better through therapy. Here's a brief preview of what these sections will be like.

Personality does not always function smoothly. Each perspective on personality has its own view about why problems occur.

ASSESSMENT

Personality psychologists give considerable attention to the process of measuring personality, for at least three reasons. First, psychologists want to be able to portray the personalities of specific individuals, in much the same way as you characterize the personalities of people you know. To be confident these pictures are accurate, psychologists need good ways to measure personality.

A second reason for assessing personality concerns the effort to study personality. To study qualities of personality, psychologists have to measure those qualities. Without good ways to assess individual differences or intrapersonal functioning, it's impossible to study them. Good assessment, then, lies at the heart of personality research.

A third reason to measure personality strays a bit from the main focus of this book. Specifically, assessing people's personality is an important part of applied psychology. For example, organizational psychologists use personality to help make hiring decisions (e.g., you might want to be sure you're hiring someone with a desired pattern of motives). Clinical psychologists also use personality assessment to help diagnose problems.

Assessment is a goal that's important throughout personality psychology. Some issues in assessment are the same for all viewpoints. (These are addressed in Chapter 3.) In other ways, assessment is viewed somewhat differently from different perspectives. As a result, theoretical views often differ in the assessment techniques they emphasize. In discussing assessment in each later chapter, we focus on how assessment from that viewpoint has its own special character.

PROBLEMS IN BEHAVIOR, AND BEHAVIOR CHANGE

The other topic included in each theory chapter concerns the fact that people's lives don't always go smoothly. Each view of normal personality also suggests a way to think about the nature of problems (more formally, *psychopathology*). Indeed, it can be argued that a theory of personality gains in credibility from saying useful things about problems. To clarify how each approach to personality views problems, we briefly take up this issue in each chapter from that chapter's viewpoint. As with assessment, our emphasis is on the special contribution made by that theoretical orientation to thinking about problems.

Finally, we describe how the theoretical orientation under discussion contributes to understanding the therapeutic management of problems. If each view has a way of thinking about normal processes and about how things can go wrong, each view also has a way to think about how to try to deal with the problems. Each suggests ways to turn problematic functioning back into effective and satisfying functioning.

· SUMMARY ·

Personality is a hard concept to define. Thinking about how people use the concept, however, suggests three reasons for its use. People use it to convey a sense of consistency or continuity within a person, to convey the sense that the person is the origin of behavior, and to convey the sense that the essence of a person can be summarized or captured in a few salient qualities.

The field of personality addresses two fundamental themes. One is the existence of differences among people. The other is how best to conceptualize intrapersonal functioning—the processes that take place within all persons, giving form and continuity to behavior.

Much of this book deals with theories. *Theories* are summary statements, sets of principles that pertain to certain classes of events. Theories have two purposes: to explain things that are known and to predict possibilities that haven't yet been examined. One way to evaluate the worth of a theory is to ask whether research supports its predictions. Scientific psychology has a continuing cycle between theory and research, as theories are tested, modified on the basis of results, and tested again.

Theories can be evaluated on several grounds other than research. For example, a theory shouldn't be based on a single kind of information. Theories benefit from being *parsimonious*—from having relatively few assumptions (or concepts). Theories also are judged as better when they fit well with one's intuitions and when they stimulate interest (and thus efforts to test them).

The theories described in this book derive from seven different perspectives, or viewpoints, on human nature. They are identified with the terms *dispositional, biological, psychoanalytic, neoanalytic, learning, phenomenological,* and *cognitive self-regulation.* Each theory chapter focuses on assumptions about the nature of personality within a particular theoretical framework. Also included are a discussion of assessment from the viewpoint of the theory under discussion, and a discussion of problems in behavior and how they can be remedied.

· GLOSSARY ·

Individual differences   Differences in personality from one person to another.

Intrapersonal functioning   Psychological processes that take place within the person.

Metatheory   A set of orienting assumptions about reality that provides guidelines for what kinds of ideas to use to create theories.

Parsimony   The quality of requiring few assumptions; simplicity.

Personality   A dynamic organization, inside the person, of psychophysical systems that create the person's characteristic patterns of behavior, thoughts, and feelings.

Theory   A summary statement, a principle or set of principles about a class of events.

CHAPTER 2

Methods in the Study of Personality

Sam and Dave are at the lounge taking a break from studying. Sam says, "My roommate got a letter yesterday from his girlfriend at home—breaking up with him. People around here better watch out 'cause he's gonna be looking for some serious partying to help forget her."

"What makes you think so?"

"What kind of question is that? It's obvious. That's what *I'd* do."

"Huh. I know several guys whose hometown girls dumped them, and *none* of them did that. It was exactly the opposite. They lay around for a few weeks moping. I think you're wrong about how people react to this kind of thing."

W HEN PEOPLE try to understand personality, where do they start? When people create theories, where do the theories come from? How are theories tested? How do personality psychologists decide what to believe? These are all questions about the methods of science. They can be asked in all areas of scientific study, from astronomy to zoology. They are particularly challenging, though, when applied to personality.

Gathering Information

SOURCES: OBSERVE YOURSELF AND OBSERVE OTHERS

A simple way to gather information about personality is to look inward to your own experience (a process called *introspection*). This technique (used by Sam in the opening example) is open to everyone. Try it. You have a personality. If you want to understand personality in general, per-haps you should take a look at yours as an example. Sit back and think about recent events in your life. Think about what you did and how you felt, and pull from those recollections a thread of continuity. From this might come the start of a theory—a set of principles to explain your thoughts, feelings, and actions.

Examining your own experience is an easy beginning, and it can be a useful one, but it has a drawback. Specifically, your own consciousness has a special relationship to your memories (and to your present behavior) because they're your own. It's hard to be sure that this special relationship doesn't distort what you're seeing. For instance, you can misrecall something you experienced yet feel sure your memory is correct.

This problem lessens when you look at someone else instead of yourself (as Dave did in the opening example). That's the second method of gathering information: observe someone else. This method also has a problem, though—the opposite of introspection's problem. Specifically, it's impossible to be "inside another person's head," to really know what that person is thinking and feeling. This difference in perspective can create vast differences in understanding (cf. Jones & Nisbett, 1971). It can lead to misinterpretation.

Which starting point is better? Most psychologists would say that each has a place in the search for truth, though each also has problems. Each can lead to theories and research.

SEEKING DEPTH: CASE STUDIES

Some psychologists interested in personality seek explicitly to understand the entire person at once, rather than just part of the person. Henry Murray (1938), who emphasized the need to study persons as coherent entities, coined the term **personology** to refer to this effort. Many other early personality theorists took a similar view.

This view leads to the use of a technique called the **case study.** A case study involves in-depth examination of one person. It usually entails a long period of observation and typically includes unstructured interviews. Sometimes it involves spending a day or two interacting with the person or just being around the person to see how he or she interacts with others. The repeated observations let the observer confirm initial impressions or correct impressions that were wrong. Confirming or disconfirming an impression is hard to do if you make only one observation. The depth of probing that's possible in a case study can reveal detail about the person that otherwise wouldn't be apparent. This, in turn, can yield important insights.

Case studies are rich in detail and can create vivid descriptions of the person under study. Particularly compelling incidents or examples can be seen as illustrating broader themes in the person's life. There are other advantages to case studies, as well. Because they examine the person in his or her life situation, instead of settings created by the researcher, the information pertains directly to normal life. Because they're open ended, the observer can follow whatever leads seem interesting, rather than asking only questions chosen ahead of time.

Many case studies (though not all) are also *clinical studies*. That is, people who do case studies often focus on persons who have some kind of problem. Typically, these are therapists studying people they're treating. Clinical case studies give information about ways personality goes awry, as well as information about the normal workings of the person. Indeed, several theories of personality arose largely from case study observations in the context of therapy.

As an illustration of how a case study might be used to generate broader ideas about personality, consider this excerpt from the brief case study of a college student who's having personal difficulties: John is 19 years old, slender, and of medium height. His typical manner of dress conveys no particular style other than "average college student." The middle of three sons, he grew up in a small city in the Midwest. His father is a factory worker, and his mother works as an aide in a nursing home. Their combined income provides a modest living and lets the sons attend the state university, but does not permit many luxuries. John's older brother (by four years) had been a star athlete in high school, but his college career ended with an injury, and he now works in the same factory as his father. John's younger brother (by three years) shows a talent for math and science, and his father refers to him as "the engineer," clearly reflecting his hope for the boy's future.

Asked to talk about his high school years, John said he thought they had been mostly good, but maybe not as good for him as for others. Asked to clarify this, he related several minor disappointments in high school, none of which seemed to carry much weight by itself. Then he described an incident in which he had done poorly on a test for which he'd felt fully prepared. He shrugged, as if to suggest that the event wasn't important, but he seemed more tense than at other times during the conversation (or in other interviews).

John has had consistent academic difficulties at the university, despite having higher than average SAT scores. Academic Services referred him to the university's counseling center in the hope of resolving the difficulties. At first, John was all bravado with his counselor, but he didn't maintain that stance for long. In their second meeting, John said to his counselor that he didn't want to disappoint his parents, but he had doubts about whether he belonged in college. Other people in his dorm never seemed to question their abilities, but John felt a constant nagging sense that he wasn't up to the challenge.

After just a few discussions, it became apparent to John's counselor that he was lacking in self-esteem. As the counselor updated her notes on the case, she thought again about an idea that had crossed her mind more than once before: Students low in self-esteem don't seem to perform up to their potential in college. This idea has many implications, and the counselor made some more notes on it.

Thus, a series of observations—even brief observations—made in the course of examining one person's life situation can lead an observer to conclusions about how personality is involved in important categories of events.

SEEKING GENERALITY: STUDIES OF MANY PEOPLE

Case studies can provide insights into the human experience. They provide useful information for researchers and often serve as an important source of ideas. But currently they aren't the main source of information about personality. In large part, this is because a case study, no matter how complete, is lacking in an important respect: It deals with just one person. When you're forming theories or drawing conclusions from observations, you want them to apply to many people—if possible, to *all* people.

The breadth of applicability of a conclusion is called its **generality** or its **generalizability.** For a conclusion to be generalizable, it must be based on many people, not just one or two. The more people you look at, the more convinced you can be that what you see is true of people in general, instead of only a few people. In most research on personality done today, researchers look at tens—even hundreds—of people to increase the generality of their conclusions.

To truly ensure generality, researchers should study people of many ages and from all walks of

The generality of a conclusion can be established only by studying a mix of people from different backgrounds.

life—indeed, from all cultures. For various reasons, this isn't always done, though it is becoming more common. As a matter of convenience, a lot of research on personality has examined only college students.

Do college students provide a reasonably good cross-section of the processes that are important in personality? Maybe yes, maybe no. College students differ from older adults in several ways; for one, they have a less fully formulated sense of self. This may make a difference in the research findings. How big a difference is a matter of conjecture. It does seem clear, though, that we should be cautious in assuming that conclusions drawn from research on college students always apply to "people in general."

Similarly, most observations on personality come from research done in the United States and western Europe. Most of the research has been done with middle- to upper-middle-class people. Some of it has used only men or only women. One must be cautious in assuming that the conclusions of a study apply to people from other cultures, other socioeconomic groups, and (sometimes) both genders.

Generalizability, then, is a kind of continuum. Rarely does any study range broadly enough to ensure total generalizability. Some are better than others. How broadly a conclusion can be generalized is an issue that must always be kept in mind in evaluating results of studies.

The desire for generality and the desire for in-depth understanding of a person represent competing pressures for observers of personality. They force a trade-off. That is, given the same investment of time and energy, you can know a great deal about the life of one person (or a very few people), or you can know a little bit about the lives of a much larger number of people. It's nearly impossible to do both at once. As a result, researchers tend to choose one path or the other, according to which pressure they find more important.

Establishing Relationships among Variables

Insights from introspection, observation, or systematic examination of a person by a case study can suggest relationships between variables. A **variable** is a dimension along which variations exist. There must be at least two values or levels on that dimension, though some variables have an infinite number of values. For example, *sex* is a variable with values of *male* and *female*. *Self-esteem* is a variable that has a virtually limitless number of values (from *very low* to *very high*) as you make finer discriminations among people.

It's important to distinguish between a variable and its values, because conclusions about relationships involve the whole dimension, not just one end of it. Thus, researchers always study at least two levels of the variable they're interested in. For example, you can't see effects of low self-esteem by looking only at people low in self-esteem. If there's a relationship between self-esteem and academic performance, the only way to find out is to look at people with *different levels* of self-esteem (see Figure 2.1). If the relationship does exist, people with very low self-esteem should have poor grades and people with higher self-esteem should have better grades.

The last part of that statement is every bit as important as the first part. Knowing that people

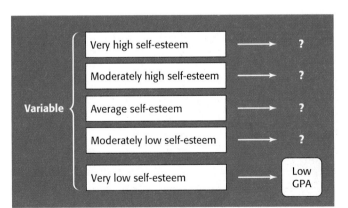

FIGURE 2.1

Whether a relationship exists between variables can be determined only by looking at more than one value on each variable. For instance, knowing that people low in self-esteem have poor academic performances leaves open the question of whether everyone else's performances are just as poor. This question is critically important in establishing a relationship between the two variables.

A correlation between two variables means they covary in some systematic way. Here there is a correlation between height and place in line.

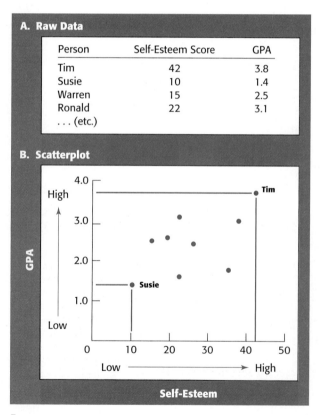

FIGURE 2.2

Thinking about the meaning of correlation (with hypothetical data): (A) For each person, there are two pieces of information, a self-esteem score and a grade-point average (GPA). (B) The data can be arranged to form a scatterplot by plotting each person's self-esteem score along the horizontal dimension and GPA along the vertical dimension, thereby locating the combination in a two-dimensional space.

low in self-esteem have poor grades isn't informative if people high in self-esteem also have poor grades. It can be hard to keep this in mind. In fact, people often fail to realize how important this issue is. If you don't keep it in mind, though, you can make serious errors in the conclusions you reach (for illustrations, see Chapman, 1967; Crocker, 1981).

The need to examine people across a range of variability is a second reason why it's important to go beyond case studies. (The issue of generality was the first reason.) Indeed, the importance of examining a range of variability is what leads to the methods on which we focus for the rest of this chapter.

CORRELATION BETWEEN VARIABLES

There are two kinds of relationship that can be found between variables. The first is called **correlation**. A correlation between two dimensions means that as you examine them across many examples or instances, the values tend to go together in a systematic way. There are two aspects of this relationship, which are separate from each other: the *direction* of the correlation and the *strength* of the correlation. To clarify what these terms mean, let's return to the example of self-esteem and academic performance.

Suppose you've decided to investigate whether these two variables go together. You've gone out and found 40 students to study. They've completed a measure of self-esteem and given you their current grade-point average (GPA). You now have two pieces of information for each person (Figure 2.2, A). One way to organize this information is to create a scatterplot, (Figure 2.2, B). In a scatterplot, the two variables are represented by lines at right angles (the axes of the graph). The point where the lines meet is zero for both variables. Being farther away from zero on each line means having a higher value on that variable. Because the lines are at right angles, the combination of any score on one variable and any score on the other variable can be portrayed as a point in a two-dimensional space. For example, in Figure 2.2, Tim has a self-esteem score of 42 (thus being to the right side on the horizontal line) and a GPA of 3.8 (thus being toward the top on the vertical line). The scatterplot for your study would be the points that represent the combinations of self-esteem scores and GPA for each person in the study.

To ask whether the two variables are correlated means (essentially) asking the following question about the scatterplot: When you look at points that represent low versus high values on the *horizontal* dimension, do they differ in how they line up regarding the *vertical* dimension? If low values tend to go with low values and high values tend to go with high values (as in Figure 2.3, A), the two variables are said to be *positively* correlated. If people low in self-esteem tend to have low GPAs and people high in self-esteem tend to have high GPAs, you would say that self-esteem correlates positively with GPA. This finding has, in fact, emerged from actual studies of these variables (Scheirer & Kraut, 1979; Wylie, 1979).

Sometimes, however, a different kind of correlation occurs. Sometimes high values on one dimension tend to go along with low values on the other dimension (and vice versa). When this happens (Figure 2.3, B), the correlation between the variables is termed *inverse*, or *negative*. This kind of correlation might have emerged if you had studied the relation between GPA and the frequency of going to parties. That is, you might have found that students who party the most tend to have lower GPAs, whereas those who party the least tend to have higher GPAs.

The *direction* of the association between variables (positive versus negative) is one aspect of correlation. The second aspect—entirely separate from the first—is the *strength* of the correlation. Think of strength as the "sloppiness" of the association between the variables. More formally, it refers to the degree of accuracy with which you can predict values on one dimension from values on the other dimension. For example, assume a positive correlation between self-esteem and GPA. Suppose that you knew that Victoria had the second-highest score on self-esteem in your study. How accurate a guess could you make about Victoria's GPA?

The answer to this question is determined by how strong the correlation is. Because the correlation is positive, knowing that Victoria is on the high end of the self-esteem dimension would lead you to predict a high GPA. If the correlation is also *strong*, you're very likely to be right. If the correlation is weaker, you're less likely to be right. A perfect positive correlation—the strongest possible—means that the person who has the very highest value on one variable also has the very highest value on the other, the person next highest on one is also next highest on the other, and so on, throughout the list (Figure 2.4, A).

The strength of a correlation is expressed by a number called a **correlation coefficient** (often labeled with a lowercase *r*). An absolutely perfect positive correlation (as in Figure 2.4, A) is expressed by the number 1.0. This is the largest numerical value a correlation can take. It indicates a totally accurate prediction from one dimension to the other. If you know where the person is on one variable, you can tell with complete confidence where he or she is on the other.

The scatterplot of a somewhat weaker correlation is shown in Figure 2.4, B. As you can see, there's more "scatter" among the points than in the first case. There's still a noticeable tendency for higher values on one dimension to match up with higher ones on the other and for lows to match up with lows, but the tendency is less exact.

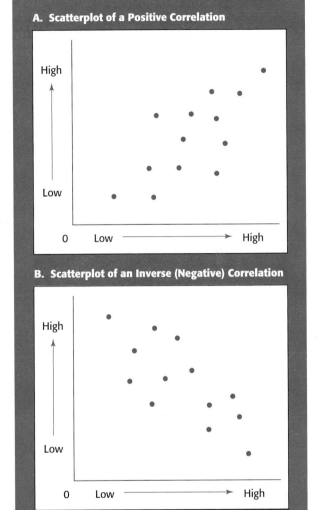

FIGURE 2.3
(A) If high numbers on one dimension tend to go with high numbers on the other dimension (and low with low), there is a positive correlation. (B) If high numbers on one dimension tend to go with low numbers on the other dimension, there is an inverse, or negative, correlation.

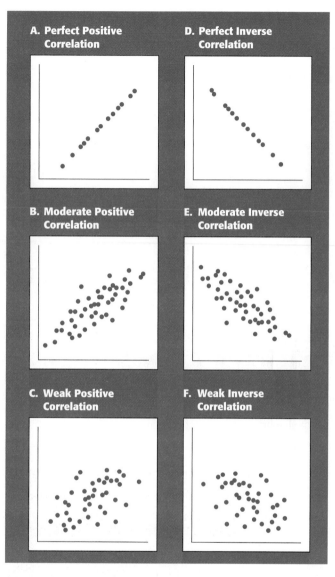

FIGURE 2.4

Six correlations: (A) Perfect positive correlation, (B) Moderate positive correlation, (C) Weak positive correlation, (D) Perfect inverse correlation, (E) Moderate inverse correlation, and (F) Weak inverse correlation. The weaker the correlation, the more "scatter" in the scatterplot.

As the correlation becomes weaker, the number representing it becomes smaller (thus, virtually all correlations are decimal values). Correlations of 0.6 to 0.8 are strong. Correlations of 0.3 to 0.5 are moderately strong. Below 0.3 or 0.2, the prediction from one variable to the other is getting poorer. As you can see in Figure 2.4, C, weak correlations have even more scatter. The tendency toward a positive relation is there, but it definitely isn't strong. A correlation of 0.0 means the two variables aren't related to each other at all. A scatterplot of a zero correlation is random dots.

As we said before, a correlation's strength is entirely separate from its direction. *Strength* refers only to degree of accuracy in prediction. Thus, it is eminently sensible to talk about a perfect inverse (negative) correlation as well as a perfect positive correlation. A perfect inverse correlation (Figure 2.4, D) means that the person who had the highest value on one variable also had the very lowest value on the other variable, the person with the next-highest value on one had the next-to-lowest value on the other, and so on.

Negative correlations are expressed in numbers, just as are positive correlations. But to show that the relationship is an inverse one, a minus sign is placed in front. Thus an r value of -0.75 is precisely as strong as an r value of 0.75. The first represents an inverse correlation, though, whereas the second represents a positive correlation.

TWO KINDS OF SIGNIFICANCE

We've been describing the strength of correlations in terms of the size of the numbers that represent them. Although the size of the number gives information about its strength, the size of the number by itself doesn't tell you whether the correlation is believable or real. Maybe it's a fluke. This is a problem, in fact, for all kinds of statistics. You can't tell just by looking at the number or looking at a graph whether the result is real. You need to know whether the result is **statistically significant.**

Significant in this context has a very specific meaning: It means that the correlation would have been that large or larger only rarely if no true relation exists. When the probability is small enough (just under 5%), the correlation (or whatever statistic it is) is said to be statistically significant (see also Box 2.1). At that point, the researcher concludes that the relationship is a real one rather than a random occurrence.

A second use of the word *significant* has also become common in psychology. This use more closely resembles the use of the word in day-to-day language. An association is said to be **clinically significant,** or **practically significant,** if the effect is both statistically significant (so it's believable) and large enough to have some practical importance. How large it has to be varies from case to case. It's possible, though, for an

BOX 2.1 STATISTICS AND STATISTICS

Description versus Inference

When people think of *statistics,* they often think of the statistics that portray a set of events—for example, "The average American earns $37,000 a year," or "She averaged 21.6 points per game." These are called **descriptive statistics** because their purpose is to give a description.

Psychologists also use statistics in a different way, discussed in the body of the chapter. These statistics are called **inferential statistics** because they let the researcher make inferences. The information they provide guides the scientist in deciding whether to believe something is true. Interestingly enough, it isn't possible to *prove* something is true. What statistics do is show how probable the finding was, provided that there was no true relation. If it can be shown that the effect was very *unlikely*

to have occurred, the researcher infers that it's real.

An example of the ability of inferential statistics to reveal patterns, and the limitations on what they can say, took place after the 2000 presidential election in the United States. Voters in Palm Beach County, Florida, had encountered an unfamiliar and confusing ballot format on election day. Many later reported accidentally voting for one candidate (Pat Buchanan) while trying to vote for another one (Al Gore). The election, won by George W. Bush, was extremely close. Its outcome might have turned on such errors. Were these people just complaining because their candidate lost? Or was there really a problem with the ballot?

Social scientists Greg Adams and Chris Fastnow (2000) used inferential statistics to test whether the pattern of votes in Palm Beach County differed from patterns in other Florida coun-

ties. In every county but Palm Beach, the more votes cast for Bush, the more votes also cast for Buchanan. If Palm Beach had been like every other county in Florida, Buchanan would have gotten around 600 votes instead of 3,407. The inference was clear: The chances were extremely small that this difference in pattern would have occurred if there were no true relation. Something apparently was throwing off the voting pattern in Palm Beach.

We say "apparently" to emphasize something about the nature of inferential statistics. Whenever you use them to make a judgment, the conclusion is always probabilistic. The odds that the inference was wrong in this case are *extremely* small. But the possibility does exist. Inferential statistics thus are best viewed as procedures that allow us to attach "confidence units" to our judgments, rather than procedures that lead infallibly to correct choices.

---

association to be statistically significant but to account for only a tiny part of the behavior. The practical significance of such an association usually isn't very great.

CAUSALITY AND A LIMITATION ON INFERENCE

Correlations tell us whether two variables go together (and in what direction and how strongly). But they don't tell us *why* the variables go together. The *why* question takes us beyond the realm of correlation into a second kind of relationship. This relationship is called **causality**—the relationship between a cause and its effect. Correlational research isn't able to provide evidence on this second kind of relationship. A correlational study often gives people strong *intuitions* about causality, but no more.

Why? The answer is illustrated in Figure 2.5. Each arrow there represents a possible path of causality. What this figure shows is that there are always three ways to account for the results of a correlation. Consider the correlation between self-esteem and academic performance. What causes that association? Your intuition may say the best explanation is that having bad academic outcomes causes people to have lower self-esteem, whereas having good outcomes causes people to feel good about themselves (arrow 1 in Figure 2.5). Or maybe you think the best explanation is that having low self-esteem causes people not to try as hard in their courses, thus resulting in poorer performances (arrow

Random assignment is an important hallmark of the experimental method. The experimenter randomly assigns participants to a condition, much as a roulette wheel randomly catches the ball in a black or red slot.

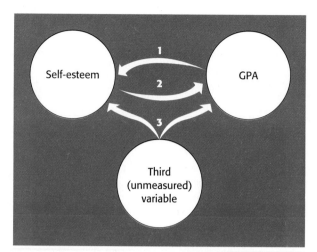

Self-esteem
GPA
1
2
3
Third
(unmeasured)
variable

FIGURE 2.5
Correlation does not imply cause and effect, because there are always three possibilities: (1) variations in one variable (academic performance) may be causing variations in the second (self-esteem); (2) variations in the second may be causing variations in the first; or (3) a third variable may actually be causing both observed effects. Knowing only the single correlation between self-esteem and GPA doesn't allow you to distinguish among these possibilities.

2). Both of these explanations are plausible, though they represent opposite cause–effect relationships.

It could also be, however, that a third variable—not measured, perhaps not even thought of—actually exerts a causal influence over both variables that were measured (the pair of arrows labeled 3). Perhaps having a high level of intelligence causes a positive sense of self-esteem and also causes better academic performance. In this scenario, both self-esteem and academic performance are effects, and something else is the cause.

The possible involvement of another variable behind a correlation is sometimes called the **third-variable problem.** It's a problem that can't be handled by correlational research. That method cannot tell which of the three possibilities shown in Figure 2.5 is actually correct.

SEARCH FOR CAUSALITY: EXPERIMENTAL RESEARCH

There *is* a method that allows one to demonstrate cause and effect, however. It's called the **experimental method.** Think of it as having two defining characteristics. First, in an experiment, the researcher "manipulates" one variable—creates the existence of at least two levels of it. The one the researcher is manipulating is called the **independent variable.** It's the one the researcher is testing as the possible *cause* in a cause–effect relationship. When we say the researcher is "creating" two (or more) levels of this variable, we mean exactly that. There's some kind of event that *actively creates* a difference between the experience of some people and the experience of other people.

Sometimes researchers do experiments in order to better understand what they've seen in correlational studies. Let's illustrate the experimental method by doing just that. Let's pursue further the example we just discussed. Suppose you have a hunch that variations in academic performance have a causal effect on self-esteem. (Unlike John's counselor, you think poor performances make people get down on themselves and good performances make them happy with themselves.) To study this possibility, you conduct an experiment in which you hypothesize (predict) that academic outcomes affect self-esteem.

You can't really manipulate GPA in this experiment, but it's fairly easy to manipulate other things with overtones of academic performance. For instance, you could arrange to have some people experience a success and others a failure (using a task rigged to be easy or impossible). By arranging this, you would *create* the difference between success and failure. You'd manipulate it—not measure it. You're sure that a difference now exists between the two sets of people in your experiment, because you *made* it exist.

As in all research, you'd do your best to treat every participant in your experiment exactly the same in all ways other than that one. Treating everyone the same—in fact, making everything be exactly the same except for what you manipulate—is called **experimental control.** Exerting a high degree of experimental control is important to the logic of the experimental method, as you'll see momentarily.

Control is important, but you can't control everything. It's rarely possible to have every person be in the research at the same time of day or the same day of the week. More obviously, perhaps, it's impossible to be sure the people in the experiment are exactly alike. One of the main themes of this book, after all, is that people differ. Some people in the experiment are just naturally going to have higher self-esteem when they walk in the door than are others. How can these differences be handled?

This question brings us to the second defining characteristic of the experimental method: Any variable that can't be controlled—such as individual differences—is treated by **random assignment.** In your experiment, you would randomly assign each participant to either the success experience or the failure experience. Random assignment is often done by such means as tossing a coin or using a list of random numbers.

The use of random assignment rests on a specific assumption: that if you study enough people in the experiment, any important differences between people (and from other sources as well) will balance out between the groups. Each group is likely to have as many tall people, fat people, depressed people, and confident people as the other group—*if* you have a fairly large number of participants and use random assignment. Anything that matters should balance out.

So you've brought people to your research laboratory one at a time, randomly assigned them to the two conditions, manipulated the independent variable, and exerted experimental control over everything else. At some point, you would then measure the variable you think is the effect in the cause-and-effect relationship. This one is termed the **dependent variable.**

In this experiment, your hypothesis was that differences in success and failure cause people to differ in their self-esteem. Thus, the dependent measure would be a measure of self-esteem (for example, self-report items asking people how they feel about themselves). After getting this measure for each person in the experiment, you would compare the groups to each other (by statistical procedures that need not concern us here). If the difference between groups was statistically significant, you could conclude that the experience of success and failure *causes* people to differ in self-esteem.

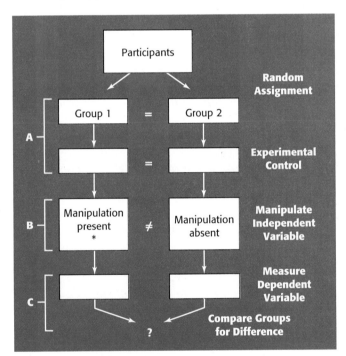

What would make you so confident in that cause-and-effect conclusion? The answer, despite all the details we've gone through, is really quite simple. The logic is displayed graphically in Figure 2.6. At the beginning of the experiment, you separated people into two groups. (By the way, the reasoning applies even if the independent variable has more than two levels.) If the assumption about the effect of random assignment is correct, the two groups don't differ from each other at this point. Because you exercise experimental control throughout your procedures, the groups still don't differ as the experiment unfolds.

At one point, however, a difference between groups is introduced—when you manipulate the independent variable. As we said before, you know there's a difference now, and you know *what* the difference is, because you created it yourself. For this reason, if you find the groups differ from each other on the dependent measure at the end, you know there's only one thing that could have caused the difference (Figure 2.6). It *had* to come from the manipulation of the independent variable. That was the only place where a difference between groups was created. It was the only thing that could have been responsible for causing the effect.

FIGURE 2.6
The logic of the experimental method: (A) Because of random assignment and experimental control, there is no systematic difference between groups at first. (B) The experimental manipulation creates—for the first time—a specific difference. (C) If the groups then are found to differ in another fashion, the manipulation must have caused this difference.

This reasoning is straightforward. We should note, however, that this method isn't entirely perfect. Its problem is this: When you do an experiment, you show that the *manipulation* causes the difference on the dependent measure—but you can't always be completely sure *what it was* about the manipulation that did the causing. Maybe it was the aspect of the manipulation that you were focused on, but maybe it was something else.

For example, in the experiment we've been considering, low self-esteem may have been caused by the failure and the self-doubt to which it led. But it *might* have been caused by other things about the manipulation. Maybe the people were worried that they had spoiled the results of your experiment by not solving the problems. They didn't feel a sense of *failure* but were angry with themselves for creating a problem for you. This interpretation of the result wouldn't mean quite the same thing as your first interpretation of it. This issue requires us always to be a bit cautious in how we view results, even from experiments.

RECOGNIZING TYPES OF STUDY

When you read about correlational studies and experiments later in this book, how easy is it going to be for you to tell them apart? At first glance, it seems simple. An *experiment* makes a comparison between groups, and a *correlational study* gives you a correlation, right? Well, no. Results of correlational studies aren't always reported as correlations. Sometimes the study compares two (or more) groups with each other on a dependent measure, and the word *correlation* is never even mentioned.

Suppose you studied some people who were 40% overweight and some who were 40% underweight. You interviewed them individually and judged how sociable they were, and you found that heavy people were more sociable than thin people. Would this be an experiment or a correlational study? Recall the two defining characteristics of the experiment: manipulation of the independent variable and random assignment of people to groups. You didn't randomly assign people to be heavy or thin (and didn't *create* these differences). Therefore, this is a correlational study. The limitation on correlational research (the inability to conclude cause and effect) applies to it.

A good rule of thumb is that any time groupings reflect *naturally occurring differences* or are formed on the basis of a *characteristic that you measure,* the study is correlational. This means that all studies of personality differences are, by definition, correlational.

Why do personality researchers make their correlational studies look like experiments? Sometimes it's because they select participants from the extreme ends of some personality variable—people who are very low and very high, respectively, on some dimension of personality. This strategy maximizes the chances of finding differences. That is, removing the people who are average on that dimension helps to remove clutter and make the picture clearer. It has the side effect, however, of making it hard to express the finding as a correlation. The result is correlational studies that look at first glance like experiments.

WHAT KIND OF RESEARCH IS BEST?

Another question that's often asked is, Which kind of research is better, experiments or correlational studies? The answer is that both have advantages, and the advantage of each is the disadvantage of the other. The advantage of the experimental method, of course, is its ability to show cause and effect, which the correlational method cannot do.

But experiments also have drawbacks. For one (as noted), there's sometimes uncertainty about which aspect of the manipulation was important. For another, experiments on people usually involve events of relatively short duration in carefully controlled conditions. The correlational method, in contrast, lets you examine events that take place over long periods (even decades) and events that are much more elaborate. Correlational studies also let us get information about events in which experimental manipulation would be unethical—for example, the effects of being raised by a divorced parent or the effects of cigarette smoking.

Personality psychologists sometimes also criticize experiments on the grounds that the kinds of relationships they reveal often have little to do with the central issues of personality. Even experiments that seem to bear on important issues in personality may tell less than they seem to. Consider the hypothetical experiment described earlier, in which you manipulated academic success and failure and measured self-esteem. Assume for the moment that participants given a failure had lower self-esteem afterward than participants given a success. You might be tempted to infer from this experiment that having poor academic outcomes over the course of one's life causes people to develop low self-esteem.

This conclusion, however, may not be justified. The experiment dealt with a brief task outcome, manipulated in a particular way. The broader conclusion you're tempted to reach deals with a basic quality of personality. This latter quality may differ in many ways from the momentary state you manipulated. The "reasoning by analogy" you're tempted to engage in is dangerous, and it can be misleading.

To many personality psychologists, the only way to really understand personality is to look at naturally occurring differences between people (Underwood, 1975). These psychologists are willing to accept the limitation on causal inference that's inherent in correlations; they regard it as an acceptable price to pay. On the other hand, many of these psychologists are comfortable *combining* the correlational strategy with experimental techniques, as described next.

MULTIFACTOR STUDIES

We've been talking about studies as though they always involved predicting a dependent variable from a single predictor variable (either an experimental manipulation or an individual difference). In reality, however, studies often look at the effects of several predictors at once by using multifactor designs. In a **multifactor study,** two (or more) variables are varied *separately,* which means creating all combinations of the various levels of the predictor variables. The study shown in Figure 2.7 has two factors, but more than two can be used. The more factors in a study, of course, the larger is the resulting array of combinations, and the trickier it is to keep track of things.

Sometimes the factors are all experimental manipulations. Sometimes they're all personality variables. Often, though, experimental manipulations are crossed by individual-difference variables. The example shown in Figure 2.7 is such a design. The self-esteem factor is the level of self-esteem the people had when they came to the study. This is a personality dimension (thus correlational). The success–failure factor is an experimental manipulation, which takes place during the session. In this particular experiment, the dependent measure is performance on a second task, which the participants attempt after the experimental manipulation.

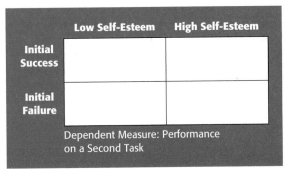

FIGURE 2.7
Diagram of a hypothetical two-factor study. Each square represents the combination of the value listed above it and the value listed to the left. In multifactor studies, all combinations of values of the predictor variables are created in this fashion.

These designs allow researchers to examine how different types of people respond to variations in situations. They thus offer a glimpse into the underlying dynamics of the individual-difference variable. Because this type of study combines experimental procedures and individual differences, it is often referred to as **experimental personality research.**

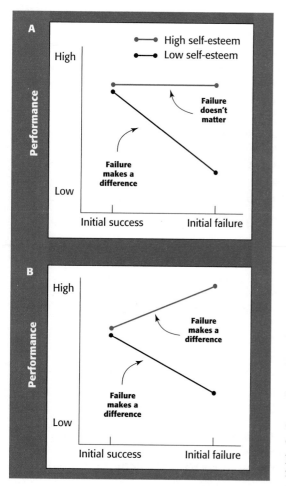

READING FIGURES FROM MULTIFACTOR RESEARCH

Because multifactor designs are more complex than single-factor studies, what they can tell you is also potentially more complex. Indeed, people who do experimental personality research use these designs precisely for this reason.

You don't *always* get a complex result from a multifactor study. Sometimes you find only the same outcomes you would have found if you had studied each predictor variable separately. When you find that a predictor variable is linked to the outcome variable in a systematic way, completely separate from the other predictor, the finding is referred to as a **main effect**. For example, the study outlined in Figure 2.7 might find only that people of both self-esteem levels perform worse after a failure than after a success.

The complexity occurs when a study finds what's termed an **interaction**. Figure 2.8 portrays two interactions, each a possible outcome of the hypothetical study of Figure 2.7. In each case, the vertical dimension portrays the dependent measure: performance on the second task. The two marks on the horizontal line represent the two values of the manipulated variable: initial success versus failure. The color of the line depicts the other predictor variable: the color line is participants high in self-esteem, and the black line is those low in self-esteem.

We emphasize that these graphs show *hypothetical* outcomes. They are intended only to give you a clearer understanding of what interactions are about. Figure 2.8, A, portrays a finding that people who are low in self-esteem perform worse after an initial failure than after a success. Among people high in self-esteem, however, this doesn't occur. Failure

FIGURE 2.8
Two hypothetical outcomes of a two-factor study looking at self-esteem and an initial success-versus-failure experience as predictors of performance on a second task. (A) This graph indicates that experiencing a failure causes people low in self-esteem to perform worse later on than if they had experienced a success, but that experiencing a failure does not have any effect on people high in self-esteem. (B) This graph indicates that experiencing a failure causes people low in self-esteem to perform worse later on, but that experiencing a failure causes people high in self-esteem to perform *better* later on. Thus, the failure influences both kinds of people but does so in opposite ways.

apparently has no effect on them. Thus, the effect of one variable (success versus failure) differs across the two levels of the other variable (degree of self-esteem). That is the meaning of the term *interaction*. In the case in Figure 2.8, A, a failure has an effect at one level of the second variable (in the low self-esteem group) but has no effect at the other level of the second variable (the high self-esteem group).

Two more points about interactions: First, to find an interaction, it's *absolutely necessary* to study more than one factor at a time. It's impossible to find an interaction unless both variables involved in it are studied at once. This is one reason researchers often use complex designs: They allow the possibility for interactions to emerge.

The second point is revealed by comparing Figure 2.8, A, with Figure 2.8, B. This point is that interactions can take many forms. In contrast to the interaction we just described, the graph in panel B says that failure has effects on both kinds of people, but opposite effects. People low in self-esteem perform worse after failure (as in the first graph), but people high in self-esteem actually perform better after a failure, perhaps because the failure motivates them to try harder.

These two graphs aren't the only forms of interactions. Exactly what an *interaction* means always depends on the form it takes. Thus, exploring interactions always requires checking to see in what way each group was influenced by the other variable under study.

· SUMMARY ·

Research in personality relies on observations of both the self and others. The desire to understand a person as an integrated whole led to *case studies,* in-depth examinations of specific persons. The desire for *generalizability*—conclusions that would apply to many rather than to a few people—led to studies involving systematic examination of many people.

Gathering information is only the first step toward examining relationships between and among variables. Relationships among variables are examined in two ways, corresponding to two kinds of relationships. *Correlational research* determines the degree to which two variables tend to go together in a predictable way when measured at different levels along the dimensions. This technique determines two aspects of the relationship: its direction and its strength. The special relationship of cause and effect cannot be determined by this kind of study, however.

A second technique, called the *experimental method,* allows testing for cause and effect. In an experiment, an independent variable is manipulated, other variables are controlled (made constant), and anything that cannot be controlled is treated by random assignment. An effect caused by the manipulation is measured in the dependent variable. Experimental and correlational techniques are often combined in multifactor studies. This is termed *experimental personality research*. Multifactor studies permit the emergence of interactions.

· GLOSSARY ·

Case study   An in-depth study of one individual.

Causality   A relationship such that variation in one dimension produces variation in another.

Clinically significant   An association large enough to have some practical importance.

Correlation   A relationship in which two variables or dimensions covary when measured repeatedly.

Correlation coefficient   A numeric index of the degree of correlation between two variables.

Dependent variable   The variable measured as the outcome of an experiment; the effect in a cause–effect relation.

Descriptive statistics   Statistics used to describe or characterize some group.

Experimental control   The holding constant of variables that are not being manipulated.

Experimental method   The method in which one variable is manipulated to test for causal influence on another variable.

Experimental personality research   A study involving a personality factor and an experimental factor.

Generality (generalizability)   The degree to which a conclusion applies to many people.

Independent variable   The variable manipulated in an experiment, tested as the cause in a cause–effect relation.

Inferential statistics   Statistics used to judge whether a relationship exists between variables.

Interaction   A finding in which the effect of one predictor variable differs depending on the level of another predictor variable.

Main effect   A finding in which the effect of one predictor variable is independent of other variables.

Multifactor study   A study with two (or more) predictor variables.

Personology   The study of the whole person, as opposed to studying only one aspect of the person.

Practical significance   An association large enough to have practical importance.

Random assignment   The process of putting people randomly into groups of an experiment so their characteristics balance out across groups.

Statistical significance   The likelihood of an obtained effect occurring when there is no true effect.

Third-variable problem   The possibility that an unmeasured variable caused variations in both of two correlated variables.

Variable   A dimension along which two or more variations exist.

CHAPTER 3

Issues in Personality Assessment

On the first day of class, Jeff saw a woman he didn't know, and he's been trying ever since to get an idea of what she's like. He watches how she acts and dresses, listens to what she says to people. He asks friends if they know anything about her. After a while he starts to wonder how "good" the information he's gathering is. Pat always sees things in a slanted way, so whatever she says has to be taken with a grain of salt. Jennifer hardly notices things that are right in front of her, so who knows what to make of what she says? When the stranger raises her hand and gives opinions in class, do they represent who she really is, or is she trying to convince the teacher she's an intellectual? When she turned down a date with Chris after class the other day, was that a trace of scorn in her voice? Or was she just flustered?

THE MEASURING of personality is called **assessment.** It's something we all do informally, all the time. We want to have an idea of the personalities of the people we interact with so we know what to expect of them. For this reason, we develop ways of gauging people, judging what they're like. You probably don't think of this as *assessment*, but what you're doing informally is much the same—in principle—as what psychologists do more formally.

Forming impressions of what other people are like can be hard. It's easy to get misleading impressions. Personality assessment is also hard for psychologists. All the problems you have, they have too. But personality psychologists work hard to deal with those problems.

Sources of Information

Informal assessment draws information from many sources, and so does formal assessment. In fact, as you'll see, each way of getting information that was mentioned in the opening example has a counterpart in a formal assessment technique.

Many measures of personality come from someone other than the person being assessed (Funder, 1991; Paunonen, 1989). The broad name for this technique is **observer ratings.** There are many kinds of observer ratings. Sometimes observers make judgments about the person being assessed without interacting directly with the person. The judgments may be based on watching the person's actions. The judgments may be opinions, ratings made by people who know the person well enough to say what he or she is like.

Other observer assessments involve interviews. People being assessed may talk in their own words about themselves, and the interviewer draws conclusions from what's said and how it's said. Sometimes the people being interviewed talk about something *other than* themselves. In so doing, they reveal something indirectly to the interviewer about what they're like.

Though many techniques of assessment rely on the impressions of outside observers, not all do. A great many measures of personality—indeed, the vast majority—are **self-reports.** In self-reports, people themselves indicate what they think they're like or how they feel or act. Self-reports thus resemble the process of introspection described in the last chapter. Although self-reporting can be done in an unstructured descriptive way, usually it's not. Most self-reports ask people to respond to a specific set of items.

There are many different types of observer ratings. Here an observer is directly rating a research participant's overt behavior.

Self-report scales can be created in many formats. An example is the true–false format, where you read statements and decide whether each one is true or false for you. Another common format is a multipoint rating scale. Here a wider range of response options are available—ranging, for example, from "strongly agree" to "strongly disagree."

Some self-reports focus on a single quality of personality. Often, though, people who develop tests want to assess *several* aspects of personality in the same test (as separate scales). A measure that assesses several dimensions of personality is called an **inventory.** The process of developing an inventory is no different from the process of developing a single scale. The only difference is that in this case, you must go through each step of development for *each scale of the inventory,* rather than just one.

As you can see, the arsenal of possible assessment techniques is large. All require two processes, though. First, in each case the person who's being assessed produces a sample of "behavior." This may literally be an action that someone else observes, it may be internal behavior such as a change in heartrate, or it may be the behavior of answering self-report items. Second, someone then uses the behavior sample as a guide to some aspect of the person's personality.

Some measures are termed **subjective,** whereas others are termed **objective.** In subjective measures, an interpretation is part of the measure. An example is an observer's judgment that a person he or she is watching looks nervous. The judgment renders the measure subjective, because it's an *interpretation* of the behavior. If the measure focuses on a concrete physical reality that requires no interpretation, it's said to be objective. For example, you could count the number of times a person stammers while talking. This would involve no interpretation yet. Although this count might later be used to infer nervousness (an interpretation), the measure itself is objective.

To some extent, this issue cuts across the distinction between observer ratings and self-reports. An observer can make objective counts of acts, or can develop a subjective impression of the person. In the same way, a person making a self-report can report counts of specific events, or can give a subjective impression of what he or she is like. It should be apparent, though, that self-reports are particularly vulnerable to incorporating subjectivity. Even reports of specific events, if they're retrospective, permit unintentional interpretations to creep in.

Reliability of Measurement

All techniques of assessment confront several kinds of problems, or issues. One issue is termed **reliability** of measurement. The nature of this issue can be conveyed by putting it as a question: Once you've made an observation about someone, how confident can you be that if you looked again a second or third time, you'd see about the same thing? When an observation is reliable, it has a high degree of *consistency,* or *repeatability.* Low reliability means that what is measured is less consistent. The measure isn't just reflecting the person being measured. It's also including a lot of randomness, termed **error.**

All measurement procedures have sources of error. (Error can be reduced but not eliminated.) When you use a telescope to look at the moon, a little dust on the lens, minor imperfections in the glass, flickering lights nearby, and swirling air currents can all contribute error to what you see. When you use a rating scale to measure how independent people think they are, the way you phrase the item can be a source of error because it can lead to different interpretations. When you have an observer watching a child's behavior, the observer is a source of error because of variations in how closely he's paying attention, thinking about what he's seeing, or being influenced by a thousand other things.

How do you deal with the issue of reliability in measurement? The general answer is to repeat the measurement, make the observation more than once. Usually this means measuring the same quality from a slightly different angle or using a slightly different measuring device. This lets the diverse sources of error in the different devices cancel each other out.

Reliability actually is a family of problems, not just a single problem, because it crops up in several different contexts. Each version of the problem has a separate name, and the tactic used to treat each version differs slightly from the tactics used on the others.

INTERNAL CONSISTENCY

The simplest act of assessment is the single observation or measurement. How can you be sure it doesn't include too much error? Let's take an illustration from ability assessment. Think about what you'd do if you wanted to know how good someone was at a particular type of problem—math problems or word puzzles. You wouldn't give the person just a *single* problem to solve, because whether he or she solved it easily might depend too much on some quirk of that particular problem. If you want to know (reliably) how well the person solves that kind of problem, you'd give him or her *several* problems.

The same strategy applies to personality assessment. If you were using a self-report to ask people how independent they think they are, you wouldn't ask just once. You'd ask several times, using different items that all reflect independence, but in different words. In this example, *each item* is a measuring device. When you go to a new item,

Human judges are not infallible. They sometimes perceive things inaccurately.

you're shifting to a different measuring device, trying to measure the same quality in the same person. In effect, you're putting down one telescope and picking up another.

The reliability question is whether you see about the same thing through the different telescopes.

This kind of reliability is termed **internal reliability** or **internal consistency.** This is reliability within a set of observations of a single aspect of personality. Because different items have different sources of random error, using many items should tend to balance out the error. The more observations, the more likely it is that the random error will cancel out. Because people using self-report scales want good reliability, most scales contain many items. If the items are reliable enough, they're then used together as a single index of the personality quality.

How do you find out whether the items you're using have good internal reliability? Just having a lot of items doesn't guarantee it. Reliability is a question about the correlations among people's responses to the items. Saying that the items are highly reliable means that people's responses to the items are highly intercorrelated.

As a practical matter, there are several ways to investigate internal consistency. All of them examine correlations among people's responses across items. Perhaps the best way (although it's cumbersome) is to look at the average correlation between each pair of items taken separately. A simpler way is to separate the items into two subsets (often odd- versus even-numbered items), add up people's scores for each subset, and correlate the two subtotals with each other. This provides an index called **split-half reliability.** If the two halves of the item set measure the same quality of personality, people who score high on one half should also score high on the other half, and people who score low on one half should also score low on the other half. Thus, a strong positive correlation between halves is evidence of internal consistency.

INTER-RATER RELIABILITY

As noted, personality isn't always measured by self-reports. Some observations are *literally* observations, made by one person watching and assessing someone else. Use of observer ratings creates a slightly different reliability problem. In an observer rating, the *person making the observation* is a measuring device. There are sources of error in this device, just as in other devices. How can you judge reliability in this case?

Conceptually, the answer is the same as it was in the other case. You need to put down one telescope and pick up another. In the case of observer ratings, you need to check this observer against another observer. To the extent that both see about the same thing when they look at the same event, reliability is high. This dual observation is logically the same as using two items on a questionnaire. Raters whose judgments correlate highly with each other across many ratings are said to have high **inter-rater reliability.**

In many cases, having high inter-rater reliability requires the judges to be thoroughly trained in how to observe what they're observing. Judges of Olympic diving, for example, have witnessed many thousands of dives and know precisely what to look for. As a result, their inter-rater reliability is high. Similarly, when observers assess personality, they often receive considerable instruction and practice before turning to the "real thing," so their reliability will be high.

If all judges are seeing the same things when they rate an event, then inter-rater reliability will be high.

Table 3.1 Three Kinds of Reliability. Each assesses the consistency or repeatability of an observation by looking a second time, either with the same measuring device or with a slightly different one.

Type of Reliability	Measuring Device	Type of Consistency
Internal reliability	Test item	Consistency within the test
Inter-rater reliability	Rater	Agreement between raters
Test–retest reliability	Entire test	Consistency across time

STABILITY ACROSS TIME

There's one more kind of reliability that's important in the measurement of personality. This type of reliability concerns repeatability across time. That is, assessment at one time should agree fairly well with assessment done at a different time.

Why is this important? Remember, personality is supposed to be stable. That's one reason people use the word—to convey a sense of stability. If personality is really *stable*—doesn't fluctuate from minute to minute or from day to day—then *measures* of personality should be reliable across time. People's scores should stay roughly the same when measured a week later, a month later, or four years later.

This kind of reliability is termed **test–retest reliability.** It's determined by giving the test to the same people at two different times. A scale with high test–retest reliability will yield scores the second time (the retest) that are fairly similar to those from the first time. People with high scores the first time will have high scores the second time; those with lower scores at first will have lower scores later on. (For a summary of these three types of reliability, see Table 3.1.)

Validity of Measurement

Reliability is a starting point in measurement, but it's not the only issue that matters. It's possible for measures to be highly reliable but completely meaningless. Thus, another important issue is what's called **validity.** This issue concerns whether what you're measuring is what you *think* you're measuring (or what you're *trying* to measure). Earlier we illustrated the concept of reliability in terms of random influences on the image in a telescope as you look through it at the moon. To extend the same analogy, the validity issue is whether the image you're seeing is really the moon, or just a street light (see also Figure 3.1).

How do you decide whether you're measuring what you want to measure? There are two ways to answer this question. One is an "in-principle" answer, the other is a set of tactics. The in-principle answer is that people decide by comparing two kinds of definitions with each other. When you see the word *definition,* what probably comes to mind is a conceptual, or dictionary, definition, which spells out the word's meaning in terms of conceptual qualities or attributes. It tells us what information the users of a language have agreed the word conveys. Psychologists also talk about another kind of definition, however, called an **operational definition.** This is a description of some kind of physical event.

The difference between the two kinds of definition is easy to illustrate. Consider the concept of *love.* Its conceptual (dictionary) definition might be something like "a strong affection for another person." There are many ways, however, to define *love* operationally. For example, you might ask the person you're assessing to indicate on a rating scale how much she loves someone. You might measure how often she looks into that person's eyes when interacting with him. You might measure how willing she is to give up events she enjoys in order to be with him. These three measures differ considerably from one another. Yet each might be taken as an operational definition (or operationalization) of *love*.

The essence of the validity issue in measurement can be summarized in this question: How well does the *operational* definition (the event) match the *conceptual* definition (the abstract quality that you have in mind to measure)? If the two are close, the measure has high validity. If they aren't close, validity is low.

How do you decide whether the two are close? Usually, psychologists poke at the conceptual definition until they're sure what the critical elements are and then look to see whether the same elements are in the operationalization. If they aren't (at least by strong implication), the validity of the operationalization is questionable.

The validity issue is important. It's also tricky. It's the subject of continual debate in psychology, as researchers try to think of better and better ways to look at human behavior (Borsboom, Mellenbergh, & van Heerden, 2004). The reason the issue is important is that researchers and assessors form conclusions about personality in terms of what they *think* they're measuring. If what they're really measuring isn't what they think they're measuring, they will draw false conclusions. Likewise, a clinician may draw the wrong conclusion about a person if the measure doesn't measure what the clinician thinks it measures.

Validity is important whenever anything is being observed. In personality assessment, the validity question has been examined closely for a long time. In trying to be sure that personality tests are valid, theorists have come to distinguish several aspects of validity from one another. These distinctions have also influenced the practical process of establishing validity.

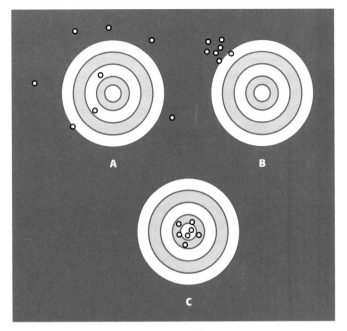

FIGURE 3.1

A simple way to think about the difference between reliability and validity, using the metaphor of target shooting. (A) Sometimes when people shoot at a target, their shots go all over. This result corresponds to measurement that's neither reliable nor valid. (B) Reliability is higher when the shots are closer together. Shots that miss the mark, however, are not valid. (C) Good measurement means that the shots are close together (reliable) *and* near the bull's-eye (valid).

CONSTRUCT VALIDITY

The idea of validity you have in mind at this point is technically called **construct validity** (Campbell, 1960; Cronbach & Meehl, 1955). Construct validity is an all-encompassing validity, and is therefore the most important kind (cf. Hogan & Nicholson, 1988; Landy, 1986). Construct validity means that the measure (the assessment device) reflects the construct (the conceptual quality) that the psychologist has in mind. Although the word *construct* sounds abstract, a construct is just a concept. Any trait quality, for example, is a construct.

Establishing construct validity for a measure is a complex process. It uses several kinds of information, each treated as a separate aspect of the validation process. For this reason, the various qualities that provide support for construct validity have names of their own. Several are described in the following paragraphs.

CRITERION VALIDITY

One important part of showing that an assessment device has construct validity is showing that it relates to other manifestations of whatever quality it's supposed to measure (Campbell, 1960). The other manifestation usually is a behavioral index, or the judgment of a trained observer, as an external *criterion* (a standard of comparison). The researcher collects this information and sees how well the assessment device correlates with it. This aspect of validity is sometimes referred to as **criterion validity** (because it uses an external criterion) or **predictive validity** (because it tests how well the measure predicts something else it's supposed to predict).

As an example, suppose you were interested in criterion validity for a measure of dominance you were developing. One way to approach this problem would be to select people who score high and low on your measure and bring them to a laboratory one at a time to work on a task with two other people. You could tape each group's discussion and score the tape for the number of times each person made suggestions, gave instructions, took charge of the situation, and so on. These behaviors would be viewed as criteria of dominance. If people who scored high on your measure did these things more than people who scored low, it would indicate a kind of criterion validity.

Another way to approach the problem would be to have a trained interviewer spend 20 minutes with each of the people who completed your scale and rate each person's dominance after the interview. The interviewer's ratings would be a different kind of criterion for dominance. If the ratings related to scores on your measure, it would indicate a different kind of criterion validity for the measure.

Criterion validity is usually regarded as the most important way to support construct validity. In recent years, though, a controversy has arisen over the process of establishing it. Howard (1990; Howard, Maxwell, Weiner, Boynton, & Rooney, 1980) has pointed out that people often assume the criterion that's chosen is a perfect reflection of the construct. In reality, though, this is almost never true. In fact, far too often, researchers choose criterion measures that are *poor* reflections of the construct. We raise this point to emphasize how critical it is to be careful in deciding what criterion to use. Unless the criterion is a good one, associations with it are meaningless. Despite this issue, however, criterion validity remains the keystone of construct validation.

CONVERGENT VALIDITY

Another aspect of support for construct validity involves showing that the measure relates to characteristics that are similar to, but not the same as, what it's supposed to measure. How is this different from criterion validity? It's just a very small step away from it. In this case, though, you know the second measure aims to assess something a little different from what your measure assesses. Because this sort of information gathering often proceeds from several angles, it's often termed **convergent validation** (Campbell & Fiske, 1959). That is the findings converge on the construct you're interested in, even though any single finding by itself won't clearly reflect the construct.

For example, a scale intended to measure dominance should relate at least a little to measures of qualities such as leadership (positively) or shyness (inversely). The correlations shouldn't be perfect because those aren't quite the same constructs, but they shouldn't be zero either. If you developed a measure to assess dominance and it didn't correlate at all with measures of leadership and shyness, you'd have to start wondering whether your measure really assesses dominance.

DISCRIMINANT VALIDITY

It's important to show that an assessment device measures what it's intended to measure. But it's also important to show that it does *not* measure qualities it's *not* intended to measure—especially qualities that don't fit with what you have in mind as a construct (Campbell, 1960). This aspect of the construct validation process is termed establishing **discriminant validity** (Campbell & Fiske, 1959).

The importance of discriminant validity can be easy to overlook. However, discriminant validation is a major line of defense against the third-variable problem in correlational research, discussed in Chapter 2. That is, you can't be sure why two correlated variables correlate. It may be that one influences the other. But it may be that a third variable, correlated with the two you've studied, is really responsible for their correlation. In principle, it's always possible to attribute the effect of a personality dimension on behavior to some other personality dimension. In practice, however, this can be made much harder by evidence of discriminant validity. That is, if research shows that the dimension you're interested in is unrelated to another variable, then that variable can't be invoked as an alternative explanation for the effect of the first.

To illustrate this, let's return to an example used in discussing the third-variable problem in Chapter 2: a correlation between self-esteem and academic performance. This association *might* reflect the effect of an unmeasured variable, for instance, IQ. Suppose, though, that we know this measure of self-esteem is unrelated to IQ, because someone checked that possibility during the process of its validation. This would make it difficult to claim that IQ is what really underlies the correlation between self-esteem and academic performance.

The process of discriminant validation is never ending because new possibilities for third variables always suggest themselves. Ruling out alternative explanations thus is a challenging task, but it's also a necessary one.

FACE VALIDITY

There's one more kind of validity that should be mentioned. It's much simpler, a little more intuitive, and most people think it's less important. It's called **face validity.** Face validity means that the assessment device appears, on its face, to be measuring the construct it was intended to measure. It *looks* right. A test of sociability made up of items such as "I prefer to spend time with friends rather than alone" and "I would rather socialize than read books" would have high face validity. A test of sociability made up of items such as "Green is my favorite color" and "I prefer imported cars" would have low face validity.

Many researchers regard face validity as a convenience, for two reasons. First, some believe that face-valid measures are easier to respond to than measures with less face validity. Second, researchers sometimes focus on distinctions between qualities of personality that differ in subtle ways. It often seems impossible to separate these qualities from each other except by using measures that are high in face validity.

On the other hand, face validity can occasionally be a detriment. This is true when the assessment device is intended to measure something that the person being assessed would find threatening or undesirable to admit. In such cases, the test developer usually tries to obscure the purpose of the test by reducing its face validity.

Whether face validity is good, bad, or neither, it should be clear that it does not substitute for other aspects of validity. If an assessment device is to be useful in the long run, it must undergo the laborious process of construct validation. The "bottom line" is always construct validity.

CULTURE AND VALIDITY

Another important issue in assessment concerns cultural differences. In a sense, this is a validity issue; in a sense, it's an issue of generalizability. Let's frame the issue as a question: Do the scores on a personality test have the same meaning for a person from an Asian culture or a Latino culture or an African American culture as they do for a middle–American European culture?

There are at least two aspects to this question. The first is whether the psychological construct *itself* has the same meaning from one culture to another. This is a fundamental question about the nature of personality. Are the elements of personality the same from one human group to another? Many people assume the basic elements of personality are universal. That may, in fact, be a dangerous assumption.

The second aspect of the question concerns how the items of the measure are interpreted by people from different cultures. If an item has one meaning for middle-class Americans but a different meaning for people in some other culture, responses to the item will also have different meanings in the different cultures. A similar issue arises when a measure is translated into a different language. This usually involves translating into the new language and then translation back into the original language by someone who's never seen the original items. This process sometimes reveals that items contain idiomatic or metaphorical meanings that are hard to translate. Adapting a measure from one culture for use in another culture is a complex process (Butcher, 1996). It must be done very carefully, if the measure is to be valid in the new culture.

RESPONSE SETS AND LOSS OF VALIDITY

Any discussion of validity must also note that there are problems in self-reporting that can interfere with the validity of the information collected. We've already mentioned that biases in recall can distort the picture and render the information invalid. In the same way, people's motivational tendencies can also get in the way of accurate reporting.

There are at least two biases in the way people respond in assessment. These biases are called **response sets.** A response set is a psychological orientation, a readiness to answer in a particular way (Berg, 1967; Jackson & Messick, 1967; Rorer, 1965). Response sets create distortions in the information assessed. Personality psychologists want their assessments to provide information that's free from contamination. Thus, response sets are problems.

Two response sets are particularly important in personality assessment. One of them emerges most clearly when the assessment device is a self-report instrument that, in one fashion or another, asks the person questions that require a yes-or-no response (or a response on a rating scale with *agree* and *disagree* as the opposite ends of the scale). This response set, called **acquiescence,** is the tendency to say yes (Couch & Keniston, 1960).

Everyone presumably has a bit of this tendency, but people vary greatly on it. That's what causes the problem. If the set isn't counteracted somehow, the scores of people who are highly acquiescent become inflated. Their high scores reflect the response set instead of their personality. People who have extreme personalities but not much acquiescence will also have high scores. But you won't know whose high scores are from personality and whose are from acquiescence.

Many view acquiescence as an easy problem to combat. The way it's handled for self-reports is this: Write half the items so that *yes* indicates being at one end of the personality dimension. Write the other half of the items so that a *no* response means being at that end of the personality dimension. In the process of scoring the test, then, any bias that comes from the simple tendency to say yes is canceled out.

This procedure takes care of the problem of overagreement, but not everyone is convinced it's a good idea. Negatively worded items often are harder to understand or more complicated to answer than positively worded items. The result can be responses that are less accurate (Converse & Presser, 1986; Schriesheim & Hill, 1981). For this reason, some people feel it's better to live with the acquiescence problem than to introduce a different kind of error by using complex wording.

The tendency to provide socially desirable responses can sometimes mask a person's true characteristics or feelings.

A second response set is perhaps more important than acquiescence and also more troublesome. It's called **social desirability,** reflecting the fact that people tend to portray themselves in a good light (in socially desirable ways) whenever possible. Once again, this tendency is stronger among some people than others (see Crowne & Marlowe, 1964; Edwards, 1957). As with acquiescence, if it isn't counteracted, people with strong concerns about social desirability will produce scores that reflect the response set, rather than their personalities.

For some personality dimensions, this isn't much of a problem. This is because there's really no social approval or disapproval at either end of the dimension. In other cases, though, there's a consensus that it's better to be one way (for example, honest or likable) than the other (dishonest or unlikable). In these cases, assessment becomes tricky.

In general, psychologists deal with this problem by trying to phrase items so that the issue of social desirability isn't salient. As much as anything else, this is a process of trying to avoid even bringing up the idea that one kind of person is approved of more than the other. Sometimes this means phrasing undesirable responses in ways that make them more acceptable. Sometimes it means looking for ways to let people admit the undesirable quality indirectly. A different way to deal with the problem is to include items that assess the person's degree of concern about social desirability and use this information as a correction factor in evaluating the person's responses to other items. In any event, this is a problem that personality psychologists must constantly be aware of and constantly guarding against in trying to measure what people are like.

Two Rationales behind the Development of Assessment Devices

Thus far, this chapter has considered issues that arise in trying to measure any quality of personality. What it hasn't taken up yet is how people decide what qualities to measure in the first place. This question won't be answered completely here, because the answer depends partly on the theoretical perspective underlying the assessment. There is, however, a general issue to address. In particular, development of personality measures usually follows one of two paths, each of which has its own kind of logic.

RATIONAL, OR THEORETICAL, APPROACH

One strategy is termed a **rational,** or **theoretical, approach** to assessment. This strategy is based on theoretical considerations from the very start. The psychologist first develops a rational basis for believing that a particular dimension of personality is important. The next task is to create a test in which this dimension is reflected validly and reliably in people's answers. This approach to test development often leads to assessment devices that have a high degree of face validity.

It's important to realize that the work doesn't stop once a set of items has been developed. Instruments developed from this starting point must be shown to be reliable, to predict behavioral criteria, and to have good construct validity. Until these steps are taken, the scale shouldn't be considered a useful measure of anything.

It's probably safe to say that the majority of personality measurement devices that now exist were developed using this path. Some of these measures are single scales; others are inventories. Most of the measures that are discussed in later chapters were created by first deciding *what* to measure and then figuring out *how* to measure it.

EMPIRICAL APPROACHES

The theoretical approach isn't the only way to start in scale development, though. A second strategy is usually characterized as an **empirical,** or data-based, **approach.** The basic characteristic of this approach is that it relies on data, rather than on theory, to decide what items go into the assessment device.

There are two important variations on this theme. One of them is an inductive approach in which the person developing the measure uses the data to decide what qualities of personality even exist (Cattell, 1947, 1965, 1979). Because this line of thought is an important contributor to trait psychology, we're going to wait to discuss it until the chapter on trait psychology. We'll focus here on another empirical approach. This one reflects a very pragmatic orientation to the process of assessment. It's guided less by a desire to understand personality than by a practical aim of sorting people into categories. If a quick or inexpensive technique can be found to do this, the technique provides an important benefit.

Instead of developing the test first and then validating it against a criterion, this approach works in the opposite direction. The groups into which people are to be sorted represent the criteria for the test. Developing the test is a matter of starting out with a very large number of possible items and finding out which items are answered differently by members of one criterion group than by other people. This is termed the **criterion keying** approach to test development. This label reflects the fact that the items retained are those that empirically distinguish between the *criterion* group and other people. If such an item set can be found for each criterion group involved, then the entire test (all the item sets together) can be used to tell who belongs to which group.

In the point of view reflected in this approach, it doesn't matter at all what the items of the assessment device look like. It only matters that they distinguish people who fit a criterion from those who don't. Items in a scale based on this approach are chosen because members of a specific group (defined on some other basis) tend to answer them differently than other people.

The best illustration of the use of this method is the Minnesota Multiphasic Personality Inventory, better known as the MMPI (Hathaway & McKinley, 1943), revised in 1989 as the MMPI-2 (Butcher, Dahlstrom, Graham, Tellegen, & Kaemmer, 1989). The MMPI was a very long true–false inventory developed as a measure of abnormality. The first step in its development was to collect a large number of self-

Table 3.2 Content Scales of the MMPI-2 and Interpretation of Each Scale's Meaning.
Source: MMPI-2TM (Minnesota Multiphasic Personality Inventory-2) TM Manual for Administration, Scoring, and Interpretation, Revised Edition. Copyright © 2001 by the Regents of the University of Minnesota. Used by permission of the University of Minnesota Press. All rights reserved. "MMPI-2" and "Minnesota Multiphasic Personality-2" are trademarks owned by the Regents of the University of Minnesota.

Clinical Scales	Interpretation
Hypochondriasis	High scorers are cynical, defeatist, over-concerned with physical health
Depression	High scorers are despondent, distressed, depressed
Hysteria	High scorers report frequent symptoms with no apparent organic cause
Psychopathic deviate	High scorers are adventurous, have disregard for social or moral standards
Masculinity/femininity	Scores provide indication of level of "traditional" male/female interests
Paranoia	High scorers are guarded and suspicious, feel persecuted
Psychasthenia	High scorers are anxious, rigid, tense, and worrying
Schizophrenia	High scorers exhibit social alienation, bizarreness in thinking
Hypomania	High scorers are emotionally excitable, impulsive, hyperactive
Social introversion	High scorers are shy, withdrawn, uninvolved in social relationships

descriptive statements. The statements then were given to a group of normal persons and to groups of psychiatric patients—people already judged by a clinician to have a specific disorder. Thus, the criterion already existed. The next step was to test the items. Do people with one psychiatric diagnosis either agree or disagree with the item more often than normal people and people with different diagnoses? If so, that item was included in the scale for that psychiatric diagnosis.

The original MMPI was developed long ago using a sample that had a narrow age range and was restricted ethnically and geographically (largely from Minnesota). Concern arose that scores from other populations might not be interpreted properly. In addition, some of the items were hard to understand. The people developing the MMPI-2 reworded about 20% of the original items for clarity, wrote 154 new ones, and distilled the total to 567. They collected data from people who varied more widely in ethnicity, age, and gender. Thus, interpretation of responses is now more consistent with the contemporary U.S. populace.

As was true of the original, the MMPI-2 has ten basic content scales (see Table 3.2). It also has six validity scales. The content scales indicate similarity of a person's responses to those of patients with a particular diagnosis. The validity scales provide an estimate of how meaningful the person's response profile is. For example, the Lie scale measures people's tendencies to present themselves too favorably to be true. As another example, frequent "cannot say" responses—an inability to choose the true or false option—may mean that the person is being evasive. If too many of these responses are made, the meaning of the other responses is called into question.

Better Assessment: A Never-Ending Search

As was just described, even one of the most widely used tests in the world wasn't considered "finished" just because it was widely used. It was subjected to further refinement, additional data gathering, and a continuing examination of how people respond to its items. The result was an improvement in what the test can tell the psychologists who use it.

The MMPI isn't the only measure to be re-examined and revised in this way. Most personality scales in widespread use have been revised once or more and restandardized periodically. The process of establishing construct validity requires not just a single study but many. It thus takes time. The process of establishing discriminant validity is virtually never ending. Tremendous effort is invested in creating and improving tests of personality. This investment of effort is necessary if people are to feel confident of knowing what the tests measure. Having that confidence is an important part of the assessment of personality.

The characteristics of personality tests discussed in this chapter distinguish these tests from those you see from time to time in newspapers, magazines, on TV, and so forth. In some cases, the items in a magazine article were written specifically for that article. It's unlikely that anyone checked on their reliability. It's even less likely that anyone checked on their validity. Even if the items were taken from a carefully developed instrument, the entire set of items usually isn't used; it can be hard to be sure how well the ones that were chosen reflect the entire scale. Unless the right steps have been taken to create an instrument, you should be careful about putting your faith in the results that come from it.

· SUMMARY ·

Assessment (measurement of personality) is something that people constantly do informally. Psychologists formalize this process into several distinct techniques. Observer ratings are made about people by someone else—an interviewer, someone who watches, or someone who knows the people well enough to make ratings of what they are like. Observer ratings often are somewhat subjective, involving interpretations of the person's behavior. Self-reports are made by the people being assessed, about themselves. Self-reports can be single scales or multiscale inventories. Assessment devices can be subjective or objective. Objective techniques require no interpretation as the assessment is made. Subjective techniques involve some sort of interpretation as an intrinsic part of the measure.

One issue for all assessment is *reliability* (the reproducibility of the measurement). Reliability is determined by checking one measurement against another (or several others). Self-report scales usually have many items (each a measurement), leading to indices of internal reliability, or internal consistency. Observer judgments are checked by inter-rater reliability. Test–retest reliability assesses the reproducibility of the measure over time. In all cases, high correlation among measures means good reliability.

Another important issue is *validity* (whether what you're measuring is what you want to measure). The attempt to determine whether the operational definition (the assessment device) matches the concept you set out to measure is called *construct validation*. Contributors to construct validity are evidence of criterion, convergent, and discriminant validity. Face validity is not usually taken as an important element of construct validity. Validity is threatened by the fact that people have response sets (acquiescence and social desirability) that bias their responses.

Development of assessment devices proceeds along one of two paths. The rational path uses a theory to decide what should be measured and then figures out the best way to measure it. Most assessment devices developed this way. The empirical path involves using data to determine what items should be in a scale. The MMPI was developed this way, using a technique called *criterion keying,* in which the test developers let people's responses tell them which items to use. Test items that members of a diagnostic category answered differently from other people were retained.

· GLOSSARY ·

Acquiescence   The response set of tending to say yes (agree) in response to any question.

Assessment   The measuring of personality.

Construct validity   The accuracy with which a measure reflects the underlying concept.

Convergent validity   The degree to which a measure relates to other characteristics that are conceptually similar to what it's supposed to assess.

Criterion keying   The developing of a test by seeing which items distinguish between groups.

Criterion validity   The degree to which the measure correlates with a separate criterion reflecting the same concept.

Discriminant validity   The degree to which a scale does *not* measure unintended qualities.

Empirical approach (to scale development)   The use of data instead of theory to decide what should go into the measure.

Error   Random influences that are incorporated in measurements.

Face validity   The scale seeming on its face to measure what it's supposed to measure.

Internal reliability (internal consistency)   Agreement among responses made to the items of a measure.

Inter-rater reliability   The degree of agreement between observers of the same events.

Inventory   A personality test measuring several aspects of personality on distinct subscales.

Objective measure   A measure that incorporates no interpretation.

Observer ratings   An assessment in which someone else produces information about the person being assessed.

Operational definition   The defining of a concept by the concrete events through which it is measured (or manipulated).

Predictive validity   The degree to which the measure predicts other variables it should predict.

Rational approach (to scale development)   The use of a theory to decide what you want to measure and then deciding how to measure it.

Reliability   Consistency across repeated measurements.

Response set   A biased orientation to answering.

Self-report   An assessment in which people make ratings pertaining to themselves.

Social desirability   The response set of tending to portray oneself favorably.

Split-half reliability   Assessing internal consistency among responses to items of a measure by splitting the items into halves and then correlating them.

Subjective measure   A measure incorporating personal interpretation.

Test–retest reliability   The stability of measurements across time.

Theoretical approach   See **Rational approach.**

Validity   A measure's "truthfulness," or the degree to which it actually measures what it is intended to measure.

PART 2

The Dispositional Perspective

The Dispositional Perspective: Major Themes and Underlying Assumptions

A key theme of the *dispositional perspective* on personality is the idea that people display consistency in their actions, thoughts, and feelings. A human being's dispositional nature doesn't shift aimlessly from moment to moment—it endures across changes in time and place. Indeed, the very concept of *disposition* is a way of representing the fact that people remain the same people, even as time passes and as they move from one situation to another. Dispositions are qualities that people carry around with them, that belong to them, that are part of them.

Certainly, we all experience periods in which we're unpredictable, in which we may feel buffeted by the psychological winds around us. But for most people that experience is the exception rather than the rule. It certainly isn't the essence of personality. Rather, personality implies stability, constancy, something that doesn't vary too much from one time to another. You—like most people—undoubtedly feel within yourself a sense of coherence, a kind of permanence across time, events, and experiences. You're the person you are, and you'll still be that person tomorrow, and next week, and next year. This is the core meaning of disposition.

A second theme of the dispositional perspective derives from the fact that people differ from each other in many ways. As indicated in Chapter 1, the entire field of personality psychology is guided in part by an emphasis on differences among people. This emphasis is particularly central to the dispositional perspective. From this perspective, each person's personality consists of a pattern of dispositional qualities. The composition of the pattern differs from one person to another. The intersection among these dispositions in any given person constitutes the defining nature of that person's personality.

These assumptions are important throughout the dispositional perspective. They're dealt with differently, however, by different kinds of theorists. One approach emphasizes the mere existence of dispositions. It focuses primarily on trying to measure and catalog them in better ways, to reach a clearer understanding of what the dimensions are that are most important in personality and to find better ways to place people on those dimensions. This trait-and-type approach is discussed in Chapter 4. This trait approach most clearly exemplifies the dispositional perspective.

This isn't the only way to approach the concept of disposition, though. A second way is to think of dispositions as enduring motivational characteristics that vary in strength from person to person. These differences in the motive tendencies that underlie people's actions are reflected in differences in the qualities that the people display in their behavior. This needs-and-motives approach to dispositions is examined in Chapter 5.

Types, Traits, and Interactionism

"I want you to meet a friend of mine from high school. He's really outgoing. He's friendly, but he doesn't go along with the crowd all the time. You might say he's sociable, but he's also independent."

"My psychology professor is *so* predictable. He's smart, but he's such a geek. He must spend all his time in his office. I can't imagine him doing anything interesting or fun. He can't help it, I guess. It's just his personality."

IT'S COMMON to assume that each person has a set of dispositions that are fairly easy to observe. When you find out what people are like, you know what to expect of them in the future. This idea applies to all of personality psychology, of course. But it's particularly prominent in the trait-and-type view of personality. The words *trait* and *type* convey slightly different meanings. They converge, though, on the idea that people have stable characteristics that they display across different circumstances and across time.

Types and Traits

The idea that people could be divided into different types, or categories, goes back at least to Hippocrates (about 400 B.C.), whose ideas were later embellished by Galen (about A.D. 150). People were thought to form four groups: *choleric* (irritable), *melancholic* (depressed), *sanguine* (optimistic), and *phlegmatic* (calm). Each personality type was thought to reflect an excess of one of four basic bodily fluids.

More recently, Carl Jung (1933) argued that people are either introverts or extraverts. An **introvert** tends to be alone a lot and prefers solitary activities. When facing stress, introverts tend to withdraw into themselves. An **extravert** prefers to spend time with others rather than be alone. When facing stress, extraverts tend to seek out other people.

In true typologies, the **types** are regarded as distinct and discontinuous categories. An example of a discontinuous category is *gender:* People are either male or female. Jung often portrayed the categories of introvert and extravert as discontinuous in the same way (see Figure 4.1). Type theories have generally faded from personality psychology. (For dissenting views, see Gangestad & Snyder, 1985; Meehl, 1992; Robins, John,

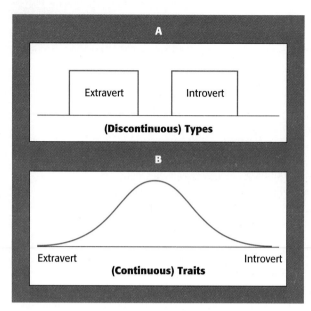

FIGURE 4.1
(A) Early type theories assumed a discontinuity between or among categories of people. (B) Trait theories assume that traits are continuous dimensions of variability on some characteristic and that the degree of presence versus absence of the characteristic is distributed across a population.

Caspi, Moffitt, & Stouthamer-Loeber, 1996; Strube, 1989; York & John, 1992.)

In contrast to categorical typologies, **trait** theories assume that people occupy different points on continuously varying dimensions (Figure 4.1). For that reason, this is sometimes called a *dimensional* approach. In trait theories, differences among people are seen as *quantitative* rather than qualitative. People are seen as differing in *how much* of various characteristics they incorporate in their personalities.

This difference in terminology has been maintained by most theorists, but not all. Hans Eysenck (1967, 1970, 1975) muddied the water a little, using the word *type* not to indicate discontinuity, but to imply a *supertrait*—a trait that's very broad and important.

NOMOTHETIC AND IDIOGRAPHIC VIEWS OF TRAITS

Thus far, we've implied that traits pertain to every person and that people just vary in how much of each quality they have. The belief that traits exist in the same way in every person is called a **nomothetic** view of personality (Allport, 1961). The term *nomothetic* derives from the Greek word meaning *law*. This view holds that everyone stands somewhere on each trait that exists. This allows comparisons among people. (You can't compare people unless the trait is the same for everyone.) The nomothetic view has dominated trait psychology for at least 50 years.

In contrast is the **idiographic** view (Allport, 1961), which emphasizes each person's uniqueness (see also Lamiell, 1981). The term *idiographic* has the same source as *idiosyncratic*. This view holds that traits are individualized. A given trait may be possessed by only one person in the world. This view suggests that people often can't be compared, because everyone is on a different scale. Even if the same term applies to two people, its connotations will differ between people (Dunning & McElwee, 1995). Even if the connotations are the same, the trait may differ in importance, so the people can't be compared meaningfully (Britt & Shepperd, 1999).

Does the nomothetic view deny uniqueness? No, not really. Those who favor the nomothetic view think instead that uniqueness means unique *combinations* of levels on many trait dimensions, though the dimensions themselves are the same for everyone. As Eysenck put it, "the unique individual is simply the point of intersection of a number of quantitative variables" (1952, p. 18).

Psychologists who emphasize the idiographic view believe that nomothetic views always are oversimplifications (even though they sometimes use them). To Allport, we should never lose sight of that fact: Even traits that people share always have a special flavor (maybe from differences in how the trait is expressed) that varies from person to person.

Most trait psychologists do keep this point in the back of their minds. But most tend to disregard the strongest version of the idiographic approach: the idea that traits themselves differ from person to person.

What Traits Matter?

Thinking of personality in terms of traits quickly leads to this question: *What are the traits that make up personality?*

This is a hard question to answer with complete certainty. In fact, there have been serious disagreements about where to *start* in answering it. Before we describe this disagreement, let's back up and consider a problem that all trait theorists share, and a tool that helps deal with it.

A KEY TOOL: FACTOR ANALYSIS

Personality is reflected in many ways—for example, in descriptive words. If each word describing personality meant a different trait, a psychologist would go crazy trying to organize things. That, in a nutshell, is a problem every trait psychologist faces: bringing order to such diversity. Perhaps, however, the many words may reflect a small number of underlying trait dimensions. If so, how do you figure out what the dimensions are?

A tool that's often used for this is a statistical technique called **factor analysis.** The basic idea is simple: If two qualities correlate when assessed across many people, they may reflect a trait that contributes to both of them. *Patterns* of correlation, then, may reveal trait dimensions that lie beneath the measured qualities. Factor analysis is essentially a more complex version of correlation. Instead of looking at one correlation between *two* variables, a factor analysis looks at correlations among *many* variables. Because the process is very complex, it was not widely used until the computer age. The huge rise in computing power over the years has led to far greater sophistication in these procedures (Bentler, 1990; Jöreskog & Sörbom, 1979).

The process starts by collecting measurements on many variables from large numbers of people. The measures can take any form, but typically they are self-reports or observer ratings. Once the data are collected, correlations are computed between every pair of variables (see Box 4.1). The set of correlations is then put through a procedure called *factor extraction*. This distills the correlations to a smaller set of **factors.** Each factor represents shared variations (underlying commonalities) among several of the measures (rather than two at a time).

Once the factors are extracted, each can be described by a set of **factor loadings.** Think of these as correlations between the factor and each item (rating) that contributes to its existence. Items that correlate strongly with the factor (usually higher than 0.30 or so) are said to "load on" that factor. Items that don't correlate strongly with the factor are said not to load on it. The items that load on the factor tell you what the factor is about.

The final step in the analysis is labeling the factors. Remember that a factor is defined by which items load on it. Thus, you choose a label to denote as closely as possible the essence of those items, particularly those with the highest loadings. In analyses on personality, the factor is viewed as the statistical reflection of a trait. When you name the factor, you are naming the trait.

Factor naming is very subjective. Several names might seem equally good. Which name is chosen, however, can have important consequences. People often forget that the label is an inference from the pattern of correlations. They rely on the label to tell them what the trait is. If the label you choose is misleading, it can create problems of interpretation later.

Factor analysis as a tool in trait psychology does three things. First, it reduces the multiple reflections of personality to a smaller set of traits (tells you what traits underlie the reflections). Second, it provides a basis for arguing that some traits matter more than others. That is, if a factor accounts for a lot of variability in the ratings, it reflects an important trait; if it accounts for less, it's less important. Third, factor analysis helps in developing assessment devices. You keep items (or ratings) that load strongly (greatly reflect the trait) and discard items that don't. Through repeated item creation and analysis, items that don't do a good job of measuring a particular trait are replaced by better ones.

Box 4.1 A Closer Look at Factor Analysis

The process of factor analysis is complex, but its logic is fairly simple. It's an attempt to find patterns of association in a set of variables.

The first step is collecting data. This is more complicated than it might seem. First you have to decide what aspects of behavior you want to measure. Do you want self-reports? Observer ratings? As you can see, the first step—collecting data—entails many decisions.

Let's use an example. Imagine you're interested in how people cope with stress (Lazarus & Folkman, 1984). You've decided to use self-reports: people's ratings of how much they did certain things during their most stressful event of the past year. To "collect data," get 300 or so of your friends to recall a stressful event and respond to each of 28 items (listing things people sometimes do under stress). Among the items are these:

1. Took action quickly, before things could get out of hand
2. Refused to believe that it was real
3. Did something concrete to make the situation better
4. Tried to convince myself that it wasn't happening
5. Went on thinking things were just like they were
6. Changed or grew as a person in a new way
7. Tried to look on the bright side of things

The second step is to compute the correlation of every item with every other item (panel A, right). Each correlation reflects the degree to which the 300 people tended to answer one item the same as the other item. There are strong correla-

tions between items 1 and 3; between 6 and 7; and between 2 and both 4 and 5 (which also strongly relate to each other). The others are quite weak.

Because you had people rate 28 items (instead of just these seven), your correlation matrix is huge (each item with each other item). Interpreting the pattern of correlations would be a real chore. The chore is lessened by the third step, called *factor extraction*. It reduces your matrix to a smaller number of underlying dimensions (for example, the links among items 2, 4, and 5 would contribute to one dimension). These dimensions of underlying commonality are called *factors*. Factors are hazy entities you can imagine but can't see.

The next step is to compute the *factor loadings* of each item on each factor. Loadings tell you the relations between the items and the factors (panel B, right). Each loading indicates how much the item reflects the underlying dimension. A large number (a high loading) means the item is closely linked to that dimension, a small number means it's not. As shown, items 1 and 3 load on factor A (but no other factor), items 6 and 7 load on factor B (but no other factor), and items 2, 4, and 5 load on factor C (but no other factor). Similar loadings emerge for all your 28 items, letting you know which items go together.

Once it's clear which items form which factors, you're at the final step: naming the factors. You want to convey the essence of the underlying quality, but your only guide is which items load on it. Often the items are ambiguous or have several elements, clouding the picture. In our example, a

A. Hypothetical Correlation Matrix

Item	1	2	3	4	5	6	7
1	*	0.10	0.75	−0.05	0.03	0.12	0.00
2		*	−0.02	0.52	0.61	−.007	−0.08
3			*	0.17	0.00	0.09	0.15
4				*	0.71	0.11	0.08
5					*	0.06	−0.04
6						*	0.59
7							*

B. Hypothetical Factor Loadings

Factor	A	B	C
Item 1	(0.62)	0.15	0.01
Item 2	0.03	−0.08	(0.49)
Item 3	(0.54)	0.04	−0.20
Item 4	0.10	0.11	(0.56)
Item 5	0.07	0.08	(0.50)
Item 6	−0.02	(0.72)	0.12
Item 7	0.08	(0.48)	0.08

couple of factors are easy. The items on factor A show a tendency to try to solve the problem. This might be called *problem-focused coping*. Given the content of items 2, 4, and 5, factor C might be *denial*. Factor B seems to be *positive reinterpretation* or *posttraumatic growth* or *looking on the bright side,* but it's hard to be sure which is best. It's important to be careful, though, because the name you use will guide your future thinking.

Factor analysis is a very useful tool. It's only a tool, though. What we've told you has a big hole in it. We haven't said anything about *what measures to collect in the first place*. A factor analysis can tell you only about what you put into it. Thus, the decision about what to measure has a huge impact on what emerges as traits.

How do you decide what measures to collect? As noted earlier, different people have started off differently. Let's now return to that question.

LET REALITY REVEAL ITSELF: CATTELL'S APPROACH

The answer some give is that researchers should determine *empirically* what traits make up person-

Whereas extraverts prefer exciting activities involving other people, introverts like to be alone.

ality, not impose preconceptions. If you start with preconceptions, you'll lead yourself astray. This was the argument of Raymond Cattell, an early contributor to trait psychology and one of the first users of factor analysis (Cattell, 1947, 1965, 1978; Cattell & Kline, 1977). This reasoning had a strong influence on many other trait researchers (Goldberg, 1993b).

One empirical approach focused on language as a source of information (see Goldberg, 1982). A language that's evolved over thousands of years has words to describe many human qualities. Presumably, any trait that matters has words that describe it. In fact, the more words for a quality of personality, the more it probably matters. This is called the **lexical criterion** of importance. Following this idea, Cattell (1947, 1965) took a set of trait terms, removed obvious synonyms, collected ratings on the terms, and factor analyzed the ratings. The resulting factors were the traits he believed are important.

Cattell came to believe that personality is captured in a set of 16 dimensions (see Table 4.1). The dimensions re-emerged in analyses across various types of data, and he saw them as the primary traits in personality. These 16 primary factors provided a name for the resulting inventory: the 16 Personality Factor inventory, or 16PF (Cattell, Eber, & Tatsuoka, 1977).

Table 4.1 The 16 Factors in Cattell's View of Personality (as defined by the characteristics of high and low scorers on each trait dimension). The factors are listed in order of variance accounted for by each factor. The labels listed are the currently used verbal approximations for the content of each factor. *Source:* Copyright © 1993 by the Institute for Personality and Ability Testing, Inc., Champaign, IL 61824-1188. Reproduced by permission.

Reserved	Warm	Trusting	Vigilant
Concrete-reasoning	Abstract-reasoning	Practical	Imaginative
Reactive	Emotionally stable	Forthright	Private
Deferential	Dominant	Self-assured	Apprehensive
Serious	Lively	Traditional	Open to change
Expedient	Rule-conscientious	Group-oriented	Self-reliant
Shy	Socially-bold	Tolerates disorder	Perfectionist
Utilitarian	Sensitive	Relaxed	Tense

START FROM A THEORY: EYSENCK'S APPROACH

Not all agreed that an empirical starting point is best. Another major contributor to trait psychology, Hans Eysenck (e.g., 1967, 1970, 1975, 1986; Eysenck & Eysenck, 1985) argued that we should begin instead with well-developed ideas about what we want to measure. Then we should set about measuring those qualities well.

In framing his theory, he began with the typology of Hippocrates and Galen and related observations made by Jung and Wundt (Eysenck, 1967). He set out to investigate whether the four types identified by Hippocrates and Galen (and re-identified by others) could be created by combining high and low levels of two supertraits.

The two supertraits Eysenck posed as the key dimensions of personality are introversion–extraversion and emotionality–stability (or neuroticism). The extraversion dimension concerns tendencies toward sociability, liveliness, activeness, and dominance (all of which characterize extraverts). The neuroticism dimension concerns the ease and frequency with which the person becomes upset and distressed. Moodiness, anxiety, and depression reflect greater neuroticism.

These dimensions can create more diversity than you might guess. Table 4.2 portrays four sets of people, with combinations of highs and lows on these dimensions. The ancient type label for each group is printed in color. In considering these people, keep two things in mind: First, although the form of Table 4.2 suggests discontinuity, both dimensions are continuous. Second, the descriptions apply to fairly extreme and clear-cut cases. Most people are closer to the middle on both dimensions and thus have less-extreme characteristics.

As Table 4.2 indicates, people who are introverted and also emotionally stable tend to be careful, controlled, calm, and thoughtful in their actions. The combination of introversion and emotional *instability,* on the other hand, creates a more moody sense of unsociable reserve, a pessimistic and anxious quality. Thus, introverts can differ substantially, depending on their levels of emotional stability or instability.

Table 4.2 Traits Common among Four Categories of People Deriving from the Two Major Personality Dimensions Proposed by Eysenck. Each category results from combining introversion or extraversion with either a high or a low level of emotional stability. *Source:* Adapted from Eysenck, 1975.

	Emotionally Stable		Emotionally Unstable	
Introvert	Passive Careful Thoughtful Peaceful Controlled Reliable Even tempered Calm	Phlegmatic	Quiet Pessimistic Unsociable Sober Rigid Moody Anxious Reserved	Melancholic
Extravert	Sociable Outgoing Talkative Responsive Easygoing Lively Carefree Leaderly	Sanguine	Active Optimistic Impulsive Changeable Excitable Aggressive Restless Touchy	Choleric

So can extraverts. When extraversion combines with emotional stability, the result is an easygoing, carefree sociability. Emotional *instability* in an extravert introduces an excitable aggressive quality. Thus, the impact of one dimension differs as a function of the person's location on the other trait dimension. In the terms used in Chapter 2, the traits *interact*.

Eysenck assessed these dimensions by a self-report measure called the Eysenck Personality Questionnaire, or EPQ (Eysenck & Eysenck, 1975). He used factor analysis to help create it, but he did so with a different goal in mind than Cattell had. Cattell used factor analysis to find out what dimensions *exist*. Eysenck used factor analysis to refine his scales by selecting items that loaded well and to confirm that the scales measure two factors, as he intended.

Although Eysenck and Cattell started out very differently, they produced trait structures with distinct similarities. The two dimensions Eysenck saw as supertraits resemble two of the first three factors of Cattell's 16PF (Table 4.1). The similarities are even stronger in **second-order factors** from the 16PF. A second-order analysis tells whether the factors *themselves* form factors (correlate in clusters). One second-order factor from the 16PF is virtually identical to extraversion (Cattell & Kline, 1977); another is similar to neuroticism.

Another reflection of the convergence can be seen in Eysenck's argument that extraversion and neuroticism are at the top of an unfolding hierarchy of qualities (see Figure 4.2). Each supertrait is made of component traits (which resemble Cattell's primary traits). Component traits contribute to the supertrait. Component traits, in turn, reflect habits, which derive from specific responses. Eysenck believed all levels are involved in behavior, but he saw supertraits (which he called *types*) as the most important.

Two more points about Eysenck's view: First, he believed that extraversion and neuroticism link to aspects of nervous system functioning. That aspect of his theory comes up in Chapter 7. Second, there's a third dimension in Eysenck's view, which has had less attention than the others, called *psychoticism* (Eysenck & Eysenck, 1976). It involves, in part, a tendency toward psychological detachment from, and lack of concern with, other people. People high in this trait tend to be hostile, manipulative, and impulsive (Eysenck, 1992).

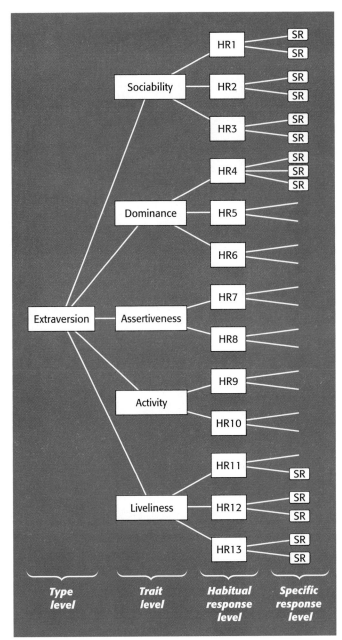

FIGURE 4.2
Eysenck's hierarchical view of personality as applied to extraversion. The top level of the model (types) subsumes the elements represented at the next-lower level (traits). These elements, in turn, are made up of yet lower-order qualities (habits), which are made up of associations between stimulus and response. *Source: Adapted from* The Biological Basis of Personality *(1967, p. 36), by H. J. Eysenck. Reprinted courtesy of Charles C Thomas, Publisher, Springfield, IL.*

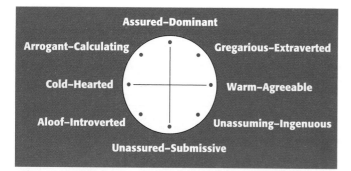

FIGURE 4.3

The *interpersonal circle,* a set of personality patterns portrayed in terms of their relative prevalence of two traits: love (the horizontal dimension) and dominance (the vertical dimension). The midpoint of each trait is the point where the lines cross.

Source: Adapted from Wiggins, Phillips, & Trapnell, 1989.

ANOTHER THEORETICAL STARTING POINT: THE INTERPERSONAL CIRCLE

Another theoretical starting point emphasized interpersonal aspects of personality. Jerry Wiggins and his colleagues (Wiggins, 1979; Wiggins, Phillips, & Trapnell, 1989) argued that the core human traits influence interpersonal life. Wiggins proposed a set of eight patterns, which he calls the **interpersonal circle,** arrayed around two dimensions that underlie human relations (see Figure 4.3). The core dimensions are dominance (or status) and love.

Wiggins argued (as did Eysenck) that diverse personalities arise from combinations of values on the two core dimensions. A person who's high in dominance and toward the cold-hearted end of love will seem arrogant and calculating. Put the same degree of dominance with warmth on the love dimension, though, and you get a person who's gregarious and extraverted.

Introversion and extraversion appear on this interpersonal circle (in lower-left and upper-right corners), but here they aren't a fundamental dimension. Instead, they are seen as resulting from the intersection of two other qualities.

The Five-Factor Model: The Basic Dimensions of Personality?

Despite the different starting points taken by various people, a substantial consensus has begun to emerge about what traits are basic. The emerging consensus has overtones of several ideas we've already presented, but it extends beyond them. The emerging consensus is that the basic structure of personality may incorporate five superordinate factors. These are often referred to as the *five-factor model,* or the *"big five"* (Goldberg, 1981; McCrae & Costa, 2003; Wiggins, 1996).

Evidence in support of a five-factor view of personality structure accumulated slowly for a long time (Digman, 1990). In 1949, Fiske couldn't reproduce Cattell's sixteen factors but instead found five. That finding sat in obscurity until the early 1960s, when Norman (1963), Borgatta (1964), and Smith (1967) all addressed the same general issue with different measures. Each reached the same conclusion: Five factors provided the best account of the data.

During the 1980s and 1990s, there was an explosion of work on this topic, which has continued to the present. Diverse samples have been collected, including teachers' ratings of children (Digman & Inouye, 1986) and peer ratings (McCrae & Costa, 1987). Some studies used a kind of self-rating called a *Q-sort* (Lanning, 1994; McCrae, Costa, & Busch, 1986); others assessed frequencies with which people engage in particular kinds of actions (Botwin & Buss, 1989); others used nonverbal assessments (Paunonen, Jackson, Trzebinski, & Forsterling, 1992). The model was also tested against measures developed from entirely different lines of thought (Costa & McCrae, 1988a; McCrae & Costa, 1989a). Peabody and Goldberg (1989; Peabody, 1984) used scales that were chosen to be sure there were enough *common* trait words instead of words that mean more to psychologists than to other people. Haas (2002) even explored the idea that proverbs capture the five factors.

Data have now been collected from many cultures and languages. The findings as a group suggest that the five factors may transcend many boundaries of language and culture (e.g., Benet-Martínez & John, 1998; Church, 2001; Katigbak, Church,

Guanzon-Lapeña, Carlota, & del Pilar, 2002; McCrae & Costa, 1997; McCrae, Zonderman, Costa, Bond, & Paunonen, 1996; Paunonen et al., 1992; Saucier & Ostendorf, 1999; Somer & Goldberg, 1999; Stumpf, 1993). The cultures examined in this work are as diverse as those of Turkey (Somer & Goldberg, 1999) and the Philippines (Katigbak et al., 2002). One study of observer ratings collected data in 50 cultures (McCrae, Terracino, et al., 2005). It has even been argued (Gosling, 2001) that the factors (or at least some of them) apply to lower animals!

There have been some failures to find the pattern and some imperfections in the findings (e.g., Benet & Waller, 1995; Church & Burke, 1994; Di Blas & Forzi, 1991; Lanning, 1994). And Saucier and Simonds (2006) caution that the pattern is clearest in Western languages and not at all easy to find in some other languages. Yet the body of work as a whole is impressive in the fit to the five-factor model (Digman, 1990; John, 1990; McCrae & Costa, 1997, 2003; McCrae & John, 1992; Ozer & Reise, 1994).

WHAT ARE THE FIVE FACTORS?

Given what we've said so far, what comes next may surprise you. There's still a fair amount of disagreement as to exactly what the five dimensions *are* (Briggs, 1989; John, 1990; Johnson & Ostendorf, 1993; Pytlik Zillig, Hemenover, & Dienstbier, 2002; Saucier, 1992).

The disagreement has at least two sources. First, recall that naming factors can be hard. You do it by looking at the items that load on the factor and trying to extract the underlying thread that connects them. But most words have several connotations, and trait terms often represent blends of factors rather than one factor per word (Hofstee, de Raad, & Goldberg, 1992). Naturally, then, there are disagreements in interpretation.

Second, exactly what a factor looks like depends on what items are in the study. If a particular quality is left out or is not well represented in the items, its importance to a trait will be missed (Peabody & Goldberg, 1989). Thus, studies with slightly different measures can lead to different conclusions about the meaning of the factors, even when there's agreement that more or less the same factors have emerged.

Table 4.3 displays the five traits, using a variety of names for each. Peabody and Goldberg (1989) suggested that the five factors are the metaphorical equivalent of a piece of music, in which there's a theme and a series of variations on it. That's pretty much what you see in Table 4.3. The labels listed under each factor all share a theme, but there are also variations. Some of the basis for the variation is displayed in Table 4.4, which lists examples of the descriptive terms that loaded on the five factors in one study or another.

Table 4.3 Labels Used by Various Authors to Refer to the "Big Five" Factors in Personality. Labels in the rows are from (in order) Fiske (1949), Norman (1963), Borgatta (1964), Digman (1990), and Costa and McCrae (1985). The final row provides a characterization by Peabody and Goldberg (1989) of the life domain to which the trait pertains.

1	2	3	4	5
Social adaptability	Emotional control	Conformity	Will to achieve	Inquiring intellect
Surgency	Emotionality	Agreeableness	Conscientiousness	Culture
Assertiveness	Emotionality	Likeability	Responsibility	Intelligence
Extraversion	Neuroticism	Friendly compliance	Will to achieve	Intellect
Extraversion	Neuroticism	Agreeableness	Conscientiousness	Openness to experience
Power	Love	Work	Affect	Intellect

Table 4.4 Bipolar and Unipolar Adjective Scales Reflective of the Five Major Personality Factors. *Source:* Based on Digman & Inouye, 1986; McCrae & Costa, 1987; Norman, 1963; Peabody & Goldberg, 1989.

Factor	Item	
Extraversion	Bold–timid	Gregarious
	Forceful–submissive	Outspoken
	Self-confident–unassured	Energetic
	Talkative–silent	Happy
	Spontaneous–inhibited	Seclusive (inverse)
Neuroticism	Nervous–poised	Concerned
	Anxious–calm	Nervous
	Excitable–composed	Fearful
	Relaxed–high strung	Tense
Agreeableness	Friendly–unfriendly	Jealous (inverse)
	Warm–cold	Considerate
	Kind–unkind	Spiteful (inverse)
	Polite–rude	Touchy (inverse)
	Good natured–irritable	Complaining (inverse)
Conscientiousness	Cautious–rash	Neat
	Serious–frivolous	Persevering
	Responsible–irresponsible	Planful
	Thorough–careless	Careful
	Hardworking–lazy	Eccentric (inverse)
Intellect	Imaginative–simple	Knowledgeable
	Intellectual–unreflective	Perceptive
	Polished–crude	Imaginative
	Uncurious–curious	Verbal
	Uncreative–creative	Original

The first factor is usually called *extraversion,* but there's a good deal of variation in what it includes. This helps account for the different labels. Sometimes it seems based in assertiveness, sometimes in spontaneity and energy. Sometimes it's based in dominance and confidence, sometimes in a tendency toward happiness. Extraversion is often thought of as implying a sense of sociability (Watson, Clark, McIntyre, & Hamaker, 1992), but some argue that that's actually a by-product of other features of extraversion (Lucas, Diener, Grob, Suh, & Shao, 2000).

There's more agreement (though still not unanimity) about the meaning of the next factor. *Neuroticism,* or *emotional stability,* is regarded by most people as being what Eysenck referred to with those labels. Digman and Takemoto-Chock (1981) called it *emotional disorganization,* because items loading on it convey more than mere presence of emotion. What's at the heart of this factor, though, seems to be the subjective experience of anxiety and general distress.

The next factor in Table 4.4 is most commonly called *agreeableness.* This trait is often characterized as being concerned with the maintaining of relationships. Digman and his colleagues (Digman, 1990; Digman & Inouye, 1986; Digman & Takemoto-Chock, 1981) held that it's not just a quality of being warm and likeable versus being cold; it may extend to a kind of docile compliance. It can also imply nurturance and emotional supportiveness, which requires inhibition of negative affect (Graziano &

Eisenberg, 1999). The opposite pole of this dimension has an oppositional or antag-onistic quality verging toward hostility (Digman, 1990). Fitting this, people low in agreeableness choose displays of power as a way of resolving social conflict more than people higher in agreeableness (Graziano, Jensen-Campbell, & Hair, 1996). There's also evidence that they actually *experience* more conflicts (Asendorpf & Wilpers, 1998).

The essence of the next factor is also a little hard to capture. The most commonly used label is *conscientiousness*. However, this label doesn't fully reflect its qualities of planning, persistence, and purposeful striving toward goals (Digman & Inouye, 1986). Indeed, because the word *conscientious* itself has two shades of meaning, it loads both on this factor and on agreeableness, which hints that conscientiousness may not be the perfect name for this factor. Noting that this quality relates to educational achieve-ment, Digman (1990) suggested that it be thought of as will to achieve, or simply *will*. Other suggested names include *constraint* and *responsibility*. Roberts, Walton, and Bogg (2005) recently examined the qualities various theorists consider part of conscien-tiousness and concluded that no measure includes all of them.

The largest disagreement may concern the next factor. The disagreement stems at least partly from differences in measures. Early on, Cattell measured qualities of *intel-ligence*. Then he stopped doing so and started using the term *culture* to refer to the qualities that remained. The label stuck. Peabody and Goldberg (1989) pointed out, though, that when intelligence-related measures are reintroduced, they join with cul-ture. These authors suggested the factor should more properly be labeled *intellect*. Costa and McCrae (1985) favor yet another label: *openness* to experience.

Peabody and Goldberg (1989) argued that Costa and McCrae's measure of this factor taps one aspect of intellect (the imaginative side) but misses the other side (the logical side). They said that when both sides are measured, they merge (implying that this factor is really intellect). McCrae and Costa (1987) disagreed. They argued that intelligence just provides a basis for the broader sense of openness. The concept of openness to experience is newer to psychology than is intelligence. However, McCrae (1996) has reviewed a wide range of ways in which openness relates to social experi-ence and shown that it may be far more important than people realize.

REFLECTIONS OF THE FIVE FACTORS IN BEHAVIOR

Until fairly recently, most work on the five-factor model was aimed at the factors themselves: showing that they exist in diverse cultures and emerge from many ways of assessment. More recently, however, researchers have turned more to looking at how these five traits are reflected, or expressed, on the broader canvas of people's lives.

Let's start with the traits that are most social in nature: extraversion and agree-ableness. Several projects have focused on the idea that extraversion and agreeableness are both tied to social situations, but in different ways. Extraversion seems to relate to *having social impact;* agreeableness seems to relate to *maintaining positive relations with others* (Jensen-Campbell & Graziano, 2001). Fitting this, extraversion predicts being prominent in fraternities and sororities (Anderson, John, Keltner, & Kring, 2001), but agreeableness does not. In a study of adolescents (Jensen-Campbell, Adams, Perry, Workman, Furdella, & Egan, 2002), extraversion and agreeableness both related to peer acceptance, but agreeableness also protected against being victimized by peers. Adults high in agreeableness also feel they have greater social support from family members (Branje, van Lieshout, & van Aken, 2004). All of this makes sense, if agree-ableness is largely about maintaining good relations.

A variety of other findings fit that idea, as well. Agreeableness predicts endorse-ment of conflict resolution tactics among children (Jensen-Campbell, Gleason, Adams,

People high in agreeableness care about maintaining positive relations with others.

& Malcolm, 2003). Agreeable adults get less angry over bad outcomes caused by other people than do less agreeable adults (Meier & Robinson, 2004). In fact, agreeableness seems to short circuit aggressive responses (Meier, Robinson, & Wilkowski, 2006).

Agreeableness has been found to predict more empathy and responsiveness in parenting (Clark, Kochanka, & Ready, 2000), less negativity in marital interactions (Donnellan, Conger, & Bryant, 2004), less seeking of revenge after being harmed (McCullough & Hoyt, 2002), and greater attempts to control negative emotions (Tobin, Graziano, Vanman, & Tassinary, 2000). Agreeableness also predicts less poaching of romantic partners and less responsiveness to poaching attempts by others (Schmitt & Buss, 2001). Agreeableness has also been linked to less substance abuse (Chassin, Flora, & King, 2004; Lynam, Leukefeld, & Clayton, 2003; Walton & Roberts, 2004) and less antisocial behavior (J. D. Miller, Lynam, & Leukefeld, 2003).

Extraversion is helpful socially. Extraverted men interact better with women they don't know than introverts do (Berry & Miller, 2001), and extraverts have the firm handshake that conveys confidence (Chaplin, Phillips, Brown, Clanton, & Stein, 2000). But there can be a dark side to the desire for social impact. There's evidence that extraverts are less cooperative than introverts when facing a social dilemma over resources, whereas agreeableness relates to being more cooperative (Koole, Jager, van den Berg, Vlek, & Hofstee, 2001).

Studies have also found that these two traits relate in consistent ways to personal values and life goals. Extraversion relates to valuing achievement and stimulation; agreeableness relates to valuing benevolence and tradition (Roccas, Sagiv, Schwartz, & Knafo, 2002). Extraversion relates to the desires for a high-status career, political influence, an exciting lifestyle, and children; agreeableness relates to desires for goals of group welfare and harmonious family relations and actually relates inversely to desires for wealth, political influence, and an exciting lifestyle (Roberts & Robins, 2000).

Conscientiousness has also received a good deal of attention in recent years. Greater conscientiousness predicts avoidance of unsafe sex (Trobst, Herbst, Masters, & Costa, 2002) and other risky behaviors (Markey, Markey, & Tinsley, 2003). Conscientious people are less likely to try to steal someone else's romantic partner, and are less responsive to being lured away (Schmitt & Buss, 2001). Conscientiousness has been linked to more responsive parenting of young children (Clark et al., 2000) and to use of negotiation as a conflict-resolution strategy (Jensen-Campbell & Graziano, 2001). Conscientiousness has been related to a desire for a career, but not necessarily a high standard of living (Roberts & Robins, 2000). Conscientiousness in adolescence predicts higher religiousness in adulthood (McCullough, Tsang, & Brion, 2003) and higher academic achievement (Chamorro-Premuzic & Furnham, 2003).

Conscientiousness also seems to have health implications. In a study of cancer risk, conscientiousness led to more restrictive household bans on smoking (Hampson, Andrews, Barckley, Lichtenstein, & Lee, 2000). People who are high in conscientiousness even seem to live longer, presumably because they take better care of themselves (Christensen et al., 2002; Friedman et al., 1995). Consistent with this, conscientiousness relates to various kinds of health-linked behaviors (Bogg & Roberts, 2004; Roberts et al., 2005). In fact, conscientiousness in childhood has been related to health behaviors 40 years later (Hampson, Goldberg, Vogt, & Dubanoski, 2006). Conscientiousness has also been related to lower levels of substance abuse (Chassin et al., 2004; Lynam et al., 2003; Roberts & Bogg, 2004; Walton & Roberts, 2004) and to less antisocial behavior more generally (J. D. Miller et al., 2003).

Openness to experience has been found to predict greater engagement with the existential challenges of life (Keyes, Shmotkin, & Ryff, 2002). Openness relates to more favorable inter-racial attitudes (Flynn, 2005). Openness relates to greater sexual satisfaction in marriage (Donnellan et al., 2004). People high in openness say they desire artistic expression, and they devalue traditional marriage and the possibility of an easy, lazy life (Roberts & Robins, 2000). On the other hand, openness has also been found to predict more prior arrests among prisoners (Clower & Bothwell, 2001).

Neuroticism has been studied for decades. High levels of neuroticism relate to distress in a wide variety of difficult circumstances. For example, it relates to more difficult interactions among married partners (Donellan et al., 2004) and less satisfaction in marriages. People who are highly neurotic are also more likely to distance themselves from their partners after a negative event (Bolger & Zuckerman, 1995). Neuroticism impairs academic performance (Chamorro-Premuzic & Furnham, 2003), and it even predicts a negative emotional tone when writing stories about oneself (McAdams et al., 2004).

THE FIVE-FACTOR MODEL IN RELATION TO EARLIER MODELS

Today, when people think of trait psychology, they tend to think first of the five-factor model. However, recall from earlier in the chapter that several other trait models preceded this one. Let's consider how the five-factor model relates to them.

The easiest comparison is to Eysenck's theory. It's obvious from Table 4.3 that two of the "big five" are virtually the same as Eysenck's supertraits: extraversion and emotional stability. It's been suggested that Eysenck's third dimension, psychoticism, is a blend of agreeableness and conscientiousness (Goldberg, 1993b; Zuckerman, Kuhlman, Joireman, Teta, & Kraft, 1993).

A second similarity to Eysenck is that the five factors are superordinate traits, incorporating narrower traits. For example, Paul Costa and Robert McCrae (1985, 1992) developed a measure called the NEO Personality Inventory (NEO-PI-R; NEO stands for *neuroticism, extraversion,* and *openness;* agreeableness and conscientiousness were added after the name was coined; the R stands for *revised*). The NEO-PI-R includes measures of six narrow traits for each domain of the five-factor model. The six narrow traits combine into a score for that supertrait. Thus, many people who use the five-factor model share with Eysenck the idea that the core traits are supertraits, which in turn are composed of more specific facet traits.

Another useful comparison is with the interpersonal circle of Wiggins and his colleagues. The basic dimensions there are *dominance* and *love*. Love may be equivalent to agreeableness. If dominance were seen as roughly equivalent to extraversion, the interpersonal circle would comprise two factors of the five-factor model (McCrae & Costa, 1989b; Peabody & Goldberg, 1989). Trapnell and Wiggins (1990) expanded a measure of the interpersonal circle to have additional scales and an even better fit to the five-factor model (see also Saucier, 1992).

This comparison with the interpersonal circle also raises an issue, however. As noted earlier (Figure 4.3), Wiggins saw extraversion as a combination of two qualities in the circle, not as a basic dimension. Doesn't that conflict with the five-factor model? It depends on how you define *extraversion*. Remember, there are diverse opinions on how to view that factor. If it's really about dominance and assertiveness, it would fit with the interpersonal circle.

To summarize some of the points made in this part of the chapter, the five-factor model of personality structure has emerged as a candidate to integrate a variety of earlier models. The data make this set of broad traits look very much as though they represent universal aspects of personality (McCrae & Costa, 1997). Remember, though, that what comes out of a factor analysis depends on what goes into it. It can be dangerous to draw solid conclusions too quickly. Nonetheless, at present the five-factor model seems to offer the best promise of a consensus about the dimensions of personality that trait psychology has ever seen.

SOME ADDITIONAL VARIATIONS AND SOME CAUTIONS

Consensus is not the same as *unanimity,* however. People have disagreed with this view for a variety of reasons (e.g., Block, 1995, 2001; Eysenck, 1992, 1993; Zuckerman, 1992). One line of dissent claims that work from the lexical approach omitted a set of words that shouldn't have been left out—words that are purely evaluative (e.g., *excellent, evil*). When these words are included, two more factors emerge: *positive valence* and *negative valence* (Almagor, Tellegen, & Waller, 1995; Benet & Waller, 1995).

We should also note that there are other influential trait models that differ from the five-factor model in various ways. One of them is Tellegen's (1985) model. It greatly resembles that of Eysenck (1975, 1986) in having three supertraits, though with somewhat different origins and different overtones. Tellegen (1985) recast *neuroticism* as a tendency to experience negative emotions, and he recast *extraversion* as a tendency to experience positive emotions. Positive emotionality (like extraversion) has been tied to social success and negative emotionality (like neuroticism) to various indices of poor adjustment (Shiner, Masten, & Tellegen, 2002). Tellegen's third factor, called *constraint,* resembles psychoticism in Eysenck's model, but viewed from the opposite direction. It predicts the same kinds of outcomes, too. Low constraint has been linked to criminal and antisocial behavior (Krueger, 2002; Shiner et al., 2002) and (in interaction with high negative affectivity) to drug use (Shoal & Giancola, 2003).

The idea of five factors was carried in another direction by Zuckerman and his colleagues (1993), who proposed an "alternative five." Remember that what comes out of the factor analysis depends partly on what goes into it. Zuckerman et al. (1993) put slightly different things in. The sociability factor in this model resembles extraversion (if you view extraversion as mostly social). Neuroticism–anxiety is most of neuroticism but without the hostility that others include there. That hostility is incorporated in aggression–hostility, which otherwise looks like agreeableness (reversed). Impulsive sensation seeking looks like conscientiousness (reversed). The last factor in this model is *activity.* What may be the most important difference between this and the other five-factor model is that Zuckerman et al., located hostility outside neuroticism. There are reasons to believe that's a better location for it (Carver, 2004; Jang, Livesly, Angleitner, Riemann, & Vernon, 2002; Peabody & DeRaad, 2002; Saucier & Goldberg, 2001).

The idea that what comes out depends on what goes in is reflected in several other findings. Saucier and Goldberg (1998) found evidence of several dimensions beyond the five factors but concluded that they lie outside personality (for example, religiousness and attractiveness). Paunonen and Jackson (2000) looked at the same evidence and saw nine or ten dimensions that they thought should be viewed as traits, albeit narrow ones (religiousness, dishonesty, seductiveness, humorousness, and conventionality). They argued that some of these narrow traits might even coalesce to form *honesty,* which might be a sixth supertrait (see also Ashton, Lee, & Son, 2000).

Ashton and his colleagues have carried this argument even further. They found a sixth supertrait in multiple studies involving seven languages (Ashton et al., 2004). They refer to it as *honesty/humility.* Subsequent work established that that factor can also be found in analyses of English words (Ashton, Lee, & Goldberg, 2004).

Ashton and his colleagues argue that this trait is a distinct quality that tends to be absorbed into agreeableness but stands out on its own, if allowed to do so.

Although some researchers have argued for more factors, others have argued that the five-factor model can be distilled into two dimensions (Digman, 1997). That is, putting the five traits into a higher-order analysis yields two factors. The first is defined by agreeableness, conscientiousness, and (low) neuroticism. Digman characterized it as reflecting *socialization,* because these qualities all influence whether people get along in social units. The second is defined by extraversion and openness. Digman characterized it as reflecting *personal growth,* because these two qualities influence whether people expose themselves to new things, thereby fostering growth.

These various lines of work all represent qualifications on the idea that the "big five" are the basic dimensions of personality. It should be clear that a number of issues still must be resolved. In sum, the consensus on the five-factor model is substantial, but not complete.

ARE SUPERORDINATE TRAITS THE BEST LEVEL TO USE?

At least one more question needs to be raised, even if you accept the five-factor model. As we said, this is a model of supertraits. Supertraits have facets. As noted earlier, Costa and McCrae's NEO-PI-R measures six facets of each factor. Those who use the five-factor model sometimes point to the utility of examining patterns of traits within each factor (Costa & McCrae, 1995; Goldberg, 1993a), but this strategy is not used very often.

Is anything lost when lower-level traits are combined to form the supertraits? This is essentially what Cattell and Eysenck argued about when they disagreed about the meaning of second-order factors (see also Briggs, 1989; H. E. P. Cattell, 1993; Funder, 1991; John, 1990). The evidence now suggests that something is indeed lost when facet traits are merged.

Paunonen and Ashton (2001a) compared the "big five" factors to specific facet scales as predictors of 40 behaviors, which were measured by self-reports and peer ratings. The behaviors were chosen because they had some social importance (altruistic behavior, smoking, alcohol consumption, religiosity, and so on). For a substantial number of these behaviors, facet scales added significantly to prediction after the five factors had been entered as predictors. Thus, something was lost if only the "big five" were used. Conceptually similar findings have come from a number of other studies (Mershon & Gorsuch, 1988; Paunonen, 1998; Paunonen & Ashton, 2001b; Schimmack, Oishi, Furr, & Funder, 2004; Wolfe & Kasmer, 1988).

Better prediction from specific narrow traits comes at a cost, though. The cost is that to understand the findings, you have to hold a larger number of traits in mind at once. In general terms, that's the trade-off: Using supertraits creates a picture that's more intuitive and easier to hold in mind. Using the narrower traits may often give greater accuracy.

Traits, Situations, and Interactionism

We turn now to a very different part of the trait approach. Trait psychology experienced an important controversy from about 1970 to about 1990. How researchers reacted to this controversy had a big impact on today's views of traits, although this impact is separate from anything we've discussed so far.

IS BEHAVIOR ACTUALLY TRAITLIKE?

The question that shook the foundations of trait psychology in the early 1970s is whether behavior actually shows traitlike consistency. Traits are assumed to be *stable* aspects of personality that influence behavior in a *wide range of settings*. The reason for assuming traits in the first place was to account for consistency in people's thoughts and actions across time and circumstances. Differences on a trait should predict differences in trait-related behaviors.

It was somewhat surprising, then, that trait measures and behavior often didn't correlate well (Mischel, 1968; P. E. Vernon, 1964). Walter Mischel (1968) coined the phrase **personality coefficient** to characterize the modest correlations between trait self-reports and actual behavior, which often were around 0.30. This correlation means that the trait accounts for less than 10% of the variation in the behavior, with the remaining 90% unaccounted for. Later estimates ranged a little higher (around 0.40). Even so, the proportion of variance accounted for didn't seem high.

What, then, are we to think about traits? If traits don't predict people's actions, then why should the trait concept be considered useful? (Indeed, some people went so far as to ask why the concept of *personality* should be considered useful.)

SITUATIONISM

An extreme form of the attack on traits was called **situationism.** This is the idea that situational forces determine behavior, not personality. This view was held by some social psychologists, who traditionally emphasize the role of the social environment, rather than personality, as a cause of actions. This view argued that correlations between traits and behavior were low because situational variables overwhelmed the effect of personality. This turned out to be quite wrong.

Funder and Ozer (1983) pointed out that effects of situations and effects of traits usually are reported with different statistics. This makes it hard to compare them. Funder and Ozer returned to several famous studies of the impact of situations on behavior and converted the original statistics to correlations. To the astonishment of many, these correlations were *about the same size* as the personality coefficients that had been criticized so sharply.

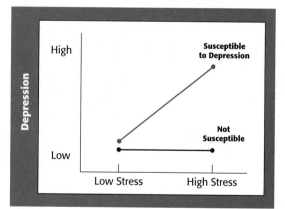

INTERACTIONISM

Another approach to understanding inconsistency between traits and actions is called **interactionism** (e.g., Ekehammer, 1974; Endler & Magnusson, 1976; Magnusson & Endler, 1977; Ozer, 1986; Pervin, 1985). Interactionism is the idea that traits and situations interact to influence behavior. Neither the setting alone nor the person alone provides a complete account.

FIGURE 4.4
Sometimes there is an interaction between a situation and a trait variable, such that variations in the situation affect some people but not others. This particular interaction is one that has, in fact, been hypothesized by Abramson, Seligman, and Teasdale (1978). The type of interaction displayed here is only one type of potential interaction between people and situations (see text).

The term *interactionism* is tied in part to an "analysis-of-variance" understanding of how two variables (or in this case, two classes of variables) influence an outcome. To explain this, we return to an idea from Chapter 2. We described there how experimental personality research often combines two variables as factors in a single study. We now state that point again in terms of persons and situations.

When a situation and a trait are examined in the same study, there are three systematic sources of influence on behavior. Sometimes variations in the *situation* have an effect on all persons—for example, stressful situations may induce depression. Sometimes variations on a *trait* have an effect in all situations—for example, people who are susceptible to depression may be more depressed across situations than people who are less susceptible.

It's also possible, however, for the situation and trait to *interact* (see Figure 4.4). An interaction here means that variations in situation affect some people in one way and others in a different way. For example, stress may cause an increase in depression among people who are prone to depression but not among others. This interaction may occur in addition to one or both of the overall effects, or it may occur *instead of them*. In the latter case, it would create a picture of weak effects for both the trait and the situation.

In this analysis-of-variance view, situations and dispositions can interact in several ways to determine behavior. Perhaps most obvious (the case shown in Figure 4.4) is that a situation may influence one kind of person but not others. Sometimes a situational variable causes one behavior in one person and a *different* behavior in another person. For example, a stressful situation may cause extraverts to seek out others and introverts to withdraw from others.

Here's another way to describe such interactions: Some situations permit easy expression of personality. Other situations force behavior into channels, thus preventing expression of personality (Monson, Hesley, & Chernick, 1982; Schutte, Kenrick, & Sadalla, 1985). The first set is called *weak* situations; the second set is called *strong* situations (Mischel, 1977). As an example, the lawn of a college campus on a Sunday afternoon is a weak situation. Individual differences can be expressed easily; in fact, the situation seems to invite it. An army boot camp is a strong situation. It dampens any expression of individual differences.

INDIVIDUAL DIFFERENCES IN CONSISTENCY

Apparently, dispositions can also be strong and weak in the same sense. That is, some people are so consistent that they overwhelm the situations they're in. Other people are more willing to let situational influences guide them and thus are less consistent.

This depiction fits a trait called *self-monitoring* (M. Snyder, 1974, 1987). People high in self-monitoring like to fit smoothly into situations they encounter. They look to others for cues about what actions are appropriate, and they bend to the needs of the situation. People low in self-monitoring behave the way they think they *are*, no matter the situation. It follows that high self-monitors should be less consistent from one situation to another than low self-monitors. This turns out to be true (see M. Snyder, 1987).

There is also evidence that people vary in consistency on *specific* traits. People who saw themselves as being inconsistent on a trait acted in ways that didn't relate well to their trait self-reports (Bem & Allen, 1974). Among those who reported being consistent, however, the trait reports predicted their actions quite well. Others have found much the same things (Kenrick & Stringfield, 1980; Woodruffe, 1985; Zuckerman, Bernieri, Koestner, & Rosenthal, 1989; Zuckerman, Koestner, DeBoy, Garcia, Maresca, & Sartoris, 1988).

Some situations act to constrain behavior and hide individual differences. Other situations allow personality free expression.

People exercise choice over the settings they enter, which influences the behaviors they engage in. Some people choose to go to football games, other people do not.

OTHER ASPECTS OF INTERACTIONISM

The analysis-of-variance model derives from lab research, a context in which researchers put people into identical situations. It tends to imply that people outside the lab also enter identical situations. This, of course, is wrong—a point made by a number of authors (D. M. Buss, 1984; Emmons & Diener, 1986; Emmons, Diener, & Larsen, 1986; Magnus, Diener, Fujita, & Pavot, 1993; Plomin, DeFries, & Loehlin, 1977; Scarr & McCartney, 1983; M. Snyder & Gangestad, 1982). In life outside the lab (and rarely, but occasionally, even in the lab), people exercise considerable choice over which environments they enter.

Some people choose to go to church, others choose not to. Some people choose to go to basketball games, some to rock concerts, some to country meadows. By exercising choice over the settings they enter, people thereby influence the behaviors they engage in. Indeed, there's evidence that people choose their *marriage partners* partly by whether the partner lets them be who they are (Caspi & Herbener, 1990). The choices that people make about what situations to enter depend partly on their personalities (Brandstätter, 1983; Emmons & Diener, 1986; Emmons et al., 1986).

Another way persons and situations interact is that people differ in the kinds of responses they elicit from others (Scarr & McCartney, 1983). Some people naturally bring a smile to your face, others can make you frown just by entering the room. Introverts tend to steer conversations in one direction, extraverts in another (Thorne, 1987). Indeed, people actively manipulate each other using such tactics as charm, coercion, and silence (Buss, Gomes, Higgins, & Lauterbach, 1987). All these effects change the situation, so *the situation is actually different for one person than it is for another.* This reciprocal influence is another way persons and situations interact.

WAS THE PROBLEM EVER REALLY AS BAD AS IT SEEMED?

Trying to understand weak links from trait to behavior has led to a great deal of information about how they relate. We should note, however, that doubt has arisen about whether the problem ever was actually as bad as it seemed to be.

After Mischel (1968) said that personality correlated with behavior around 0.30, others pointed out that the studies leading to that conclusion weren't the best of studies (Block, 1977; Hogan, DeSoto, & Solano, 1977). There seems to have been some truth to that. More recent studies, which were more carefully designed (e.g., Conley, 1985; Deluty, 1985; Funder & Block, 1989; Funder & Colvin, 1991; Moskowitz, 1994; Woodruffe, 1985), have found much stronger relationships than those Mischel had summarized.

There also turn out to be statistical reasons why a correlation of 0.30 isn't so bad! Many actions are influenced by more than one trait. For example, when you get to a party where you don't know anyone, what you'll do next will depend on how extraverted you are, but it will also depend on how anxiety prone you are. As it happens, whenever a behavior is influenced by several traits at once, the *mere fact of multiple influence* puts limits on how strong a correlation can be for any single trait (Ahadi & Diener, 1989). This limit looks, in fact, very nearly the same as the much maligned personality coefficient.

Maybe the core problem really wasn't ever as bad as it seemed in 1968. But the work addressing the problem has told us a lot about how behavior emerges. Indeed, this work has led many people to hold a more elaborate view of the trait construct than they might otherwise hold. We consider this view next.

Interactionism Becomes a New View of Traits: Context-Dependent Expression of Personality

Psychologists put a lot of effort into developing the ideas known collectively as *interactionism*. Nonpsychologists, however, seem to approach traits naturally with what seems an interactionist mentality. That is, people seem to recognize intuitively that whether a trait influences behavior varies from setting to setting. You shouldn't expect a given trait to operate all the time—only in situations to which it's relevant.

This is reflected in the fact that people often use verbal hedges in discussing personality (Wright & Mischel, 1988). A *hedge* (in this context) means a word or phrase that limits a trait's applicability. As examples, you might describe someone as "shy *with strangers*" or "aggressive *when teased*." The ultimate hedge is *sometimes*. Using a hedge implies you think the trait-based behavior occurs only in certain kinds of situations (see also Shoda, Mischel, & Wright, 1989).

Such evidence, along with the insights of interactionism more generally, led Mischel and Shoda (1995) to a more elaborated analysis of how traits influence behavior (see also Cervone, 1997, 2004; Mischel, Shoda, & Mendoza-Denton, 2002). In this view, traits are not freestanding tendencies to act, but patterns of linkages between situation and action. Given situation *x*, action *y* is likely. A key point of this idea is that a given action shouldn't be expected to occur all the time, because the situation that brings it out isn't always present. Thus, a person's behavior may appear inconsistent across situations, especially situations that differ a lot. But in situations that seem similar to the person, the behavior is consistent (Furr & Funder, 2004). Thus, there's a lot of consistency, despite the variability (see also Box 4.2).

Another key point in this theory is that the pattern of linkage between situation and behavior differs from one person to another. This is a source of individuality, uniqueness: the pattern of situation–behavior links the person has established over time and experience. Even if two people tend toward the same kind of behavior, the situations that elicit that behavior may differ from one person to the other. If so, these two people will act differently from each other in many situations, even though they have the same trait. This, in fact, may be a way in which idiographic traits can exist. Each person's unique pattern of links from situation to action creates a trait that is just a little different from that of any other person.

The idea that traits represent patterns of situation–action links opens other possibilities as well. For example, imagine a person who is mostly an introvert but occasionally acts like an extravert—for example, by becoming talkative. From the perspective of the linkage model, this would mean that there are classes of situations (perhaps infrequent in their occurrence) that link to those actions for this person. From this way of thinking, there would be no contradiction in the idea that a person can display qualities from one end of a trait dimension in one situation and qualities from the opposite end of the dimension in another.

Considerable support for this argument has been reported by Fleeson (2001). For example, he found that most people do things that reflect the entire range of a trait

Box 4.2 How Consistent Is Personality over *Long* Periods?

When we talk about consistency and stability in personality, we often focus on fairly short time periods. However, the trait concept implies stability over much longer periods. We should also ask about whether people's personalities stay the same even years later.

Several projects have contributed information on this issue (for more, see Caspi, Roberts, & Shiner, 2005). Helson and Moane (1987) described women who were studied as college seniors, then at age 27, and again at age 43. Across each span, traits had high test–retest correlations. On the other hand, the women also changed as a group, becoming more dominant and independent from age 27 to 43. How can that be? The answer is that there was a lot of rank-order stability in the group over time. Even as the women became more independent as they all grew older, the ones who were most independent at 22 were still the most independent at 27 and at 43.

Wink and Helson (1993) found that the change toward more competence and self-confidence continued to age 52. There was also evidence that women who changed the most were those who had begun families or had career development during this period—activities that changed role demands, which changed how the women saw themselves. Analyses of even later assessments showed that dominance and independence had peaked in middle age but that various kinds of change continued into old age (Helson, Jones, & Kwan, 2002).

Several studies have looked at the transition from adolescence to young adulthood. Robins, Fraley, Roberts, and Trzesniewski (2001) looked at personality reports across the college years and found some change in mean levels, but large correlations over time. Roberts, Caspi, and Moffitt (2001) found changes from ages 18 to 26 that were consistent with a group shift toward greater maturity. For the most part, though, correlations of traits across time were quite strong. Yet people appear to think their personality has changed more over this period than it really has (Robins, Noftle, Trzesniewski, & Roberts, 2005).

One interesting project focused on two specific qualities of childhood personality—shyness and temper—and how they predict adult behavior (Caspi, Elder, & Bem, 1987, 1988). This study started with mothers of 8- to 10-year-old children describing what the children were like. The children themselves were interviewed when they were 30 and 40, along with their spouses and their own children. Boys with frequent temper tantrums in childhood grew up to be ill-tempered men. Girls with frequent tantrums in childhood were seen by their *families* as ill-tempered mothers, but this didn't come across in interviews with the researchers. Childhood shyness also reverberated later on. Shy boys married late and were slow to establish stable careers. Shy girls weren't slower to marry but were more likely to follow a conventional pattern of family and homemaking than were less-shy girls.

On the whole, research seems to confirm two ideas. They may seem at first glance to be contradictory, but they really aren't. First, people change as they age. They become more conscientious and more agreeable (Helson, Kwan, John, & Jones, 2002; Roberts et al., 2005)—more "mature" (Caspi et al., 2005). Second, there is a lot of rank-order stability within any given group over long periods of time. Indeed, a review of the evidence from 152 longitudinal studies found that correlations of personality grow increasingly strong from college, through midadulthood, to later adulthood (Roberts & Del Vecchio, 2000; see also Costa & McCrae, 1988b, 1989; McCrae, 1993). This kind of consistency is one more reason to believe that traits are real.

---

dimension. It's just that the things they do most often reflect a narrower portion of that dimension (see Figure 4.5). In the same way, more recent research (Fleeson, Malanos, & Achille, 2002) shows that the positive emotions that are tied to extraversion vary from hour to hour, right along with the degree of extraverted behavior the person is engaging in.

The linkage viewpoint seems to deal well with some problems people have had in thinking about traits. It doesn't distort the trait concept, but it clearly adds something to the concept, as it was discussed in the first part of this chapter. This theory has other elements that are considered in Chapter 16. For now, the point is that the impact of traits seems to be context dependent (see also Fleeson & Leicht, 2006). This conclusion is very consistent with an interactionist view of personality.

Fitting the Pieces Together: Views of Traits and Behavior

Let's pull these ideas together with what came earlier. If you had read only the first half of this chapter, you might have been tempted to assume that most trait theorists hold the view in Figure 4.6, panel A or B, in which traits have a *constant* influence on behavior. People who discuss the five-factor model tend not to talk much about how traits and situations interact. It can be easy to infer from their statements that that's what they assume.

But traits don't work that way. Research described in the previous sections makes that clear. Traits sometimes influence behavior a lot, and sometimes not at all. Whether the trait matters depends on the situation (Figure 4.6, C). This dynamic approach to the role of traits in the constantly varying social environment recognizes complexities in the creation of behavior.

This picture is certainly more compelling than the simple ones. Interestingly enough, though, the core idea isn't all that new. Some trait theorists of earlier years said much the same thing. They didn't say it in as much detail as it's being said today, however. As early as 1937, Gordon Allport wrote that "traits are often aroused in one situation and not in another" (p. 331). His conception of a trait explicitly included the assumption that the trait doesn't influence all behaviors and that it may not influence a given category of behavior at all times (Zuroff, 1986). Rather, the effect of the trait depends on whether it's evoked in that situation. Allport even believed that people have *contradictory* traits. The fact that the different traits are aroused by different situations keeps this from being a problem (Fleeson, 2001, 2004).

Allport also anticipated another contemporary theme when he noted that people choose the situations they enter and actively change the situations they're in (Zuroff, 1986). Thus, the ideas that would become known as *interactionism* have roots that go back a long way.

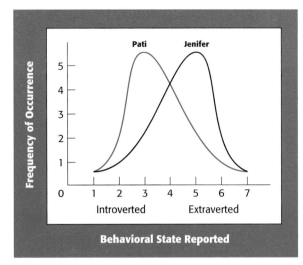

FIGURE 4.5
Traits as situation-linked frequency distributions of states. People occasionally act extraverted, even if they are essentially introverts (such as Pati); people occasionally act introverted, even if they are essentially extraverts (such as Jenifer). The person's generalized trait is reflected in the fact that particular sorts of behavioral states are most frequent. *Source: Based on Fleeson, 2001.*

Assessment

More than is true of most viewpoints on personality, the trait approach focuses a great deal on the process of assessment. Indeed, the first part of this chapter discussed how various theorists developed measures. In this section, we consider briefly how the measures are used.

COMPARING INDIVIDUALS: PERSONALITY PROFILES

The trait approach makes extensive use of self-report inventories. Those self-reports ask people to describe their view of themselves by making ratings of one kind or another. The most common ratings involve indicating whether a descriptive adjective applies to you or not, or where on a dimension (anchored by opposing adjectives) you'd fall, or whether you agree or disagree with a statement. The ratings may be made as yes–no or agree–disagree decisions, or they may be made on multipoint scales.

Recall that traits are seen as fundamental qualities of personality, reflected in diverse behaviors. For this reason, self-reports of traits usually include ratings for several reflections of each trait being measured. A scale using adjectives would have several adjectives for each trait; a scale made up of statements would include statements implying diverse ways the trait might be expressed.

Regardless of the exact form of the inventory, the nomothetic version of trait psychology assumes that anyone can be placed somewhere along each trait dimension

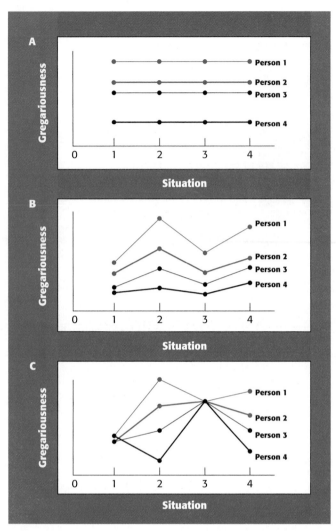

FIGURE 4.6

Three models of the effects of traits on behavior (portrayed for the trait of gregariousness). (A) A naive model, in which people are assumed to display their traits at a relatively constant level, no matter what situation they're in (what Magnusson & Endler, 1977, called *absolute consistency*). (B) A model in which situations influence the *overall* levels at which the trait is displayed, but people retain the same ordering (*relative consistency*). (C) An *interactionist model,* in which some situations (2 and 4) permit or even elicit individual differences, whereas others (1 and 3) don't do so.

assessed. Inventories measuring these traits are used to create *profiles.* A personality profile describes a person's place on each trait dimension the inventory measures (see Figure 4.7). Knowing the dimensions and the person's place on each can create a sense of what the person is like and how the person will behave in a variety of situations.

The profile in Figure 4.7 illustrates the kind of information a personality inventory gives. At first glance, a profile can seem like nothing more than a string of beads. (Allport [1961] said that's exactly what they are.) Perhaps a better metaphor is the bar code used by supermarkets to identify products. Nomothetic theorists believe that the profile is where uniqueness lies. You can see from Figure 4.7 that a shift on a single trait changes the balance of a person's qualities. It can thereby change how the person will act in various settings and how the person will seem to someone else. Since everyone has a unique combination of trait levels, everyone is different from everyone else.

Further, trait theorists believe traits can *interact* with one another. To put it differently, how a given level of one trait influences behavior may differ from person to person, as a function of where the people are on other traits. For example, two adventuresome people may display their boldness differently as a function of how sociable they are. The highly sociable one may engage in risky interpersonal exchanges, the less sociable one may climb mountains. Thus, a given trait can be reflected in unique ways for each person because of the modifying effect of differences on *other* traits (recall the earlier discussion of extraversion and emotionality and Table 4.2). This is true even though any particular trait dimension is the same from one person to another.

Problems in Behavior, and Behavior Change

The trait approach was the starting point for some of the earliest efforts to assess disorder. Those efforts were based on the idea that problems directly reflect people's traits. Differences among categories of problems occur because each trait (or group of traits) relates to a different kind of problem.

The attempt to understand psychopathology from this trait-based viewpoint was largely an attempt to categorize it. Categorizing was a matter of determining the trait indicators in people's behavior that relate to a given class of problem. This process led to a taxonomy for identifying and labeling problems (Wiggins, 1973), which has been revised several times.

Some traits relate to problems because the trait itself *is* problematic. As noted earlier, Eysenck's model has a dimension termed *psychoticism*. Psychoticism is a tendency toward certain kinds of problem behaviors, such as antisocial actions and alcohol and drug abuse (Sher, Bartholow, & Wood, 2000). Because people vary in psychoticism, they will vary in the degree to which they can be expected to display those problems. *Neuroticism* is a tendency toward experiencing emotional distress. Many psychopathologies are characterized by high levels of distress. Thus, people who are high in neuroticism are more likely to display those problems than people lower in neuroticism.

THE FIVE-FACTOR MODEL AND PERSONALITY DISORDERS

The emerging influence of the five-factor model of personality has led especially to renewed interest in the traits related to personality disorders (see Costa & Widiger, 2002; Watson & Clark, 1994). A *personality disorder* is a stable, enduring pattern of behavior that deviates from normal cultural expectations and interferes with a person's life or the lives of others. Many theorists are interested in whether personality disorders are essentially extreme manifestations of several of the "big five" traits (Larstone, Jang, Livesley, Vernon, & Wolf, 2002; Markon, Krueger, & Watson, 2005; Widiger, Trull, Clarkin, Sanderson, & Costa, 2002).

Recent research indicates this might be the case. For example, O'Connor and Dyce (2001) found that all personality disorders are represented within the five-factor model. Reynolds and Clark (2001) also found that the "big five" did a good job of representing personality disorder and that the facet scales (the narrow scales within the five domains) did even better. An edited volume containing diverse reviews of relevant evidence, and theoretical statements on the relation between the "big five" and the personality disorders is now in its second edition (Costa & Widiger, 2002). One recent study has even found that clinicians find the "big five" more useful clinically than the categories of the diagnostic system (Samuel & Widiger, 2006).

This exploration of the five factors and disorder is not limited to personality disorder. The question is being raised more generally about abnormalities of all types (Krueger, Watson, & Barlow, 2005; Nigg et al., 2002; O'Connor, 2002). Might they turn out to reflect extremes of specific traits? This area of work is likely to continue to be an important focus for more exploration in future years.

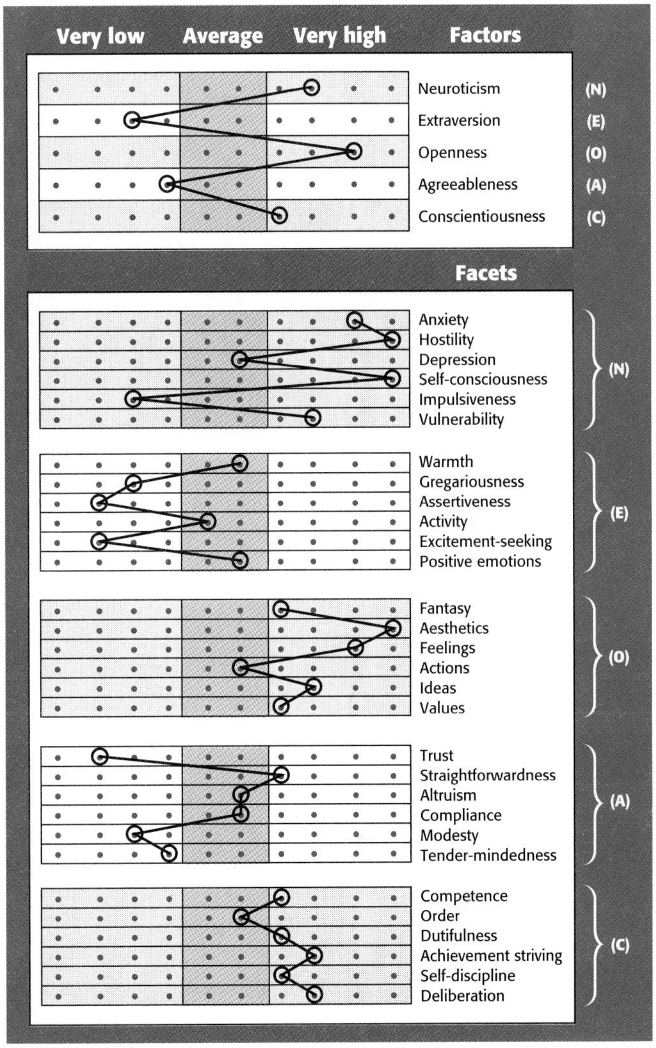

FIGURE 4.7
An illustration of a personality profile, adapted from the NEO-PI-R. The NEO-PI-R provides both an overall profile of the five major factors (top portion) and a profile of the facets within each of the "big five" (lower portion). The top profile provides a quick and simple summary for the person's personality; the other provides a more detailed picture.
Source: Reproduced by special permission of the Publisher, Psychological Assessment Resources, Inc., 16204 North Florida Avenue, Lutz, Florida 33549, from the NEO Personality Inventory Revised, by P. T. Costa, Jr., and R. R. McCrae, PhD, copyright 1978, 1985, 1989, 1992 by Psychological Assessment Resources, Inc. (PAR). Further reproduction is prohibited without permission of PAR.

Even a person prone to experiencing fear will not experience fear unless a fear-producing situation is encountered.

INTERACTIONISM IN BEHAVIOR PROBLEMS

As described earlier in the chapter, evidence suggesting a poor relationship between traits and actions led to development of *interactionism*. The logic of interactionism is useful not just for understanding normal behavior, but also for understanding problems.

One basic idea of interactionism is that individual differences matter in some situations but not others. As applied to problems, the idea takes on slightly different connotations. They are easiest to understand if you think of a trait as a *vulnerability* or *susceptibility* to a problem. Saying a person is susceptible to a problem doesn't mean that the person *has* the problem. It means the problem will emerge more easily for this person than for someone else. To put it in terms of interactionism, there are situations in which the susceptibility matters and others in which it doesn't (recall Figure 4.4).

The susceptibility usually matters in situations involving a lot of stress. Therefore, this approach to problems is called a **diathesis-stress model.** (*Diathesis* means susceptibility.) In this model, an interaction is required between the diathesis and a stress before the problem will develop (Meehl, 1962). Diathesis-stress models have been quite common in thinking about psychological problems.

BEHAVIOR CHANGE

What of the process of therapeutic behavior change? The trait approach is inherently a little pessimistic about change. If traits define a person's personality, how much can problems be resolved without changing the person's personality? Traits are stable. Any change that therapy produces is likely to be in how traits are displayed, rather than in the traits themselves.

On the other hand, the interactionist approach also has an implication here. If problems arise through an interaction between susceptibilities and difficult situations, then it should be helpful for the susceptible person to avoid entering situations in which the relevant stresses are likely to occur. Avoiding such situations should prevent the problems from arising.

This, of course, is something that people often do on their own. As we said earlier in the chapter, people exercise some control over what situations they choose to enter. Just as some people choose to go to church and some do not, some people choose to avoid situations in which their vulnerabilities place them at risk. Shy people may avoid singles bars. People with short tempers may try to avoid arguments. People who routinely overspend their credit cards may cancel the cards and switch to using only cash. Avoidance isn't always possible. Yet if people learn which stressors they can and cannot handle, this knowledge should make them more effective in managing their lives.

Trait Psychology: Problems and Prospects

The trait view is in many respects the most basic approach to personality of all. The very concepts of type and trait arose literally thousands of years ago, to account for consistency in behavior across time and circumstances. The concepts have been elaborated and embellished over the years, but in some ways their core remains the same.

Although the trait view on personality is the most basic, some people find it unsatisfying. It's been criticized on several grounds in recent years. (For opinions on both sides, see Pervin, 1994, and commentaries that follow it.) One problem is that trait theories have had little to say about how personality works (Block, 1995) or how the person gets from trait to action (Pervin, 1994). A clear exception to this characterization is the more recent work of Mischel and Shoda (1995), their colleagues, and others pursuing their ideas. This work is not at all typical of the trait approach of years past, but it may represent the trait approach of the future.

To put it differently, until the recent past, the trait approach has had little to say about intrapersonal functioning. This has resulted in a picture of personality that feels static and empty. McAdams (1992) called *trait psychology* the "psychology of the stranger," because it provides information that would be important if you knew nothing about a person, but it doesn't portray the dynamic aspects of personality. Labeling a person as *friendly,* or *sociable,* or *dominant* gives a name to what you see. But it doesn't tell you much about how or why the person acts that way. This is a major criticism of the trait concept.

The idea that the trait viewpoint has had little to say about the process side of personality is often made jointly with a second, related criticism. This second criticism is that trait theories sometimes resort to circular explanation in trying to deal with causality. As an example, imagine a woman who acts in a dominant manner—not just occasionally but often; not just in one situation or with one set of people, but in many situations, with whoever else is around. You might conclude from this that she has a high level of the trait of dominance.

But that can be a hollow conclusion. Ask yourself two questions and think about your natural responses. Question: Why does she behave that way? (Answer: Because she's dominant.) Question: How do you know she's dominant? (Answer: Because she behaves that way.) The problem is that the information about behavior is being used to infer the existence of a trait, which is being used in turn to explain the behavior. This is called *circular reasoning,* because it can go around and around in an endless circle. There's no point here at which the presumed trait is used to predict anything but the evidence that was used to presume it initially. The circularity can be broken if the trait is used to predict something new, and sometimes trait theorists do that. However, this view on personality is more vulnerable than most to the criticism of circularity.

A final problem that was raised in years past concerns the issue of consistency. As noted earlier, the concepts of trait psychology were developed to account for consistency in behavior across time and situations. The discovery that people's behavior sometimes fails to display this consistency created a crisis. There have been many creative and thoughtful responses to this discovery. Thus, this problem has served to promote evolution in this viewpoint. There has been a growing awareness among trait theorists that to view traits as having a constant impact on behavior is too simple. This view is being replaced by approaches in which situational forces and the interaction between situations and dispositions are taken into account. These insights hold further promise for the possibility of linking the trait approach to other views that have a more prominent place for process.

A final point favoring the future of the trait approach is this: No matter how hard various people have tried to dispense with the use of traits as explanatory mechanisms, the trait concept has retained an active place in the working vocabulary of the personality psychologist. The long history of these concepts attests to their hardiness. Somehow it appears as though the personality psychologist needs them. The fact that they've endured the test of time seems to imply a fundamental correctness that is hard to deny.

· SUMMARY ·

The trait-and-type approach begins with the assumption that personality consists of stable inner qualities, which are reflected in behavior. *Types* are discontinuous categories of personalities, with each person falling into one category or another. This concept has largely disappeared from use in personality psychology. *Traits* are continuous dimensions of variability, along which any person can be placed. Most trait approaches are nomothetic, emphasizing how people differ but assuming that the trait dimensions are the same for everyone. The idiographic approach emphasizes persons' uniqueness and treats some dimensions as unique to specific persons.

Factor analysis is a tool used by many trait psychologists. Factor analysis tells what items (or ratings, etc.) go together. Further, the more variability in ratings a factor accounts for, the more important the factor. Factor analysis also lets you tell which observations do and don't reflect a factor well, thus helping refine scales.

An important question in trait psychology is what traits are basic and important. Some theorists believe we must let reality tell us the structure of personality. Others believe we must start with a theory. Several theoretical views have been developed, including one that emphasizes traits that have a long history in ideas about personality (extraversion and neuroticism) and one that emphasizes traits that are relevant to social interaction (the interpersonal circle).

Many now favor the idea that there are five major factors in personality. Evidence to that effect is strong, and a relatively successful attempt has also been made to fit these five factors to the models of personality structure already mentioned. There is disagreement about the precise nature of the five factors, but commonly used labels for them are *extraversion, agreeableness, conscientiousness, emotionality,* and *openness.* Recent research has examined how these traits relate to behaviors and experiences in people's lives.

A question about the usefulness of the trait concept was raised by the finding that people's behavior often wasn't well predicted from trait self-reports. This led some to question whether traits actually influence behavior. *Situationism,* the idea that behavior is controlled primarily by situational influences, was a poor alternative. *Interactionism* holds that personality and situations interact in several ways to determine behavior. For example, some situations permit or even elicit individual differences, whereas other situations don't. People also choose which situations to enter, and then they influence the nature of situations by their own actions. Indeed, people also vary in how consistent they are, and they often know whether they're consistent or not.

The idea that the influence of traits on behavior is dependent on situations has expanded into a broader view of personality structure, in which traits are individualized linkages between situations and actions. This view accounts for stability over time within the person as well as for variability across situations. This view of the nature of traits provides a sense of process for trait models.

Personality assessment from the viewpoint of trait psychology is a matter of developing a personality *profile* of the person being assessed—a description of where the person falls on all the dimensions being measured by the inventory. To these psychologists, the profile holds the key to understanding the person's uniqueness.

Regarding problems in behavior, trait theorists say that some problems result from having a trait that is intrinsically problematic, such as psychoticism or neuroticism. Other kinds of problems stem from having an extreme position on some trait dimension. Interest in the relation between personality disorder and the five-factor model is growing. The interactionist position suggests the following possibility (termed a *diathesis-stress model*): Certain dispositions may create a susceptibility to some kind of problem, but the problem occurs only under certain conditions, usually involving stress. Therapeutic behavior change, from the trait perspective, may mean changing how a trait is reflected in behavior, because a person's traits are not easily altered. Alternatively, it may mean avoiding situations in which the problem behavior arises.

· GLOSSARY ·

Diathesis-stress model   A theory holding that a vulnerability plus stress creates problems in behavior.

Extravert   A person who is outgoing and prefers social and exciting activities.

Factor   A dimension that underlies a set of interrelated measures, such as items on a self-report inventory.

Factor analysis   A statistical procedure used to find basic dimensions underlying a set of measures.

Factor loading   A correlation between a single measure and the factor to which it is being related.

Idiographic   Pertaining to an approach that focuses on an individual person's uniqueness.

Interactionism   The idea that situations and personality interact to determine behavior.

Interpersonal circle   Personality patterns deriving from varying levels of dominance and love.

Introvert   A person who prefers solitary activities.

Lexical criterion   An index of the importance of a trait from the number of words that refers to it.

Nomothetic   Pertaining to an approach that focuses on norms and on variations among persons.

Personality coefficient   A stereotypic correlation between personality and behavior of about 0.30.

Second-order factor   A factor that emerges from a factor analysis performed on a set of previously found factors.

Situationism   The idea that situations are the primary determinants of behavior.

Traits   Dimensions of personality on which people vary.

Types   Distinct and discontinuous categories of persons.

Needs and Motives

"I'm in the pre-med program here, and I really want to get into a good medical school. The courses aren't that easy for me, so I have to study more than some people. I can't even take time off on weekends because I'm taking an extra heavy load. I don't mind, though, because I'm really motivated to go to med school, and that makes it worth the effort."

"I've been going with my boyfriend for over two years now. I care for him a lot. But lately I've been wondering if this is really the right relationship for me. It's hard to describe it. It's not anything about *him*, exactly, but it's like the relationship isn't meeting my needs. I don't know how else to put it."

THINK ABOUT the concerns that occupy your daily thoughts. Many college students are concerned about what they will do after college. Some have ambitions they're already pursuing full speed (for example, the pre-med student quoted above). Others aren't sure what they want to do, and worry about it. Yet others don't think it's a big deal one way or another.

Many college students are concerned about close relationships. Some envision being married in the years to come and wonder whether the person they're with is the right one. Some don't have this kind of relationship but wish they did. For some people, this is the most serious issue in their lives. For others, it's not a big deal.

These two concerns are probably familiar to you. Work and love are issues in everyone's life. They aren't everything, of course. Most of us have other things on our minds a lot of the time. Some people are trying to find order and meaning in life's experiences. Some seek truth, some seek beauty. For others, what really matters isn't truth *or* beauty but having the laundry done, the kitchen clean, or new high-performance tires on their SUV.

There's a lot of diversity in the concerns we've touched on here. Despite the diversity, they have something in common. They imply the existence of needs and motives behind people's thoughts and actions. How do people describe their preoccupations? I *need* to find a lover. I *need* to have a direction for my future. I *want* to do well in school. I *need* to find a sense of purpose in life. I *have* to get caught up on my chores. I *need* to get an A on this test. There are also individual differences here. For any aspect of life you might imagine, some people feel a deep need within it, others don't.

If needs and motives influence people's thoughts and actions this way, they're surely important. It can even be argued that they define who a person is. This idea forms the basis for the viewpoint on personality that's examined in this chapter.

Basic Theoretical Elements

NEEDS

The fundamental principle of this approach is that human behavior is best understood as a reflection of needs. A **need** is an internal state that's less than satisfactory, a lack of something that's necessary for well-being. Henry Murray (1938), who began this approach to personality (see Box 5.1), defined a need as an internal directional force that determines how people seek out or respond to objects or situations in the environment.

Some needs are based in our biological nature (needs for food, water, air, sex, and pain avoidance). Murray called these **primary needs.** Others, such as the need for power and the need for achievement, either *derive* from biological needs or are inherent in our *psychological* makeup. Murray called these **secondary needs.**

When you take up need theories, it's easiest to start with biological needs, because biology is a good model for how needs work. Biological needs must be satisfied

Box 5.1 THE THEORIST AND THE THEORY:

Henry Murray and Human Motives

The history of Henry Murray, the father of the motive view of personality, contains tantalizing suggestions about how his theory drew on his life's experiences. Murray was born to a wealthy family in New York in 1893. He got on well with his father but had a poor relationship with his mother, feeling that she gave him less attention than his sister and brother. The emotional separation created a deep-seated need to stand on his own, which was central to his personality. It's tempting to speculate that this experience led Murray to be especially aware of social needs, and may have led him toward the idea that such needs are the determinants of personality.

Murray's education was varied, but none of it was in psychology (he disliked his only psychology course). He majored in history, completed medical school, got a master's degree in

biology, did an internship in surgery, and then earned a Ph.D. in biochemistry. His focus after college was on the biology of human functioning. This biological emphasis is also apparent in Murray's thinking about personality. As noted, the ideas behind his theory are most easily illustrated by biological motives. Indeed, he believed that even psychological motives have biological roots.

Murray's medical background also influenced his approach to research. The program he led at the Harvard Psychological Clinic was very much a team approach. This seems to reflect the view that personality is best assessed by a team of specialists working together, much as a team of physicians collaborates on diagnosing patients.

A turning point in Murray's life occurred seven years into his marriage, when he fell in love with Christiana Morgan. This was a turning point in at least two ways. First, Murray was faced with a serious conflict. He didn't want

to leave his wife, but neither did he want to give up his lover. Wanting both women in his life surely made Murray acutely aware of the conflicting pressures that differing motives exert on a person.

The experience was a turning point in a second way, as well. Morgan had been fascinated by the psychology of Carl Jung. At her urging, Murray visited Jung in Switzerland. Jung, it turned out, was living in much the same situation as Murray but without discomfort. Jung's advice was to continue with both relationships, which Murray proceeded to do for 40 years (see Douglas, 1993; Robinson, 1992). The experience of bringing a problem to a psychologist and receiving an answer that seemed to work had a great impact on Murray, leading him to seriously consider psychology as a career (J. W. Anderson, 1988). When given the opportunity to assist in founding the Harvard Psychological Clinic, which was being set up to study personality, he jumped at the chance.

Every need has associated with it some category of "goal objects." When thirsty, you need water, not food.

repeatedly over time. As time passes, the needs gradually become more intense, and the person acts in ways that cause the need to be satisfied. For example, over time your body starts to need food. When the need gets strong enough, you'll do something to get some food. That reduces the need.

The strength of a need influences the intensity of the related behavior. The stronger the need, the more intense the action. Intensity can be reflected in several ways: vigor, enthusiasm, and thoroughness. But intensity can also be expressed in less obvious ways. For example, need strength can help set priorities—which action you do first versus put off until later. The stronger the need, the sooner it's reflected in action. Figure 5.1 shows how this prioritizing can create a continually changing stream of actions, as need strengths build and subside. The need that's greatest at any given point is the one that shows up in behavior.

Needs are directive: They help determine which of many possible actions occurs at a given time. They are directive in two senses. First, when you have a need, it's a need for something in particular. When you need water, you don't just *need;* you need *water.* Needs thus pertain to classes of goal objects or events. Needs are also directive in that they create movement either *toward* the object or *away* from it. A need is either to get something or to avoid something. Thirst reflects a water-related need, but it's more than just water *related.* After all, fear of going swimming also reflects a water-related need. Thirst reflects a need to *get* water. Moving toward versus moving away is part of the directionality of all needs.

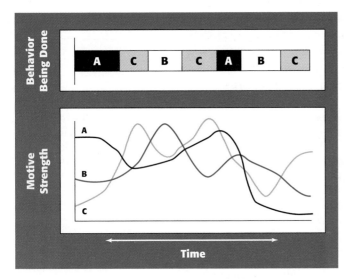

Time

FIGURE 5.1

A graphic display of how changes in behavior over time can be explained by variations in the relative strengths of several motives over the same time. The letters at the top of the diagram indicate which of three activities the person is engaged in at any given time (shifting from one to the other). The three lines indicate the levels of the three motives related to these three activities. As one motive rises above the other two, the behavior changes. *Source: Adapted from Seltzer, 1973.*

MOTIVES

Theorists assume that needs work through **motives.** Motives take the underlying need and move it a step closer to behavior. David McClelland (1984), an important contributor to this view of personality, said motives are clusters of *cognitions with affective overtones, organized around preferred experiences and goals.* Motives appear in your thoughts and preoccupations. The thoughts pertain to goals that are either desired or undesired. Thus they are affectively toned. Motives eventually produce actions.

To illustrate, the need for food occurs in the tissues of the body, but it gives rise to a motive state called *hunger.* Unlike the need for food, hunger is experienced directly. It creates mental preoccupation and leads to behavior that will reduce the hunger (and the need for food). Thus, people who distinguish needs from motives do so partly by whether there is a subjective experience. The need is a physical condition you don't sense directly. It creates a motivational state that you *do* experience subjectively.

PRESS

Motives are influenced by internal needs, but they're also influenced by external events. Murray (1938) used the term **press** to refer to such external influences. A press (plural is also *press*) is an external condition that creates a desire to obtain (or avoid) something. It thus has a motivational influence, just as does an internal need (see Figure 5.2).

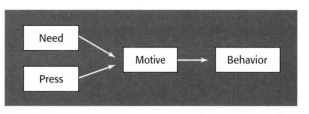

It's probably easiest to get a feel for the effects of need and press with a biological motive. Imagine your need for food creates a hunger motive. You respond by eating lunch. Your peanut butter sandwich, though dry and crumbly, satisfies the need for food. But just as you finish, someone walks in with an extra-large pizza (or whatever you find irresistible). Suddenly you don't seem as satisfied as you did a moment before. The motive to eat has been rekindled—not by a need but by a press.

The concept of press also applies to motives from secondary needs. Seeing someone else receive an honor can increase your motive for recognition. Being around someone who's in a close relationship may increase your motive to be with someone. Being around a new mother brings out caretaking motives in some people, making them wish they had a baby to care for. These are all examples of motive states induced by environmental press.

Although needs and motives clearly *can* be distinguished from each other, people don't always do so. One reason is that it's harder to keep the concepts distinct for psychological needs than biological needs. A need for achievement involves no deficit in the body. It's hard to say how the need to achieve differs from the motive to achieve. For this reason, it's common for people writing about needs and motives in personality to use the two terms interchangeably.

FIGURE 5.2
Internal need states and external press can both influence motives to engage in particular kinds of action, which in turn become realized in overt behavior.

Needs, Motives, and Personality

When motives are strong, they influence behavior. Motive strength has two aspects, however. There are temporary variations in needs across time and situations. But people also vary in *dispositional* needs. That is, some people naturally have more of a given need much of the time than other people do. Such dispositions begin to form a picture of the person's personality.

MOTIVE STATES AND MOTIVE DISPOSITIONS

We've already shown how to think about temporary fluctuations of needs (Figure 5.1, earlier). People shift from doing one thing to doing something else, as one need is satisfied and others build up. Ongoing behavior reflects whichever need is now greatest. That model provides a sense of how people shift from one action to another over time.

Now let's add the idea that people vary in their dispositional levels of needs. This can be portrayed as differences in the overall heights of the lines. Such differences can have large effects on moment-to-moment behavior. For example, John has a high dispositional need for achievement, whereas George's dispositional need for achievement is lower. Assume that the achievement motive goes up and down in the same pattern for both across time. Assume also that they have identical patterns in all their other needs.

As Figure 5.3 shows, John and George would display quite different patterns of behavior over time. Why? Because *even when John's other needs are also up, his need for achievement is so high it tends to remain above the others*. As a result, he tends to do achievement-related things a lot of the time. For George, the achievement motive rarely gets

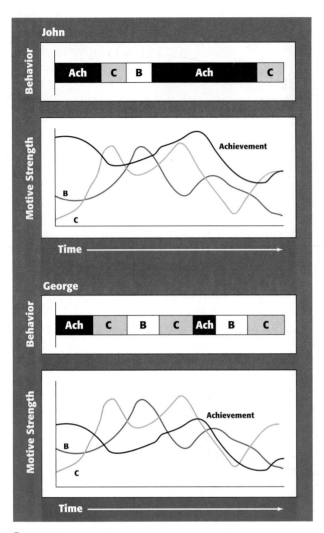

FIGURE 5.3
John has a high dispositional need for achievement; George's is lower. Assume this need fluctuates for both of them in the same pattern across time. John's and George's levels of two other needs are identical (and also fluctuate). The difference in the dispositional need for achievement creates a great difference in the overt actions John and George display (the bars above the lines).

high enough to be the strongest motive. Thus, George doesn't engage in achievement-related behavior very often.

MURRAY'S SYSTEM OF NEEDS

Murray (1938) developed a view of personality organized in terms of needs, press, and motives. He and his colleagues made a list of needs, emphasizing the secondary ones. Some of them are listed in Table 5.1. These, to Murray, are the motives that underlie important human behavior, the needs that form personality. Murray believed that everyone has all these needs but that everyone has a dispositional tendency toward *some particular level* of each need.

Each need stands on its own, but Murray argued that needs can also interrelate in several ways. Needs sometimes *fuse* and are expressed in the same act. For example, Sarah's mother has a high need to dominate and a high need to nurture. She often acts toward Sarah in a caring way (nurturing) but at the same time disregards Sarah's wishes and preferences (dominating). A single action thus satisfies two needs for her at the same time.

Needs can also act *in the service of* one another. For instance, a person may have a need for order, which works to the benefit of a more general need for achievement. As another example, sexual activity, which is motivating in its own right, can serve and support a variety of other motives (Cooper, Shapiro, & Powers, 1998). Needs can also *conflict* with one another. For instance, the need for independence can conflict with the need for intimacy. Someone with a strong need to be independent and also a strong need to share experiences with someone else may feel conflicted in social relations.

Just as needs can interrelate in complex ways, so can needs and press. As one need can work in the service of another, a press can work in the service of a need. For example, Jane, who has a high need for achievement, works at an advertising firm. Her office surrounds her with challenging tasks; each of them is a press for achievement. Having this constant press at work facilitates and supplements her already high motive to achieve.

MEASURING MOTIVES: THE THEMATIC APPERCEPTION TEST

To study the motive approach to personality, researchers had to measure motives. For several reasons, they began not by just asking people about their motives but with another strategy. This turns out to have been a very fortuitous decision. *Why* gets us ahead of our story, however.

What was this alternative strategy? Morgan and Murray (1935) suggested that needs are *projected* into a person's fantasy, just as a movie is projected onto a screen. (This idea derives from psychoanalytic theory; we'll say more about it in Chapter 9.) Murray termed the process of projecting imagery **apperception.** The idea that people

Table 5.1 Partial List of Psychological Needs. *Source:* Adapted from Murray, 1938.

Domain	Need for . . .	Representative Behavior
Pertaining to Ambition		
	Achievement*	Overcoming obstacles
	Recognition	Describing accomplishments
	Exhibition	Attempting to shock or thrill others
Pertaining to Inanimate Objects		
	Acquisition	Obtaining things
	Order	Making things neat and orderly
	Retention	Hoarding things
	Construction	Building things
Pertaining to Defense of Status		
	Inavoidance	Concealing a handicap or a failing
	Defendance	Giving an explanation or excuse
	Counteraction	Retaliating for something
Pertaining to Human Power		
	Dominance*	Directing others' behavior
	Deference	Cooperating with or obeying someone
	Autonomy	Standing up to authority
	Contrariance	Being oppositional
	Aggression	Attacking or belittling others
	Abasement	Apologizing or confessing
	Blame avoidance	Stifling blameworthy impulses
Pertaining to Affection between People		
	Affiliation*	Spending time with others
	Rejection	Snubbing others
	Nurturance*	Taking care others
	Succorance	Being helped by others
	Play	Seeking diversion through others
Pertaining to Exchange of Information		
	Cognizance	Asking questions of others
	Exposition	Delivering information to others

* Needs that have received the most research attention.

normally do this led to the **Thematic Apperception Test,** or TAT (Morgan & Murray, 1935; Murray, 1938; C. P. Smith, 1992).

When your motives are being assessed by TAT, you view a set of pictures in which it isn't clear what's going on. You're asked to create a story about each one. Your story should describe what's happening, the characters' thoughts and feelings, the relationship among characters (if there's more than one), and the outcome of the situation. Through apperception, the themes in your stories should reflect your implicit motives.

Do fantasy stories really reflect people's needs? Yes. Several early validation studies were done. One of them looked at a biological need, the need for food. Participants were deprived of food for varying lengths of time, so they'd have different needs for food. They turned out to differ in their food-related TAT imagery (Atkinson & McClelland, 1948).

Other research manipulated people's achievement motive, by giving some a success and others a failure. A failure should temporarily increase the achievement need, because it creates an achievement deficit (just as passing time creates a food deficit). A success should reduce the achievement motive because it satisfies the need. As predicted, success and failure led to differences in TAT achievement imagery (McClelland, Atkinson, Clark, & Lowell, 1953). In another study, people who were led to be concerned about their social acceptability displayed more affiliation imagery (Atkinson, Heyns, & Veroff, 1954).

Studies of Specific Dispositional Needs

Once it had been validated by such studies, the TAT was used extensively to measure individual differences in *dispositional* needs. Researchers studied several dispositional needs in detail.

NEED FOR ACHIEVEMENT

Of the various needs identified by Murray, the first to receive research attention was the **need for achievement.** This motive has been studied for decades by David McClelland, John Atkinson, and many other people (e.g., Atkinson & Birch, 1970; Atkinson & Raynor, 1974; Heckhausen, 1967; Heckhausen, Schmalt, & Schneider, 1985; McClelland et al., 1953).

Achievement motivation is *the desire to do things well, to feel pleasure in overcoming obstacles.* The need for achievement is reflected in TAT responses that mention performing well at something, reaching goals or overcoming obstacles to goal attainment, having positive feelings about success, or negative feelings about failure.

People who differ in achievement motivation differ in several ways in achievement-related situations. Consider, for instance, the very act of choosing a task. Tasks (or problems within a task) can be easy, hard, or somewhere in between. Given a choice, which would you prefer? (When you plan your course schedule for next semester, do you choose easy courses and professors, hard ones, or ones in between?)

People with low need for achievement prefer tasks that are either very easy or very hard (Atkinson, 1957). It's easy to understand the easy ones. There isn't much achievement pressure in an easy task, and it's nice to get something right, even if everyone else gets it right too. Why, though, would people with low achievement needs choose a hard task? Apparently it's not for the challenge. It seems to be more that doing poorly on a hard problem doesn't reflect badly on you. And there's always the possibility (however remote) that you'll get lucky and succeed. People high in the need for achievement, in contrast, tend to prefer tasks of moderate difficulty. They also work harder on moderately difficult tasks than on very hard or very easy ones (Clark & McClelland, 1956; French, 1955).

Persons high in achievement motivation have a strong need to succeed.

Why do those high in achievement motivation prefer tasks of middle difficulty? Maybe because these tasks give the most information about ability (Trope, 1975, 1979). If you *do well* at an *easy* task, you don't learn much about your ability, because *everyone* does well. If you *fail* at a *hard* task, you don't learn much about your ability, because almost *no one* does well. In the middle, though, you can find out a lot. Perhaps people high in achievement motivation want to find out about their abilities. Trope (1975, 1980) tested this by having people choose test items. He figured out a way to manipulate (separately) the items' difficulty and their **diagnosticity** (how much they tell about ability). People with high achievement needs had a strong preference for diagnostic items (see Figure 5.4), whereas difficulty in itself turned out not to be important.

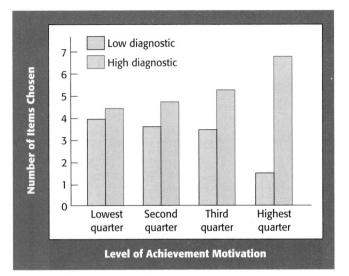

Effects of achievement motivation have been studied in a variety of domains. The need for achievement relates to persistence in the face of failure (e.g., Feather, 1961). It relates to task performances (e.g., Lowell, 1952) and to grades in school (Schultz & Pomerantz, 1976). This need thus plays an important role in a variety of achievement-related behaviors. Indeed, it's even been suggested that the need for achievement may play a role in the economic rise and decline of entire cultures. This idea led to studies of literature from several civilizations, at several distinct points in their history. The literature is interpreted for its themes, in much the same way as TAT responses are interpreted. The economic growth and decline of that civilization are then plotted over the same period.

One impressive study of this sort was done by Bradburn and Berlew (1961), who examined the literature and economic history of England from 1500 to just after 1800. They divided this period into 50-year segments and coded achievement imagery and economic development in each. Achievement imagery was stable for 100 years, fell off, then rose sharply. The index of economic development followed a nearly identical pattern of falling then rising—but 50 years later. This suggests that shifts in achievement motives had economic consequences.

Another, even more complex study of this sort was done by D. C. McClelland (1961). This study focused on a much more narrow period (1925 to 1950) but looked at 23 cultures across the world. McClelland coded achievement imagery from children's schoolbooks at both points in history. He developed two measures of economic growth over the intervening period and compared the achievement imagery to economic growth. A moderately strong association emerged between achievement imagery in 1925 and economic growth from 1925 to 1950. As in the Bradburn and Berlew study, there was virtually no relation between economic growth and later achievement imagery. This pattern suggests that motivation (reflected in the imagery) produced the economic achievement, not vice versa.

Achievement motivation predicted economic success in these studies, but in some situations a need for achievement can be a problem. For example, people who serve in high-level managerial or political positions don't have opportunities for personal achievement. Their task is to mobilize others (which draws on a different need). If people in this situation try to do too much themselves, it can backfire, producing worse outcomes. Consistent with this idea, Spangler and House (1991) found that the need for achievement related inversely to the effectiveness of U.S. presidents.

FIGURE 5.4
Participants in this study chose items to work on that they expected to be either highly diagnostic of their abilities or not diagnostic. This figure divides participants into four levels of achievement motive, ranging from very low to very high. There is an increasingly strong preference for highly diagnostic items among those with higher levels of achievement motivation. *Source: Adapted from Trope, 1975.*

An interesting aspect of the literature on the achievement motive is that at first, far more was known about its effects among men than among women, because most early studies included only males. Eventually, however, researchers looked at achievement needs among women. Some of this work suggests that achievement needs are expressed in varying ways among women, depending on the direction taken by their lives.

Elder and MacInnis (1983) recruited two sets of 17- to 18-year-old girls. One group was family oriented, the other group had a mix of family and career interests. Achievement motives, assessed at the same time, predicted different outcomes in the two groups as they moved into adulthood. Among family-oriented women, those with high achievement needs invested energy in activities leading to marriage and family. In effect, they expressed achievement by creating and sustaining a family. Among career-minded women, high achievement needs led to putting off marriage and family. Presumably this was because they were focusing on their careers. Thus, what women value as a goal determines what behaviors follow from achievement needs.

Another way of putting this is to say that women with achievement needs pursue achievement in ways that fit their views of themselves and the world they live in. It seems reasonable that this principle should also influence what careers women consider. Jenkins (1987) looked at career choices made by women who were college seniors in 1967. Those high in the need for achievement were likely to become teachers but not to go into business. Why? Teaching gave them an outlet for their achievement needs but didn't conflict with traditional women's roles. Business careers didn't fit those roles as well. Thus, the achievement needs of these women were channeled by other aspects of their social environments.

Need for Power

Another motive that's been studied extensively by David Winter (1973) and others is the **need for power.** The need for power is *the motive to have impact on others, to have prestige, to feel strong* compared to others. TAT responses that reflect the need for power have images of forceful, vigorous action—especially action that evokes strong emotional responses in others. Responses showing concern about status or position also reflect need for power.

What kinds of behavior reflect the power motive? Not surprisingly, people high in the need for power seek out positions of authority and influence and surround themselves with symbols of power (Winter, 1972, 1973). For example, students high in the power motive are likely to be office holders in student organizations (Greene & Winter, 1971). People high in this motive also are more sexually active than persons lower in this motive (Schultheiss, Dargel, & Rohde, 2003). People high in the need for power are concerned about controlling the images they present to others (McAdams, 1984). They want to enhance their reputations. They want others to view them as authoritative and influential. Not surprisingly, they tend to be somewhat narcissistic, absorbed in their importance (Carroll, 1987).

This quality can work for you or against you. People high in the power motive are less likely to make concessions in diplomatic negotiations than those lower in this motive (Langner & Winter, 2001), which can lead to better outcomes in the negotiations. Power-motivated people learn more from victories than do other people (Schultheiss, Wirth, Torges, Pang, Villacorta, & Welsh, 2005). On the other hand, they learn less from failures than other people.

There's evidence that the power motive can enhance effectiveness in managing others. For example, among U.S. presidents, those high in the power motive were more effective than those lower (Spangler & House, 1991). One way in which this motive may enhance effectiveness is by fostering a more active response to problems. For example, people high in the need for power respond to inefficiency in work groups by becoming more aroused or activated (Fodor, 1984).

Who do power-motivated persons relate to in their personal lives? Men with high power needs are more likely than those with lower power needs to say that the ideal wife is a woman who's dependent (Winter, 1973). An independent woman is a potential threat. A dependent woman allows the man to feel superior. A later study found that the wives of men high in the need for power were indeed less likely to have careers of their own than other wives (Winter, Stewart, & McClelland, 1977).

The need for power is often expressed in the tendency to acquire high-status possessions and to surround oneself with symbols of power.

This isn't to say that the need for power is something that matters only among men. Women vary in this need as well, and it has proved to predict important outcomes among women. One study (Jenkins, 1994) found that women high in the need for power had more power-related job satisfactions than women lower in this need but also more *dis*satisfactions. These women also made greater strides in career development over a 14-year period—but only if they were in power-relevant jobs.

The level of a person's need for power can also influence the manner in which the person relates to others. The need for power relates to taking an active, assertive, controlling orientation in peer interactions (McAdams, Healy, & Krause, 1984). Power-motivated students are also more argumentative in class and eager to convince others of their point of view (Veroff, 1957). The desire for dominance is reflected in the social signals that are rewarding to them. That is, people high in the need for power are rewarded by low-dominance expressions from others and they're disrupted by high-dominance expressions (Schultheiss, Pang, Torges, Wirth, & Traynor, 2005). Not surprisingly, they are also more attentive to low-dominance expressions (Schultheiss & Hale, in press). The dominating style of interacting that characterizes the need for power can also have more ominous overtones: Men high in power needs are more likely than men with lower power needs to physically abuse their female partners during arguments (Mason & Blankenship, 1987).

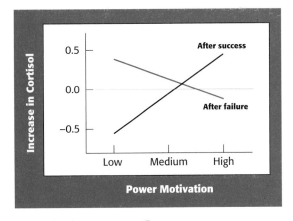

FIGURE 5.5
Increase in the stress hormone cortisol after a failure was greater among persons *higher* in the need for power; increase in cortisol after a success was greater among persons *lower* in the need for power. *Source: Adapted from Wirth et al., 2006.*

The desire for dominance sometimes leads to success but sometimes is frustrated by failure. Both of these experiences can be stressful but for different people (see Figure 5.5). Those with a high need for power have an increase in the stress hormone cortisol after a failure (Wirth, Welsh, & Schultheiss, 2006). But people with low power needs have an increase in cortisol after a success! Apparently, what constitutes a stressor differs between these two sorts of people. Stress seems to be the occurrence of an outcome other than the one you are motivated for or accustomed to.

Oliver Schultheiss and his colleagues have found that the need for power also relates to the sex hormone testosterone. (We say more about this hormone and its influence on personality in Chapter 7.) There is a slight link between power needs and baseline testosterone (Schultheiss et al., 2005). More interesting, however, is what happens to testosterone after success and failure. Among men, higher need for power related to a larger increase in testosterone after a success and also to a greater reduction in testosterone after a failure. Among women, however, the associations were much more complex.

Winter has suggested that the power motive is manifested in two paths, depending on whether the person has acquired a sense of responsibility during socialization (Winter, 1988; Winter & Barenbaum, 1985). For those high in the sense of responsibility, the power motive yields "conscientious" pursuit of prestige, where power is expressed in socially accepted ways. For those lower in responsibility, though, the need for power can lead to more problematic ways of influencing others—what Winter calls "profligate, impulsive" power. This includes aggressiveness, sexual exploitation, and alcohol and drug use.

Winter and Barenbaum (1985) found considerable support for this argument. In one sample of low-responsible men, the need for power related to drinking, fighting, and sexual possessiveness. Among high-responsible men, the need for power related inversely to all these tendencies. Similar findings have emerged from other samples. It has since been found that men with high need for power without the sense of responsibility also have a rise in testosterone when imagining and experiencing a power-related success (Schultheiss, Campbell, & McClelland, 1999; Schultheiss & Rohde, 2002).

NEED FOR AFFILIATION

Another motive that received a good deal of early attention in motive research is the motive to affiliate. The **need for affiliation** is *the motive to spend time with others and form friendly social ties.* This isn't a need to dominate others but to be in social relationships, to interact with others. Social interactions here aren't a means to an end; they're a goal in their own right. In TAT responses, the need for affiliation is reflected in concern over acceptance by others and by active attempts to establish or maintain positive relations with others.

Studies have uncovered several reflections of this motive. For example, people who want to affiliate want to be seen as agreeable. If a group exerts pressure on them, they will more likely go along than will people with lower affiliation needs (Hardy, 1957). People with a high affiliation need get nervous if they think others are judging their interpersonal skills (Byrne, McDonald, & Mikawa, 1963). They show a strong preference for interaction partners who are warm compared to those who are reserved (Hill, 1991). They're more likely to make concessions in negotiations (Langner & Winter, 2001) and more likely to initiate contacts and try to establish friendships (Crouse & Mehrabian, 1977). They are especially sensitive to angry expressions from others (Schultheiss et al., 2005).

The active initiation of social contact suggests that affiliative needs go beyond worry about acceptance from others. These needs can also lead to active participation in social events. For example, Sorrentino and Field (1986) studied the emergence of leadership in discussion groups, which met in five weekly sessions. At the end, group members were asked to indicate whom they viewed as group leaders. People high in the need for affiliation were nominated more often than people lower in the need for affiliation.

As suggested by the Sorrentino and Field research, people with a strong affiliation motive spend more time engaged in social activities than people lower in this motive. They make more phone calls (Lansing & Heyns, 1959), and when paged, they're more likely to be engaged in social activities—conversing or letter writing (Constantian, 1981; McAdams & Constantian, 1983). When they're alone, they're more likely to express a wish to be interacting with others (McAdams & Constantian, 1983; Wong & Csikszentmihalyi, 1991).

The affiliation motive influences satisfaction in relationships (Meyer & Pepper, 1977) in a complex way. Happiness depends partly on the balance of affiliation needs between partners. That is, well-adjusted husbands and wives had affiliation needs that *correlated* with each other. To put it concretely, if you have a low affiliation need, you're best off with someone else with a low affiliation need. If your affiliation need is high, you're best off with someone whose affiliation need is also high.

We noted in Chapter 4 a difference of opinion about whether traits should be measured as broad supertraits or as more narrow traits. A similar question has been raised about affiliation motivation, and by implication about the entire motive approach to personality. Hill (1987) pointed out that affiliation can occur for several reasons. Perhaps the different reasons for affiliation should be considered as separate motives.

To do this, Hill developed self-report scales for four affiliation needs: social comparison, emotional support, positive stimulation, and attention from others. He then created hypothetical situations, each of which related to a particular type of affiliation need. For example, one of them described a job interview that was confusing and ambiguous; this should relate to a need for social comparison (but not to other affiliation motives). As expected, the social comparison scale predicted responses to this situation better than any other scale. The same pattern held for each situation: In each case, the theoretically relevant scale was the best predictor of responses.

These findings have a more general implication. They suggest that there is merit in focusing on specific, rather than global, needs. As with traits, the question seems to be whether the better prediction is worth the trade-off of having to hold more variables in mind.

Need for Intimacy

Another motive that has emerged as a research focus is the **need for intimacy.** It's been studied intensively by Dan McAdams (1982, 1985, 1989) and his collaborators. Intimacy motivation is *the desire to experience warm, close, and communicative exchanges with another person, to feel close to another person.* Carried to an extreme, it's the desire to merge with another person. Intimacy motivation shares with affiliation motivation a wish to be with others as an end, rather than as a means. It goes beyond the need for affiliation, though, in its emphasis on closeness and open sharing with another person.

Interestingly, intimacy motivation wasn't on Murray's list. McAdams proposed it partly because he felt the need for affiliation didn't focus enough on the positive, affirmative aspects of relationships. Additionally, the need for affiliation is an active, striving, "doing" orientation, whereas the need for intimacy as McAdams views it is a more passive "being" orientation (McAdams & Powers, 1981). The two aren't entirely distinct, of course. McAdams and Constantian (1983) reported a correlation of 0.58 between them.

What kinds of behaviors reflect the intimacy motive? In one study, people higher in the need for intimacy reported having more one-to-one exchanges with other people, though not more large-group interaction (McAdams et al., 1984). The interactions reported by intimacy-motivated people involved more self-disclosure, as well. To put it differently, people with a high intimacy need are more likely to share with friends their hopes, fears, and fantasies. The sharing goes both ways: People with a

Need for intimacy is the desire to experience warm, close, and meaningful relationships with others.

high intimacy need report doing more *listening* than people with a low intimacy need, perhaps because they are more concerned about their friends' well-being. Indeed, intimacy seems to entail both self-disclosure and partner disclosure (Laurenceau, Feldman Barrett, & Pietromonaco, 1998).

Because close interactions are important to people with high intimacy needs, it should be no surprise that these people define their lives partly in terms of such interactions. McAdams (1982) collected autobiographical recollections among students high and low in intimacy needs. They were asked to report a particularly joyful or transcendent experience from their past and then an important learning experience. The content of each was coded several ways. For instance, some events involved considerable psychological or physical intimacy with another person; others did not. Analysis revealed that intimacy motivation was strongly correlated with memory content that also implied intimacy.

How do people high in the intimacy motive act when they're with others? They laugh, smile, and make more eye contact when conversing than people with lower intimacy needs (McAdams, Jackson, & Kirshnit, 1984). They don't try to dominate the social scene. (People with the need for power do that.) Instead, they seem to view group activities as chances for group members to be involved in a communal way (McAdams & Powers, 1981).

There's evidence that the desire for intimacy may be good for people. Men in this study (McAdams & Vaillant, 1982) wrote narrative fantasies at age 30 and were assessed 17 years later. Men with higher intimacy motivation at 30 had greater marital and job satisfaction at 47 than did those with less intimacy motivation. Another study found that women high in the intimacy motive reported more happiness and gratification in their lives than those low in the intimacy motive—unless they were living alone (McAdams & Bryant, 1987). On the other hand, intimacy needs (needing to be close) don't coexist well with power needs (needing to influence or dominate others). Persons who are high in both needs are often poorly adjusted (Zeldow, Daugherty, & McAdams, 1988).

Patterned Needs: Inhibited Power Motive

Thus far, we've mostly discussed needs individually. Indeed, for many years that's how they were examined—one at a time. However, some have examined patterns involving several needs at once, sometimes in combination with other characteristics. One well-known pattern combines a low need for affiliation with a high need for power, in conjunction with the tendency to inhibit the expression of the latter. This pattern is called **inhibited power motivation** (McClelland, 1979). The reason for interest in this pattern depends on the context in which it's examined.

One context is *leadership*. The line of reasoning goes as follows: A person high in the need for power wants to influence people. Being low in the need for affiliation lets the person make tough decisions with no worry about being disliked. Being high in self-control (inhibiting the use of power) means the person will want to follow orderly procedures and stay within the framework of the organization. Such a person should do very well in the structure of a business.

This pattern does seem to relate to managerial success (McClelland & Boyatzis, 1982). Those with the inhibited power pattern moved to higher levels of management in a 16-year period than others, but only those who were nontechnical managers. Among managers whose jobs rested on engineering skills, personality didn't matter. This is understandable, because the managerial value of those people depends heavily on their particular skills.

There is also evidence that people with this pattern are especially effective at persuasion (Schultheiss & Brunstein, 2002). Their persuasiveness stems both from greater verbal fluency and from an effective use of nonverbal cues such as gesturing. Presumably being more persuasive helps these people be effective in mobilizing others.

The pattern of high power motivation and low affiliation motivation may be good for getting others mobilized, but even this may be a mixed blessing. Winter (1993) has argued that this pattern is actually conducive to starting wars! Historical data show that high levels of power imagery and low levels of affiliation imagery in the statements of politicians predicted going to war. For example, speeches by the rulers of Great Britain contained more power imagery than affiliation imagery in the year before Britain entered a war, whereas the reverse was true during years before a no-war year (see Figure 5.6). In another case (the Cuban Missile Crisis of 1962), greater affiliation than power imagery occurred before the successful avoiding of a war.

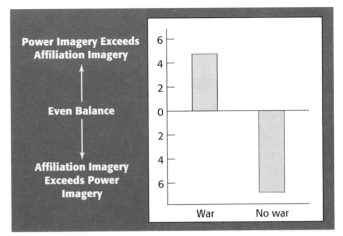

FIGURE 5.6
Balance of power motive imagery versus affiliation motive imagery in sovereign's speeches during the year before Great Britain entered a war (18 cases) compared to the year before Britain did *not* enter a war (36 cases). *Source: Adapted from Winter, 1993, Table 3.*

Implicit and Self-Attributed Motives

As we noted earlier in the chapter, the motivational view is that personality is a system of multiple needs. Every motive exists in every person. Behavior at any given time depends partly on how intense various motives are.

INCENTIVE VALUE

This analysis sounds reasonable, but it's missing something. It predicts that if your need for affiliation is more intense than your other needs, you'll engage in an affiliative act. But what act? Additional concepts are needed to address that question (McClelland, 1985).

One such concept is **incentive,** the degree to which a given action can satisfy a need for you. It's sort of a personalized weighting of how relevant an act is to the need. Incentive values determine how a motive is expressed behaviorally. For example, a person with a high need for affiliation who values long conversations with special friends but not impersonal crowds will avoid parties. Avoiding parties might seem strange for a person with a high need for affiliation. But people don't engage in all conceivable need-related behaviors. They choose ways to satisfy their needs, based on the incentive values that various activities have for them.

We didn't introduce the concept of *incentives* earlier in the chapter. It should be clear, however, that something like it is needed to account for behavior's diversity. People vary in the activities they engage in, even when satisfying the same need. As noted earlier, some women satisfy the need for achievement through careers, others by achieving strong family lives. These activities differ greatly, yet each can satisfy the need to achieve.

This principle relates to a point made in Chapter 4 regarding interactionism: We said there that people choose for themselves which situations to enter and which to avoid, thus creating an interaction between person and situation. We didn't say *why* different people choose different situations. One answer is that various situations have different *incentive* values to different people, even if the situations fulfill the same need.

Needs and incentives both influence behavior but in different ways. McClelland (1985) said that need strength relates to long-term *frequencies of need-relevant actions of any type.* Incentive values, on the other hand, should relate to *choices within a domain of action.* In this view, needs influence behavior primarily at a nonconscious level, whereas values influence the more conscious process of choice.

IMPLICIT MOTIVES ARE DIFFERENT FROM SELF-ATTRIBUTED MOTIVES

The last paragraph was deceptively simple, but it has a great many implications. Earlier in the chapter, we described development of the TAT to assess needs. We said there that the decision to use that strategy instead of asking people about their needs was fortuitous. Why? Because it allowed the discovery of something that today seems very important.

The TAT was used in the vast majority of the work described thus far. We feel relatively confident from the wide range of findings that it does assess people's motives. Given the large effort required to score the TAT, however, other researchers created self-report scales to assess motives. They intended those self-reports to measure the same motives as the TAT. But the self-reports turn out to correlate poorly with TAT assessment (McClelland, Koestner, & Weinberger, 1989; Pang & Schultheiss, 2005; Schultheiss & Brunstein, 2001). Why? What's going on?

McClelland and his colleagues argued that the two kinds of assessments are, in fact, measuring different things (McClelland et al., 1989). They used the term **implicit motive** to refer to what the TAT measures. They called the motives *implicit* because the person may or may not be aware of them. They used the term **self-attributed motive** to refer to what's measured by self-reports. An increasing body of evidence indicates that implicit motives and self-attributed motives are different from each other. Implicit motives seem to be what we have been calling *motives.* Self-attributed motives are closer to what was described in the preceding section as *incentives.*

McClelland et al. (1989) held that implicit motives are the more basic. They are the recurrent preferences for classes of affective experiences that McClelland believed lie at the heart of motives (the feeling of "doing better" for the achievement motive, the feeling of "being strong" for the power motive, the feeling of "being close" for the intimacy motive). Implicit motives are thought to be primitive and automatic (Schultheiss, 2002). Because they are basic, they are good predictors of broad behavioral tendencies over time. In contrast, self-attributed motives relate to specific action goals. They tell how a person will act in a particular situation. For this reason, they're better at predicting responses in structured settings.

This distinction has been pursued further in several projects. Brunstein and Maier (2005) expanded on the idea that both implicit and self-attributed achievement motives play important, but distinct, roles in achievement behavior. They found evidence that the implicit achievement motive acts primarily as an energizer, boosting effort when the person falls behind. The self-attributed achievement motive, in contrast, acts primarily as an influence on decision making, influencing how people seek information about their skills compared to other people (for example, by choosing whether to continue a task or not).

Evidence that these qualities are distinct also comes from research in which people first completed TAT and self-report measures and then kept records of memorable experiences over 60 days (Woike, 1995). The records were coded for motive relevance and for feelings. Strength of implicit motives (TAT) related to the frequency of reporting feelings that relate to that motive, but strength of self-attributed motives did not. Self-attributed motives related to the frequency of reporting motive-related events with no feelings (but TAT scores did not). It seems, then, that the two aspects of motivation link to different aspects of memory. Further evidence that they link to different aspects of memory comes from studies showing that self-attributed motives predict recall of general memories related to the self-concept, whereas implicit motives predict recall of specific events (Woike, Mcleod, & Goggin, 2003).

As a final example of the value of distinguishing between implicit and self-attributed motives, consider a set of studies by Baumann, Kaschel, and Kuhl (2005). They argued that people sometimes form motive-related intentions (conscious) that fit poorly with their implicit motive dispositions (thus making it clear the two are different). When this happens, the person is stressed, which has adverse effects on well-being. Finally, they argued that this tendency is particularly pronounced among persons who are poor at regulating negative emotions. Evidence from three studies fits that picture.

McClelland believed that both the implicit motive and the self-attributed motive are important, but that they should be viewed separately. The evidence appears to support that belief. Sometimes it makes sense to expect an implicit motive to predict an outcome but not a self-attributed motive. Sometimes the opposite is true. For this reason, it's important to be sure which one you want to measure and to measure it correctly (McClelland, 1989). The distinction between implicit and self-attributed motives is one aspect of the motive view on personality that is receiving increasingly close attention.

Approach and Avoidance Motives

Another distinction that is also becoming increasingly important is between *approach* and *avoidance*. As noted early in the chapter, a motive is either a readiness to approach something or a readiness to avoid something. Thus far, we've written only about approach: for example, people who want to achieve try to approach success. But whenever there's an achievement task, the possibility of failure is also present. It seems likely that the desire to avoid failure also plays a motivational role here. Just as Atkinson (1957) tied the need for achievement to the capacity to feel pride in success, the motive to avoid failure relates to a tendency to feel shame after failure (McGregor & Elliot, 2005).

A simple way to avoid failure is to avoid achievement situations altogether. Never trying keeps you from failing. Another way to avoid failing is *by the very act of succeeding*. It may be that some people who struggle to achieve don't care so much about gaining success as they care about the fact that gaining success lets them avoid failure.

Much early research on achievement actually measured both of these motives. A lot of it derived from Atkinson's (1957) theory of achievement behavior. That theory makes its clearest predictions for people whose only motivation is to approach success and people whose only motivation is to avoid failure. Predictions are less clear for people high in both motives and people low in both motives. For that reason, studies often included only the two groups who were high in one motive and low in the other.

That strategy was guided by theory, but it has a bad side effect: It completely confounds the two motives. This causes ambiguity in interpretation (Chapter 2). If the groups act differently, is it because of the difference in the motive to approach success, or because of the difference in the motive to avoid failure? There is no way to know, though interpretations tend to focus on the motive to approach success.

In recent years, the distinction between approach and avoidance motivation has re-emerged as a focus for research on achievement, much of it by Andrew Elliot and his colleagues (e.g., Elliot, 2005; Elliot & Harackiewicz, 1996; Elliot & McGregor, 2001). Part of their theory is that achievement can reflect either of these motives. Which motive is central, however, will influence many aspects of the person's experience.

Elliot and McGregor (2001) found that the motive to succeed in mastering course material (approach) related to study strategies that involved thoughtfully elaborating on the material. The avoidance motive related to memorization. Avoidance motivation also related to having difficulty organizing study time effectively. Elliot and Sheldon (1997) found that the two motive tendencies also had different effects on subjective experiences. People who spent their effort trying to avoid failure reported less emotional well-being and less satisfaction with their performances than did people who were trying to approach success.

Though it might generally be better to approach than to avoid, there is also evidence that people do better when they're doing what's familiar to them. Specifically, people with high fear of failure are made uneasy and upset by imagining success (Langens & Schmalt, 2002). As suggested in the context of the power motive, it may be that what is stressful to you is what you're unfamiliar with.

APPROACH AND AVOIDANCE IN OTHER MOTIVES

Once you grasp the idea of separate approach and avoidance motives, you realize that the idea has implications for *every* motive you can think of (see also Carver, Lawrence, & Scheier, 1999; Higgins, 1997; Ogilvie, 1987). Try it out. Pick a motive from Table 5.1 (or think of one that's not there). Identify a behavior that reflects that motive. Then see if you can spot the opposing motive that might create the same behavior. For example, acts of affiliation can come from the desire to *be with others* (need for affiliation), but they can also come from a desire to *avoid being alone* (Boyatzis, 1973; Pollak & Gilligan, 1982). These aren't the same. One is a motive to approach; the other is a motive to avoid. The same issue can be raised for any need you can think of.

Just as with achievement behavior, evidence is beginning to accumulate that approach and avoidance motives have different consequences in other domains. A powerful example is a study of commitment among romantic partners. Frank and Brandstätter (2002) found that commitment based in approach predicted more relationship satisfaction six and thirteen months later. However, commitment based in avoidance (i.e., avoiding the process of breaking up) predicted lower relationship satisfaction at the follow-ups.

The idea that a given behavior can be based on either an approach motive or an avoidance motive (or some combination of the two) raises very broad questions about why people do the things they do. Are people generally moving toward goals, or are they trying to avoid or escape from things? Do actions differ, depending on which motive is more prominent? Do the feelings that go with the actions differ? The general idea that any approach motive has a corresponding avoidance motive has very broad implications. It complicates the picture of human behavior enormously. We will put this idea aside for the rest of this chapter, but you should keep in mind that it's always in the background.

The Methods of Personology

Research examining the effects of motive patterns tends to take one of two forms. Some studies examine how people respond to particular events, in the laboratory or in the field. Other studies collect evidence of a dispositional motive (or set of motives) at one time and relate the motive to some outcome that occurs considerably later.

These two ways of studying motives both differ greatly from the approach favored by Henry Murray, the father of this viewpoint. Murray believed the way to understand personality is to study the *whole person* and to do so over an extended period. The work on which he based his theory was an intensive study of 51 college men (Murray, 1938). Each was tested in many ways and also interviewed by a staff of professionals. These people then presented their impressions to what Murray called the Diagnostic Council, the most experienced members of the team. This group came to know each participant's personality quite thoroughly.

This approach was idiographic. It focused on the pattern of qualities that made each person unique. Murray disliked nomothetic methods. He thought their focus on comparison prevented them from probing deeply into a person's life. To Murray, the nomothetic approach yielded only a superficial understanding.

In fact, Murray's concern about the inadequacies of nomothetic approaches led him to coin the term **personology** to refer to the approach he preferred. He defined *personology* as the study of individual lives and the factors that influence their course. He believed that personology was more meaningful than other approaches because of its emphasis on the person's life history. According to Murray (1938, p. 604), "The history of a personality *is* the personality."

Recent years have seen a resurgence of interest in this way of thinking about personality. For example, Dan McAdams, whose work on intimacy motivation was described earlier, has written extensively on the idea that identity takes the form of an extended narrative—a life story that each of us writes and lives out over time (McAdams, 1985; McAdams & Pals, 2006). This narrative has chapters, heroes, and thematic threads that recur and permeate the story line (see also Rabin, Zucker, Emmons, & Frank, 1990).

As an example of how individual narratives can differ from person to person, the themes they express sometimes emphasize growth ("I found out how to make our relationship better") and sometimes safety ("I hope that never happens again"; Bauer, McAdams, & Sakaeda, 2005). As another example of a narrative focus, McAdams (2006) has identified a constellation of themes focused on personal redemption—a transition from a state of suffering to a better psychological state—which characterizes the lives of some middle-aged Americans.

From this point of view, the person's identity lies in keeping a coherent narrative going across time (McAdams & Pals, 2006; Singer, 2004). This way of thinking speaks directly to the uniqueness of each person, because every life story is unique (Singer, 2005). Whether this approach will become more prominent in personality psychology in the future remains to be seen, but it surely is a development that Murray would have applauded.

Assessment

Assessment of personality from the motive viewpoint is a matter of determining the dispositional levels of a person's needs. As noted earlier, there are several ways to assess this information. The assessment technique most distinctly associated with assessment of needs, however, is the TAT (C. P. Smith, 1992; Winter, 1996).

BOX 5.2   THE PROCESS BEHIND THE TAT

Take a good look at the picture on the right. Something's happening in the minds of these people, but what? Decide for yourself. Make up a story that fits the picture. Include the following information (and whatever else you want to include): *What's just happened to these people? What's the relationship between them? What are their present thoughts and feelings? What will be the outcome of the situation?* Take your time, and make your story as long and detailed as you wish.

What you've just done is similar to what people do when completing the Thematic Apperception Test, or TAT (Morgan & Murray, 1935). The idea is that people's needs will show up in the

thoughts they generate from their imaginations when they try to make sense out of ambiguous pictures. The ambiguity of the picture makes it less likely that environmental press will dictate your story's content and more likely that your needs will influence what you write. When people complete the TAT, they write stories for several pictures. One of them is completely blank, the ultimate in ambiguity!

Different pictures tend to elicit stories with different themes. Some pictures naturally elicit achievement-related stories; others are more amenable to stories with affiliation themes. Over the course of several pictures, however, dispositional tendencies emerge in the narratives

that people compose. Presumably these storytelling tendencies reflect the motives that characterize the person's personality. If you're interested in the motives that dominate your own personality, look at the story you wrote to see if there's evidence of the motives listed back in Table 5.1.

Illustration by Stephen P. Scheier. Reproduced by permission.

Earlier in the chapter, we described the essence of the procedure by which the TAT is administered (see also Box 5.2). People who are completing the TAT view a set of ambiguous pictures, in which it isn't clear what's happening. They're asked to create a story about each picture. The story should describe what's happening, the characters' thoughts and feelings, their relationship to each other (if there's more than one character), and the outcome of the situation. Through apperception, the themes that are manifested in the stories reflect implicit motives.

Scoring people's responses can be complex (Winter, 1994), but here's a simple version. Look to see what kinds of events take place in the story and what themes and images are in it. Events that involve overcoming obstacles, attaining goals, and having positive feelings about those activities reflect the achievement motive. Events in which people choose to be with other people and stories that emphasize relationships among people reflect the affiliation motive. Stories with images of one person controlling another reflect the power motive. More than one theme can occur in a given story. These can be scored separately, so the story can be used to assess several different motives at the same time.

The use of stories written in response to ambiguous pictures is the core method for assessing motives in research deriving from this theoretical viewpoint. It's not just stories that can be scored for motive imagery, of course. Anything that is written can potentially be scored in the same way (Winter, 1994). However, variations on the TAT remain the most popular method of assessing implicit motives.

The TAT is widely used to measure motives, but it has had its share of criticism. Questions have been raised about its relatively low internal consistency and test–retest reliability (Entwisle, 1972; Lilienfeld, Wood, & Garb, 2000). Defenders of the technique reply that there are good reasons for both of these to be low. The pictures in the TAT vary considerably in content. It's not surprising that they bring out different kinds of stories. This reduces internal consistency. It is also arguable that being instructed to tell several stories creates some implicit pressure to avoid repetition. This can reduce both internal consistency and test–retest reliability (e.g., Atkinson & Raynor, 1974). There's evidence, though, that the reliability of the TAT need not be as low as was once believed (Lundy, 1985; Schultheiss & Pang, in press).

Another criticism of the TAT is far more pragmatic. It takes a lot of time and effort to give and score it. This is a key reason people wanted to develop self-report measures of motives. Several attempts were made to create self-reports of the needs Murray saw as basic. An early effort was the Edwards Personal Preference Schedule (Edwards, 1959). A more recent one was the Personality Research Form, or PRF (Jackson, 1984). As with any inventory, these can be used to create personality profiles. In this case, however, the traits measured are self-attributed motivational traits.

As was noted earlier in the chapter, there is now substantial evidence that self-attributed motives (assessed by self-report scales) and implicit motives assessed (by story imagery) are not the same. Each captures something different about human motivational experience.

MOTIVES AND THE FIVE-FACTOR TRAIT MODEL

Do the qualities measured by inventories of motives resemble those that are measured by scales with different starting points? Chapter 4 described the idea that the basic traits of personality fall largely within five supertraits. Does the five-factor model absorb the qualities that Murray saw as important?

Several researchers have addressed this question. As a starting point, several analyses of the PRF yielded five factors. Stumpf (1993) concluded that all of the "big five" except neuroticism were captured in the PRF. Costa and McCrae (1988a) looked at associations of PRF scales with the NEO-PI-R, a "big five" measure. Their findings also suggested that many PRF scales reflect underlying qualities of the five-factor model. On the other hand, several PRF scales loaded on two or more of the five factors, rather than one. This appears to indicate that those motives relate to several traits. For example, the need for dominance related to openness, extraversion, and (inversely) agreeableness. It seems, then, that the five-factor model doesn't perfectly absorb the needs reflected in the PRF.

This general pattern of loadings has been replicated by Paunonen et al. (1992). In contrast, somewhat better support for a fit to the five-factor model has been found using the Edwards measure of needs (Piedmont, McCrae, & Costa, 1992).

TRAITS AND MOTIVES AS DISTINCT AND COMPLEMENTARY

Although the attempt to fit these motives to the five-factor model can be seen as an effort to integrate across theoretical boundaries, some believe that the effort is misguided and that traits and motives are fundamentally different from each other (Winter, John, Stewart, Klohnen, & Duncan, 1998). In taking this position, Winter et al. noted that all the evidence reviewed in the previous section involved self-attributed motives, not implicit motives. The fact that self-attributed and implicit motives are not strongly related is reason enough to be cautious about concluding that traits and motives are the same. In fact, there is separate evidence that implicit motives relate poorly to the five-factor model (Schultheiss & Brunstein, 2001).

Winter et al. (1998) proposed an integration, but of a different sort: They proposed that motives are fundamental desires and that traits channel how those desires are expressed. Thus, they argued, motives and traits interact to produce behavior. In some respects, this resembles the argument described earlier in the chapter about

Table 5.2 Sample Hypothesis about the Interaction between the Affiliation–Intimacy Motive and the Trait of Introversion–Extraversion. *Source:* Adapted from Winter et al., 1998.

	Affiliation–Intimacy Motive	
	Low	High
Extravert	Intimate relationship not salient as a desire	Desire for intimate relationship leads to single stable relationship
Introvert	Intimate relationship not salient as a desire	Desire for intimate relationships but difficulty maintaining them, because high focus on inner world is disruptive of a connection to the other person

implicit motives and incentive values. In the view taken by Winter et al., traits may represent patterns of incentive preferences.

In support of their argument, Winter et al. (1998) presented two studies of the trait of extraversion and (TAT-derived) needs. The studies examined women's lives across many decades. Winter et al. (1998) predicted that intimacy needs would have different effects among introverts and extraverts (see Table 5.2). For women with a low intimacy need, it shouldn't matter much whether they are introverts or extraverts. Intimacy isn't a big need for them. The complicated situation occurs among those with high intimacy needs.

An extravert with a high intimacy need should do fine in relationships, because extraverts are comfortable with and good at various kinds of social interaction. In contrast, introverts with high intimacy needs should have more problems. Their highly inner-directed orientation should interfere with relationships. Their partners may see them as remote or withholding. The result should be more likelihood of marital problems. This is exactly what Winter et al. (1998) found.

Problems in Behavior, and Behavior Change

People working within the motive approach to personality have been interested in specific domains of human activity (e.g., achievement, affiliation, power, intimacy) and in the more general idea of motivation as a concept. They haven't addressed the question of problems in behavior in great detail, nor have they suggested a particular approach to therapy. Nevertheless, the literature in this area has at least tentative links to some problems in behavior and to the processes of behavior change.

NEED FOR POWER AND ALCOHOL ABUSE

It's been suggested that the need for power can play a role in developing a drinking problem (McClelland, Davis, Kalin, & Wanner, 1972). This idea stems partly from the finding that drinking alcohol leads to feelings of power. Thus, a person with a need for power can satisfy that need, at least somewhat, by drinking. This doesn't satisfy the need for long, of course, because the feeling of power is illusory. It goes away when the person sobers up.

The idea that alcohol abuse may reflect a need for power leads to some recommendations for treatment. In particular, it suggests that people who are using alcohol this way aren't aware of doing so. They'd probably benefit from realizing what they're doing. By encouraging other ways to satisfy the power motive, a therapist can treat the issue productively, rather than simply treating a symptom. Evidence from one study (Cutter, Boyatzis, & Clancy, 1977) indicates that this approach can be more effective than traditional therapies, yielding nearly twice the rate of rehabilitation at one-year follow-up.

FOCUSING ON AND CHANGING MOTIVATION

Those contributing to the motive approach to personality have also had relatively little to say about therapeutic behavior change. Murray, the father of this approach, was a thera-

Motivation seminars are often used to enhance achievement motivation among people in business.

pist, but he didn't develop new therapy techniques. In general, he tended to apply the currently existing psychodynamic techniques to people's problems.

It would seem, however, that one of the studies just discussed makes some suggestions about behavior change. As indicated, some people appear to use alcohol as a way of temporarily satisfying a desire for power. A treatment program developed for these people had two focuses. It made them more aware that this motive was behind their drinking. It also helped them to find other ways to satisfy the need for power, thus making drinking unnecessary.

A broader implication of this discussion is that people may *often* be unaware of the motives behind problem behaviors. Many problem behaviors may reflect needs that are being poorly channeled. If so, taking a close look at the person's motive tendencies might tell something about the source of the problem. Knowing the source may make it easier to make changes.

Another program of work with indirect implications for therapy was conducted by McClelland and his colleagues (McClelland, 1965; McClelland & Winter, 1969). This training program was developed to raise achievement motivation among businesspeople (see also Lemann, 1994). It was rooted in the idea that thinking a lot about achievement-related ideas increases your motive to achieve.

The program began by describing the nature of the achievement motive and instructing people on how to score TAT protocols for achievement imagery. People then were taught to use achievement imagery in their thoughts as much as possible. By teaching themselves to think in terms of achievement, they increased the likelihood of using an achieving orientation in whatever activity they undertook.

Achievement-related thinking is important. By itself, however, it isn't enough. A second purpose of the training was to link these thoughts to specific concrete action patterns. It's also important to be sure the patterns work outside the training program. Participants were encouraged to think in achievement terms everywhere—not just in training sessions—and to put the action patterns into motion. People who completed the course wrote down their plans for the next two years. They were encouraged to plan realistically and to set goals that were challenging but not out of reach. Creating this plan was a way of turning the achievement orientation they had learned into a self-prescription for a course of activity. This prescription then could be used in guiding actual achievement later on.

Was the course effective? The answer seems to be yes. In a two-year follow-up, participants had greater business achievement, were more likely to have started new business ventures, and were more likely to be employing more people than previously compared to control participants (McClelland & Winter, 1969).

The outcomes of this program show it's possible to change people's achievement-related behavior, but a question remains about whether their underlying needs are

Box 5.3 Theoretical Controversy:

Are Motives Biologically Based or Rooted in Cognition?

As we've noted, McClelland and his colleagues developed a training program to increase achievement motive. This program seemed to produce the desired results, but its success raises questions about the nature of the achievement motive—indeed, about all psychological motives.

Early motive theorists such as Murray assumed that even psychological and social needs derive from biological processes. Biology is used here more as a metaphor than an explanatory device. Still, it's generally assumed that individual differences in need profiles are stable, determined by the person's basic nature.

McClelland (1965), on the other hand, came to believe that psychological motives are learned and thus can be altered. The success of his program

stands as a testament to this idea. The program is very simple. Participants get a clear understanding of what the motive is and how it shows up in thought and action. They're then taught to think and act that way. Because McClelland knew a lot about how need for achievement is manifested, it was easy for him to tell people what to do.

These procedures produced the intended changes, but they raise questions. If motives are so easily altered—if motives are learned—why have the concept of motive at all? There are, after all, some psychologists who see the concept of motive as useless and even misleading (Chapters 12 and 13). Isn't this a case in which a motivational theorist is turning around and embracing a competing approach?

Another question is raised by the training program's emphasis on cognitive processes. The program entails elaborately coding in memory the nature of the motive the people are

trying to acquire. It also includes drawing explicit mental associations between that motive and concrete actions and emphasizing the monitoring of outcomes. These processes look suspiciously like the things that would be emphasized by people who take a cognitive or self-regulation approach to personality (Chapters 16 and 17). Are the effects of the program, then, really motivational?

One possible response to these questions is that the program developed by McClelland may change people's motives but not their needs. Recall that theorists sometimes distinguish needs from motives and that motives are influenced by both needs and press. It's possible to think of McClelland's training program as teaching people how to surround themselves with press to evoke the achievement motive. This way of thinking would account for the fact that the motive changes but still allow the assumption that needs are enduring dispositions.

---

changed, as well (see Box 5.3). It also remains uncertain how much these effects can be generalized to the domain of therapy. Nonetheless, the studies do seem to provide intriguing suggestions about behavior change.

Need and Motive Theories: Problems and Prospects

The chapter before this one dealt with trait theorists. As a group, those theorists are more concerned about describing the structure of personality than in describing the mechanics by which traits are expressed. Theorists of *this* chapter, in contrast, look to motivational processes and the pressures they place on people as a way to specify how dispositions influence actions. By providing a way to think about how dispositions create behavior—by specifying a type of intrapersonal functioning—this approach to dispositions evades one of the criticisms of trait theories.

A criticism that's harder to evade is that decisions about what qualities to study have been arbitrary. Murray developed his list of needs from his own intuition (and other people's lists). Others working in this tradition have tended to go along uncritically. Yet McAdams noted one omission from that list—the need for intimacy—that is strikingly obvious as a human motive. This suggests that Murray's intuitive list was incomplete. A response to this criticism is that the motives that have been examined most closely in research are those that fit with ideas also appearing elsewhere in psychology, including trait psychology. This convergence across views suggests that the needs in question really are fundamental.

Another criticism bears less on the theory than on its implementation. Murray was explicit in saying that the dynamics of personality can be understood only by considering multiple needs at once. However, research from the motive approach to personality has rarely done that. More often, people have studied one motive at a time to examine its dynamics. Occasionally, researchers have stretched to the point of looking at particular clusters of two or three needs, but this has been rare. On the other hand, it's important to keep in mind that, despite Murray's wishes, the motive view of dispositions is not the same as the practice of personology. It's certainly possible to investigate the former without adopting the latter.

Despite these limitations, work on personality from the viewpoint of motive dispositions has continued into the present. Indeed, such work has enjoyed a resurgence in the past decade or so. The idea that people vary in what motivates them has a good deal of intuitive appeal. Further appeal derives from the idea that motive states wax and wane across time and circumstances. This builds in a way to incorporate both situational influences and dispositional influences in an integrated way. Given these pluses, and a growing interest in understanding how implicit motives and self-attributed motives work together, the future of this approach seems strong.

· SUMMARY ·

The motive approach to personality assumes that behavior reflects a set of underlying needs. As a need becomes more intense, it is more likely to influence what behavior occurs. Behavior is also influenced by press: external stimuli that elicit motivational tendencies. Needs (and press) vary in strength from moment to moment, but people also differ from each other in patterns of chronic need strength. According to this viewpoint, this difference is the source of individual differences in personality.

Murray cataloged human needs, listing both biological (primary) and psychological (secondary) needs. Several of the psychological motives later received systematic study by others. One (studied by McClelland, Atkinson, and others) was the need for achievement: the motive to overcome obstacles and to attain goals. People with high levels of the achievement motive behave differently from those with lower levels in several ways: the kinds of tasks they prefer, the level of task difficulty they prefer, their persistence, and their performance levels. Early research on achievement tended to disregard how approach and avoidance motives might separately influence behavior. More recent work has begun to examine those distinct influences.

The need for power—the motive to be strong compared to other people—has also been studied extensively. People who score high in this need tend to seek out positions of influence, to surround themselves with the trappings of power, and to become energized when the groups they are guiding have difficulties. People with a high level of the power motive tend to choose as friends people who aren't influential or popular, thereby protecting themselves from undesired competition. Power-motivated men prefer wives who are dependent, and these wives tend not to have their own careers. The power motive can lead to unpleasant forms of social influence unless it's tempered by a sense of responsibility.

The need for affiliation is the desire to spend time with other people, to develop and maintain relationships. People who score high in this need are responsive to social influence, spend a relatively large proportion of their time communicating with other people, and when alone often think about being with others. A related motive that isn't represented in Murray's list but has received research attention in recent years is the need for intimacy. People high in this need want warm, close, and communicative relationships with other persons. People with a strong intimacy need tend to spend more time in one-to-one interaction and less in groups. They tend to engage in interactions that involve lots of self-disclosure and are especially concerned about their friends' well-being.

Recent research has also begun to investigate patterns of motives, such as inhibited power motive. This pattern is defined by having more of a need for power than a need for affiliation and by restraining the power need. People with this pattern do well in managerial careers, but the pattern has also been linked to political orientations preceding wars.

Theorists of this view also use other concepts in talking about behavior. Incentive value—the extent to which a given action will satisfy a given need for a person—helps to explain why people with the same need express the need in different ways. Indeed, the concept of incentive provides an opening into a broader issue. Specifically, assessment of needs by the Thematic Apperception Test (TAT) does not relate well to assessment by self-report. The former have come to be called *implicit motives* and the latter, *self-attributed motives.* The former are thought to function mostly nonconsciously and the latter consciously. One active area of interest is how these two aspects of motives function.

Murray emphasized the study of individual lives in depth over extended periods of time. He coined the term *personology* to refer to the study of the whole person, and he saw personology as his goal. This emphasis has not been strong in the work of most others, but it has re-emerged more recently in the work of McAdams and his colleagues.

The contribution to assessment that is most identified with the motive approach is the TAT. It is based on the idea that people's motives are reflected in the imagery they *apperceive,* that is, read into ambiguous stimuli—a set of pictures depicting people in ambiguous situations. There are also self-report measures of needs, which appear to measure something different from what the TAT measures.

The motivational approach to personality has largely ignored the issue of analyzing problems in behavior, although at least some evidence links the need for power to the misuse of alcohol. It's possible to infer from this evidence, however, that many problems in behavior may stem from inappropriate channeling of motives. It's also reasonable that people can be helped by increasing their awareness of the motive that underlies the problem, so the motive can be channeled in alternative ways. Research on increasing the need for achievement suggests that it may be possible to alter people's dispositional levels of the motives that make up personality.

· GLOSSARY ·

Apperception   The projecting of a motive onto an ambiguous external stimulus via imagery.

Diagnosticity   The extent to which a task provides information about something.

Implicit motive   A motive assessed indirectly by fantasy or other narrative.

Incentive   The degree to which an action can satisfy a particular need for a person.

Inhibited power motivation   The condition of having more need for power than for affiliation but restraining its use.

Motive   Cognitive–affective clusters organized around readiness for a particular kind of experience.

Need   An unsatisfactory internal condition that motivates behavior.

Need for achievement   The need to overcome obstacles and attain goals.

Need for affiliation   The need to form and maintain relationships and to be with people.

Need for intimacy   The need for close communication with someone else.

Need for power   The need to have influence over other people.

Personology   The study of the entire person.

Press   An external stimulus that increases the level of a motive.

Primary need   A biological need, such as the need for food.

Secondary need   A psychological or social need.

Self-attributed motive   A motive that is consciously reported.

Thematic Apperception Test (TAT)   A method of assessing the strength of a motive through narrative fantasy.

part 3

The Biological Perspective

The Biological Perspective: Major Themes and Underlying Assumptions

We human beings are biological creatures, members of the animal kingdom. We carry around all of the characteristics implied by citizenship in that kingdom. We eat, drink, breathe, void wastes, and engage in sexual activities that ensure the continuation of our species. We're also influenced by a number of more subtle forces that reflect our animal nature.

How deeply rooted are these biological pressures? How pervasive is their influence? Are the qualities of personality determined by genes? Is the existence of personality itself a product of evolution? How much of an influence do biological processes have on personality? What adaptive functions do these influences serve? These are some of the questions that underlie the biological perspective on personality.

Biological approaches to personality have varied widely in focus over the years. Some theories of this group are only vaguely biological. Others are tied to specific biological processes and structures. The nature of the research also varies widely, from studies of inheritance to studies examining the nature of biological functions. In some ways, the biological perspective is still a scattered approach to personality. There are, however, threads of thought running below the fragmented surface, linking many of the pieces together.

The biological orientation to personality has two main thrusts. Theorists of the first group focus on the idea that personality characteristics are genetically determined. The biological mechanisms by which inherited differences influence behavior aren't well understood yet, and until recently, they were rarely explored. That is changing quickly, however. The interest of this group lies largely in knowing what characteristics of personality and social behavior are influenced by heredity. The view of these theorists is something of a cross between the biological perspective and the dispositional perspective.

Many of these same people are also interested in the broader idea that the qualities of personality resulted from the evolutionary pressures that produced the human species. This view has grown rapidly in recent years. It's now suggested that far more of human social behavior is a product of our evolutionary heritage than anyone would have guessed two decades ago. These two ideas—that many personality characteristics are genetically determined and that human behavioral tendencies derive from our evolutionary history—form the basis of Chapter 6.

The second focus of the biological perspective is the idea that human behavior is produced by a complex biological system. The processes that make up this system reflect the way we're organized as living creatures. In this view, many ongoing biological processes have systematic influences on people's behavior and experience. To understand these influences, theorists first try to follow the biological systems that exist, to see exactly what they're about and how they work. They then think about how the workings of these systems might influence the kinds of phenomena that are identified with personality.

This idea has its roots in antiquity, but it's been revolutionized by methodological advances of the recent past. The component processes and functions of the nervous system are becoming better understood. We're also coming to understand how hormones affect behavior. The viewpoint represented in this work is a process approach to personality, looking at how biological functions influence human action. As you'll see, however, this focus on process doesn't mean ignoring individual differences. That is, the processes often operate to different degrees in different people, thereby creating the patterns of uniqueness we know as personality. This type of biological approach to personality is considered in Chapter 7.

Inheritance, Evolution, and Personality

Two 3-day-old babies are lying in cradles behind the glass window. One of them lies peacefully for hours at a time, rarely crying and moving only a little. The other thrashes his arms and legs, screws up his face, and rends the air with piercing yowls. What could possibly have made these two children so thoroughly different from each other so soon in life?

A group of young men, 16 to 18 years old, have been hanging around the pool hall all afternoon, acting cool, eyeing women who pass by, and trying to outdo one another with inventive insults. Occasionally tempers flare, the lines of faces harden, and there's pushing and taunting. This time, though, the one doing the taunting went too far. There's a glint of dark steel, and the hot air is shattered by gunshots. Later, the dead one's grieving mother cries out, "Why do men do these things?"

P ART OF who you are is the body you walk around in. Some people have big bodies, some have small ones. Some bodies are strong, some are frail. Some bodies are coordinated, some are klutzy. Some bodies turn toward dolls at a certain stage of life, others turn to Legos.

Your body is not your personality. But does it influence the personality you have? The idea that our bodies determine our personalities goes back at least to Hippocrates and Galen. As was said in Chapter 4, Hippocrates proposed four personality types; Galen added the idea that each type reflects an excess of some bodily fluid. The idea that people's physical makeup determines their personalities has re-emerged repeatedly ever since.

The term *physical makeup* has meant different things to theorists at different times, however. In the early and mid-twentieth century, it meant physique, or body build (see Box 6.1). Today, physical makeup means genes. Many people now believe most qualities of personality are partly— maybe even largely—genetically determined.

Box 6.1 Early Biological Views

Physique and Personality

The idea that people's bodies relate to their personalities is reflected in popular stereotypes: the jolly fat man, the strong adventurous hero, the frail intellectual. Is there any truth to it?

Several theorists have thought so over the years. Kretschmer (1925) classified people as *thin, muscular,* or *obese,* and found that each group was prone to a different set of disorders. William Sheldon (1942) expanded the idea from categories to dimensions and looked at normal personality. What he called a **somatotype** is defined by placing a person on three dimensions corresponding to Kretschmer's categories. It's designated by three numbers (from 1 to 7), indicating the degree to which the person has that quality. Sheldon believed each quality reflects an emphasis on one of three layers of the embryo. For that reason, he named them after the layers.

Endomorphy is the tendency toward plumpness (reflecting an emphasis on digestion). Endomorphs are soft and round. **Mesomorphy** is the tendency toward muscularity (reflecting a predominance of bone, muscle, and connective tissue). Mesomorphs are rectangular, hard, and strong. **Ectomorphy** is the tendency toward thinness (reflecting predominance of skin and nervous system). Ectomorphs are delicate and frail, easily overwhelmed by stimulation.

Most people have a little of each quality. Someone who's generally muscular but a little pudgy might be a 4-6-2 (endo-meso-ecto). A person who's frail but has a potbelly might be a 6-1-7. A person who's absolutely average would be a 4-4-4.

In parallel with the physical dimensions, Sheldon proposed three aspects of *temperament.* **Viscerotonia** is qualities such as relaxation, tolerance, sociability, love of comfort, goodwill, and easygoingness. **Somatotonia** is qualities such as boldness, assertiveness, and a desire for adventure and activity. **Cerebrotonia** includes avoidance of social interaction, restraint, high pain sensitivity, and a mental intensity approaching apprehensiveness. As with somatotypes, most people have some of each of these three temperaments.

As he'd predicted, Sheldon found that temperaments and somatotypes go together. Mesomorphy related to somatotonia, endomorphy to viscerotonia, and ectomorphy to cerebrotonia. Later studies also supported this view in ratings of children (Walker, 1962), in self-reports (e.g., Cortes & Gatti, 1965; Yates & Taylor, 1978), and in other ways (M. A. Davidson, McInnes, & Parnell, 1957; Glueck & Glueck, 1956; Parnell, 1957).

These studies all say that body types relate to personality. But why? Does physique cause personality? Is the link more roundabout? The body types reflect well-known stereotypes, which include expectations about how people act. If we have such expectations, we may induce people to act as expected (Gacsaly & Borges, 1979). This can produce an association between physique and behavior. It would stem from social pressure, though, not body type per se.

It's hard to know why associations exist between body type and personality. Partly for this reason, many people were skeptical and interest waned. Sheldon's ideas as such are no longer influential, but he stressed a theme that re-emerged only a couple of decades later. He believed that personality, along with body type, was inherited. He didn't test this belief. Indeed, in his time, it wasn't widely understood *how* to test it. Others found ways to do so, however, leading to the findings presented in the first half of this chapter.

Determining the Role of Inheritance in Personality

How do researchers decide whether a given quality is inherited? Family resemblance is a starting point, but it has a serious problem. Family members could be similar for two reasons: They may be similar because of inheritance. Or they may be similar because they're around each other a lot and have learned to act like each other (see Chapter 13).

To get a clearer picture requires better methods. Psychologists turned to the discipline of genetics for ideas. The result was a mix of psychology and genetics called **behavioral genetics.** This is the study of genetic influences on behavioral qualities, including personality qualities, abnormalities, and even cognitive and emotional processes (Plomin, 1997; Plomin, DeFries, & McClearn, 1990; Plomin & Rende, 1991).

TWIN STUDY METHOD

A method that's widely used in behavioral genetics is the **twin study.** It takes advantage of two unusual events in reproduction, which produce two types of twins. One kind of event occurs shortly after conception. A fertilized egg normally divides into two cells, then four, then eight, eventually forming a person. Sometimes, though, the first two cells become separated, and each grows *separately* into a person. These persons are identical twins, or **monozygotic (MZ) twins.** Because they came from what was a single cell, they are 100% alike genetically.

The second kind of event occurs in conception itself. Usually, only one egg is released from the mother's ovary, but occasionally, two are. If both happen to be fertilized and begin to develop simultaneously, the result is fraternal twins, or **dizygotic (DZ) twins.** Genetically, DZ twins are like any pair of brothers, pair of sisters, or brother and sister. They just happen to be born at the same time rather than separately. As with any pair of **siblings** (brothers or sisters), they are, on the average, 50% alike genetically (though the overlap of specific pairs ranges from 0% to 100%). Interestingly enough, many twins are wrong about which kind they are, and errors are just as common for MZ as DZ twins. One study found that in about 30% of pairs, one twin was wrong; in about 12% of pairs, both twins were wrong (Scarr & Carter-Saltzman, 1979).

In a twin study (see Figure 6.1), pairs of identical twins are related to each other on the characteristic of interest by a correlation; the same is done with pairs of same-sex fraternal twins. The two *correlations* are then compared. If identical twins are more similar to each other than fraternal twins, presumably it's because of the difference in degree of genetic similarity.

The index of genetic influence on personality is termed a **heritability** estimate. This index represents the amount of interpersonal variability in the trait under study that's accounted for by inheritance. The higher the heritability, the stronger the evidence that genes matter in some way. It's important to be careful here, because people sometimes read too much into this term. It does *not* represent the probability that a behavioral characteristic is inherited, *nor* does it mean we know *why* genes matter, only that they seem to matter.

The twin study method is based on the assumption that co-twins who are raised together are exposed to much the same life experiences as each other, *whether they are identical or fraternal twins.* This

Comparisons between identical and fraternal twins can provide information about the heritability of characteristics.

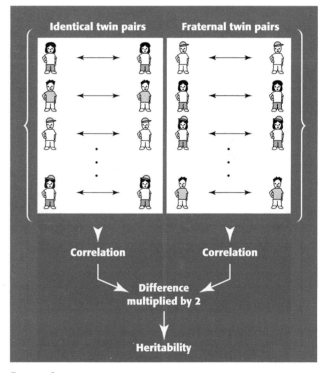

FIGURE 6.1

A basic twin study method examines pairs of identical and same-sex fraternal twins raised together. Members of each twin pair are assessed on the variable of interest, and a separate correlation is computed for each type of twin. The correlation for fraternal (DZ) twins is subtracted from the correlation for identical (MZ) twins. Multiplying this difference by 2 gives an index of the heritability of the characteristic—an estimate of the proportion of variance in that characteristic that is accounted for by inheritance.

is critically important. You couldn't conclude that a difference between correlations comes from heredity if parents treated DZ twins differently from MZ twins. The difference in genetic overlap would be confounded with the difference in treatment.

Are the two kinds of twin pairs treated more or less the same? The answer seems to be a very cautious yes. MZ twins are more likely than DZ twins to be dressed alike, but the differences are slight (Plomin et al., 1990). MZ twins also don't seem to resemble each other more in personality if they were treated alike than if they were not (Loehlin & Nichols, 1976). On the other hand, one study found that DZ twins who thought they were MZ twins were more alike than other DZ twins (Scarr & Carter-Saltzman, 1979). A more recent study found that MZ pairs recalled somewhat more similar experiences than DZ twin pairs, but these similarities did not relate to personality similarity (Borkenau, Riemann, Angleitner, & Spinath, 2002).

ADOPTION RESEARCH

Another way to study inheritance is termed the **adoption study.** An adoption study looks at how the adopted child resembles the biological parents and the adoptive parents. Resemblance to biological parents is viewed as genetically based, whereas resemblance to the adoptive parents is environmentally based.

Another method combines features of the twin study with features of the adoption study. It's sometimes possible to study MZ twins who were adopted and raised separately (see Box 6.2). Because they grew up in different homes, environmental impacts should cause *differences*, rather than similarities. Similarity between these

---

BOX 6.2 TWINS SEPARATED AT BIRTH, REUNITED AS ADULTS

Some Startling Similarities

Our emphasis here is on systematic studies of genetics and personality. However, some of the most striking indications that personality qualities can be inherited are more anecdotal. The information comes from identical twins who were separated early in life, raised in different homes, and then reunited later on (Segal, 1999).

This combination of circumstances occurs when identical twins are put up for adoption separately as newborns, a practice that once was fairly common but no longer is. In many cases, the infants grew into adults who had no idea they were twins. In some cases, though, they were reunited as adults. Imagine the surprise of discovering someone else who looks just like you!

What's it like to discover your identical twin after you're both grown?

Reunited twins sometimes discover astonishing similarities (Rosen, 1987; Segal, 1999). Fascinating stories have emerged from projects studying twins raised apart, such as the Minnesota Center for Twin and Adoption Research. Two of their participants, brothers from New Jersey, didn't meet—didn't even know the other existed—until they were adults. At that time, both were volunteer firefighters, both held their beer bottles in the same unusual way, both drank the same brand, and both tended to make the same remarks and gestures when joking, which both did frequently. Another pair of twins discovered that they both smoked the same brand of cigarettes, drove the same kind of car, and did woodworking as a hobby.

A pair of women from Finland provide another amazing example. They were raised in economic circumstances that were very different from each other, but both grew up to be penny pinchers. Each had a fear of heights, each had had a miscarriage, then three healthy children. Not long after they first met, they were so in tune with each other that they began finishing each other's sentences—all this despite being raised totally separated from each other.

Examples such as these are striking, but it's hard to say how much they capitalize on chance. That is, although reunited twins do tend to be similar in many ways, not every pair of twins displays such dramatic patterns of unlikely similarities. Nonetheless, dramatic examples such as these do tend to stick in people's minds and influence their thinking about the nature of personality. Such illustrations convey the impression that inheritance not only influences broad qualities such as activity level and emotionality but also affects personality in more subtle ways.

pairs can be contrasted with MZ twins raised together and DZ twins raised together. If heredity is important to the trait under study, then MZ twins—even if they were raised apart—should be more similar than DZ twins. If heredity is *really* important, then MZ twins raised apart should be nearly as similar as MZ twins raised together.

What Personality Qualities Are Inherited?

Twin and adoption study methods have been used for over three decades to study genetic influences on personality. An early body of work focused on **temperaments.** This term has been used in several ways. Some people have used *temperament* (singular) to refer to a person's overall "emotional nature" (Allport, 1961; Gallagher, 1994; Kagan, 1994). Arnold Buss and Robert Plomin (1984) used the plural *temperaments* to refer to "inherited personality traits present in early childhood."

TEMPERAMENTS: ACTIVITY, SOCIABILITY, AND EMOTIONALITY

Buss and Plomin (1984) argued that three normal personality qualities deserve to be called temperaments: *activity level, sociability,* and *emotionality.* Each of these is a dimension of individual differences.

Activity level is the person's overall output of energy or behavior. This temperament has two aspects that differ conceptually but are highly correlated: *vigor* (the intensity of behavior) and *tempo* (speed). People high in vigor prefer high-intensity action. People whose tempo is high prefer fast-paced activities. Those whose vigor and tempo are lower take a more leisurely approach to things.

Sociability is the tendency to prefer being with other people, rather than alone. Sociability is a desire for other people's attention, sharing activities, and the responsiveness and stimulation that are part of interaction. Sociability is *not* a matter of desiring social rewards such as praise or respect. Rather, to be sociable is to value intrinsically the process of interacting with others.

Emotionality is the tendency to become physiologically aroused—easily and intensely—in upsetting situations. This temperament was conceptualized as pertaining to distress, anger, and fear, and the measure of temperaments for adults has three subscales, measuring proneness to these three emotions. It's of interest that anger proneness isn't highly correlated with the others (Buss & Plomin, 1984). Perhaps this temperament of emotionality is actually two distinct traits.

Temperaments influence many kinds of behavior; for example, activity level expresses itself through the kinds of leisure activities people choose to engage in. Some activities are more laid back, others are more fast paced and require lots of energy.

The temperaments proposed by Buss and Plomin resemble those proposed earlier by Sheldon more than is usually recognized (see Box 6.1). The resemblances are quite intriguing. Activity level—and the impact on the world this concept implies—resembles somatotonia. Sociability was part of viscerotonia. Emotionality (apprehensiveness) was part of cerebrotonia.

What's the evidence that these temperaments are inherited? In several twin studies, parents rated their children on these qualities (Buss & Plomin, 1975; Plomin, 1974;

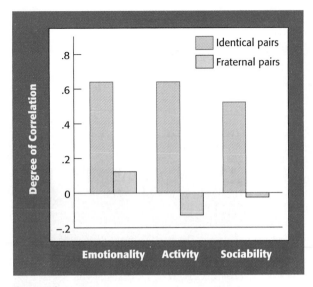

FIGURE 6.2

Average correlations for parental ratings of identical and fraternal twins on temperaments of emotionality, activity level, and sociability. (Correlations are averaged across four samples, totaling 228 pairs of identical twins and 172 pairs of fraternal twins, with an average age of 5 years, 1 month. *Source: Adapted from Buss & Plomin, 1984.*

Plomin & Rowe, 1977). Correlations between parent ratings of activity, emotionality, and sociability were strong for MZ twins; they were next to nonexistent for DZ twins (see Figure 6.2).

Concerns have been raised, though, about rater bias when parents rate their children (Neale & Stevenson, 1989; Saudino, McGuire, Reiss, Hetherington, & Plomin, 1995). If DZ twins fail to much resemble each other, parents tend to contrast the two, which would amplify differences. Parents of MZ twins, seeing more similarity, wouldn't do this. There's also evidence that mothers of young children aren't very good reporters of their children's behavior (Seifer, Sameroff, Barrett, & Krafchuk, 1994).

It's important, then, that other sources of evidence exist. Adoption research (Loehlin, Willerman, & Horn, 1985) also supports a genetic influence for activity level and sociability. This study compared adopted children with their biological parents and their adoptive parents. Measures were self-reports, with several scales that reflect sociability and activity level. Table 6.1 shows some of the correlations from this study. Although the children had spent their lives with their adoptive parents (from a few days after birth), there was remarkably little resemblance between them (column A). On the other hand, despite the separation from their biological parents, there was a pattern of moderate correlations between them (column B).

The data also allowed comparisons between the adopted children and both biological and adoptive siblings (columns C and D). The pattern is less consistent than for parents, but the same general picture emerges: Adopted children are more like their biological brothers and sisters than their adoptive brothers and sisters.

OTHER VIEWS OF TEMPERAMENTS

Developmental researchers have become increasingly interested in temperaments in the past two decades. Mary Rothbart and her colleagues have argued for the existence

Table 6.1 Correlations between Adopted Children and (A) Their Adoptive Parents, (B) Their Biological Parents, (C) Their Adoptive Siblings, and (D) Their Biological Siblings, on Three Measures of Sociability and Two Measures of Activity. *Source:* Data adapted from Loehlin, Willerman, & Horn, 1985. Parent correlations are averages of child–father and child–mother correlations; sibling correlations are also averaged.

Measure	(A) Adoptive Parent	(B) Biological Parent	(C) Adoptive Siblings	(D) Biological Siblings
Sociability (CPI)*	0.04	0.17	0.04	0.22
Social presence (CPI)	0.12	0.34	−0.08	0.70
Sociable (TTS)**	0.02	0.18	−0.13	0.38
Active (TTS)	0.02	0.16	−0.12	0.06
Vigorous (TTS)	0.06	0.33	0.18	0.42

* CPI is the California Psychological Inventory.
** TTS is the Thurstone Temperament Schedule.

of basic temperaments for approach and avoidance (e.g., Derryberry & Rothbart, 1997; Rothbart, Ahadi, & Evans, 2000; Rothbart, Ahadi, Hershey, & Fisher, 2001; Rothbart & Bates, 1998; Rothbart, Ellis, Rueda, & Posner, 2003; Rothbart & Posner, 1985; see also Eisenberg, 2002; Eisenberg et al., 2004; Kochanska & Knaack, 2003; Nigg, 2000). To some extent, the avoidance temperament resembles Buss and Plomin's (1984) view of emotionality. There also seems to be some resemblance between the approach temperament and sociability, though that resemblance is a little less clear.

Rothbart also proposes a third temperament termed **effortful control.** This temperament is about being focused and restrained. In part, it reflects attentional management (e.g., persistence of attention during long-lasting tasks). It also reflects the ability to suppress an approach behavior when doing so is situationally appropriate. This temperament seems to imply a kind of planfulness versus impulsiveness. High levels of this temperament early in life relate to fewer problems with antisocial behavior later in life (Kochanska & Knaack, 2003).

In thinking about this temperament, it is very interesting that Buss and Plomin (1975) originally saw impulsivity as a possible temperament. They dropped it, because evidence of heritability had not been strong. Later on, a new study found a genetic effect on impulsiveness (Pedersen, Plomin, McLearn, & Friberg, 1988). This later study was unusual in that it examined older adults (average age 58), whereas Buss and Plomin had relied mostly on parent ratings of children.

Another possible candidate to be a temperament is intelligence. Intelligence is not usually regarded as a *personality* trait (for a dissenting opinion see Eysenck & Eysenck, 1985), but it has the characteristics Buss and Plomin used to define temperaments. It's genetically influenced (Bouchard, Lykken, McGue, Segal, & Tellegen, 1990; Loehlin, Willerman, & Horn, 1988; Plomin, 1989), and its effects on behavior are broad, manifest early in life, and continue throughout the life span. Perhaps intelligence should also be seen as a temperament.

INHERITANCE OF TRAITS

We began this discussion with temperaments. Are other traits genetically influenced? Yes. An early twin study (Loehlin & Nichols, 1976) found correlations among MZ twins were higher than among DZ twins on a wide range of characteristics (an average of about 0.50 versus an average of about 0.30). Other early studies (reviewed by Carey, Goldsmith, Tellegen, & Gottesman, 1978) found similar results.

Early twin studies were done before trait theorists had begun to converge on the idea that personality is described by five basic factors. With the emergence of the five-factor model, however, work has increasingly focused on whether those dimensions are genetically influenced (Bergeman et al., 1993; Heath, Neale, Kessler, Eaves, & Kendler, 1992; Jang, Livesley, & Vernon, 1996; Jang, McCrae, Angleitner, Riemann, & Livesley, 1998; Loehlin, 1992; Tellegen et al., 1988; Viken, Rose, Kaprio, & Koskenvuo, 1994). The answer again is yes. Indeed, the effects are substantial and remarkably consistent across factors (Bouchard, 2004).

Most twin studies of adult personality use self-reports or reports of people close to the twins. This suggests the same criticism as was made when mothers rated their infants. That is, the potential exists for contrast effects that exaggerate differences between twins that are only slightly dissimilar. To deal with this possibility, Borkenau, Riemann, Angleitner, and Spinath (2001) did a twin study in which participants were videotaped and then rated by people who didn't know them. They also found evidence of genetic contribution to all five factors.

TEMPERAMENTS AND THE FIVE-FACTOR MODEL

The supertraits that make up the five-factor model are broad and pervasive in influence. In that respect, they're a lot like temperaments. In fact, the five factors have considerable conceptual similarity to qualities that others call temperaments (Digman & Shmelyov, 1996; Halverson, Kohnstamm, & Martin, 1994; Loehlin, 1992). One obvious similarity is that the temperament Buss and Plomin (1984) called *emotionality* and Rothbart and Posner (1985) called an *avoidance* temperament closely resembles neuroticism.

Extraversion from the "big five" has overtones of not one but two temperaments (plus some other qualities). Extraversion suggests a preference for being with others, implying a possible link to sociability (Depue & Morrone-Strupinsky, 2005). Eysenck (1986) also included activity in his view of extraversion. This suggests extraversion may blend sociability with activity level. On the other hand, extraversion has come to be viewed partly in terms of social dominance or agency (Depue & Collins, 1999), which isn't directly implied either by sociability or by activity.

Another of the five factors—agreeableness—also has overtones of sociability, although again not being identical to it. Agreeableness suggests liking to be with people. It goes beyond that, however, in having connotations of being easy to get along with. Whether agreeableness derives from a temperament of sociability is something of an open question.

Examination of conscientiousness suggests that it's defined partly by the absence of impulsiveness. That is, conscientiousness is a planful, persistent, focused orientation toward life's activities. The possibility that impulsivity, or effortful control, is a temperament (Pedersen, Plomin, McClearn, & Friberg, 1988; Rothbart et al., 2003) suggests another link between temperaments and the five-factor model.

The last of the "big five" is openness to experience, or intellect, culture, or intelligence. Given the diverse labels for this factor, it's unsure whether this is the same as intelligence, mentioned earlier as a potential temperament. (Indeed, it's not entirely clear exactly what intelligence is, cf. Sternberg, 1982.) But if this part of the five-factor model did reflect what intelligence tests measure, there would be yet another link between temperament and trait models.

In sum, although the fit is not perfect, the set of qualities proposed as biologically based temperaments bears a great deal of resemblance to qualities in the five-factor model. The places where the resemblance is less clear serve partly to raise interesting questions. For example, why should activity and sociability be considered fundamental, rather than extraversion? Is extraversion really one trait, or two? As we said in Chapter 4, there are many ways to divide up the qualities of behavior, and it's hard to know which is best.

It's likely that these questions will continue to be of interest. More specifically, it seems likely that the five-factor model will continue to have an increasing influence on how behavioral genetics researchers decide which qualities of personality to study in their research.

GENETICS OF OTHER QUALITIES: HOW DISTINCT ARE THEY?

The evidence that inheritance influences personality goes beyond studies of traditional traits. A number of other effects have emerged, some of which relate fairly readily to personality. For example, there's a genetic effect on risk of divorce (McGue & Lykken, 1992), which operates through personality (Jockin, McGue, & Lykken, 1996). There's a genetic effect on having impactful life events, which again appears to operate via personality (Saudino, Pedersen, Lichtenstein, McClearn, & Plomin, 1997). Heredity influences how much social support people have (Kessler, Kendler, Heath, Neale, & Eaves, 1992), which probably reflects personality (Brissette, Scheier, &

Carver, 2002; Kendler, 1997). There's also a genetic contribution to people's attitudes on various topics (Eaves, Eysenck, & Martin, 1989; Olson, Vernon, Harris, & Jang, 2001; Tesser, 1993), which again seems likely to reflect personality.

Findings such as these raise a question: To what extent are the various effects distinct and separate? The temperaments and supertraits discussed earlier are very broad. When evidence is found that a quality is genetically influenced, it raises a question. Is this a *separate* effect? Or is the effect there because the quality under study relates to a temperament or supertrait?

The question of how many distinct qualities are *separately* influenced by inheritance is one that hasn't been explored much. However, it's an important question in understanding how inheritance affects personality. One recent study began to explore it, within the framework of the five-factor model (Jang et al., 1998). This study found that not only were the five supertraits heritable, but so were most of the facet traits. Indeed, the genetic influences on facets were separate from the genetic influences on the overall traits. This suggests that *many* distinct qualities may be genetically influenced, not just a few broad ones.

INHERITANCE AND SEXUAL ORIENTATION

A topic about which there's been much discussion in recent years is the possible role of genetics in determining a person's sexual orientation. Some people would regard this topic as outside the realm of personality, but others would say it's very much a part of personality.

Evidence of a possible genetic role in sexual orientation goes back over 40 years, with the report of a higher incidence of homosexuality among men whose MZ twin was gay than men whose DZ twin was gay (Eysenck, 1964a). Later on, twin studies were done with homosexual men (Bailey & Pillard, 1991) and homosexual women (Bailey, Pillard, Neale, & Agyei, 1993). In both cases, a co-twin was more than twice as likely to be homosexual if the twins were MZ than if they were DZ. (Similar findings were also reported by Whitam, Diamond, and Martin [1993].) A later twin study of men found much weaker effects (Bailey, Dunne, & Martin, 2000), but it did find evidence of genetic influence on childhood gender nonconformity (low feelings of male gender identity and participation in gender-typed activities).

Other research has found evidence of a genetic basis for male homosexuality using an entirely different approach. A study of families of gay men found there were more gay male relatives on the mother's side (maternal uncles and sons of maternal aunts) than on the father's side. This suggests that a gene related to homosexuality might be on the X chromosome (because a son always receives it from his mother). Examination of genetic material revealed a region of the X chromosome that was similar among most of the gay participants. This suggests a genetic basis for at least some instances of homosexuality. Genetics cannot explain all of the instances, though, because this region was *not* similar for all gay men (see also Pool, 1993). A later study found further (and more complicated) evidence of the involvement of the X chromosome in men's sexual orientation (Bocklandt, Horvath, Vilain, & Hamer, 2006).

It's long been wondered why homosexuality hasn't died out over generations, because gay men don't reproduce at the same rate as other men. If the gene is on the X chromosome, that would account for it. That is, the X chromosome is carried by women as well as men. The gene can be passed on without being reflected in behavior.

The biological basis for homosexuality almost certainly involves several paths, rather than one. The findings just reviewed focus on a particular chromosome. However, there is other evidence that multiple gene locations are involved (Mustanski, Dupree, Nievergelt, Bocklandt, Schork, & Hamer, 2005).

Indeed, other possibilities are biological without being genetic. For example, the probability of a man's being homosexual increases with the number of older brothers he has but not with the number of older sisters (Blanchard, 2004; Blanchard, Cantor, Bogaert, Breedlove, & Ellis, 2006). This led to the idea that mothers develop antibodies to male qualities when pregnant with boys. Repeated occurrence (having more sons) causes the antibody response to strengthen to the point that it prevents full masculinization of the fetal brain.

MOLECULAR GENETICS AND NEW SOURCES OF EVIDENCE

In the preceding discussion, a new issue crept in. Specifically, there now are ways to study genetic influences that weren't available even a short time ago. The effort to map the human **genome**—the genetic blueprint of the body—was wildly successful. A first draft was completed in 2000, years ahead of schedule. It's increasingly possible to identify specific genes that cause differences among people. Differences range from vulnerability to physical and psychological disorders to normal personality qualities. Many believe the ability to identify genes linked to such differences will revolutionize medicine, psychiatry, and psychology (Plomin, 1995; Plomin & Crabbe, 2000; Plomin, DeFries, Craig, & McGuffin, 2003).

A huge proportion of the human genome is identical for everyone. Interest focuses on the parts that vary. When different forms or patterns of DNA (genetic material) occur at a particular location, they are called **alleles.** The existence of the differences is called a **polymorphism.** A **genotype** difference between persons means the persons have different alleles at some particular location. Whereas twin research is referred to as quantitative behavioral genetics, the attempt to relate differences in particular gene locations to other measurable differences among persons is often called **molecular genetics** (Carey, 2003).

The question for personality, then, is which locations influence a given personality quality. The answer to this is not likely to be at all simple. It is very likely that many genes relate to a given personality quality (Plomin & Crabbe, 2000). Indeed, different genes may connect to different aspects of behavior that all relate to the same trait.

The first discoveries in this area were mostly single genes relating to broad outcomes, such as disorders (which we return to later on). A few genes have also been identified that have clear relevance to normal personality. For example, a gene has been identified that relates to the use of dopamine in the brain. This gene has several alleles, one of which is longer than the others. Two research teams (Benjamin, Li, Patterson, Greenberg, Murphy, & Hamer, 1996; Ebstein et al., 1996) found almost simultaneously that people with the long allele have high scores on personality scales that relate to novelty seeking. A different candidate gene for dopamine function has also been linked to a different measure of fun seeking (Reuter, Schmitz, Corr, & Hennig, 2006). Some have been able replicate such associations, but a good many others have not. Ebstein (2006) recently reviewed a series of meta-analyses (involving many specific studies) and concluded that the support is not very strong after all.

Another gene has been identified that appears to relate to use of serotonin in the brain. Several groups have found a link of the short allele of that gene to high scores on neuroticism and low scores on agreeableness (e.g., Greenberg et al., 2000; Lesch et al., 1996; Sen et al., 2004). There is even some suggestion that this gene is partly responsible for the moderately high inverse correlation between neuroticism and agreeableness (Jang et al., 2001). Again, the association has been difficult to replicate. Several meta-analyses have also been done on studies of this polymorphism, and support for a relation to neuroticism is not strong overall (Ebstein, 2006). It is important to note, however, that these meta-analyses have all failed to look at the association with agreeableness. There is reason to believe that that one may be the more important of the two (Carver & Miller, 2006).

Single-gene discoveries such as these have received huge publicity when first announced. We repeat, though, that it's very likely that most genetic influences on behavior will involve small contributions from many genes (Plomin & Crabbe, 2000). Indeed, that may be one reason why the discoveries have been hard to replicate. News programs and magazines will probably continue to trumpet every new discovery as *the* gene for something, but that's misleading (Kendler, 2005). Despite this caution, it's clear that the tools of molecular genetics have greatly changed the way in which researchers pursue the genetic contributions to many aspects of the human experience, including personality.

Environmental Effects

There are two more issues to raise in this part of the chapter. They concern the other effects in twin and adoption studies—the part we haven't emphasized. Specifically, studies always find that nonhereditary factors contribute to personality. The issues are how great a contribution they make and what kind of contribution they make.

THE SIZE OF ENVIRONMENTAL INFLUENCES

A topic that's been debated as long as twin and adoption studies have been done is the size of genetic versus environmental influence. The argument seems easy enough to resolve. Don't the statistics of the study tell you? Unfortunately, it's not that simple. There are reasons why the statistics may have built-in biases. The arguments are subtle and complex. Here are two of them.

Dickens and Flynn (2001) said that there often are unrecognized correlations between genetic influences and environmental influences on the same outcome. The example they used is intelligence. People with high intelligence gravitate to environments that foster learning more than do people with less intelligence. In those environments, they learn more. Their IQs go up. The *environment* had an effect on their IQ. But the possibility for that to happen stemmed indirectly from their genetic makeup. Thus, the two influences are correlated.

Why does this matter? The size of an environmental effect on an outcome is judged by how much variability is not explained by the genetic effect. If an environmental effect is mistaken to be a genetic effect (because they're correlated), the genetic effect gets the credit for what the environment is doing. The genetic statistical effect from the study is larger than it should be, and the environmental statistical effect is smaller than it should be.

Dickens and Flynn (2001) made this argument in the context of IQ, but it also can be applied to personality. As was said in Chapter 4, people gravitate to environments that suit their interests, that let them be who they are. Maybe those environments even induce people to have more of the quality that first led them there. Someone who's slightly introverted and who starts reading more or keeping a diary may discover the joys of solitary pursuits and become even more introverted. Someone who's slightly extraverted and who gets involved in group activities may discover he or she likes being in charge of groups and develop greater extraversion.

Another argument begins with the fact that influences on societies as a whole change over extended periods of time. These broad influences may have an impact on personality. There is evidence, for example, that people of a given age in the United States were more anxious in 1993 than in 1952 (Twenge, 2000). Indeed, in that study, the average child in the 1980s reported more anxiety than did children who were psychiatric patients in the 1950s! Age-cohort effects have also been found for extraversion (Twenge, 2001) and self-esteem (Twenge & Campbell, 2001).

Why does this matter? It matters because these seem to be environmental influences on personality (perhaps across the entire population). But this very broad environmental influence is never included in the computations of genetic and environmental effects in twin studies. It's controlled out of the entire analysis (Twenge, 2002). Again, this would mean that the genetic effects seem larger in the studies than they really are.

The Nature of Environmental Influences

The studies that establish a powerful role for inheritance in personality also show an important role for nonhereditary factors. Surprisingly, however, the evidence on the whole suggests that families don't make children alike, as you might assume. The environment has an impact on personality but primarily at an *individual* level (Plomin & Daniels, 1987).

What might be the sources of nonshared environmental influence? There isn't a lot of information on this. Several guesses sound reasonable, though (Dunn & Plomin, 1990; Rowe, 1994). For example, siblings often have different sets of friends, sometimes totally different. Peers have a big influence on growing children—some think even stronger than the influence of parents (Harris, 1995). Differences in peer groups may cause children's personalities to become different. If that happens, it's an environmental influence, but it's not shared by the siblings.

Another point is that siblings in families don't exist side by side. In their interactions, they develop roles that play off each other (e.g., Daniels, 1986; Hoffman, 1991). For example, if one child often helps another child with schoolwork, the two are developing styles of interacting that diverge. As another example, parents sometimes favor one child over another. This can affect the children's relationship, perhaps inducing differences between them. Again, the effects would be environmental, but they would differ from one child to the other.

The exact manner in which the environment influences personality remains to be clarified. Questions also remain about the impact of the shared versus the unshared environment. When behavior measures are used instead of rating scales, the shared environment seems to matter more (Turkheimer, 1998). For example, in the study described earlier, in which videotaped behavior was rated by strangers, Borkenau et al. (2001) found a much larger effect for shared environment than is typically found. Thus, variations in research methods may influence what conclusion emerges.

Evolution and Human Behavior

We now change directions somewhat. Evidence that inheritance plays a role in personality is one contributor to the emergence of a broader current of thought. The broader current is the idea that evolutionary processes have a major influence on present-day human behavior. This line of thought is tied to several labels, including behavioral ecology, sociobiology, and evolutionary psychology (Barkow, Cosmides, & Tooby, 1992; Bjorklund & Pellegrini, 2002; D. M. Buss, 1991, 1995; Caporael, 2001; Heschl, 2002; Segal, 1993; Tooby & Cosmides, 1989, 1990). Work deriving from this group of ideas has grown explosively in recent years.

SOCIOBIOLOGY AND EVOLUTIONARY PSYCHOLOGY

Sociobiology (Alexander, 1979; Barash, 1977, 1986, 2001; Crawford, 1989; Crawford, Smith, & Krebs, 1987; Dawkins, 1976; Lumsden & Wilson, 1981; Wilson, 1975) is the study of the biological basis of social behavior. The core assumption is that many—perhaps all—of the core elements of social interaction in humans are products of evolution. That is, the patterns were retained genetically because at some point in pre-history they conferred an adaptive advantage.

In some respects this view resembles one presented earlier by people working in **ethology,** the study of animals' behavior in their natural environment. Two ideas from ethology are often mentioned in psychology. One is *imprinting,* in which the young of many species attach to their mothers (Hess, 1973). Another is the idea that animals mark and defend territories (cf. Ardrey, 1966). Ethologists suggested that humans have similar patterns.

Ethologists addressed human behavior mostly by making analogies. Sociobiologists, in contrast, focused on evolutionary genetics and the question of how behavior patterns might get built in (see also Box 6.3). This view is more radical. To a sociobiologist,

---

Box 6.3 THEORETICAL ISSUE

Specieswide Adaptations and the Existence of Individual Differences

The basic concepts of natural selection and population genetics are simple. If a characteristic differs from person to person, it means each gene behind that characteristic has several potential forms, or alleles. Some people have one allele, some have another one. (Actually, it's even more complicated, because everyone has two of each chromosome, so you can also have mixed alleles even if there are only two versions available.)

Selection means one form of the gene is more likely to show up in the next generation because it's been help-ful in survival or reproduction, or is less likely to show up because it's *interfered* with survival or reproduction. This is **directional selection.** It means a shift toward a greater proportion of the adaptive allele in the population's next generation. If it goes on long enough, directional selection reduces or even eliminates individual differences. Over many generations, those without the

adaptive allele fail to reproduce, and a larger proportion of the next generation have the adaptive one. In principle, this is how a characteristic can become uni-versal in the population.

Many characteristics might influence survival. For example, in a world where strength matters (which probably was true during human evolution), strength makes you more likely to survive long enough to reproduce. That sends genes for strength into the next gener-ation. As long as these genes are well represented in the population, the pop-ulation will tend to survive and create yet another generation.

But wait. If some characteristics are more adaptive than others, why are there individual differences at all? Why aren't we all large and strong and smart and stealthy and whatever else is a good thing to be? A tricky thing about selection is that whether a particular value is adaptive depends on the con-text. Sometimes a value that's useful in one environment is not just useless—but fatal—in another. In the long run, genetic variability in the population is necessary for it to survive in a world that changes over time. Thus, the importance of another kind of selec-

tion, termed **stabilizing selection,** which maintains genetic variability (Plomin, 1981). Stabilizing selection occurs when an intermediate value of some characteristic is more adaptive than the value at either extreme. Presumably, intermediate values reflect combinations of alleles, rather than a specific allele, and probably involves multiple genes. Predominance of inter-mediate values thus implies genetic variability.

How can an intermediate value of a characteristic be more adaptive than an extreme value? Consider this example. It's important for people to have some sociability because we are such a social species. Having too little sociability isn't adaptive. But neither is it adaptive to have too *much* sociability. A person with extremely high sociability can hardly bear to be alone, and life some-times requires people to be alone.

Intermediate values are especially adaptive in many of the domains that are relevant to personality. That's why personality traits vary from person to person: There's genetic diversity on those traits. Otherwise, there'd be only a single personality, which everyone would have.

Evolutionary psychologists believe that even acts of altruism, such as doing disaster relief work for the Red Cross, may have a genetic basis.

a behavior pattern might exist in humans *but in no other species* because of a unique adaptation among humans.

This reasoning led in some surprising directions. For example, it led to a way to account for altruism, a tendency that seems very hard to explain in evolutionary terms. *Altruism* is acting for the welfare of others, to the point of sacrificing one's own well-being (potentially one's life) for someone else. Altruism would seem to confer a biological *dis*advantage. That is, being altruistic may help someone, but it also might get you killed. This would prevent your genes from being passed on to the next generation. If the genes aren't passed on, a genetically based tendency toward altruism should disappear very quickly.

Sociobiologists point out, however, that the process of evolution isn't really a matter of individual survival. What matters is a *gene pool,* distributed across a population. If one *group* in a population survives, prospers, and reproduces at a high rate, its genes move onward into subsequent generations more than other groups' genes.

This means there are ways to get your genes carried forward besides reproducing on your own. Your genes are helped into the next generation by anything that helps *your part of the gene pool* reproduce, an idea called **inclusive fitness** (Hamilton, 1964). If you act altruistically for a relative, it helps the relative survive. If an extremely altruistic act (in which you die) saves a great many of your relatives, it helps aspects of your genetic makeup be passed on because your relatives resemble you genetically. This process is sometimes called *kin selection.*

Thus, it's argued, the tendency to be altruistic may be genetically based. This argument implies that people will be more altruistic toward those in their kinship group than strangers (especially competitors). This seems to be true (Burnstein, Crandall, & Kitayama, 1994). Also fitting this view, there seems to be a genetic contribution to empathic concern for others, which may underlie altruism (Burnstein et al., 1994; Matthews, Batson, Horn, & Rosenman, 1981; Rushton, Fulker, Neale, Nias, & Eysenck, 1986). Indeed, there's evidence that emotional closeness, which increases with genetic relatedness, underlies the effect of relatedness on altruism (Korchmaros & Kenny, 2001).

The idea that altruistic tendencies are part of human nature has been extended to suggest an evolutionary basis for cooperation even among nonrelatives. The idea is essentially that our far ancestors survived better by cooperating than by being individualists. Thus, they acquired a tendency toward being helpful more generally. One person helps the other in the expectation that the help will be returned, an idea termed **reciprocal altruism** (Trivers, 1971).

Can this possibly have happened? Wouldn't people cheat, and take without giving? Sometimes. But those who do get punished (Fehr & Gächter, 2002). From an evolutionary view, the issue is whether cooperation leads to better outcomes for the group. There's evidence that it does, at least in the cooperative situations studied by psychologists (Axelrod & Hamilton, 1981). This has led some to conclude that a tendency to cooperate is part of human nature (Guisinger & Blatt, 1994; Kriegman & Knight, 1988). There's also evidence that punishing those who don't cooperate leads to better group outcomes (Fehr & Gächter, 2002). Maybe punishing those who don't go along with the group is also genetically built into human nature.

GENETIC SIMILARITY AND ATTRACTION

The idea that people act altruistically toward relatives has been extended by Philippe Rushton and his colleagues (Rushton, 1989a; Rushton, Russell, & Wells, 1984) to what he calls **genetic similarity theory.** The basic idea is what we've said before: A gene "survives" (is represented in the next generation) by any action that brings about reproduction of any organism in which copies of itself exist. That may mean being altruistic to your kinship group, but Rushton says it means other things as well.

Rushton and his colleagues (1984) argued that genetic similarity has an influence on who attracts you. Specifically, you're more attracted to strangers who resemble you genetically than to those who don't. How does this help the survival of the gene? If you're attracted to someone, you may become sexually involved, which may result in offspring. Offspring have genes from both parents. By making you attracted to someone with genes like yours, your genes increase the odds that genes like themselves will be copied (from one parent or the other or both) into a new person, surviving into the next generation.

Are people attracted to others whose genes resemble their own? Maybe so. Rushton (1988) had couples take blood tests that give a rough index of genetic similarity. He found that sexually involved couples had in common 50% of the genetic markers. When he took the data and paired people randomly, the pairs shared only 43% of the markers, significantly less. Rushton went on to compare couples who'd had children with those who hadn't. Those with a child shared 52% of the genetic markers; those with no child shared only 44%. Thus, among sexually active couples, those most similar were also most likely to have reproduced.

This attraction effect isn't limited to the opposite sex. People also tend to form friendships with others who are genetically similar to them. Rushton (1989b) repeated his study with pairs of men who were close friends (all heterosexual). The pairs of friends shared 54% of the genetic markers, the random pairs shared only 48%. Again, genetic similarity related to attraction.

How would friendships with genetically similar people of the same sex be adaptive? The point is to get the genes into offspring. Having same-sex friends won't do that directly. There are two ways it can help, though. The first is similar to the idea discussed earlier about altruism and kin selection. You're more likely to be altruistic for a close friend than a stranger, making the friend more likely to live to reproduce. The second possibility is that you may meet the same-sex friend's opposite-sex sibling. If the sibling is also genetically similar to you, an attraction may develop, with potential sexual activity, resulting in offspring.

How do people detect genetic similarity in others? It's hard to say. One possibility is that we are drawn to others who share our facial and body features. People who look like you seem like family and therefore attract you. Another possibility is that genetic similarity is conveyed by smell. Consistent with this, there is evidence that women prefer the odor of men who are genetically similar to their fathers (Jacob, McClintock, Zelano, & Ober, 2002). Outside your awareness, you may recognize those who are like you by subtle physical cues.

It's also likely that culture plays a role here. If you are descended from eastern Europeans, you may feel more comfortable around people who share your (eastern European) traditions. It might be the familiar traditions that bring you close, but the result is that you are drawn to people who come from your part of the gene pool.

The general idea that people choose mates on the basis of particular characteristics is called **assortative mating** (Thiessen & Gregg, 1980). Mating definitely isn't

Both men and women are in competitions for desirable mates.

random. People select their mates on the basis of a variety of characteristics, though there are limitations on how fine grained this selection is (Lykken & Tellegen, 1993). Often the features that influence mate selection are similarities to the self (Buss, 1985; Rushton & Bons, 2005).

MATE SELECTION AND COMPETITION FOR MATES

We've talked at some length about the importance of getting genes to the next generation. (From this viewpoint, it's sometimes said that a person is a gene's way of creating another gene [Barash, 2001].) Obviously, then, the evolutionary view on personality focuses closely on mating (Gangestad & Simpson, 2000). Indeed, from this view, mating is what life's all about (although other issues do arise when you think about the complexities of mating). Just as certain qualities confer survival advantage, certain qualities also confer reproductive advantage.

Mating involves competition. Males compete with one another; females compete with one another. But what's being competed for differs between the sexes. Trivers (1972) argued that males and females evolved different strategies, based on their roles in reproduction. Female humans have greater investment in offspring than males: They carry them for nine months, and they're more tied to caring for them after birth. The general rule across species is that the sex with the greater investment can generate fewer offspring over the life span, because of the commitment of time and energy to each. It thus is choosier about a mate (though not everyone agrees on this; see Small, 1993). The sex with less investment can generate more offspring and thus is less discriminating.

Given the difference in biological investment, the strategy of women is to tend to hold back from mating until they identify the best available male. "Best" here is defined as quality of genetic contribution, parental care, or material support for the mate and offspring. In contrast, the strategy of males is to maximize sexual opportunities, copulating as often as possible. This means seeking partners who are available and fertile (Buss, 1994a, 1994b). In this view, men tend to view women as *sex objects,* whereas women tend to view men as *success objects.*

These differences in orientation should produce different strategies for trying to get the opportunity to mate (which both males and females want). David Buss and David Schmitt (1993) examined differences in how men and women compete for and select mates and how the strategies differ from short term to long term (see also Buss, 1994a, 1994b; Feingold, 1992; Schmitt & Buss, 1996). If men are interested in finding fertile partners, women should compete by emphasizing their attributes that relate to fertility—youth and beauty. If women want to find partners that will provide for them and their babies, men should compete by emphasizing their status, personal dominance and ambition, and wealth or potential for wealth (Sidanius, Pratto, & Bobo, 1994; Sprecher, Sullivan, & Hatfield, 1994).

What do men and women actually *do* to compete for mates? College students report doing pretty much what we just described (Buss, 1988). Women enhance their beauty with makeup, jewelry, clothing, and hairstyles. Women also play hard to get, to incite widespread interest among many males. This permits the women to be choosy once candidates have been identified (see also Kenrick, Sadalla, Groth, & Trost, 1990). Men brag about their accomplishments and earning potential, display expensive possessions, and flex their muscles. In fact, just seeing women around makes men display these qualities even more (Roney, 2003).

Buss (1989) examined mate preferences in 37 different cultures around the world. Cultural differences were relatively rare. The preferences of U.S. college students didn't differ much from those of people elsewhere. Males (more than females) were drawn to cues of reproductive capacity. Females (more than males) were drawn to cues indicating resources (see also Singh, 1995). The resource issue may not be a case of "more is better." It may just be that men who aren't at an acceptable level are out of the running (Kenrick, Sundie, Nicastle, & Stone, 2001). Females are also drawn to cues of dominance and high status (Cunningham, Barbee, & Pike, 1990; Feingold, 1992; Kenrick et al., 1990; Sadalla, Kenrick, & Vershure, 1987), especially dominance expressed in socially positive ways (Jensen-Campbell, Graziano, & West, 1995).

Despite these gender differences, the qualities just listed don't always rank high in people's lists of desired characteristics. This leads some to be skeptical of their importance. But rankings can also be deceiving. Other research gave people tight "budgets" for getting what they want in a partner (Li, Bailey, Kenrick, & Linsenmeier, 2002). In this situation, men treated physical attractiveness as a necessity rather than an option, women treated status and resources as necessities, and both treated kindness and intelligence as necessities. That is, given that they couldn't be choosy about everything, they went for these qualities first.

People have investigated implications of the evolutionary model in several ways. For example, research shows that men prefer younger women, especially as they themselves grow older, consistent with the seeking of reproductive capacity. This comes from a study of the age ranges specified in singles' ads (Kenrick & Keefe, 1992). As can be seen in Figure 6.3, men past age 25 specified a range that extended increasingly below their own age. Women, in contrast, tended to express a preference for men slightly older than themselves.

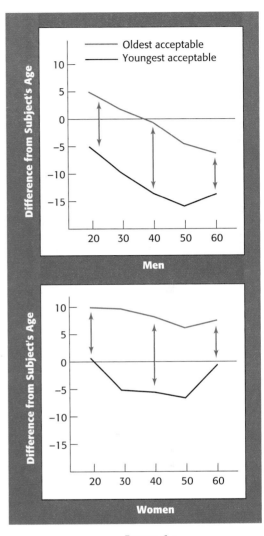

FIGURE 6.3
Singles' ads placed by men and women often specify the age range of persons of the opposite sex whom the placer of the ad would like to meet. In this sample of ads, as men aged, they expressed an increasing preference for younger women. Women tended to prefer men slightly older than they were, and the extent of that preference didn't change over time.
Source: Adapted from Kenrick & Keefe, 1992.

Also consistent with predictions from the evolutionary model are results from several other studies of gender differences (see also Table 6.2). Men are more interested in casual sex than are women (Bailey, Gaulin, Agyei, & Gladue, 1994; Buss & Schmitt, 1993; R. D. Clark & Hatfield, 1989; Oliver & Hyde, 1993), want more sexual variety (Schmitt, 2003), and are less selective in their criteria for one-night stands (Kenrick, Groth, Trost, & Sadalla, 1993). Men are more easily turned on by visual erotica than are women (Bailey et al., 1994). Men's commitment to their relationship is shaken by exposure to a very attractive woman, whereas women's commitment is shaken by exposure to a very dominant man (Kenrick, Neuberg, Zierk, & Krones, 1994). Men's confidence in their own value as a mate is shaken by exposure to a very dominant man (but not an attractive one), and women's confidence in their value as a mate is shaken by exposure to a very attractive woman (but not a dominant one; Gutierres, Kenrick, & Partch, 1999). Men overinterpret women's smiles and touches as implying sexual interest, and women are overly conservative in judging men's commitment in relationships that are forming (Buss, 2001).

Both men and women experience jealousy, but it has been suggested that there's a difference in what creates this emotion. In theory, it's evolutionarily important for men

Table 6.2 Summary of Predictions from Evolutionary Psychology for Sex Differences in Mating Tendencies.

Issue	Females	Males
Reproductive constraints	Can produce only a limited number of children over life	Can reproduce without limit through life
Optimal reproductive strategy	Locate and hold onto best-quality mate	Mate as widely and often as possible
Desired quality in potential mate	Resources to protect and support them and offspring	Childbearing capability
Basis for evaluating mate potential	Earning capacity, status, possessions, generosity	Physical attractiveness, health, youth
Prime basis for jealousy	Partner's emotional attachment to another	Partner's sexual infidelity

to be concerned about paternity. (They want to support their *own* children, not someone else's.) Thus, men should be especially jealous about sexual infidelity. In theory, women are most concerned about whether the man will continue to support her and her children. Thus, women should be jealous about a man's having emotional bonds with another woman, rather than sex per se.

Data from several studies fit this view: Men were more disturbed by thoughts of sexual infidelity, and women were more disturbed by thoughts of emotional infidelity, (Buss, Larsen, Westen, & Semmelroth, 1992; see also Bailey et al., 1994). This particular finding has been challenged, however, partly because asking the question differently erases the gender difference (DeSteno, Bartlett, Braverman, & Salovey, 2002; Harris, 2002, 2003) and partly because it's been hard to obtain the effect in non-student samples (Sabini & Green, 2004).

Jealousy is partly about what your partner may have done, but it's partly about the presence of rivals. Again, there is evidence of a gender difference in what qualities matter. Men are more jealous when the potential rival is dominant than when he is physically attractive; women are more jealous when the potential rival is physically attractive (Dijkstra & Buunk, 1998).

MATE RETENTION AND OTHER ISSUES

The first challenge in mating is getting a mate. The next challenge is *keeping* the mate. Men and women both have the potential to stray, and other people sometimes try to make that happen (Schmitt, 2004; Schmitt & Buss, 2001). People use various tactics to prevent this (Buss & Shackelford, 1997). Some are used by men and women alike, but others differ by gender. For example, men report spending a lot of money and giving in to their mates' wishes. Women try to make themselves look extra attractive and let others know their mate is already taken.

Use of retention tactics also relates predictably to other factors in the relationship but differently for men and women. Men use their tactics more if they think their wife is physically attractive. Men also work harder at keeping a wife who is young, independent of the man's age and the length of the relationship. In contrast, women work harder at keeping husbands with higher incomes. They also make more efforts if their husbands are striving for high status (independent of current income).

Although mating strategies are the starting point for much of this research on gender differences, others have applied the theme more broadly. (As noted earlier, issues involved in mating lead to several other complexities in life.) Several have suggested that evolutionary differences cause men and women to have very different styles—indeed different *needs*—in communication (e.g., J. Gray, 1992; Tannen, 1990). Men are seen as having an individualistic, dominance-oriented, problem-solving approach. Women are seen as having an inclusive, sharing, communal approach. The argument is also made that these differences in goals and patterns of communication lead to a good deal of misunderstanding between men and women.

We should note that our discussion has emphasized gender differences, not similarities. There are, of course, many similarities. Both genders are looking for partners who have a good sense of humor and a pleasing personality (Feingold, 1992), who are agreeable and emotionally stable (Kenrick et al., 1993), intelligent (Li et al., 2002), and kind and loving (Buss, 1994b). Both also seem to prefer partners whose faces are symmetrical (Grammer & Thornhill, 1994). The way men and women look at each other goes far beyond seeing each other as sex objects and success objects (Buss, 1994b). Nevertheless, gender differences also seem important.

AGGRESSION AND THE YOUNG MALE SYNDROME

Competition for mating opportunities leads to a lot of male posturing. It has also been blamed for many problem aspects of young men's behavior, including their risky driving (Nell, 2002). But it can also lead to more. When males face hard competition for scarce resources (females), the result sometimes is confrontation and potentially serious violence of several sorts (Hilton, Harris, & Rice, 2000).

This pattern has been referred to as the *young male syndrome* (Wilson & Daly, 1985). It's viewed as partly an effect of evolutionary pressures from long ago and partly a response to situations that elicit the pattern. That is, although the pattern of behavior may be coded in every man's genes, it's most likely to emerge when current situations predict reproductive failure. The worst case would be a single man who is unemployed and thus a poor candidate as a mate.

In line with this analysis, there's clear evidence that homicide between competitors is primarily a male affair (Daly & Wilson, 1990). Figure 6.4 displays the homicide rates in Chicago during a 16-year period, omitting cases in which the person killed was a relative. Males are far more likely to kill one another than are females. It's also obvious that the prime ages for killing are the prime ages for mating. According to Daly and Wilson, these killings come largely from conflicts over "face" and status (see also Wilson & Daly, 1996). Trivial events escalate into violence, and someone is killed.

Why killing instead of ritualized displays of aggressiveness? No one knows for sure. It is certain that easy access to guns in the United States plays a role. When weapons aren't there, the same pressures are more likely to result in punching and shouting. Deadly violence certainly is possible without weapons, but weapons make it far more likely.

We should point out explicitly that the theory underlying this area of study is very different from ideas about aggression and human nature of only a few years ago. This view isn't that aggression is part of human nature, expressed indiscriminately. Rather,

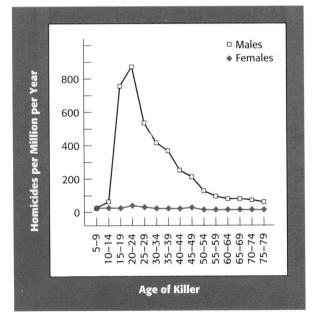

FIGURE 6.4
Homicide rates for males and females killing nonrelatives of the same sex in Chicago during the period 1965–1981.

Source: Adapted from Daly & Wilson, 1990.

physical aggression is seen as largely a male phenomenon, which occurs specifically as a result of sexual selection pressures in the competition for mates (Buss, 2005b).

Our focus here is on violence by young men toward their genetic competitors. It's worth noting that genetic competition also may play a role in violence within family units. In particular, children—especially very young children—are far more likely to be killed by stepparents than by genetic parents (Daly & Wilson, 1988, 1996). The overall frequency of this event is low; most parents don't kill children. Yet if it happens, a stepparent is far more likely to be the perpetrator than a biological parent. As is true of the young male syndrome, this finding may reflect a deep-rooted desire to help one's own genes into the next generation instead of a competitor's genes.

We noted earlier that part of mating is retaining one's mate. People have a variety of tactics for doing this. Most of them are quite benign. Some can even be viewed as efforts at solidifying the relationship to make it resistant to temptation. However, some tactics of mate retention are coercive. Some men are so concerned about losing their mates—or unknowingly supporting a rival's child—that they become quite controlling. Tactics to control the woman sometimes escalate to violence against her (Hilton et al., 2000; Wilson & Daly, 1996). Sometimes that violence is a warning: Don't stray. Sometimes the violence is murder, ending all possibility of straying (Buss, 2005b). When killings occur *within* families, most victims are wives.

Although male violence against women is cause for great concern, we should also be clear that it is not just men who do this. Aggression against partners also occurs among women (Hilton et al., 2000).

Assessment

The orientation to personality that was discussed in the first part of this chapter developed as a branch of the dispositional perspective. In general, its ways of assessing personality reflect the dispositional view. What it offers primarily is content—some ideas about which traits to assess. As we said earlier, those who take the genetic view on personality feel that certain dispositions are inherited as biological substrates of personality. These, then, are the qualities to assess.

A second point made by this approach to personality concerns a more general issue regarding assessment in research. The issue is what kind of data to collect to measure the trait you want to study (an issue also discussed in Chapter 3). For example, in some twin studies, the data were self-report scales. In other studies, children were rated by their parents or by teachers. Occasionally, but not often, behavioral observations have been made of children at play.

It turns out that it may matter considerably which of these sources of data is used in the research, because different types of data don't always give the same answers about degree of genetic influence (Plomin & Foch, 1980). In general, parent ratings of children and self-ratings indicate genetic influence more reliably than do behavioral observations. (In fact, they may well overestimate the size of genetic effects [Saudino et al., 1995].) This raises questions about which kind of data to be most confident in. The importance of deciding which kind of measure to use is not unique to the biological approach. But it may be particularly important here because of the fact that twin studies are difficult and expensive.

Given the rise in influence of molecular genetics, some have raised the possibility that gene assessment will eventually be done as a better way of determining personality. Although it is too soon to be sure, many people prominent in this area see this as unlikely (e.g., Plomin & Crabbe, 2000). The reason is the belief that personality traits are influenced by many, many genes, each exerting a small effect. It will be hard enough to identify those genes, never mind use them as convenient personality tests.

Problems in Behavior, and Behavior Change

Let's turn now to problems in behavior. The genetic approach has made a major contribution here. Behavior geneticists have examined the possibility that several kinds of vulnerabilities to problems may be influenced by inheritance (see also Box 6.4). Molecular genetics is also starting to weigh in, but with the same problem as it has with respect to normal personality: that many genes are likely to be involved in any given problem rather than one or two.

SCHIZOPHRENIA AND BIPOLAR DISORDER

For many years, research on the behavior genetics of problems focused mainly on schizophrenia and bipolar disorder. Most of the research has been on schizophrenia, which is characterized by disorientation, confusion, cognitive disturbances, and a separation from reality.

BOX 6.4 LIVING IN A POSTGENOMIC WORLD

The human genome is mapped. Researchers today know more than ever about the makeup of the human body and the functions of some of our genes (Plomin et al., 2003). The technology behind these advances is continuing its rapid development, with no signs of slowing down.

Mapping the human genome will surely yield benefits. Some disorders are caused by single genes. Knowing the map makes it easier to locate the genes. (For example, the gene for cystic fibrosis is in the middle of chromosome 7.) This information can be used in genetic counseling. People can be warned if they carry a gene for a disorder they may pass on to a child. Another benefit is genetic therapies, which now exist for some disorders—for example, to correct defects in producing blood cells. Some say the map of the genome, by allowing identification of genetic weaknesses, will usher in a new era of preventive medi-

cine, dramatically changing the way we deal with disease (Lewin, 1990).

The mapping of the genome excites imaginations, but it also raises concerns (Buchanan, Brock, Daniels, & Wikler, 2000; Fukuyama, 2002; Lynn, 2001; Stock, 2002). Knowing what genes control body and behavior raises serious ethical issues. For example, a great deal of pressure will doubtlessly arise to modify genes to create specific characteristics in new children, creating so-called designer babies (Plomin & Crabbe, 2000; Stock, 2002). Should this happen? Who is to decide what characteristics should be created? What happens to people whose genetic characteristics are viewed by society as inferior?

Knowledge about disorders also raises ethical issues. Will there be discrimination against people with particular genetic profiles? What happens to the cost of medical insurance when it's possible to know who is susceptible to what diseases? Will insurance even be *available* to people with susceptibilities? This isn't an idle

question. Already, insurance policies have been cancelled for entire families because of genetic problems in specific family members (Stolberg, 1994).

The same issue arises with respect to psychological disorders. If it's known that your genes predispose you to mania or depression, will you be able to get a job? Will you be able to have insurance against the possibility of needing treatment? The other side of this issue, however, is that it is likely that many patterns now seen as disorders are simply extremes of personality (Plomin & Crabbe, 2000). Clarity on this issue would follow from knowing what genes are involved in both the problem patterns and normal patterns. Such a realization might go a long way toward removing stigma from disorders.

In short, the project to map the genome holds out much promise, but it also raises very difficult issues that will have to be addressed. You may want to start thinking about them, because they're issues that are in your future—and the future of your children.

A well-known early study of genetic influence on schizophrenia by Gottesman and Shields (1972) began by recruiting twins admitted to a hospital with a diagnosis of schizophrenia. They sought out each one's co-twin and evaluated the co-twin's status. The term **concordance** is used to describe similarity of diagnosis. A pair of twins were concordant if they were both diagnosed as schizophrenic. This study found concordance rates of 50% among identical twins and 9% among fraternal twins. It thus appears that inheritance plays a role in schizophrenia. Indeed, this conclusion follows from over a dozen studies similar to this one.

It should be noted that the twin study data also indicate that life circumstances play a role in determining who shows schizophrenic symptoms openly (Plomin & Rende, 1991). Some people have the genetic susceptibility but don't develop the disorder. This interaction between a susceptibility and a suitable context to touch it off reflects a diathesis-stress view of disorder (discussed in Chapter 4). This is a theme that recurs in studying genetics and disorder.

Molecular genetic studies have also been done to try to isolate gene locations that relate to schizophrenia. Several locations have been suggested (Faraone, Taylor, & Tsuang, 2002; Owen, Williams, & O'Donovan, 2004; Straub et al., 2002). However, findings from studies such as these are often very difficult to repeat (DeLisi et al., 2002). Thus, there remains great uncertainty about what genes may be involved in schizophrenia.

A second disorder that appears to be affected by heredity is bipolar (manic–depressive) disorder. *Mania* is characterized by episodes of frenetic, hyperactive, grandiose, and talkative behavior, accompanied by a rush of ideas. Often the manic pattern is accompanied by positive emotion, but anger is also common. The onset of this disorder is usually sudden. As with schizophrenia, twin studies reveal very strong evidence of genetic contribution (McGuffin, Rijsdijk, Andrew, Sham, Katz, & Cardno, 2003).

There has also been molecular genetics research on this problem. One study linked bipolar disorder to a specific dominant gene on chromosome 11 in a group of Amish families (Egeland, Gerhard, Pauls, Sussex, & Kidd, 1987). Two other studies, however, found no link from the disorder to that chromosome, so this gene can't be the only one responsible for the disorder (Detera-Wadleigh, Berrettini, Goldin, Boorman, Anderson, & Gershon, 1987; Hodgkinson, Sherrington, Gurling, Marchbanks, & Reeders, 1987). Scientists continue to look for genetic markers of bipolar disorder, using the techniques of molecular genetics (Badner & Gershon, 2002).

It is clear that biology plays a major role in bipolar disorder. However, it is also clear that events in the environment are important to how the disorder is expressed. In this case, at least a little is known about what environmental influences matter. For example, lack of sleep makes people with the disorder especially vulnerable to manic episodes; so does experiencing success in attaining goals (S. L. Johnson, 2005; S. L. Johnson et al., 2000). Once again, at least in the short term, there is an interaction between genetic and environmental influences.

SUBSTANCE USE AND ANTISOCIAL BEHAVIOR

Another focus of research on the genetics of problems is substance abuse. Quite some time ago, Eysenck (1964b) found that MZ twins were more likely to share tendencies toward alcoholism than DZ twins. Similar findings, with information about the metabolic processes that underlie the difference, were reported by Schuckit and Rayses (1979). Another finding provides an interesting reflection of the interweaving of genetic and environmental influences (Dick & Rose, 2002). Genetic contributions to drinking in this study increased from about a third of the variance at age 16 to half the variance—in the same sample—at age 18.

Recent research has also implicated a specific gene in the craving for alcohol that some people experience after having a little (Hutchison, McGeary, Smolen, Bryan, & Swift, 2002). The gene turns out to be the long allele of the dopamine-related gene described earlier in the chapter. That was the gene that related to measures of reward seeking. That allele has also been linked to heroin addiction (Kotler et al., 1997; Li et al., 1997; Shao et al., 2006).

Another fast-growing area of research concerns genetics and antisocial behavior. Long ago, Eysenck (1964a) reported higher concordance rates among MZ than DZ twins on childhood behavior problems and adult crime. Further research on adult criminality tends to fit the picture of a genetic influence (DiLalla & Gottesman, 1991; Wilson & Herrnstein, 1985). Other research suggests that antisocial personality disorder is genetically influenced (Rowe, 1994; Vandenberg, Singer, & Pauls, 1986; Willerman, Loehlin, & Horn, 1992), and most observers now believe there are clear genetic influences on antisocial behavior (Moffitt, 2005b; Rhee & Waldman, 2002).

Some people believe that our cultural evolution has outstripped the ability of our biological evolution to keep up.

Once again, however, there appears to be evidence of an interaction between predisposition and environment. Moffitt (2005) reviewed research on antisocial behavior, looking specifically for interactions between genetics and environment and finding them. One of her conclusions was that we should not be framing questions in terms of whether genes influence this disorder but rather who is at greatest risk when placed in circumstances that pull for problem behavior. The search for interactions between genes and environment is likely to remain an important focus for studies of diverse problems, including this one (Moffitt, Caspi, & Rutter, 2006).

EVOLUTION AND PROBLEMS IN BEHAVIOR

A somewhat different view of certain behavior problems is suggested by sociobiology. Barash (1986) argued that many difficulties in human life stem from the fact that two kinds of evolution influence people. There is biological evolution, a very slow process that occurs over millennia. There is also cultural evolution, which is much faster. Your experiences of life stem partly from what biological evolution shaped humans to be during prehistory and partly from the cultural circumstances in which you live.

Barash pointed out that biological evolution prepared us for life in a world very different from the one we live in now. Cultural evolution has raced far ahead, and biological evolution can't keep up. Being in a world to which we don't quite belong, we are conflicted and alienated. Barash's point is a general one, not specific to a particular disorder, but it's an interesting one: That is, problems emerge when behavioral tendencies that have been built in as part of human nature conflict with pressures that are built into contemporary culture.

BEHAVIOR CHANGE: HOW MUCH IS POSSIBLE?

A major question about therapeutic behavior change is raised by the view under discussion in this chapter. Biologically based personality qualities—whether temperaments or not—are by definition firmly anchored in the person's constitutional functioning. How easy can it be to alter these aspects of personality in any major way, through *whatever* therapeutic processes are used? Psychotherapy may change the person to some extent. But how far against their biological nature can people be expected to bend?

This is an interesting issue, about which little is known. It's been suggested that even true temperaments can be modified, within limits (Buss & Plomin, 1984). But what are the limits? It seems likely that some kinds of therapeutic change are more difficult to create and sustain for some people than for others. For example, it will be harder for a therapy aimed at reducing emotional reactions to be effective for some- one with high emotionality than for someone lower in that temperament. In fact, there may be some people whose constitutions make certain kinds of therapy so dif- ficult as to be impractical.

Nonetheless, it should also be recognized that the heritability of personality, though strong, is not complete. There's a good deal of influence from experiences. Thus, the data that establish a genetic influence on personality also show that genetic determination is not total. The extent to which genetically coded tenden- cies limit behavior change is an important issue. The answer is not at all clear. It is clear, however, that psychological processes do matter, even for disorders that are strongly influenced by inheritance, such as bipolar disorder. Although medication is very important in the management of this disorder (see Chapter 7), psycholog- ical treatments of various kinds have also proven beneficial (Johnson & Leahy, 2003).

Inheritance and Evolution: Problems and Prospects

The biological perspective on personality has roots that go far back in the history of ideas. Yet today's views are in many ways quite new. Research on heritability of per- sonality is still fairly recent in origin. Application of the ideas of evolutionary psychology is even more recent. With the advent of advances in molecular genetics, people are now trying to link particular genes with qualities of personality, an approach that's newer still.

In considering the usefulness of these biological ideas in thinking about per- sonality, several issues arise. For example, temperaments are broad tendencies reflected in fundamental aspects of behavior. The fact that temperaments are so basic, however, raises a question about how to view their role in personality. Does it make more sense to think of temperaments as all of personality, as part of per- sonality, or as the bedrock on which personality is constructed? Since many personality traits seem heritable and many of the traits relate conceptually to tem- peraments, perhaps we should view temperaments as the starting point from which the conceptually related traits emerge.

Another question is, How many traits are genetically influenced, and how many *look* heritable because they derive from the first group? Recent evidence suggests that facets of the five supertraits are separately heritable. This puts a different twist on the question. Maybe we should be asking whether the temperaments are really unitary, broad qualities that are just displayed in diverse ways or whether they are convenient aggregates of what are really separate traits.

A final question concerns the methods of behavioral genetics as a discipline. Although we didn't address this point in discussing the research, some have ques- tioned whether the methods in this research really tell investigators what they believe they are being told (e.g., Haviland, McGuire, & Rothbaum, 1983; Wahlsten, 1990). Questions have also been raised about what kind of bridge can be built between quantitative *behavioral genetics*—which is about identifying sources of variability in data—and *molecular genetics*—which is about particular gene locations and what they do. These are extremely different phenomena (Greenberg, 2005; Partridge, 2005), yet we are treating them as though they were closely related. The issues here are very technical, and it's difficult to know how they will be resolved. But until they *are* resolved, there will remain at least a small cloud on the horizon of the genetic approach to personality.

Another aspect of the viewpoint discussed in this chapter is sociobiology and evolutionary psychology. This view on personality has been controversial during its relatively brief existence and has been criticized on several grounds (e.g., L. C. Miller, Putcha-Bhagavatula, & Pedersen, 2002). The early arguments of sociobiology were very theoretical, with little supporting evidence. Sociobiology was seen by some as a game of speculation, rather than a serious science. More than a few people scorned the ideas under discussion as unfalsifiable and indeed untestable.

In the past decade and a half, however, this situation changed dramatically. As more precise ideas were developed about the implications of evolutionary theory, this way of thinking led to a surge of studies. Evolutionary psychology is now an area of vigorous research activity. It seems clear that evolutionary thinking provides a wealth of hypotheses for researchers. Moreover, the hypotheses are becoming more and more sophisticated.

Nevertheless, there remains concern about whether the hypotheses being studied by these researchers really *depend on* evolutionary theory, as opposed to merely *being consistent* with it. Indeed, one recent critic has argued that support for many key evolutionary hypotheses is highly ambiguous and does not support the conclusions drawn (Buller, 2005a, 2005b). One challenge evolutionary psychology faces today is that of making clear predictions that resist alternative interpretations. This issue, of course, is faced by all views on personality, not just the evolutionary one. The issue, however, seems likely to remain an especially important one for this approach for some time.

Sociobiology and evolutionary psychology have also been criticized because their statements have disturbing political and social overtones. Some regard arguments about how human nature evolved as thinly veiled justifications for unfair social conditions in today's world (Kitcher, 1987, and the succeeding commentaries; see also Lewontin, Rose, & Kamin, 1984). That is, these ideas explain why men are bullies, why there's a double standard of sexual behavior for men and women, and why race and class differences exist. These explanations provide a basis for considering such conditions to be natural. This is only a small step from saying they should continue to exist (see Pratto & Hegarty, 2000). These overtones of evolutionary thinking are seen by some as racist and sexist and have prompted considerable hostility toward the theories among some people.

One response to this sort of criticism is to point out that evolution is a natural force that works dispassionately, based on the principles of reproduction and survival. In the arena of evolution, issues of equal rights and equal opportunities have no meaning. It may well be that in today's world, some of the results of evolution work against some people because evolution prepared us to fit not this world but the world of prehistory. If people are disadvantaged by the consequences of evolution, though, it's something that must be dealt with by the cultures that people have built. The fact that the theory explains why inequity exists can't be used as an argument that the theory is wrong. As you might expect, this response is not entirely satisfying to critics.

Despite controversies such as these, there remains a huge interest in evolutionary ideas in today's personality psychology. These ideas will not go away any time soon.

· SUMMARY ·

The approach to personality rooted in inheritance and evolution has two facets. One emphasizes that your personality is tied to the biological body you inherit. This idea goes far back in history, but today's version of the idea is quite different, emphasizing the role of genes.

Behavior genetics provides ways to find out whether personality differences are inherited. In twin studies, correlations among identical twins are compared with correlations among fraternal twins; in adoption studies, children are compared with their biological and adoptive families. Studies of identical twins raised apart provide yet a different look at the effects of inheritance and environment.

Twin research has been used to look at genetic contributions to a variety of dispositions, starting with temperaments: broad inherited traits that appear early in life. Evidence supports genetic influences on activity level, emotionality, and sociability. Other temperaments have been suggested, including temperaments for approach, avoidance, and effortful control. There also is evidence of genetic influence in the "big five" supertraits and other variables. It's unclear whether the "big five" derive from (or duplicate) the temperaments studied under other names. It is also unclear whether hereditary influences on other variables depend on associations between the other variable and a temperament. Recent developments in molecular genetics provide a new tool in the search for genetic influences on personality. Now there is evidence of specific genes playing roles in traits, including novelty seeking and neuroticism.

The idea that dispositions are genetically influenced can be extended a step further, to the suggestion that many aspects of human social behavior are products of evolution. This idea is behind an area of work termed *sociobiology* or *evolutionary psychology*. Sociobiologists propose ways to account for various aspects of human behavior, even behavior that on the face of it seems not to provide an evolutionary advantage. Altruism, for example, is understood as people acting for the benefit of their family groups, so that the family's genes are more likely to be continued (kin selection). This idea has been extended to the notion that people are attracted to other people who share their genetic makeup.

The evolutionary view also has implications concerning mate selection, including the idea that males and females use different strategies. The male strategy is to mate whenever possible, and males are drawn to signs of reproductive capability. The female strategy is to seek the best male available, and females are drawn to signs of resources. People use the relevant strategies and act in ways that make them seem better candidates as mates. Mating pressures also may lead to aggression among young men. Theory suggests that violence is most likely among men of reproductive age who are in poor reproductive circumstances. Evidence seems to bear this out, along with the idea that much violence concerns conflicts over status.

The genetic approach to personality says little about assessment except to suggest what dispositions are particularly important to assess—those that have biological links. Assessment directly from genes seems unlikely soon, due to the probable involvement of many genes in any given trait. With regard to problems in behavior, there is substantial evidence that schizophrenia and manic–depressive disorder are affected by heredity, as are substance abuse tendencies and antisocial tendencies. As elsewhere, this area is beginning to use the tools of molecular biology to search for genetic influences.

With regard to therapeutic behavior change, this approach raises a question on the basis of studies of temperament: How much can people be expected to change, even with therapy, in directions that deviate from their biological makeup?

· GLOSSARY ·

Activity level   The overall output of a person's energy or behavior.

Adoption study   A study of resemblances between children and their adoptive and biological parents.

Allele   Some version of a particular gene.

Assortative mating   Mating based on choice of specific characteristics rather than random.

Behavioral genetics   The study of inheritance of behavioral qualities.

Cerebrotonia   A mental overintensity that promotes apprehensiveness and social inhibition.

Concordance   Agreement on some characteristic between a twin and a co-twin.

Directional selection   Evolution in which one extreme of a dimension is more adaptive than the other.

Dizygotic (DZ) twins   Fraternal twins (overlapping genetically 50%, on average).

Ectomorphy   A tendency toward frail thinness.

Effortful control   A tendency to be focused, restrained, and planful.

Emotionality   The tendency to become emotionally aroused easily.

Endomorphy   A tendency toward obesity.

Ethology   The study of animals in their natural environment.

Genetic similarity theory   The idea that people work toward reproducing genes similar to their own.

Genome   The sequence of the genes contained in the full complement of chromosomes.

Genotype   The particular version of a gene that a given person or group has.

Heritability   An estimate of how much variance of some characteristic is accounted for by inheritance.

Inclusive fitness   The passing on of genes through the survival of relatives.

Mesomorphy   A tendency toward muscularity.

Molecular genetics   The study of how alleles of specific genes relate to other observed differences.

Monozygotic (MZ) twins   Identical twins (overlapping genetically 100%).

Polymorphism   The characteristic of having more than one allele for a given gene.

Reciprocal altruism   Helping others with the expectation the help will be returned.

Siblings   Brothers and sisters.

Sociability   The tendency to prefer being with people over being alone.

Sociobiology   The study of the evolutionary basis for social behavior.

Somatotonia   Energetic desire for adventure and physical activity.

Somatotype   The description of a person's body configuration along three dimensions.

Stabilizing selection   Evolution in which intermediate values of a dimension are most adaptive.

Temperaments   Inherited traits that appear early in life.

Twin study   A study comparing similarity between MZ twins against similarity between DZ twins.

Viscerotonia   A relaxed sociability and love of comfort.

Biological Processes and Personality

Gina craves adventure. She always seems to be widening her circle of friends and activities. It's as though she needs the stimulation to keep her alive and happy. Her boyfriend, Leo, shies away from it. All the noise and action seem too much for him. He's more comfortable when things are less intense and he can plan his activities. Oddly enough, both of them feel their bodies are telling them what's best for them, even though what's "best" is so different from the one to the other.

THE IDEA that people's personalities are somehow embedded in the makeup of their bodies was the starting point for Chapter 6. There we focused on the idea that genetics play a big role in what people are like. That idea accounts for why people are different from one another (they inherit different traits). It also accounts for why people are the same (evolution shaped certain tendencies into the human species as a whole).

The ideas in Chapter 6 are definitely biological. If something is genetically caused, the influence has to occur through a biological process. But the ideas in Chapter 6 say little about how the effects are *exerted*. That is, knowing that traits are inherited says nothing about the process by which genes influence the behaviors that eventually emerge.

In this chapter, we take the same starting point: the idea that personality is embedded in people's bodies. This time, though, we focus on the idea that personality is influenced by the *workings* of the body. Now we consider some questions about what the body is organized to do. The view taken now is that personality reflects the operation of these processes of the body.

As in the last chapter, there's room for similarities among people and also differences. The similarities reflect the fact that everyone has a nervous system and an endocrine system. The systems have the same basic structure and functions from one person to another. The differences reflect the fact that parts of the nervous system and endocrine system are more active or more responsive in some people than in others.

Eysenck: Extraversion, Neuroticism, and Brain Functions

One of the first modern attempts to link personality to biological functions was that of Hans Eysenck (see Box 7.1). Recall from Chapter 4 that Eysenck saw personality as composed largely of two supertraits: neuroticism and extraversion. He saw both of these as rooted in the body.

EXTRAVERSION AND CORTICAL AROUSAL

Introverts are quiet, introspective, and disinterested in social activity; extraverts are outgoing, uninhibited, and immersed in social activity. Eysenck (1967, 1981) argued that this difference derives from the degree to which the cerebral cortex is activated. When the context is highly activated, the person is alert. When it's not, the person is sluggish and drowsy. Eysenck proposed that introverts normally have higher cortical arousal than extraverts. Because they have higher base levels, it's easy for them to get overaroused. They may refrain from social interaction because it gets them overstimulated. Extraverts, with lower baseline levels, seek stimulation to bring their arousal up.

BOX 7.1   THE THEORIST AND THE THEORY

The Many-Faceted Contributions of Hans Eysenck

Hans Eysenck was one of the most eclectic theorists in psychology. As described in Chapter 4, he played a major role in the dispositional view of personality. He also studied inheritance and tried to understand how the nervous system relates to personality. His interests didn't stop there, however. Eysenck wrote about topics as diverse as intelligence, politics, the links between personality and health, parapsychology, and astrology. He published more than 50 books and hundreds of articles and was often embroiled in controversy (which he appeared to relish).

Eysenck's parents were actors in Germany, where he was born in 1916. His parents divorced when he was two, and he lived with his grandmother for years afterward. Eysenck grew quickly into a self-confident and strong-willed young man. Two anecdotes illustrate his tenacity (Gibson, 1981). When he was about 8, he was called on during singing class to perform a solo passage. He declined on the grounds that his voice wasn't any good, but the teacher insisted. He finally went ahead but sang so poorly the teacher thought he was mocking the lesson. The teacher was about to punish him, but Eysenck struck first: He took the teacher's thumb in his teeth and held on like a bulldog, not letting go until the headmaster intervened.

The second incident occurred when Eysenck was in high school, during the period when the Nazis were seizing power. His teacher said that Jews were known to be lacking in military valor. Eysenck set off to explore this issue and returned with the fact that Jewish soldiers had earned an extra-high rate of military honors during World War I. This incident illustrates his tendency to take on controversy willingly and also his dedication to scientific evidence.

Eysenck later went to England for university studies. He had decided to study physics and astronomy, but he made an error that changed the path of his life—and that of psychology. Prospective students had to take a set of exams in the areas of their intended study. Eysenck inadvertently took the wrong exams, making him eligible to major only in subjects other than his chosen ones. Because psychology was the most scientific of the majors available at that point, he decided to study psychology.

In short, the qualities that mark Eysenck's contributions to personality psychology can be seen in his own life, including an extremely diverse range of interests, a tenacity about sticking with what he believed, and an enjoyment of controversy and being the center of attention. All those qualities were apparent early in his life. The same qualities also play a role in a central construct of his theory: extraversion.

Laboratory studies suggest that introverts may do better than extraverts at tasks that require the monitoring of slowly changing visual displays, as is required in the work of air traffic controllers.

This influences the kinds of situations introverts and extraverts prefer. Introverts should prefer lower levels of stimulation—but not *too* low, or it will get boring even to them. Extraverts should prefer higher levels—but not *too* high, or it will get overwhelming even to them. Research has shown not only that the two groups prefer different levels of stimulation but that they also function better with different levels of stimulation (Geen, 1984).

Other evidence also fits the idea that introverts and extraverts differ in alertness. Consider *vigilance tasks,* which require you to be alert for specific stimuli. For example, you might have to listen to a long series of numbers and press a button whenever you hear three odd ones in a row. If your mind wanders, you will miss some of what you're listening for. Introverts miss less than extraverts (Claridge, 1967). Another source of evidence is drug effects. If introverts are already alert, they shouldn't need as much of a stimulant to reach a given level of arousal. On the other hand, introverts should need *more* of a depressant drug to reach a given level of unalertness. This seems to be the case (Claridge, 1967; Eysenck, 1983).

NEUROTICISM AND EMOTIONAL AROUSAL

Eysenck also proposed a neural basis for neuroticism (emotionality). He said that people who are higher on this trait are more easily aroused in the brain's emotion centers. Eysenck thought this had two implications. First, emotional arousal causes behavioral reflections of both extraverts and introverts to emerge more fully. It makes both of them become "more of what they are."

Second, emotional arousal can set the stage for conditioning, because emotional reactions sometimes result in conditioning (see Chapter 12). Eysenck said that introverts condition easily, because they're high in cortical arousal. If they also happen to be highly emotional, they'll have emotions in many settings and thus many opportunities for conditioning. Because much of the conditioning during childhood arises from punishment, the emotions that get conditioned are mostly negative. As a result, Eysenck argued, neurotic introverts should be vulnerable to anxiety and depression.

When neuroticism combines with extraversion, the effects are different. Extraverts don't condition well, because they're less aroused cortically. Thus, they don't learn from punishment. Extraverts who happen also to be highly emotional therefore respond to the emotions especially impulsively. They display a lack of socialization.

Eysenck's effort to link personality to aspects of brain function was a path-breaking one. However, brain functioning was not as well understood when he wrote as it is now. Changes in knowledge have greatly changed people's views of how brain functions and personality relate.

Incentive Approach System

Within the past 20 years or so, a number of theorists have proposed ideas about how the nervous system relates to personality. The ideas vary in focus. Some concern what parts of the brain are involved in certain kinds of actions. Some concern what brain chemicals are involved in certain kinds of actions. As did Eysenck, all of them take what might be called a *functional approach*. That is, they ask, what *functions* do particular kinds of behavior serve? The various types of behavior then are linked to ideas about brain processes, and both are also linked to personality.

Many people are working hard on this topic, and the literature is growing explosively. There are broad areas of agreement, but there are also disagreements. There's a lot of consensus about major themes, but there are also lots of ways to slice the pie. People differ in where they draw the lines for slicing.

Behavioral Approach, Activation, Engagement, or Facilitation

Most theorists of this group believe there's a set of brain structures that cause animals to approach **incentives:** things they desire. Several theorists have made assertions about parts of the brain involved in this system, though they're not in full agreement (Cloninger, 1988; Davidson, 1992, 1995; Davidson, Jackson, & Kalin, 2000; Depue & Collins, 1999; Depue & Iacono, 1989; J. A. Gray, 1982, 1991). Although there is a great deal of ongoing effort to figure out what parts of the brain are involved, we will say only a little about that here. We will focus instead on the functional properties of the brain systems—how they are believed to be reflected in behavior and experience.

The structures involved in approach have been given several names: the *activation system* (Cloninger, 1987; Fowles, 1980), *behavioral engagement system* (Depue, Krauss, & Spoont, 1987), *behavioral facilitation system* (Depue & Iacono, 1989), and **behavioral approach system** (J. A. Gray, 1987, 1990, 1994a, 1994b), often abbreviated as **BAS.** You might think of this system as regulating the psychic gas pedal, moving you toward what you want. It's a "go" system, a reward-seeking system (Fowles, 1980).

This set of brain structures is presumed to be involved whenever a person is pursuing an incentive. It is likely that certain parts of the brain are involved in the pursuit of food, others in the pursuit of sex, and others in the pursuit of shade on a hot summer day. But it is thought that the separate parts also link up to an overall BAS. Thus, the BAS is seen as a general mechanism to go after things you want. BAS doesn't rev you up "in neutral," though, with no incentive in mind (Depue & Collins, 1999). It's engaged only in the active pursuit of incentives.

The BAS is also held to be responsible for many kinds of positive emotions (e.g., hope, eagerness, and excitement). These emotions can be viewed as reflecting the anticipation of getting incentives. Researchers have pursued this idea in studies of brain activity. Richard Davidson and his colleagues (and others) have studied what brain areas are active by recording electrical activity (Davidson, 1988, 1992, 1995; Davidson & Sutton, 1995) or by using imaging techniques that capture activity in other ways. While that's happening, the people are exposed to stimuli such as video clips or still images that were chosen to create specific kinds of emotional reactions. The question is which parts of the brain become more active in various situations.

A variety of evidence indicate that incentives (and thus positive feelings) activate the left prefrontal cortex. More left prefrontal activity has been found in adults presented with incentives (Sobotka, Davidson, & Senulis, 1992) or positive emotional adjectives (Cacioppo & Petty, 1980), and in 10-month-olds viewing their mothers approaching (Fox & Davidson, 1988). Higher *resting* levels in that area predict positive responses to happy films (Wheeler, Davidson, & Tomarken, 1993). Self-reported BAS sensitivity also relates to higher resting levels in that area (Harmon-Jones & Allen,

1997; Sutton & Davidson, 1997). Findings such as these led Davidson and his colleagues to two conclusions: First, the tendency to experience many positive emotions relates to an approach system. Second, that system is based partly in the left prefrontal cortex.

MORE ISSUES IN APPROACH

Recent evidence suggests that what underlies left-prefrontal activation is not positive feelings but something else about the approach motivational process (Harmon-Jones, Lueck, Fearn, & Harmon-Jones, 2006). Sometimes a desire to approach is thwarted. Sometimes a desire to approach is specifically a desire to inflict pain on someone. In both cases, the approach system is engaged, but the emotions—frustration and anger—have a negative valence rather than a positive one. Several studies have linked such emotional experiences to left-prefrontal activation and BAS sensitivity (Carver, 2004; Fox & Davidson, 1988; Harmon-Jones & Allen, 1997; Harmon-Jones & Sigelman, 2001; Harmon-Jones, Vaughn-Scott, Mohr, Sigelman, & Harmon-Jones, 2004).

Another project has linked BAS sensitivity to conditioning. Because the BAS responds selectively to incentives, BAS sensitivity should relate to conditioning involving *positive* outcomes, but not to conditioning involving *negative* outcomes. Research by Zinbarg and Mohlman (1998) supports this idea. A self-report measure of BAS sensitivity predicted speed at learning cues of reward in a conditioning task. This scale did not relate to speed at learning cues of punishment.

One more thing about the approach function: Some neurobiological evidence suggests that there may be social incentive and social threat systems, which overlap partially but not entirely with the more general approach and avoidance systems (Depue & Morrone-Strupinsky, 2005; Panksepp, 1998). Thus, there may be specialized sensitivities to incentives and threats *within relationships*. In support of this idea, Gable (2006) found that hope for affiliation predicted social approach goals and fear of rejection predicted social avoidance goals. Elliot, Gable, and Mapes (2006) have developed a measure to assess social approach and avoidance goals to investigate this idea further.

To sum up, people with reactive approach systems are highly sensitive to incentives, or to cues of good things about to happen. Those whose approach systems are less reactive don't respond as much (either behaviorally or emotionally) to such cues. For example, consider two people with tickets to an upcoming concert by a band they like. Melanie gets excited whenever she thinks about the concert (although it isn't until next week). Every time she thinks about it, she's ready to jump in the car. Melanie is very high in incentive reactivity, or BAS sensitivity. Barbara, on the other hand, is more calm about it. She knows she'll enjoy the concert, but she's not so responsive to thoughts of potential reward. Barbara has less incentive reactivity.

NEUROTRANSMITTERS AND THE APPROACH SYSTEM

Operation of the approach system has been tentatively linked to a specific **neurotransmitter** in the brain. A *neurotransmitter* is a chemical involved in sending messages along nerve pathways. There are many of them, and they seem to have somewhat different roles. Several theorists have argued that a neurotransmitter called **dopamine** is involved in the approach system (Cloninger, 1988; Depue & Collins, 1999; Zuckerman, 1994).

As we noted in Chapter 6, two research teams (Benjamin et al., 1996; Ebstein et al., 1996) linked dopamine to a specific gene, though subsequent research found the link wasn't as reliable as it seemed at first (Ebstein, 2006). The finding was that people with one version of that gene scored higher on personality scales related to approach (novelty seeking). That finding linked *genetics* (variation in a particular gene) to a biological *process* variable (dopamine function) to an aspect of *behavior* (approach of incentives).

Others have used very different methods to study dopamine function. One technique is to assess individual differences in dopamine reactivity using biomedical indicators of response to drug challenges. In several studies, higher dopamine reactivity related to higher trait levels of positive emotionality (Depue, 1995; Depue, Luciana, Arbisi, Collins, & Leon, 1994). Others have used similar procedures to relate dopamine to novelty seeking (Hansenne et al., 2002). Depue and Collins (1999) linked dopamine to aspects of extraversion, including social dominance, enthusiasm, assertiveness, and energy. Research using monkeys also linked dopamine function to greater social dominance (Kaplan, Manuck, Fontenot, & Mann, 2002).

Dopamine function has also been related to performance on particular kinds of tasks (Wacker, Chavanon, & Stemmler, 2006). Higher levels of dopamine relate to being able to hold larger amounts of information in working memory (Barch, 2004; Seamans & Yang, 2004). A link from dopamine to approach is suggested by the fact that people who report high BAS sensitivity also can hold more information in working memory (J. R. Gray & Braver, 2002).

It's also been suggested that low dopamine levels tend to keep people focused on one goal, whereas higher levels produce a flexible shifting among goals (Dreisbach & Goschke, 2004). Of course, shifting of goals can also be seen as distractibility. Consistent with this is evidence that links high levels of dopamine explicitly to distractibility (Frank & O'Reilly, 2006).

It has long been believed that dopamine is involved in reward-based learning (Frank & Claus, 2006; Holroyd & Coles, 2002). For example, a substance that disrupts dopamine function impairs instrumental learning and performance (Andrzejewski, Spencer, & Kelley, 2006). The idea that dopamine is involved in reward-based learning has evolved over the years. One current view is that bursts of dopamine in response to reward increase the learning (and the execution) of approach behavior and that dips in dopamine after nonreward increase the learning (and the execution) of avoidance responses (Frank, Seeberger, & O'Reilly, 2004).

It may be, however, that the effect of dopamine is more on the performance than on actual learning. Studies of mice seem to show that the mice don't need dopamine to learn from reward and that dopamine doesn't increase the value of the reward. However, dopamine is necessary for the mice to *want* the reward and *seek* it in goal-directed action (Peciña, Cagniard, Berridge, Aldridge, & Zhuang, 2003; Robinson, Sandstrom, Denenberg, & Palmiter, 2005). Some have concluded that dopamine is mainly about motivation rather than learning—more specifically, that dopamine is involved in attaching motivational importance to stimuli (Wise, 2004).

Others have looked at these effects from a different angle. Dopaminergic neurons respond intensely when a reward occurs unpredictably, but respond less to rewards that are expected, and diminish responses when an expected reward fails to occur (Schultz, 2000, 2006). This pattern has been seen as indicating that dopamine neurons are involved in detecting unexpected events of two kinds—better and worse than expected. That is, there's an increase in activation when a desirable event is better than expected, no change in activity when an event occurs as expected, and a decrease in activity when an event is worse than expected (Schultz, 2006).

Although discussion of dopamine usually focuses on the context of approach, there is also some evidence of its involvement in stressful situations. There have been a number of reports of dopamine release in animals in response to stress (see Pruessner, Champagne, Meaney, & Dagher, 2004). People undergoing a stressful, anxiety-inducing task have also been shown to experience dopamine elevation (Pruessner et al., 2004). It seems certain that dopamine has multiple functions, rather than one (Seamans & Yang, 2004). Though some of these functions relate to the management of approach, it may not be that all do.

Behavioral Avoidance, or Withdrawal, System

The prior section described an approach system. Many theorists also assume a somewhat distinct system that reacts to punishers and threats, rather than incentives. Gray (1987, 1990, 1994a, 1994b) called it the **behavioral inhibition system (BIS).** Others have labeled a threat-responsive system as an *avoidance system* (Cloninger, 1987) or *withdrawal system* (Davidson, 1988, 1992, 1995). Activity in this system may cause people to *inhibit* movement (especially if they are currently approaching an incentive) or pull back from what they just encountered. You might think of this system as a psychic brake pedal, a "stop" system. You might think of it instead as a "throw-it-into-reverse" system.

The avoidance system is responsive to cues of punishment or danger. When this system is engaged, the person may stop and scan for further cues about the threat, or the person may pull back. Since this is the system that responds to threat, danger, or other to-be-avoided stimuli, this system is also thought to be responsible for feelings such as anxiety, guilt, and revulsion.

Once again, research on cortical activity is consistent with this general view. We said earlier that left-prefrontal areas are more active when people are happy. Right-prefrontal areas are more active when people are feeling anxiety or aversion: for example, when viewing film clips that induce fear and disgust (Davidson, Ekman, Saron, Senulis, & Friesen, 1990). Higher resting levels in that area predict more negative feelings when seeing such films, and they also relate to self-reports of BIS sensitivity (Harmon-Jones & Allen, 1997; Sutton & Davidson, 1997). Findings such as these led Davidson and his colleagues to argue that anxiety relates to a behavioral withdrawal system, which involves the right-prefrontal cortex.

Research on conditioning has also examined the sensitivity of this system. The BIS was theorized to be reactive to punishments, not incentives. Thus, BIS sensitivity should relate to conditioning for *negative* outcomes, not positive ones. This was found by Zinbarg and Mohlman (1998). A self-report measure of BIS sensitivity predicted speed at learning cues of punishment (but not cues of reward). Similar results were reported by Corr, Pickering, and Gray (1997).

To sum up this section, people with reactive avoidance systems are sensitive to threat. This dimension reflects a trait of anxiety proneness. As an example of how it influences experiences, think of two people who just took a psychology test and suspect they did badly. Anxiety-prone Randy is almost in a panic about it. Jessica, who is less anxiety prone, is bothered hardly at all. One of them is reacting emotionally to the sense of threat; the other isn't.

Threat sensitivity and incentive sensitivity are thought to be relatively separate. People presumably differ from each other on both. As a result, all combinations of high and low BAS and BIS sensitivity probably exist. As an example, it might be intuitive to think of sociability as being the opposite of shyness, but that's too simple (Schmidt, 1999). It's possible to be both very sociable (drawn to social incentives) and very shy (fearful of social interaction and avoiding it).

A Revised View of BIS Function

Thus far, we've treated the label *BIS* as equivalent to the label *withdrawal system*. However, differences of opinion have arisen about what to call what. In 2000, Gray and McNaughton revised Gray's (1987, 1990) theory. In the revision, inhibition, instead of threat sensitivity, is the core feature of the BIS (fitting its label: behavioral inhibition system). In the new view, the BIS responds to conflict—of any kind—by inhibiting action and searching for more information. In the new view, a different system altogether is sensitive to threat. Thus, use of the term BIS from the newer Gray and McNaughton (2000) point of view differs from previous use.

This change obviously creates potential for confusion. To minimize confusion, in the rest of the chapter, we do not refer to *BIS* at all. We continue to refer to a threat sensitivity system as managing avoidance. Later on in the chapter, we take up the inhibition of action, because that is a very important function. When we do so, however, we use new terms altogether.

Neurotransmitters and the Avoidance System

As with incentive sensitivity, there have also been efforts to link threat sensitivity to a particular neurotransmitter, but with less consensus. **Serotonin** has long been believed by some people to be involved in threat sensitivity or anxiety (Cloninger, 1987; Handley, 1995; Lesch & Mössner, 1998). However, that view has been strongly challenged (Depue, 1995; Depue & Spoont, 1986; Panksepp & Cox, 1986; Soubrié, 1986; Zuckerman, 2005). The dispute isn't over, and the evidence is complex. Our interpretation of it, however, suggests that serotonin's main influence lies elsewhere (Carver & Miller, 2006). We return to this issue later on.

Another candidate for involvement in anxiety is *gamma-aminobutyric acid,* more commonly known as *GABA* (Roy-Byrne, 2005). There is some research linking sensitivity of GABA receptors to neuroticism (Glue, Wilson, Coupland, Ball, & Nutt, 1995). However, most of what is known about GABA and anxiety comes from studies of anxiety disorders. In fact, most of the studies focus specifically on panic disorder (Zwanzger & Rupprecht, 2005). People with panic disorder have relatively low levels of GABA (Goddard et al., 2001). Treatments that increase GABA reduce anxiety in panic patients (Zwanzger & Rupprecht, 2005).

Yet another likely contributor to the biology of threat is *norepinephrine.* Norepinephrine is produced in response to stress (Morilak et al., 2005), and there is evidence linking it to panic reactions (Bailey, Argyropoulis, Lightman, & Nutt, 2003). Recent research has also shown that problems in regulation of norepinephrine relate selectively to anxiety disorders (Cameron, Abelson, & Young, 2004). This seems to link this chemical specifically to threat sensitivity.

Although there are several candidates for involvement in the brain systems that manage anxiety and avoidance, it may be wise to resist jumping to conclusions. This is an active area of research, and it seems likely that the eventual answer will involve some complexity.

Relating Approach and Avoidance Systems to Traits or Temperaments

Let's stop and look at what we've said thus far in the chapter. Many theorists converge on the idea that one brain system manages approach of incentives and another manages withdrawal from threats (Cacioppo, Gardner, & Berntson, 1999; Watson, Wiese, Vaidya, & Tellegen, 1999). The one that manages approach also creates excitement and other positive feelings. The one that manages withdrawal creates anxiety. How do these ideas fit with ideas from previous chapters?

It's possible to draw some very strong connections. The avoidance system links easily to the trait of neuroticism. As noted in Chapter 6, although some labels for that trait are neutral, anxiety is always at its core. Thus, Larsen and Ketelaar (1991) found that neuroticism predicts susceptibility to a manipulation of anxiety; Carver and White (1994) found the same effect for a measure of threat sensitivity. In sum, neuroticism and anxiety proneness have a great deal in common. (Elliot and Thrash [2002] also provide support for this idea.) In fact, there's little doubt that the brain system we've been describing regarding avoidance is critical to neuroticism.

As also noted in Chapter 4, Tellegen (1985) postulated a temperament termed **negative emotionality.** The idea is that some people are built to have negative emotions frequently and others less frequently (see also Watson & Clark, 1984; Watson & Tellegen, 1985; Watson et al., 1999). This concept resembles both neuroticism and threat sensitivity. As noted in Chapter 6, developmental theorists have also posited an avoidance temperament (e.g., Derryberry & Rothbart, 1997; Eisenberg, 2002; Eisenberg et al., 2004; Kochanska & Knaack, 2003; Rothbart, Ahadi, & Evans, 2000; Rothbart, Ahadi, Hershey, & Fisher, 2001; Rothbart & Bates, 1998; Rothbart & Posner, 1985). Again, there is a good fit.

With respect to approach, there appears to be a link between the BAS and extraversion. Fitting these two together is a little trickier than matching neuroticism and avoidance, partly because theorists differ about what defines *extraversion.* Definitions usually include a sense of activity and agency (Morrone, Depue, Scherer, & White, 2000). Extraversion also suggests a preference for being with others, or sociability (Depue & Morrone-Strupinsky, 2005). Sometimes there's a quality of social dominance or potency (Depue & Collins, 1999). All definitions seem to include a tendency to experience positive emotions.

These various extraversion packages resemble BAS function fairly well. Extraverts are responsive to positive mood manipulations (Larsen & Ketelaar, 1991); those high in BAS sensitivity similarly have more positive feelings to impending reward (Carver & White, 1994). Measures of extraversion correlate with measures of BAS sensitivity (Carver & White, 1994). As noted in Chapter 4, Tellegen (1985) postulated a temperament termed **positive emotionality,** which relates closely to extraversion, and developmental theorists also assume an approach temperament. Zelenski and Larsen (1999) found that measures of extraversion and several BAS constructs all were interrelated, and as a set, they predicted positive feelings. Thus, there is a good deal of consistency.

THE ROLE OF SOCIABILITY

Still, when fitting extraversion to approach sensitivity, there are a couple of areas of uncertainty. Table 7.1 lists several theorists who have written about extraversion and similar traits. The table also lists some qualities the theorists see as belonging to these

Table 7.1 Several Theorists and Qualities They Believe Belong to Extraversion (and alternative traits closely related to extraversion). All incorporate pursuit of incentives and a tendency to experience positive emotions. Many, though not all, include a quality of sociability. A few also include impulsiveness.

Theorist	Preferred Term	Term Incorporates:			
		Pursuit of Incentives	Sociability	Impulsivity	Positive Emotions
Eysenck	Extraversion	X	X		X
Costa & McCrae	Extraversion	X	X		X
Depue	Extraversion	X	X	X	X
Zuckerman	Sociability	X	X		X
Tellegen	Positive emotionality	X	X		X
Cloninger	Novelty seeking	X		X	X
Gray	BAS–Impulsivity	X		X	X

traits. As you can see, there are two qualities for which some difference of opinion arises.

One issue concerns the social quality that's usually considered part of extraversion. That quality is missing from Gray's view of the BAS. That may be simply because Gray ignored sociability altogether. One way to resolve things would be to view BAS sensitivity as sensitivity to *social* incentives. Given that humans are a very social species, it might make sense to think of human approach primarily in terms of approaching social interaction. As noted earlier in the chapter, however, some postulate a separate approach subsystem that's specialized to regulate social approach. Perhaps extraversion actually is a blend of overall BAS sensitivity and social-specific BAS sensitivity.

On the other hand, several recent studies seem to suggest that sociality per se is not the core quality of extraversion. One of these projects, mentioned in Chapter 4, was by Lucas, Diener, Grob, Suh, and Shao (2000). Their studies led them to conclude that the core of extraversion is *reward sensitivity* and the tendency to experience *positive affect*. They inferred that extraverts' social tendencies stem from the fact that social interaction is one source of positive experiences. Indeed, Lucas and Diener (2001) found extraverts were drawn to situations that offered opportunities for pleasant experiences, whether social or nonsocial.

THE ROLE OF IMPULSIVITY

The second issue on which conceptualizations of extraversion differ concerns impulsivity. In this case, however, fewer people currently argue that it should be part of extraversion. Gray used the word *impulsivity* for incentive sensitivity, but it was an unfortunate choice, as he didn't seem to have issues of impulse control in mind. Cloninger includes a kind of impulsiveness in his construct of novelty seeking, but impulsiveness is also involved in his threat sensitivity construct (see Carver & Miller, 2006). Eysenck included impulsiveness in extraversion for years, but he moved it to psychoticism because it consistently related better to psychoticism than to extraversion. Depue and Collins (1999) said that impulsivity with positive affect (the key to extraversion) belongs in extraversion but impulsivity without it doesn't.

Relevant to this issue is a study by Zelenski and Larsen (1999) mentioned earlier. They factor analyzed several personality measures, including measures of impulsivity and threat and incentive sensitivity. They found that measures of impulsivity loaded on a different factor than did extraversion (which loaded on the BAS factor). Also relevant to this issue is evidence from monkey research. One study (Fairbanks, 2001) found that social dominance, which many see as part of extraversion, relates to moderate impulsivity—not high or low.

On the whole, the evidence suggests that impulsivity does not belong in extraversion. Where, then, does it belong?

Impulse, Constraint, Sensation Seeking, and Effortful Control

Many people believe that there's at least one more biologically based dimension of personality. It has had several labels. In each case, the construct incorporates a quality of planfulness versus impulsivity. One label for this dimension is **sensation seeking.** Marvin Zuckerman (e.g., 1971, 1985, 1991, 1992, 1993, 1994, 2005) and his colleagues have studied this variable extensively.

People high in sensation seeking are in search of new, varied, and exciting experiences. Compared to people lower on this trait, they're faster drivers (Zuckerman & Neeb, 1980). They are also more likely to use drugs (Zuckerman, 1979), to increase alcohol use over time (Newcomb & McGee, 1991), to do high-risk sports such as skydiving (Hymbaugh & Garrett, 1974), and to engage in risky antisocial behaviors (Horvath & Zuckerman, 1993). They are more sexually experienced and sexually responsive (Fisher, 1973), and when in relationships, they're more dissatisfied (Thronquist, Zuckerman, & Exline, 1991). In the army, they're more likely to volunteer for combat units (Hobfoll, Rom, & Segal, 1989).

FUNCTIONS OF THE SENSATION-SEEKING DIMENSION

We said earlier that theorists of this group tend to use a functional approach—that is, look for the purpose that a given system might serve. What might be the function of a dimension of sensation seeking? At least two possibilities have been suggested. An early view was that it regulates exposure to stimulus intensity (Zuckerman, 1979, 1991, 1994). High sensation seekers open themselves to stimulation; low sensation seekers protect themselves from it.

Both of these tendencies would have advantages and disadvantages. People high in sensation seeking should function well in overstimulating conditions such as combat, but they may display antisocial and even manic qualities when the situation is less demanding. People lower in sensation seeking are better adapted to most circumstances of life, but they may "shut down" psychologically when things get too intense.

Another broader view of this trait's function relates it to the demands of social living. Zuckerman (1991, 1993) found a higher-order factor he calls **impulsive unsocialized sensation seeking (IUSS).** He thinks IUSS concerns a capacity to inhibit behavior in service of social adaptation. People high on IUSS don't do this very well. IUSS relates

Sensation seekers like to seek out new, varied, and exciting experiences.

inversely to sociability and positively to trait aggressiveness (Zuckerman, 1996; Zuckerman, Kuhlman, Joireman, Teta, & Kraft, 1993). It has been implicated in antisocial personality disorder (Krueger et al., 1994; Rowe, 2001; Zuckerman, 1994). There is also evidence that IUSS involves a focus on the immediate consequences of behavior, rather than longer-term consequences (Joireman, Anderson, & Strathman, 2003). All of these qualities seem to reflect (in part) qualities of impulse versus restraint.

RELATING IUSS TO TRAITS OR TEMPERAMENTS

As with the approach system and the avoidance system, it's useful to stand back and ask how these ideas fit with ideas from previous chapters. There are strong links to several trait models, discussed in Chapter 4 (for more detail see Carver, 2005).

With regard to the five-factor model, IUSS relates inversely to both conscientiousness and agreeableness (Zuckerman, 1996). Recall that low levels of these traits relate to a variety of problems in getting along in life. IUSS also relates positively to psychoticism in Eysenck's model, which concerns disregard of social restraint in pursuit of intense sensations. Similarly, it relates inversely to constraint from Tellegen's (1985) model, which is virtually the opposite of IUSS. Constraint is the holding back of impulses. A description of constraint sounds like a reverse description of the sensation-seeking dimension.

In discussing temperaments in Chapter 6, we noted that impulsivity has been discussed as a temperament. The most elaborate view of that possibility was developed by Rothbart and her colleagues (e.g., Rothbart et al., 2000; Rothbart et al., 2001; Rothbart, Ellis, Rueda, & Posner, 2003; see also Eisenberg, 2002; Eisenberg et al., 2004; Kochanska & Knaack, 2003). The temperament that she called *effortful control* bears a good deal of resemblance to IUSS. It's about being focused and restrained, and it implies a kind of planfulness and an awareness of others' needs. High levels of this temperament early in life relate to fewer problems with antisocial behavior later on (Kochanska & Knaack, 2003).

TWO SOURCES OF IMPULSE AND RESTRAINT

In making comparisons to these trait-and-temperament models, one more thing is worth noting explicitly. In each case, whatever trait IUSS relates to is distinct and separate from the traits relating to extraversion and neuroticism (or to approach and avoidance sensitivities). Clark and Watson (1999) reviewed considerable evidence and concluded that constraint is consistently separate from extraversion (or positive affectivity) and neuroticism (or negative affectivity). Similarly, Depue and Collins (1999) reviewed 11 studies in which two or more personality inventories were jointly factor analyzed. All identified a distinct higher-order trait reflecting impulse versus constraint.

Why, then, did early views of extraversion—and some current views—incorporate impulsivity? One reason seems to be that there are two ways for the separation of impulse and restraint to occur (Carver, 2005). One possibility derives entirely from the balance between incentive sensitivity and threat sensitivity (see the bottom of Figure 7.1). A person with strong appetites and little anxiety will approach impulsively (Arnett, Smith, & Newman, 1997; Avila, 2001); a person with weak appetites and strong anxiety won't behave impulsively (and would certainly not seek out unusual sensations). But with the addition of a system that exerts effortful control (top of Figure 7.1), restraint can have a different source (as can action). People can

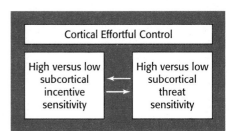

FIGURE 7.1
Impulse can arise from high subcortical incentive sensitivity compared to threat sensitivity; restraint can arise from high threat sensitivity compared to incentive sensitivity. Addition of a system of effortful control can override either of these: impulse *or* constraint.

restrain themselves in order to get along better with other people, or in order to get better outcomes over the long term (Carver, 2005). They can also make themselves do things they don't want to do, such as look happy when they get a gift they don't really like (Kieras, Tobin, Graziano, & Rothbart, 2005). These influences on behavior need not involve anxiety at all.

The planfulness of this system of effortful control is quite different in character from responses involving "grabbing" or "freezing" (or "fleeing"). The latter are more basic, more reactive. Theory relates reactive control to subcortical brain areas (Eisenberg, 2002; Rothbart & Bates, 1998). Effortful control is believed to relate to the part of the brain that manages executive functioning: the prefrontal cortex.

NEUROTRANSMITTERS AND IMPULSE VERSUS CONSTRAINT

Is there a particular brain chemical tied to sensation seeking or constraint? Zuckerman (1994, 1995) suggested a role for an enzyme called *monoamine oxidase (MAO)*. MAO helps regulate several neurotransmitters. MAO levels relate to personality traits such as sensation seeking and novelty seeking (Ruchkin, Koposov, af Klinteberg, Oreland, & Grigorenko, 2005; Zuckerman, 1994). MAO also relates to dominance, aggression (Rowe, 2001; Zuckerman, 1995), and drunk driving (Paaver, Eensoo, Pulver, & Harro, 2006). A gene related to MAO levels has been linked to aggression and impulsivity (Manuck, Flory, Ferrell, Mann, & Muldoon, 2000). Maybe MAO is one key, then, to this system.

On the other hand, some consider MAO level to be mostly an indicator of the activity of serotonergic neurons (Oreland, 2004). Perhaps the key actually lies in serotonin function. There is, in fact, quite a good deal of evidence linking low serotonin function to impulsivity (reviewed by Carver & Miller, 2006). Much of the research assesses serotonin function by responses to drug challenges of various sorts (see Box 7.2).

Sometimes serotonin function is even manipulated. In one such study, experimentally lowering serotonin led to greater hostility and aggressiveness among persons who were already high in aggressive tendencies, but it didn't do anything among persons lower in aggressiveness (Cleare & Bond, 1995). In a later study (Bjork, Dougherty, Moeller, & Swann, 2000), lowering serotonin created higher aggressiveness among highly aggressive men but had the opposite effect among those low in aggressiveness. These findings suggest that low serotonin function made people act more the way they tend to be anyway. That would fit with the idea that low serotonin function means loosening restraint of one's basic tendencies.

Another source of information is cross-sectional studies linking qualities of personality to serotonin function. Many of these studies focus on patient samples, typically comparing patients to controls. A popular group for this kind of study is people displaying impulsive aggression. A good number of studies have related lower serotonin function to a history of fighting and assault (Coccaro, Kavoussi, Cooper, & Hauger, 1997), domestic violence (George et al., 2001), and impulsive aggression more generally (Cleare & Bond, 1997). Although there is a lot of evidence linking low serotonin function to aggressiveness, most of the researchers appear to believe that the link is more directly to impulsiveness or volatility than to hostility per se.

Studies have also examined personality qualities and serotonin function among nonclinical samples. Several early studies (Cleare & Bond, 1997; Depue, 1995; Netter, Hennig, & Rohrmann, 1999) found relations between low serotonin function and elevated aggression–hostility traits, similar to the findings just described. Depue (1995) also found links from low serotonin function to the impulsivity facet of Tellegen's

BOX 7.2 RESEARCH QUESTION:

How Do You Assess Neurotransmitter Function?

Researchers are now examining the role of neurotransmitters in a wide range of behavior. Many of the techniques for studying this require a way to assess neurotransmitter functions in research participants. How is this done? It's more complicated than assessing how much of that particular neurotransmitter is lying around in the person's brain. What's actually at issue is how the neurotransmitter is being *used*.

Serotonin is a particularly interesting case. Serotonin receptors can vary in sensitivity (as can all receptors for neurotransmitters). If someone has a chronically low serotonin level (call him Eddie), the receptors adjust to become more sensitive. If someone has a

chronically high serotonin level (call him Phil), the receptors adjust to become less sensitive. Because Eddie's receptors are now very sensitive, they can do their work with relatively little serotonin. Because Phil's receptors are now relatively insensitive, they respond less to the same amount of serotonin. Phil needs more serotonin to have the same "processing" effect. Eddie has very responsive serotonin functioning, whereas Phil's is less responsive.

The responsiveness of a neurotransmitter system in humans is often assessed by a biochemical challenge. This means challenging the system's ability to regulate itself by administering an agent that perturbs or disrupts its stable state. The drug that's administered stimulates the system to see how big a response occurs.

For example, a drug called *fenfluramine* causes the release of

serotonin from presynaptic storage areas and also inhibits its reuptake. Thus, it causes an increase (that lasts several hours) in the levels of serotonin available for use in serotonergic neural transmission. Receptors in the hypothalamus sense this increase in serotonin and cause the pituitary gland to release prolactin into circulation. This eventually helps bring the serotonin level back down, but it takes a while. Prolactin concentrations are easy to assess. Researchers track the prolactin level and determine its peak increase over a period of three to five hours after the fenfluramine is taken. That peak prolactin response (the increase over baseline) is an index of how responsive the serotonin system is (e.g., Manuck et al., 2000). A large rise in prolactin means a sensitive or responsive serotonin system.

---

constraint scale, the aggression facet of Tellegen's negative emotionality scale, to two sensation-seeking subscales, and to several indices of impulsiveness. Depue also looked more closely at hostility and found the strongest relations of low serotonin function to subscales for impulsive, action-oriented aggression, rather than more passive, cognitive forms. A more recent study (Hennig, Reuter, Netter, Burk, & Landt, 2005) produced similar results.

Other research has had a broader focus. Several studies have been done using personality inventories, sometimes along with other measures. One of them (Manuck et al., 1998) used the NEO-PI-R plus additional measures in a community sample. All effects that emerged did so only among men. Low serotonin function related to greater life history of aggression and impulsiveness, consistent with previous results. Low serotonin function also related to higher neuroticism (from the NEO-PI-R) and the neuroticism facet angry hostility. (Other facets were not tested.) High serotonin function related to higher conscientiousness (from the NEO-PI-R).

There's also one more interesting twist to the evidence. Zald and Depue (2001) argued that serotonin should inhibit positive reactions as well as negative. To test this, they had men track their emotions for two weeks. They computed averages separately for positive and negative feelings and then related them to the men's levels of serotonin function. Higher serotonin function related to less negative affect, consistent with findings just reviewed. However, higher serotonin function also related to lower levels of *positive* feelings (interested, active, attentive, and enthusiastic). Thus, serotonin may provide a constraining influence over the biological systems that manage affects of both sorts.

The pattern from this research as a whole seems consistent with the view that serotonergic pathways are involved in impulse control (Depue, 1995; Depue & Collins, 1999; Depue & Spoont, 1986; Manuck, Flory, Muldoon, & Ferrell, 2003; Soubrié, 1986; Zuckerman, 2005). Further, it appears to be consistent with a view in which the resulting restraint (when it does occur) is effortful, rather than an involuntary reaction to anxiety.

Why, then, has the idea that serotonin relates to anxiety held on for so long? There probably are several reasons. As noted earlier, one of them is the common assumption that anxiety is the prime reason for restraint. Another concerns the personality measures used in the research. Some measures are better than others at keeping various qualities separate. Those used in some of the early research on this topic tend to blur threat sensitivity with impulsiveness. Indeed, even the better measures do not really sort the pieces out fully unless facets are examined (Carver & Miller, 2006).

Hormones and Personality

We turn now to a different aspect of biology and personality: *hormones.* An important group is sex hormones. They determine a developing embryo's physical sexual characteristics. They also influence physical characteristics at other stages of development. We won't explore all the ways sex hormones influence behavior (see, e.g., Le Vay, 1993; Rubin, Reinisch, & Haskett, 1981; Tavris & Wade, 1984), but we'll examine a few of them, focusing on testosterone.

HORMONES, THE BODY, AND THE BRAIN

Sex hormones are important in a variety of ways from very early in life. Normal males have higher testosterone than normal females from week 8 to week 24 of gestation, from about the first through the fifth month after birth, and again after puberty (Le Vay, 1993). Testosterone differences in gestation appear essential to changes in the nervous system that create normal male and female physical development. Many believe the hormones also change the brain in ways that result in behavioral differences (Breedlove, 1994; Le Vay, 1993).

The basic template for a human body is female. Only if hormones cause specific changes to occur does a body emerge that looks male. If a genetic male isn't exposed to androgen ("male-making") hormones at critical points in development, the result is an exterior that looks female. If a genetic female is exposed to testosterone at the same points, the result is an exterior that looks male (Breedlove, 1994). During typical fetal development, of course, only males are exposed to enough androgen to be masculinized.

The hormones that guide the body in its sexual development also affect nerve cells (Breedlove, 1992; Le Vay, 1993). They organize the developing brains of males and females differently, in subtle ways (Cohen-Bendahan, van de Beek, & Berenbaum, 2005). Animal research suggests there aren't just two patterns but a broad range of variation, with male and female patterns as the extremes (Panksepp, 1998). The genders tend to differ in linkages among synapses and in the size of some brain structures. For example, the two sides of the cortex are more fully interconnected in women than men (Le Vay, 1993). Men are more visually dominated than women (Panksepp, 1998). Interestingly, there's evidence that the brains of gay men structurally resemble those of women more than those of heterosexual men (Allen & Gorski, 1992; Le Vay, 1991).

How might these differences in the nervous system relate to personality? We said earlier that exposure to androgens may "masculinize" the nervous system. Several things may follow from this.

EARLY HORMONAL EXPOSURE AND BEHAVIOR

Early exposure to hormones, even prenatal exposure, can influence later behavior. One study (Reinisch, 1981) looked at children whose mothers had received synthetic hormones that act like testosterone while being treated for complications in their pregnancies. Each child thus was exposed to the hormones prenatally (an average of 11 years earlier) during a critical phase of development. The other group was their same-sex siblings (to match as closely as possible on genetic and environmental variables).

Each child completed a self-report measure in which six situations were described, each involving interpersonal conflict. The children made decisions about what they would do in each situation. The measure was the likelihood of responding with physical aggression, verbal aggression, withdrawal, and nonaggressive coping.

The study yielded two separate effects, both bearing on the choice of physical aggression as a response to conflict (see Figure 7.2). The first was a sex difference: Boys chose this response more than girls did. There was also an effect of prenatal exposure to the hormone. Children who'd been exposed chose physical aggression more than did those who hadn't been exposed. This was true both for boys and for girls.

This study is intriguing for a couple of reasons. It's clear that a biological variable—the hormone—influenced the behavior. It's less clear *how* it did so. Animal research indicates that exposure to male hormones during early development increases aggressive displays (Reinisch, 1981). But that wasn't the behavior measured here. This study measured no aggressive acts, just self-reports indicating the choice of aggressive acts. Thus, any masculinizing influence on the nervous system had to filter through a lot of cognition to be displayed.

In another project, Berenbaum and Hines (1992) studied children with a genetic disorder that causes high levels of androgens (masculinizing hormones) prenatally and soon after birth. Years later (ages 3 to 8), these children (and unaffected same-sex relatives) were observed as they played individually. Available were toys that had been determined to be generally preferred by boys and by girls. The question was who would play with which toys.

The androgen-exposed girls spent more time with the boys' toys and less time with the girls' toys than did unexposed girls (see Figure 7.3). In fact, they displayed a preference pattern like that of boys. Preferences among the boys were unaffected by exposure. These findings suggest that a masculinizing hormone can influence the activities children engage in much later in life.

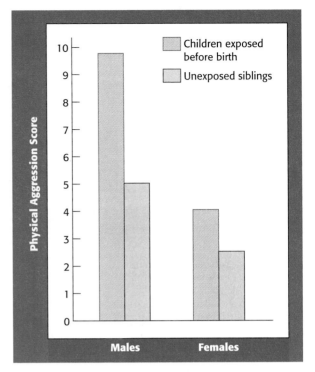

FIGURE 7.2
Average (self-report) physical aggression scores during childhood for boys and girls who had been exposed to synthetic hormones before birth and for their sex-matched siblings who had not been exposed. Exposure to the hormone produced elevated aggression scores for both boys and girls.

Source: Adapted from Reinisch, 1981.

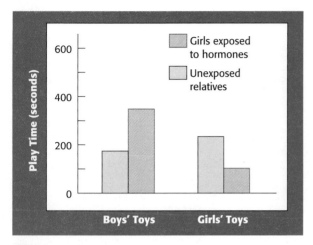

FIGURE 7.3
Amount of time two groups of girls played in a free-play setting with toys generally preferred by boys and toys generally preferred by girls. Some of the girls had been exposed to masculinizing hormones before birth and shortly afterward; the others had not been exposed. *Source: Adapted from Berenbaum & Hines, 1992.*

Androgens come from several sources. Exposure through a mother's medical treatment during pregnancy is one. Another is the adrenal glands, which secrete androgen normally. High levels of natural androgen in girls have been related to greater involvement in sports that involve rough body contact (Kimura, 1999), activities that are more typical of boys. Another study found that higher levels of naturally occurring fetal testostrone predicted lower levels of empathy at age 4 (Knickmeyer, Baron-Cohen, Raggatt, Taylor, & Hackett, 2006).

Other research suggests that hormones also influence play styles. Jacklin, Maccoby, and Doering (1983) found that testosterone levels at birth were related to boldness versus timidity in infant boys over the next 18 months. Boldness was assessed by exposing children to novel (and thus somewhat scary) toys. Higher estradiol (an estrogen) related to more timidity among the boys. No association with a hormone was significant among the girls in the study.

The findings thus are somewhat mixed, but they appear generally consistent with the idea that early exposure to masculinizing hormones can influence behavior. It can increase the potential for aggression, lead to preference for masculine toys, and enhance boldness.

TESTOSTERONE AND ADULT PERSONALITY

A good deal of research on sex hormones and personality examines how current levels of testosterone relate to behavior. That research is several steps away from examining the idea that testosterone masculinizes the nervous system. Yet it shares with it the theme that testosterone is involved in regulating important qualities of behavior. Much of the pioneering research in this area was conducted by James Dabbs and his colleagues (see Dabbs & Dabbs, 2000).

Testosterone is a sex hormone, but research focuses more often on dominance and antisocial behavior than sexual behavior. One study of men in prison (Dabbs, Frady, Carr, & Besch, 1987) found inmates high in testosterone had violated prison rules more often and were more dominant than those lower in testosterone. They were also more likely to have committed violent crimes. Similar results have come from female inmates (Dabbs, Ruback, Frady, Hopper, & Sgoutas, 1988). In a sample of men who had committed murder, those high in testosterone were more likely to have planned the act ahead of time and to have killed people they knew (Dabbs, Riad, & Chance, 2001).

Another study examined testosterone and antisocial behaviors in a noncriminal population: military veterans (Dabbs & Morris, 1990). Men higher in testosterone had larger numbers of sex partners and were more likely to abuse alcohol and other drugs. They were more likely to have gone absent without leave in the military and to have assaulted others. They were also more likely to have had trouble with parents, teachers, and classmates while growing up (see also Box 7.3). These effects were strongest by far among men of low-socioeconomic status (SES).

Being low SES can increase the ill effects of high testosterone, and research also suggests that high testosterone tends to lead men *into* lower-SES occupations (Dabbs, 1992a). This seems to be because high testosterone promotes antisocial behavior and

BOX 7.3 STEROIDS

An Unintended Path to Aggression

Discussing the effects of testosterone on behavior brings up a related topic: bodybuilding and its excesses. The appeal of bodybuilding comes partly from the result: a body that looks as though it's chiseled from rock. Cultural expectations of men's bodies (as reflected in *Playgirl* photos) have shifted over the decades, becoming increasingly dense and muscular (Leit, Pope, & Gray, 2001). These expectations create pressure on men to look that way.

The desire for a well-formed body has led many people into the use of **anabolic steroids.** The word *anabolic* means "building up." Anabolic steroids are chemicals that mimic the body's tendency to rebuild muscle tissues that have been stressed or exercised. Your body gives you small doses of such chemicals, producing growth in muscle size. Using steroids gives you a much bigger dose. Steroids thus let you speed up and exaggerate the building of muscles in ways that exercise alone can't do. That's why people use them.

Indeed, some people are using steroids and steroidlike substances without fully realizing it. So-called dietary supplements, which many use, are often potent drugs. One survey of gym users found that 18% of men said they used adrenal hormones, 25% used ephedrine, and another 5% used anabolic steroids (Kanayama, Gruber, Pope, Borowiecki, & Hudson, 2001). A survey by the National Institute on Drug Abuse found that steroid use more than doubled among high school sophomores from 1992 to 2000.

Many users don't realize that steroids are synthetic hormones. Steroids are related to testosterone (that's why men's muscles tend to be larger than women's). Testosterone is involved in many things, not just building muscle tissue. Consequently, people who use steroids for larger muscles are in for a surprise: There can be unintended and unpleasant side effects.

Some of these effects are physical. If you're a man, part of your body sees the steroids as testosterone. It reacts to what looks like too much testosterone by shutting down production of more. The results are a lowered sperm count and a decreased sex drive. (The steroids don't act like testosterone in those respects.) If you're a woman, steroids cause masculinizing effects: shrinking breasts, a deepening voice, and a growth in facial and body hair (Gruber & Pope, 2000).

Steroids also have behavioral effects, which are of particular interest here. As you've read in the main text, studies link testosterone to dominance and aggressiveness. Steroids produce much the same effects (even among hamsters; Grimes, Ricci, & Melloni, 2006). Because the doses tend to be large, so are the effects. Heavy steroid use can yield irrational bursts of anger that are popularly referred to as "roid rages." Adverse behavioral and psychological responses aren't limited to men, either. In a sample of women users, 56% reported hypomanic symptoms during steroid use, and 40% reported depressive symptoms during steroid withdrawal (Gruber & Pope, 2000). Ominously, evidence from animal research suggests that steroid use during adolescence can create aggressive tendencies that remain after the steroid is withdrawn (Harrison, Connor, Nowak, Nash, & Melloni, 2000).

These effects are bad enough in the average person. But bodybuilding and steroid use aren't limited to the average person. Bodybuilding has considerable appeal for people who already have a strong streak of dominance and aggressiveness. Add steroids to an already aggressive personality, and the result is a potential for serious violence.

disruption of education. Both of these factors then lead people away from white-collar occupations.

Differences in testosterone relate to occupations in other ways, as well, fitting a link between testosterone and social dominance (Mazur & Booth, 1998). For example, trial lawyers (of both genders) are higher in testosterone than nontrial lawyers (Dabbs, Alford, & Fielden, 1998). Actors and professional football players have high levels of testosterone (Dabbs, de La Rue, & Williams, 1990), and ministers have low levels. (College professors, if you must know, are in the middle.)

Why are actors so different from ministers? After all, they're both on stage. Dabbs et al. (1990) suggested that actors must be dominant constantly, because their reputation is only as good as their last show. Ministers are in a framework that tolerates more variability. Further, the actor's role is to seek and hold onto glory, whereas a minister's role is to be self-effacing.

Research suggests a link between testosterone level and aggression.

Effects of testosterone occur in many small ways that are related to social potency and dominance. In one study, testosterone related to deeper voices among men (Dabbs & Mallinger, 1999). In studies of brief interactions with strangers, participants higher in testosterone entered more quickly, focused more directly on the other person, and displayed more independence and confidence than those with less testosterone (Dabbs, Bernieri, Strong, Campo, & Milun, 2001). Even young children high in testosterone are more independent on the playground than those with lower testosterone (Strong & Dabbs, 2000).

The role of testosterone in dominance is displayed in other ways as well. What happens if people low in testosterone are put into positions of high status? What happens if people high in testosterone are put into positions of low status? In both cases, the people become upset and perform poorly (Josephs, Sellers, Newman, & Mehta, 2006). When the situations are reversed, however, everyone feels better and performs better.

The dominance that's linked to high testosterone is useful in many contexts, but it can interfere with relationships. Booth and Dabbs (1993) found that men with higher testosterone were less likely to have married. If they did marry, they were more likely to divorce. They were also more likely to have had extramarital sex and to commit domestic abuse. Men high in testosterone have smiles that are less friendly than men lower in testosterone, and they express more dominance in their gaze when in conversation (Dabbs, 1992b, 1997). Members of low-testosterone fraternities are friendly and smile a lot, whereas members of high-testosterone fraternities are wilder and more unruly (Dabbs, Hargrove, & Heusel, 1996).

Several studies have related testosterone to personality measures. In two studies, personality data and testosterone data were factor analyzed (Daitzman & Zuckerman, 1980; Udry & Talbert, 1988). In both cases, a factor formed around testosterone, with overtones of impulsiveness, sensation seeking, and dominance. Udry and Talbert's (1988) factor included these self-ratings: cynical, dominant, sarcastic, spontaneous, persistent, and uninhibited. Such findings may relate back to work on brain functions and impulsivity, discussed earlier in the chapter.

CYCLE OF TESTOSTERONE AND ACTION

It may be most obvious to think about testosterone in terms of stable individual differences. However, testosterone is also part of a dynamic system that changes over time and events (Dabbs, 1992b). Levels of testosterone shift in response to social situations of several types. These shifts may, in turn, go on to influence the person's later behavior.

Testosterone levels rise after certain kinds of positive experience. As shown in Figure 7.4, testosterone rises after success at a competitive event (Mazur, Booth, & Dabbs, 1992) and falls after a failure or humiliation. It rises when your team wins and falls when your team loses (Bernhardt, Dabbs, Fielden, & Lutter, 1998). It rises when you are confronted with the challenge of an insult (Nisbett & Cohen, 1996). It rises (for both men and women) after sexual intercourse (Dabbs & Mohammed, 1992). Even fooling around with a gun for a few minutes can make testosterone increase (Klinesmith, Kasser, & McAndrew, 2006).

Such changes in testosterone also have implications for subsequent behavior. Increases in testosterone make people more sexually active (Dabbs, 1992b). An increase in testosterone can also make a person more assertive and may lead him to seek out new competition and chances to be dominant (Mazur, 1985; Mazur et al., 1992). It makes people more responsive to possible reward and less responsive to possible losses (van Honk, Schutter, Hermans, Putman, Tuiten, & Koppeschaar, 2004). Decreases in testosterone after a failure may cause a person to be less assertive and avoid new competition. Thus, in either case (success or failure), there's a tendency toward a spiraling effect: A given outcome tends to promote more of the same outcome.

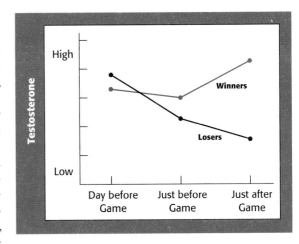

FIGURE 7.4
Testosterone levels among chess players who won or lost close matches in a citywide tournament. *Source: Adapted from Mazur et al., 1992.*

TESTOSTERONE, DOMINANCE, AND EVOLUTIONARY PSYCHOLOGY

Let's step back from these studies to consider a broader implication. The findings as a group seem to fit with one of the themes of evolutionary psychology, discussed in Chapter 6.

Recall that evolutionary thinking includes the idea that selection pressures led to certain gender differences. These differences stem from the fact that human females have greater investment than males in offspring (through the long period of pregnancy and mothering). Females are believed to be choosy about mates for this reason, trying to find one who will provide resources for their children. A gender difference in dominance and aggression is also believed to follow from the differing selection pressures.

In this view, aggression can increase males' opportunities to mate. Aggressiveness helps males establish dominance and status. Evidence for this idea comes from both monkeys and humans. One study found that when male monkeys in a troupe were threatened by an outside rival, their testosterone went up, presumably to facilitate aggression and dominance displays (Cristóbal-Azkarate, Chavira, Boeck, Rodríguez-Luna, & Veà, 2006). An extensive review of relevant literature in humans supports that conclusion and others as well (Archer, 2006). For example, when men are required to care for offspring, testosterone decreases.

There are also interesting individual differences in testosterone effects. For example, after being insulted, testosterone rises more among men from the American South than men from the North (Cohen, Nisbett, Bowdle, & Schwarz, 1996). This has been interpreted as indicating that there is a stronger culture of honor in the South, which increases the impact of insults.

Overt aggressiveness in females doesn't confer the same advantage as it does to men and may even be a disadvantage. It can create the potential for damage to an unborn or young child. It also interferes with their more important activities (bearing and raising children). Nonetheless, testosterone does relate to aggression among women as well as men (Archer, 2006). That this can be a problem for women is suggested by findings that this assertive style interferes with forming alliances in female groups (Archer & Coyne, 2005).

Dabbs (1992b, 1998) notes an interesting irony about testosterone effects. In the evolutionary view, males are high in testosterone and dominance, because physical domination over other males brought access to mates. In recent millennia, however, the rules have changed somewhat. Success is now defined partly in socioeconomic terms, rather than by physical dominance. A man who's too preoccupied with displays and posturing may have trouble gaining the skills needed for economic and social power. Thus, a quality that was important in prehistory may actually interfere with success in today's world.

RESPONDING TO STRESS: MEN, WOMEN, AND OXYTOCIN

Another hormonal influence has drawn considerable attention in recent years. It concerns responses to stress, but extends far beyond. A phrase that's well known in psychology, coined long ago by Cannon (1932) is the *fight-or-flight response*. It refers to the fact that when an animal confronts a predator or competitor, it has two obvious adaptive choices: to attack (hoping to overcome the other) or to flee (hoping to escape). Presumably, the flight response connects in some way to the avoidance that was discussed earlier in the chapter. Apparently, there's a link between the fight response and the system of impulsivity, also discussed earlier in the chapter.

It's often been assumed that these are the only important responses to threat. Shelley Taylor (2002) and her colleagues (Taylor, Klein, Lewis, Gruenewald, Gurung, & Updegraff, 2000) have argued that this assumption is wrong. As they point out, most of the evidence for that view comes from studies of males (and mostly male rats, at that). Females have been studied in a few stressful contexts, but the behavior examined in those studies hasn't been about fight or flight. Rather, the behavior has concerned affiliation, particularly affiliation with other women.

Taylor et al. (2000) argued that focusing on male behavior caused an important set of responses to stress to be widely ignored. They refer to these responses, which are stronger in females than in males, with the phrase *tend-and-befriend*. Taylor et al. think the existence of these responses reflects a difference in evolutionary pressures on males and females, due to differing investment in offspring. That is, as noted just earlier, fighting and fleeing may make good sense for males, who aren't carrying offspring (or pregnant). It makes less sense for females. Females thus may have evolved strategies that benefit both themselves and their offspring.

Tending refers to calming offspring. This protects them from harm. That is, if they don't cry, they (and you) fade into the background, where the threat is less. By extension, you do the same for adults you're close to who are stressed. By soothing them, you put them into a situation of less threat. *Befriending* means affiliating and bonding with others. This reduces certain kinds of risk (there's greater safety in numbers) and increases the chances of receiving tending from each other when needed (Taylor, 2002).

This pattern of response is believed to derive from the system that produces attachment between infant and caregiver. Attachment is often discussed from the perspective of the infant's bond to a caregiver (Chapter 11). It's less often discussed the other way around. Yet there's a good deal of research on this topic (mostly with lower animals), and aspects of the biological mechanism that creates it have been identified (Panksepp, 1998).

This system involves a hormone called *oxytocin*. It acts to relax and sedate (e.g., Light, Smith, Johns, Brownley, Hofheimer, & Amico, 2000), and it reduces fear. Both males and females have this hormone, but females seem to have more of it. Further, androgens inhibit its release under stress, and estrogen increases its effects (see Taylor et al., 2000). Thus, men and women react somewhat differently to stress. Men tend to remove themselves from social interaction; women immerse themselves in nurturing those around them (Repetti, 1989).

The idea that oxytocin is involved (along with endogenous opioids) in mother–infant bonding is a starting point. But it's also argued that oxytocin is involved in social bonding more generally (Carter, 1998; Panksepp, 1998; Taylor et al., 2000; Turner, Altemus, Enos, Cooper, & McGuinness, 1999). Animal research shows oxytocin plays a key role in adult pair bonding in some species. It is released during orgasm, childbirth, massage, and breastfeeding (Matthiesen et al., 2001; Turner et al., 1999). It has been found that greater partner support relates to higher oxytocin (Grewen, Girdler, Amico, & Light, 2005). There is also evidence that receiving a jolt of oxytocin causes people to experience an increase in trust, a willingness to take on risks in the context of a social bond with a stranger (Kosfeld, Heinrichs, Zak, Fischbacher, & Fehr, 2005).

And what of personality? There definitely are individual differences in oxytocin release to particular stimuli. But thus far there's no clear link between these differences and personality traits. This reflects the fact that human research on oxytocin is just getting momentum, in part because it's harder to study than some other hormones. If oxytocin is important in the formation of social bonds, though, it's a key biological influence on human experience. Undoubtedly, its influence on personality will be the subject of work in years to come.

Assessment

The biological view on personality discussed in this chapter assumes that personality derives from events in the nervous system and hormonal system. If personality is biological, then why not just assess the biological characteristics?

There are a couple of problems with this. In many cases, no one's quite sure what the biological mechanism is, so it's hard to know what to measure. It's also hard to assess biological functions in a way that doesn't require a sensor in the body or the drawing of blood. Nonetheless, some biological methods of assessment are now in use.

ELECTROENCEPHALOGRAMS

An indirect indication of what's going on in the brain can be obtained by recording electrical activity from the skin over the skull. The record is called an **electroencephalogram, or EEG.** The reasoning behind it is that neurons throughout the brain fire at various intervals, creating continuous fluctuations in voltage. Electrodes on the scalp sense these changes. This gives a view of aspects of the activity in the cerebral cortex. Cortical activity is very complex, but it forms patterns that relate to different subjective states.

EEGs have been used for some time as a way of investigating normal personality. In fact, some of the work discussed earlier in the chapter used EEGs. Various regions of the cortex are active to different degrees when people are in various psychological states. Mapping EEG activities in different locations shows what areas of the brain are involved in what kinds of mental activity. For example, it's possible to identify a person who's dominated by incentive motivation or by avoidance motivation by looking at left versus right frontal activation levels at rest (Harmon-Jones & Allen, 1997; Sutton & Davidson, 1997).

NEUROIMAGING

Mapping of brain activities has also moved further inside the brain. One technique is called **positron emission tomography (PET).** PET derives a picture of brain functioning from metabolic activity. The person receives a radioactive form of glucose (the brain's energy source). Later, radioactivity in different brain areas is recorded. Presumably, more active areas use more glucose, resulting in higher radioactivity there. A computer color codes the intensities, producing a brain map in which colors represent levels of brain activity.

One application of the PET procedure is measuring neurotransmitter function. To do this, the person receives a radioactively labeled drug with known effects. The person's brain activity is then compared to its activity when in a nondrugged condition. Differences between the PET scans provide information about the receptor systems involved in the drug's effects.

Another technique, called **magnetic resonance imaging (MRI),** relies on a very subtle property of nerve activity. Functioning nerve cells create magnetic fields. With a good deal of computer assistance, the magnetic resonances of a person's brain can be translated into a visual image. Typically, the image is of slices across the brain, as seen from above. Different slices give different information, because they show different parts of the brain.

At first, MRI images were used primarily to look for structural problems in the brain. For example, if you were having blackouts after an auto accident, you might be asked to undergo an MRI to look for possible damage. MRIs are also now being used in a different way. People are being studied to assess levels of activation in various brain structures, both at rest and in other mental states. The picture from this sort of study, called **functional MRI (fMRI),** is much more detailed than what comes from EEG recordings. Of particular importance is that it lets the brain be viewed in slices at different levels. The result is a very detailed three-dimensional picture about what brain centers are active during the scan. As with PET scans, the images are usually created in multiple colors, with each color representing a different level of activity.

Use of fMRI as a tool to understand how the brain works has increased at an incredible rate over the past decade. It's very expensive (it requires a giant, powerful magnet, plus a lot of skilled technical support). But the fact that it can provide a three-dimensional picture means it can show very precise locations of increases and decreases in neural activity as a function of what the person is doing. People can be placed in different motivational and emotional states while in the device and can engage in diverse tasks. This lets researchers determine which parts of the brain are involved in those various experiences. More and more researchers are thinking of possible uses for this tool. This is a research area that unquestionably will continue to grow enormously in the years to come.

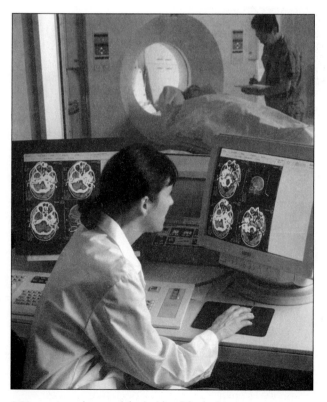

MRIs create an image of the inside of the brain.

Problems in Behavior, and Behavior Change

Let's now turn to problems in behavior. The biological process approach has made large contributions to the understanding of disorders. A full treatment is well beyond the scope of this chapter. We focus here on contributions that relate to the ideas discussed earlier in the chapter.

BIOLOGICAL BASES OF ANXIETY, DEPRESSION, AND ANTISOCIAL PERSONALITY

Recall that a basic assumption of these models is that two motivational systems in the brain manage the approach of incentives and avoidance of threats, respectively. People presumably vary in the strength or sensitivity of these systems. Being too extreme on one or the other system may set a person up for problems.

Perhaps the easiest problem to link to this view is anxiety disorders. The avoidance system creates anxiety in the presence of cues of impending punishment. A person with a very sensitive threat system will experience anxiety easily and frequently. This creates fertile ground for an anxiety disorder to develop. If these people are exposed to frequent punishment during childhood, they learn anxiety responses to many stimuli. The result may be the development of such clinical symptoms as phobias, panic attacks, and obsessive–compulsive disorders.

A related problem is depression. There's less consensus on the biological roots of depression than on those of anxiety (Davidson, Pizzagalli, Nitschke, & Putnam, 2002). Some see depression as a variant of anxiety, reflecting an oversensitive avoidance system. Others tie depression to a weak BAS (e.g., Allen, Iacono, Depue, & Arbisi, 1993; Henriques & Davidson, 1990, 1991). In this view, a person with weak BAS activation has little motivation to approach incentives. The result is the leaden behavioral qualities that typify depression.

Another problem that's often discussed in terms of biological systems is **antisocial personality.** As noted earlier, it involves impulsivity and an inability to restrain antisocial urges. It's sometimes argued that these people have an overactive BAS (Arnett et al., 1997). Thus, they pursue whatever incentive comes to mind. It's sometimes argued that they have deficits in the threat system (Fowles, 1980). Thus, they fail to learn from punishment or aren't motivated to avoid it.

Some think the failure to learn from punishment stems not from a deficient avoidance system but from a failure to stop and think before plowing ahead in pursuit of an incentive (Bernstein, Newman, Wallace, & Luh, 2000; Patterson & Newman, 1993; Schmitt, Brinkley, & Newman, 1999). This would tend to link the antisocial personality to the system that underlies impulsiveness and sensation seeking (Krueger et al., 1994; Rowe, 2001; Zuckerman, 1994). Insufficient MAO (associated with this system) may be a vulnerability, interacting with the environment. In one study (Caspi et al., 2002), boys with genes causing low MAO engaged in more antisocial behavior—but only if they also received maltreatment while growing up (see Figure 7.5). Although men with the combination of low MAO gene and severe maltreatment were only 12% of the male birth cohort, they accounted for 44% of the cohort's

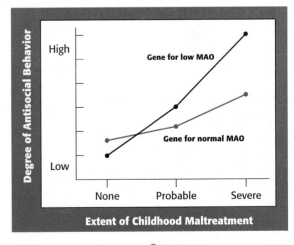

FIGURE 7.5
Scores on an index of antisocial behavior among men with a gene causing low MAO and men with a gene for normal MAO who had experienced either no maltreatment (abuse) during childhood, probably some maltreatment, or severe maltreatment.
Source: Adapted from Caspi et al., 2002.

violent convictions. Indeed, a full 85% of this group developed some sort of antisocial behavior.

Some discussions of antisocial behavior involve other biological systems. Recall that high levels of testosterone relate to various kinds of violent and antisocial behavior (Dabbs & Dabbs, 2000; Dabbs et al., 2001). There's even evidence that high testosterone relates to disruptive behavior in boys as young as 5 to 11 years of age (Chance, Brown, Dabbs, & Casey, 2000). Thus, this set of problems seems to relate to both hormonal and neural processes.

MEDICATION IN THERAPY

The biological process approach to personality also has a relatively straightforward implication for therapy. Many manifestations of problems reflect biological functions. It follows that changing the action of these biological functions should change the manifestation of the disorder. There are several disorders for which this approach seems effective. Because the treatments typically involve administering drugs, they are often called **pharmacotherapy.**

It has long been known that manic–depressive, or bipolar, disorder can be relieved by lithium. About 80% of people with bipolar disorder respond to lithium (Depue, 1979). Besides treating existing symptoms, repeated doses can ward off new symptoms. Unfortunately, lithium has serious unpleasant side effects. Nevertheless, its effectiveness supports two ideas: that the disorder is biological and that its treatment should be (at least in part) biologically based.

A similar case has also been made for treatment of schizophrenia. Research on the biological basis of schizophrenia has looked for ways to treat its symptoms. One hypothesis is that the symptoms reflect too much dopamine (see Walker & Diforio, 1997). As we said earlier, dopamine is a neurotransmitter. With too much dopamine, transmission in certain parts of the nervous system is too easy. With too many messages being sent, communication is disrupted.

This hypothesis is speculative, but it is supported by studies of biochemical treatments for schizophrenic symptoms. Drugs that remove the symptoms of schizophrenia also turn out to lower the levels of usable dopamine in the brain. Apparently the effectiveness of these drugs is related to their ability to block dopamine use. Once again, this finding suggests that the disorder is biological and that treatment should also be biologically based (at least in part).

Drug treatments are also used for disorders that are far less extreme than the two just discussed. Antianxiety drugs are among the most often prescribed of all medications. Current antidepressants—*selective serotonin reuptake inhibitors (SSRIs)*—are used by many people with moderate to mild depression. Indeed, development of this set of antidepressants has led to a far wider use of mood-altering medication than ever before.

The widespread use of these drugs raises a number of questions and issues (Kramer, 1993). One issue concerns the fact that responses to these medications often are much broader than the mere lifting of a depressed mood. People's personalities undergo changes that are subtle but profound and pervasive. People become more confident, more resilient, more decisive—almost more dominant—than they were before. In a sense, they aren't quite the same people as they were before taking the medication. Their very personalities have changed.

Seeing these changes in personality as a function of a slight alteration in brain chemistry raises questions about where personality resides. Personality may consist of the person's biological functioning and the experiences to which it gives rise. Personality may not be a stable entity that stands apart from the symptoms that bring people for therapy. Personality, in the form of the person's biological systems, may be the *source* of the symptoms.

Researchers have gone on to ask whether SSRIs affect people who don't have a disorder. One study (Knutson et al., 1998) gave people either an SSRI or a placebo for four weeks and assessed them before and after. Those given the medication later reported less hostility and negativity (but not greater positive feelings). They also displayed more positive social behavior while working on a cooperative task. Another study (Tse & Bond, 2001) found an increase on a measure of self-direction, which assesses such qualities as purposefulness and resourcefulness.

The availability of drugs with these broad effects on personality raises more questions. How widely should they be prescribed? Should people whose problems aren't severe be given medication if it will make their lives more enjoyable? Should all people have the option of changing their personalities by taking pills? These questions are a long way from being answered.

Biological Processes and Personality: Problems and Prospects

This chapter has discussed the idea that patterns of biological processes have important things to tell us about personality. We wouldn't blame you if you came away feeling that the presentation was a little fragmented. In truth, the ideas themselves are somewhat fragmented. The pieces are coming together, but they're not there yet. As a result, this way of thinking about personality has something of a disjointed feel.

One reason for this is that theories about how the nervous system and hormones influence behavior rely in part on knowledge from other sciences. Ideas in those sciences are continually evolving, causing changes in these ideas about personality. Further, work on these topics is as new as the methodological advances that permit closer looks at how the biological systems function. These methodological advances continue to march forward (Davidson et al., 2000; Lane & Nadel, 2000; Posner & DiGirolamo, 2000). The result is a kaleidoscope of new looks at biological functioning that sometimes have unexpected implications for personality.

For example, many psychologists now have access to PET scans and fMRIs, which illuminate brain functioning in ways only dreamed of a few years ago. The findings generated from these techniques have raised as many new questions as have been answered. Sorting out the picture that such methods reveal will likely be a complex process.

It's clear that there's been progress in these areas of research and thought. To a large extent, theorists agree about what they're trying to account for. There's a general consensus that approach and avoidance (and positive and negative feelings) are important focal points for biological theory building. Almost everyone seems to feel the need to include something more than that, but there's been less consensus about what else to include. Partly for this reason, this way of thinking doesn't yet stand as a fully developed personality theory. It's more of a vantage point, a place from which to look at and consider the nature of personality.

Lest you be tempted to conclude from the disagreements that these theorists aren't doing their homework carefully enough, let us point out that it's not easy to tell what's going on in the nervous system. To really know what connects to what in the brain means tracing neural pathways, which can't be done in human subjects. When animal research is done, the animals can't report directly on the psychological effects of what the researcher is doing. Thus, information often is indirect, and progress can be slow. The functions of the nervous system are being sorted out by research of several types, but there's a long way to go. Until the nature of the organization of the nervous system becomes clearer, personality psychologists of this orientation won't have definitive models.

Although criticisms can be made of various aspects of this way of thinking about personality, this line of work is one of the most active areas of personality psychology today. Many people believe that the mysteries of the mind will be revealed by a better understanding of the brain. They are committed to unraveling those mysteries and their implications for personality. At present, the prospects of this viewpoint seem quite bright indeed.

· SUMMARY ·

The idea that personality is tied to the biological functions of the body leads to a variety of possibilities involving the functions of the nervous system and the endocrine (hormone) system. An initial approach of this sort was Eysenck's theory that brain processes underlie extraversion. He argued that introverts are more cortically aroused than extraverts. Thus, introverts avoid overstimulation, whereas extraverts seek out stimulation.

Others have taken a different path, relying on newer knowledge. It is now often argued that personality rests on an approach system (BAS) that responds to incentives and an avoidance system that responds to threats. Work on emotions suggests that the approach system, which produces positive feelings, involves (in part) the left prefrontal cortex, and that the withdrawal system, which produces feelings such as fear, involves (in part) the right prefrontal cortex. The threat system seems to represent the biological basis for the trait of neuroticism. Some suggest that the BAS represents the biological basis for extraversion.

Many people now believe it is useful to assume another biological variable that is responsible for variations between impulsiveness and sensation seeking (the tendency to seek out novel, complex, and exciting stimuli) and restraint. Sensation seeking relates to Eysenck's dimension of psychoticism and Tellegen's dimension of constraint. Variation in these qualities may concern regulation of exposure to stimulation (as a protective process), and it may concern taking into account other people and long-term goals.

Another aspect of the biological view on personality focuses on the role in behavior played by hormones. Exposure to male hormones before birth can cause people years later to choose more aggressive responses to conflict; it can also increase girls' preference for boys' toys. Testosterone in adults relates to dominance behavior, sometimes expressed in antisocial ways. Testosterone also fluctuates, increasing with challenges and victories and decreasing with failures.

An emerging area of work examines the possibility that another hormone, called *oxytocin,* is important in human social behavior. Oxytocin appears to relate to female responses to stress, termed a tend-and-befriend response. The roots of this response may be in the attachment system, and it may relate to social bonding more generally.

This approach to personality suggests it may be possible to assess personality through biological functions. Although the attempt to do this is in its infancy, some believe recordings of brain activity—particularly fMRIs—hold great promise for the future.

With regard to problems in behavior, high levels of threat sensitivity activity promote disorders involving anxiety. Either a high threat response or a low approach response may contribute to depression. High approach–low avoidance can yield symptoms of antisocial personality, which also relates to impulsive sensation seeking and testosterone. This orientation to personality suggests that therapy based on medication is a means to bring about behavioral change. The idea is that medication can influence the underlying biological system, thereby altering the person's behavior and subjective experience.

· GLOSSARY ·

Anabolic steroids   Chemicals that mimic the body's tendency to rebuild muscle tissues.

Antisocial personality   A person who displays impulsive action with little thought to consequences.

Behavioral approach system (BAS)   The part of the brain that regulates pursuit of incentives.

Behavioral inhibition system (BIS)   The part of the brain that regulates anticipation of punishment.

Dopamine   A neurotransmitter believed to be especially important to approach regulation.

Electroencephalogram (EEG)   A record of overall electrical activity in higher regions of the brain.

Functional MRI (fMRI)   Use of MRI to create a picture of activity inside the brain in different mental states.

Impulsive unsocialized sensation seeking (IUSS)   Trait involving the capacity to inhibit behavior in the service of social adaptation.

Incentives   Things that people desire.

Magnetic resonance imaging (MRI)   A picture of activity inside the brain based on the brain's electromagnetic energy.

Negative emotionality   The predisposition to experience negative feelings frequently.

Neurotransmitter   A chemical involved in sending messages along nerve pathways.

Orienting response   The shift of attention to a stimulus that suddenly appears.

Pharmacotherapy   A therapy based on use of medication.

Positive emotionality   The predisposition to experience positive feelings frequently.

Positron emission tomography (PET)   A picture of activity in the brain based on the brain's metabolism.

Sensation seeking   The tendency to seek out varied, unusual, and exciting stimuli.

Serotonin   A neurotransmitter that some believe is involved in behavioral inhibition.

part 4

The Psychoanalytic Perspective

The Psychoanalytic Perspective: Major Themes and Underlying Assumptions

The *psychoanalytic perspective* originated in the writings of Sigmund Freud. His impact on personality psychology was so strong that his ideas form the essence of a distinct perspective on personality (although others have contributed to it besides him). The psychoanalytic view on personality is the subject of Chapters 8 and 9.

One theme of this perspective, which gave rise to the term *psychodynamic,* is the idea that personality is a dynamic set of processes, always in motion. They sometimes work in harmony with one another and sometimes against one another, but they are never still. Personality is a dynamo—or a bubbling spring—from which emerge forces that can be set free, channeled, modified, or transformed. As long as you're alive, these forces never come to rest.

An important implication of this dynamic quality in personality is that the forces sometimes work against each other. The processes of personality sometimes compete or wrestle for control over the person's behavior. The assumption that pressures within the personality can *conflict* with each other is another theme that's very prominent in the psychoanalytic perspective.

An additional assumption goes hand in hand with this one: Specifically, psychoanalytic thinking emphasizes the role of the unconscious in determining behavior. The conflicts that take place among the elements of personality often occur outside awareness. Many of the motives that people have are also unconscious. The emphasis on unconscious influence is a theme that permeates this perspective on personality.

Another theme in the psychoanalytic perspective is the idea that human experience is suffused with qualities of lust and aggression, sexuality and death. These assumptions tie psychoanalytic thinking to Darwin's theory of evolution (see Ritvo, 1990). They serve as a reminder that humans are—first of all—animals whose purpose in life is reproduction. Although this idea doesn't seem so odd today, the extent to which Freud emphasized the role of sexuality in human life was very unusual at the time.

Indeed, Freud's emphasis on sexuality even extended to his ideas about the development of personality. A fifth theme of the psychoanalytic perspective is that personality is strongly affected by early experiences. More specifically, Freud argued that sexuality is involved at all stages of development, even infancy. Many people found the idea of infantile sexuality either absurd or shocking. Nevertheless, the idea that the fundamentals of personality emerge from the crucible of early experience is deeply embedded in psychoanalytic thought.

Another theme that characterizes psychoanalysis is the idea that defense is an important aspect of human functioning. This idea rests on the assumption that there are things about every person that are threatening to him or her. Maybe you have what you regard as shameful desires; maybe you secretly feel you're unworthy as a human being; or maybe you're afraid the social world will reject you. Whatever it is that most threatens you, psychological processes operate to keep these desires or elements of self-knowledge from overpowering you. The notion of defense is an important aspect of psychoanalytic thought.

The psychoanalytic perspective on personality is extremely metaphorical in nature, but it's hard to point to a single metaphor for human nature that dominates this perspective. Rather, it uses multiple metaphors. Freud was a physician, and the idea of biological processes underlying mental processes often appeared in his writing. Similarly, his concepts of life instincts and death instincts resemble the dual processes of metabolic functioning, continually tearing down and building up. Freud used many other metaphors, as well. Sometimes he likened the psyche to a sociopolitical system making reference to censors, economics, compromises, and repression. Sometimes his analogies were from physics, with personality treated as an energy system and the competition among forces compared to hydraulic systems in which energy focused at one point had an inevitable consequence at another point. At other times, he treated psychological phenomena almost as though they were the products of artistic or literary efforts.

Despite the lack of a single orienting point, or perhaps because of it, the psychoanalytic viewpoint on personality may be characterized fairly as one in which the *quality* of analogy or metaphor figures prominently. Human behavior is to be understood not as the product of any one process but as a reflection of multiple processes whose functioning can be captured only imperfectly by any one metaphor.

A final theme of the psychoanalytic perspective is the idea that mental health depends on a balance of forces in one's life. It's good to express your deep desires, but it's not good to let them control your life. It's good to act morally, but a constant effort to be perfect cripples your personality. It's good to have self-control but not to be overcontrolled. Moderation and balance among these forces provide the healthiest experience of life.

CHAPTER 8

Psychoanalytic Structure and Process

John and his girlfriend, Ann, go to different colleges, a thousand miles apart. It's been hard for them to be separated for long periods of time, and John has finally decided he can't go on this way. He's decided to call Ann and break up. He picks up the phone, dials a number, and hears a voice on the other end of the line say "Hello"—at the dorm where Ann lived last year, before she moved off campus. "Now why'd I dial *that* number?" John wonders to himself.

WHY DID I do that? Most people, most of the time, find it easy to answer this question with no doubt that their answer is correct. Most of us assume a direct link between our intentions and actions. Accidents may interfere with those intentions, but accidents are random.

There's a viewpoint on the nature of personality that sharply challenges these assumptions. It sees behavior as determined partly by inner forces that lie outside your awareness and control. Accidents? This view says they rarely happen. What seems accidental, you've usually done on purpose. You just aren't *aware* of the purpose.

The approach to personality that takes this view is called *psychoanalysis.* Psychoanalytic theory is closely identified with a single theorist, an Austrian physician named Sigmund Freud (although it rests more on historical ideas than is widely realized; Ellenberger, 1970; Erdelyi, 1985). The theory, which evolved over the period from 1895 to 1940, stunned the scientific world when it was proposed (see Box 8.1). It's been one of the most influential views ever developed. Its effects have been felt not just in psychology but in anthropology, political science, sociology, and art and literature. It's hard to think of a single aspect of thought in Western civilization that hasn't been touched in some way by psychoanalytic ideas.

One sign of the impact of psychoanalytic ideas is the extent to which they've crept into everyday language. For example, people often use the term *Freudian slip* to refer to an error in speech that seems to suggest an unconscious feeling or desire. Such slips imply that behavior is caused by forces outside our awareness, an idea from psychoanalysis.

Before getting to the theory, we note two features that make it different from any other in personality psychology. First, Freud was fascinated by symbols, metaphors, and analogies. This fascination is reflected

Box 8.1 Psychoanalysis in Historical Context

The concepts of psychoanalytic theory were formed earlier than any other theory in this book (starting before the turn of the twentieth century). The cultural and scientific context in which the theory arose differed greatly from that of today, and the context strongly influenced the theory's form. To better understand why Freud's ideas took the form they did and why they had the impact they had, consider the world in which he lived.

Freud did his early writing during the latter part of the Victorian era (late 1800s), a time in which middle- and upper-class society had come to view humans as having reached a lofty state of rational self-control, civilization, and near perfection. It was a smug and self-satisfied society. By today's standards, it would be seen as stuffy and hypocritical. For example, sexuality was rarely even acknowledged publicly, never mind openly discussed.

Into this calm society, Freud dropped a cultural bomb. Instead of rational, he said we are driven by forces from the unconscious. Instead of godlike, we are primitive animals. Instead of intellectual beings, we are driven by sexual and destructive urges, even in infancy.

Freud noted that humanity's admiration of itself had suffered three traumatic shocks: The first was the discovery by Copernicus that the earth is not the center of the universe. The second was the assertion by Charles Darwin that humans evolved as animals. The third was Freud's claim that people are at the mercy of forces that are unconscious and uncontrollable. Soon the horror of World War I showed clearly that the veneer of civilization was far thinner than most assumed.

Freud's ideas jolted the scientific world when they were proposed, partly because they conflicted so sharply with widely held assumptions. Another reason was Freud's emphasis on sexuality, particularly infantile sexuality. This caused many to view him as a pervert, obscene and wicked. The fact that he was a Jew in an anti-Semitic society raised additional suspicion. Further, he presented his theories without much evidence, which didn't sit well in the scientific community. All these factors raised controversy. Ironically, the controversy only brought his ideas more attention.

Although Freud's ideas contradicted the assumptions of Victorian society, they didn't arise in an intellectual vacuum. Darwin's earlier assertion that humans were just one sort of animal carried several other assumptions. For instance, Darwin saw all

creatures as driven by instincts to survive and reproduce. Freud's sexual and life instincts resemble these. Although society at large viewed humanity as rational, philosophers such as Schopenhauer and Nietzsche argued that human behavior is often caused by unconscious irrational forces. This idea is echoed in Freud's work.

Freud was also influenced by the ideas of scientists in other fields (Ellenberger, 1970). For example, Freud's view of the human being as an energy system drew directly from then-current ideas in physics and chemistry. Nineteenth-century physicists had also developed the principle of *conservation*, the idea that matter and energy can be transformed but not destroyed. This conservation principle is reflected in Freud's belief that impulses must eventually be expressed, in one form or another.

If Freud had lived in a different time, his metaphors may well have been different. But psychoanalysis lives on in the terms Freud used. As you read this chapter, keep in mind the cultural and scientific context in which the theory was constructed. We've tried to present the theory as it applies to you, in today's world. If aspects of the concepts seem out of date metaphorically, try to keep in mind the world in which they were conceived.

---

both in the theory's form and in its content. The form of the theory uses many analogies. Freud constantly sought new metaphors. He used different ones at different times, and the metaphor used often had an impact on the theory's form. As a result, it can be hard to be sure which ideas are basic and which are metaphors (Erdelyi, 1985).

Freud's fascination with symbol and metaphor is also reflected in the theory's content. Specifically, Freud came to believe that human behavior itself is highly symbolic. People's acts are rarely quite what they seem to be. Instead, those acts symbolize other, more hidden qualities. This is an idea that permeates psychoanalytic theory.

A second feature is that it's hard to separate Freud's theory from the therapy procedures on which he based it or from the assessment that occurs continually within that therapy. Indeed, the very word *psychoanalysis* is applied to an approach to therapy, Freud's method of research, and his theory of personality. The entanglement of theory with therapy is far greater here than in any other approach to personality, and this tends to color all aspects of the theory.

When viewed in its entirety, psychoanalytic theory is very complex. Underlying this complexity, however, is a fairly small number of principles (Kahn, 2002). The theory can be confusing, because its concepts are deeply interwoven. It's hard to talk about any aspect of the theory separate from other aspects. Perhaps the best place to start, though, is Freud's view of how the mind is organized. This is often termed Freud's **topographical model** of mind.

The Topographical Model of Mind

Many people would say the mind has two regions. One region holds *conscious experience:* the thoughts, feelings, and behaviors you're aware of right now. The other contains *memories,* now outside awareness but able to come to awareness easily. Drawing on ideas of other theorists of his time (Ellenberger, 1970), Freud added a third region to this list. Taken together, the three form what Freud thought of as the mind's *topography,* or its surface configuration.

Freud used the term **conscious** much as we use it today, to mean the part of the mind that holds what you're now aware of. People can verbalize conscious experience and think about it in a logical way. The part of the mind that represents ordinary memory is termed **preconscious.** Things in the preconscious, although now not in awareness, can be brought into awareness easily. For example, if you think of your phone number or the name of the last movie you saw, you're bringing that information from the preconscious to consciousness.

Freud used the term **unconscious** in a way that's considerably different from the way it's used in everyday language. He reserved it to stand for a portion of the mind that's not directly accessible to awareness (see also Box 8.2). Freud viewed the unconscious as being (in part) a repository for urges, feelings, and ideas that are tied to anxiety, conflict, and pain (e.g., Rhawn, 1980). Being unconscious doesn't mean they're gone, though. *They exert a continuing influence* on later actions and conscious experience.

In this view, the mind is like an iceberg. The tip of the iceberg is consciousness. The much larger part—the part below water—is outside awareness. Some of it—the part you can see through the water—is the preconscious. The vast majority of it, however—the part you can't see—is the unconscious. Although the conscious and preconscious influence behavior, Freud saw them as less important than the unconscious. The unconscious is where Freud thought the core operations of personality take place.

The three levels of consciousness form the topographical model of the mind (see Figure 8.1 on page 164). Material passes easily from conscious to preconscious and back again. Material from both of these can slip into the unconscious. Truly unconscious material, however, can't be brought voluntarily to awareness because of psychological forces that keep it hidden. These regions of the mind constitute the theater in which the dynamics of personality are played out.

BOX 8.2 TODAY'S VIEWS ON THE UNCONSCIOUS

As long as psychology has existed, it has been apparent that events outside awareness influence what happens in awareness. Hardly anyone has assumed an unconscious as contentious and conflicted as Freud did. But many have found it necessary to make assumptions about what's going on in the unconscious.

In recent years, interest in how the mind works has grown dramatically, along with the field of *cognitive psychology* (more about cognitive processes comes up in Chapter 16). Theorists now view the unconscious with a vastly different lens than Freud did (Bargh, 1997; Epstein, 1994). The unconscious is still seen as part of the mind to which we don't have ready access, but for different reasons. Today's theorists sometimes talk of the *cognitive unconscious,* as opposed to the *psychodynamic unconscious* (for a thorough review see Hassin, Uleman, & Bargh, 2005).

From today's point of view, *consciousness* is a sort of workspace where you consider information and make judgments, come to decisions, and form intentions. If these processes become sufficiently routine, they begin to occur automatically, outside awareness. What makes things routine? Some processes are innately routine. You don't have to think about making your digestive juices flow or having your heart beat, and you'd have trouble bringing into consciousness the processes by which those events take place.

Other processes become routine from practice. As you practice anything (a tennis stroke, a new recipe, typing), what happens changes over repetitions. The first few times, you devote lots of attention to it. As you do it over and over, it starts to feel more fluid and go more smoothly. The more you practice, the less attention it needs. When you've done it enough, you disregard it almost totally. When an activity is *very* automatic, the processes have become unconscious. You no longer have access to them as you did when you were just starting out. One well-known study, for example, found that people couldn't accurately report the basis of a decision they'd just made; instead they fell back on stereotypes (Nisbett & Wilson, 1977). Automation seems to occur even for higher mental processes (Bargh & Ferguson, 2000). Even goals can become activated and pursued without the person being aware of it (Bargh, Gollwitzer, Lee-Chai, Barndollar, & Trötschel, 2001).

Seymour Epstein (1994) argues that all these phenomena and more reflect what he calls an *experiential* mode of processing. This mode of processing occurs in parallel to, but distinct from, rational processing. The experiential system is emotional and nonverbal, rather than deliberative and verbal. Its functioning is fast and largely out of awareness. Epstein argues that an unconscious as chaotic as the one Freud assumed is very unlikely. Being so poorly fit to reality, it couldn't possibly have survived. On the other hand, an unconscious such as Epstein argues for has much more adaptive value.

In sum, many aspects of people's experience are influenced by processes that occur outside awareness. Such influences occur when you form perceptions and impressions of other people and when you make judgments about how likely something is to happen. Such influences can also affect your mood states and your actions. Whether you agree with Freud about what defines the *content* of the unconscious, it's clear that he was right about its existence.

Aspects of Personality: The Structural Model

Freud (1962/1923) also developed a **structural model** of personality, which complements the topographical model. He saw personality as having three aspects, which work with each other to create the complexity of human behavior. They aren't physical entities but rather labels for three aspects of functioning. They are known as *id,* *ego,* and *superego.*

Id

The **id** is the original component of personality, the only one present at birth. *Id* (the Latin word meaning "it") is all the inherited, instinctive, primitive aspects of personality. The id functions entirely in the unconscious. It's closely tied to basic biological

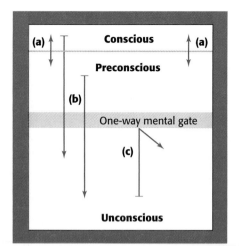

FIGURE 8.1
Graphic representation of Freud's topographical model of the mind. (A) Material can pass easily back and forth between the conscious and preconscious portions of the mind. (B) Material can also move from the conscious and preconscious into the unconscious. But once material is in the unconscious, the person is prevented from having conscious access to it because (C) a mental gate prevents retrieval.

processes, from which it draws energy. Indeed, Freud believed that *all* psychic energy comes through the id. Thus, the id is the "engine" of personality.

The id follows what's called the **pleasure principle:** that needs should be satisfied immediately (Freud, 1949/1940). Unsatisfied needs are aversive tension states. They should be gratified whenever they arise to prevent the tension. Under the pleasure principle, any increase in hunger should cause an attempt to eat. Any twinge of sexual desire should cause an attempt to get sexual gratification.

At first glance, this looks great. Who wants to walk around with inner tensions? There's a problem, though. The pleasure principle doesn't concern *how* needs are to be met. It doesn't say that needs should be met in a way that takes into account risks or problems. It just says that needs are to be met at once.

Acting totally by the pleasure principle would soon get you into a lot of trouble. There's a complex and threatening world out there. A hungry person can't just rush across a street filled with zooming cars to get to food. Social reality also presents problems. For example, if you grab your roommate's pizza before he can get to it (or if you get too friendly with his girlfriend), you may find yourself with an angry roommate on your hands.

Nonetheless, the pleasure principle means that when any tension arises, the id tries to discharge it. The id's mechanism for doing that is called the **primary process.** This entails forming a mental image (fantasy, dream, or hallucination) of an object or event that would satisfy the need and becoming involved with that image. In the case of a hungry infant, the primary process might produce an image of a mother's breast or a bottle. When you're separated from someone you love, the primary process produces images of that person. The experience of having such an image is called **wish fulfillment.**

Tension reduction by primary process has a drawback, however. The primary process can't distinguish between image and reality. Primary process thought may reduce tension briefly, but it can't do so by itself in the long run. The hungry infant that imagines sucking at a nipple won't be satisfied for long. The person who misses a loved one won't be content with fantasies, no matter how vivid. This illustrates again how the id doesn't take reality into account. It's in a world of its own wishes.

Ego

Because the id and its primary process can't deal well with reality, a second set of functions develops, termed **ego** (the Latin word for "I"). The ego evolves from the id and harnesses part of the id's energy for its own use. Ego focuses on making sure id impulses are expressed *effectively,* by taking into account the external world. Because of this concern with the outside world, most ego functioning is in the conscious and preconscious. Given the ego's ties to the id, however, it also functions in the unconscious.

The ego is said to follow the **reality principle:** the taking into account of external reality along with internal needs and urges. The reality principle brings a sense of rationality to behavior. Because it orients you toward the world, it leads you to weigh the risks linked to an action before acting. If the risks seem too high, you'll think of another way to meet the need. If there's no safe way to do so immediately, you'll delay it to a later, safer, or more sensible time.

BOX 8.3 EGO CONTROL AND DELAY OF GRATIFICATION

A major function of the ego is to delay gratification of impulses and urges until a later time. Delay of gratification is a mark of a mature personality; it's a major goal of socialization. Children must learn to wait for rewards (e.g., work now but be paid later), if they're to become full members of society. The *inability* to delay gratification predicts use of cigarettes, alcohol, and marijuana among high school students (Wulfert, Block, Santa Ana, Rodriguez, & Colsman, 2002) and may play a role in development of criminal behavior.

Delay of gratification has been studied from a variety of angles. (In fact, it comes up several more times in this book.) Most of the research was prompted by ideas other than psychoanalytic theory, but the findings are relevant to psychodynamic processes.

In most laboratory studies of this phenomenon, children are given the following choice: They can have a smaller, less desired reward now, or they can wait for a while and then get a larger, more desired reward. One focus of this research is on the determinants of delay (for reviews, see Mischel, 1966, 1974). It's harder for children to delay when the desired object is right in front of them (Mischel & Ebbesen, 1970). Delay is easier if the children can mentally transform the situation to make it seem as if the objects aren't really there—for example, to imagine the objects are only "color pictures in their heads" (Mischel & Baker, 1975; Moore, Mischel, & Zeiss, 1976). More generally, delay of gratification seems easiest when children distract themselves, shifting attention away from the desired rewards (Mischel, Ebbesen, & Zeiss, 1973). In effect, the ego tricks the id by getting it involved in something else.

A second line of research on delay of gratification concerns personality correlates of the ability to delay. Ability to delay relates to certain aspects of intelligence (Mischel & Metzner, 1962). Maybe this is because brighter children can more easily transform the situation mentally. Children who are better able to delay also seem more concerned with achievement and social responsibility (Mischel, 1961), fitting the idea that they have well-defined egos.

Longitudinal research by Funder, Block, and Block (1983) suggests that the basis for delay differs slightly from boys to girls. Among boys, delay seems to be closely related to the ability to control emotional and motivational impulses, to concentrate deeply, and to be deliberate in action. This fits the idea that delay of gratification is an ego function, aimed at control over the id's impulse expression. Delay among girls, in contrast, seems most strongly related to intelligence, resourcefulness, and competence. According to Funder et al. (1983), these gender differences stem from differences in the manner in which boys and girls are socialized (see also J. Block, von der Lippe, & Block, 1973; J. H. Block, 1973, 1979).

Thus, a goal of the ego is to *delay the discharge* of the id's tension until an appropriate object or activity is found (see Box 8.3). The ego uses what's called the **secondary process** to match the image of a tension-reducing object to a real object. Until such an object can be found, the ego keeps the tension in check. Ego's goal is *not* to block the id's desires permanently. The ego wants the id's urges to be satisfied. But it wants them satisfied at a time and in a way that's safe—that won't cause trouble because of some danger in the world (Bergmann, 1980).

The ego, using the reality principle and secondary process thought, is the source of intellectual processes and problem solving. The capacity for realistic thought allows the ego to form plans of action to satisfy needs and test them mentally to see whether they'll work. This is called **reality testing.** The ego is often described as having an "executive" role in personality, mediating between the desires of the id and the constraints of the external world.

It's easy to see how the id and ego can conflict. The pleasure principle says needs should be met *now;* the reality principle says *delay.* The pleasure principle orients to internal tensions; the reality principle orients to external constraints. The ego's function, in the short run, is to prevent the id from acting—to hold it up, so its needs can be met in a realistic way. Given all this, there is a vast potential for conflict within the personality.

Freud (1933) used the metaphor of a horse and rider to refer to this pulling of forces within personality. The id is the horse, providing power for movement. The ego is the rider, trying to direct the movement. Often the rider can direct the horse. Sometimes, though, the rider can only guide the horse in small ways, as the horse goes in the direction it wants to go.

The ego can appear to be a positive force, because it exercises restraint over the id. That can be misleading, however, because the ego has no moral sense. It's entirely pragmatic, concerned with getting by. The ego wouldn't be bothered by cheating or stealing or giving free rein to the pleasure principle, as long as there's no danger involved. The moral sense resides in the third part of personality.

SUPEREGO

The final aspect of personality—the last to develop—is the **superego** (a joining of two Latin words meaning "over I"). Freud held that the superego develops while the person resolves a particular conflict during development (discussed later in the chapter).

The superego is the embodiment of parental and societal values. It holds an image of what's right and wrong, and it strives for perfection rather than pleasure. The values in your superego stem from the values of your parents. To obtain the parents' love, the child comes to do what the parents think is right. To avoid pain, punishment, and rejection, the child avoids what the parents think is wrong. The process of "taking in," or incorporating, the values of parents (and wider society) is called **introjection.** Although other authority figures can influence the superego, Freud thought it derived largely from parents.

The superego is further divided into two subsystems. The **ego ideal** is rules for good behavior, or standards of excellence for the person. What the parents approve of, or value, is in the ego ideal. Conforming to those values makes you feel proud. The **conscience** is rules about what behaviors are bad. Prohibitions against things parents disapprove of and punish are in the conscience (Sederer & Seidenberg, 1976). Doing those things causes the conscience to punish you with guilt feelings.

The superego has three interrelated goals. First, it tries to prevent (not just postpone) any id impulse that would be frowned on by your parents. Second, it tries to force the ego to act morally, rather than rationally. Third, it tries to guide the person toward perfection in thought, word, and deed. The superego exerts a civilizing influence on the person, but its perfectionism is quite removed from reality.

Like the ego, the superego operates at all three levels of consciousness. This has important implications for how you experience its effects. When superego processes are conscious, you're aware of your feelings and where they're coming from. If you know you just insulted someone, despite your belief that insulting people is bad, the source of your guilt will be obvious. However, when the superego operates unconsciously to punish an urge of the id (also unconscious), you feel guilty but don't know why. Because guilt can be set off by primary process

DENNIS THE MENACE

"MOM TELLS ME THE STUFF I SHOULDN'T DO AND MY DAD TELLS ME THE STUFF I *SHOULD* DO!"

The superego has two parts. The conscience holds an image of undesirable behavior, and the ego-ideal holds an image of desirable behavior. *DENNIS THE MENACE® used by permission of Hank Ketcham and © by North America Syndicate.*

thought (unconscious id fantasies that don't really occur), the guilt itself may even be irrational.

BALANCING THE FORCES

Once the superego develops, the ego has a hard road. It must deal simultaneously with the desires of the id, the moral dictates of the superego, and the constraints of reality (see Figure 8.2). To satisfy all the demands, the ego would have to release all tension immediately in a way that's both socially acceptable and realistic. This, of course, is highly unlikely. It's much more likely that these forces will conflict. In the psychoanalytic view, such conflicts are part of life.

The term **ego strength** refers to the ego's ability to be effective despite these conflicting forces (Barron, 1953). With little ego strength, the person is torn among competing pressures. With more ego strength, the person can manage the pressures. It's possible, however, for the ego to be too strong. Someone whose ego is too strong is very rational and efficient but may also be very boring or cold and distant.

In fact, Freud didn't hold that any aspect of personality is better than the others. Rather, he suggested there should be a balance among them. A person whose superego is too strong may feel guilty all the time or may act in an insufferably saintly way. A person whose id is too strong may be obsessed with self-gratification and completely uninterested in other people. The healthiest personality is one in which the influences of the three aspects are well balanced.

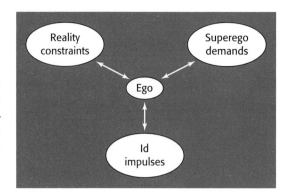

FIGURE 8.2
Graphic representation of how the ego must mediate among the often conflicting demands of the id, the superego, and the constraints of outside reality.

Motivation: The Drives of Personality

At several points we've talked in general terms about energy, impulses, tension states, drives, and urges. Let's now consider these forces more explicitly.

Ego strength refers to a person's ability to deal effectively with competing demands and taxing situations.

In thinking about motivation, Freud borrowed heavily from prevailing views in the biological and physical sciences. He saw people as complex energy systems, in which the energy used in psychological work (thinking, perceiving, remembering, planning, dreaming) is generated and released through biological processes. These biological processes, which operate through the id, have been called *instinct* and *drive*. These two terms differ from each other in other contexts (see Box 8.4), but they are used interchangeably here.

A drive has two related elements: a biological need state and its psychological representation. For example, the need state underlying thirst is a lack of sufficient water in the body's cells. This creates the psychological state of thirst, the desire for water. These elements combine to form a drive to drink water. (This portrayal isn't much different from the picture of motives presented in Chapter 5.)

Box 8.4 Have Freud's Ideas Been Distorted by Translation and Cultural Distance?

Freud wrote in German and lived in a culture very different from ours. His ideas were later translated into English. Translation of any complex or subtle idea is hard, and there is great potential for error. It's hard for any translator to know precisely what the original writer intended to convey, and it's likely that no translation is entirely faithful to the original. Less-than-perfect word choices can greatly distort meaning, however.

How faithful are the translations of Freud's writings? Not very, according to Bruno Bettelheim (1982), an important analyst in his own right. Bettelheim had the background to judge. He came from a Jewish family of Vienna, spoke German from childhood, and lived in the same cultural context as Freud. He was distressed by many aspects of the English translations of Freud. Here are some examples.

Whenever possible, Freud tried to communicate his ideas in words that his readers had used since childhood, adding new insights to those common words. Two names he chose for aspects of personality are among the first words learned by every German-speaking child. In German, the words are personal pronouns. In the pronoun *I (Ich)*, Freud chose a word that virtually forces you to think of yourself, adding the emotional qualities related to your assertive affirmation of your own existence. The translated *ego,* in contrast, is lifeless and sterile.

In the pronoun *it (Es),* Freud made an allusion that's completely lost to people who speak only English. In German, the word meaning "child" is neuter. For this reason, in early childhood, each German child is referred to as an *it.* This word, as applied to yourself, has clear emotional overtones: It's what you were called when you were so young that you hadn't learned to stifle your impulses or to feel guilty about them. A sense of personalized infancy is conveyed in the original, whereas the translated *id* has no intrinsic associations at all.

Another common word used by Freud was *Trieb,* which is commonly translated as *instinct.* Bettelheim says *drive* is better, because Freud used a different word when he wanted to refer to instincts of animals. By *Trieb,* he meant to convey an inner propulsion, a basic urge, an impulse, but not the sense that the drive was the same as an animal instinct, inborn and unalterable.

Among the few non-German terms Freud used in his theory are *Eros* and *Psyche,* which are the names of characters in a Greek myth. They were characters Freud knew intimately, as did most people to whom he was writing. (Educated people at that time read the classics.) When Freud wrote of *erotic* qualities, he meant to evoke these characters and their qualities: Eros's charm and cunning and the deep love he had for Psyche. Psyche had at first been tricked into believing that Eros was disgusting, and the message of the myth is that this was an

error. For sexual love to be true erotic pleasure, it must be filled with beauty (symbolized by Eros himself) and express the longings of the soul (symbolized by Psyche). These are connotations Freud wanted to convey with the word *erotic.* When they are stripped away (because readers don't know the myth), the word not only loses its true meaning but even takes on connotations opposite to Freud's intention.

Indeed, Bettelheim argued that the word *psyche* itself has also been misrepresented. We're used to thinking of the psyche as the mind, because that's how it's been translated. The German word for *psyche,* however, is *Seele,* which means "soul." Thus, said Bettelheim, Freud's focus was on the metaphysical, but this has been misread as a focus on the mental.

In sum, Bettelheim argued that much of the sense of Freud's ideas has been missed. Freud chose his language to evoke responses not just at an intellectual level but at an emotional level. The latter is lost in translation. Because we don't live in the cultural context in which Freud wrote, we also miss many of his nods to ideas that were common at the time.

Bettelheim also argued that Freud was aware of the distortions and chose to let them go. Why? Freud was annoyed at the U.S. medical establishment, which seemed intent on making psychoanalysis part of medicine, which Freud opposed. Apparently, he simply didn't care enough to correct them.

These processes are continuous. Drive states build up until an action causes their tension to be released. If a drive isn't expressed, its pressure continues to build. This view of motives is called a *hydraulic* model. In this view, trying to prevent a drive from being expressed only creates more pressure toward its expression.

CATHEXES AND THE USE OF ENERGY

Freud believed that psychic energy is generated continuously but gradually. Only so much is available at any given time. The idea that there's only a limited amount available within a given time span has been supported in a good deal of recent research (Baumeister, 2002; Baumeister, Bratslavsky, Muraven, & Tice, 1998; Muraven & Baumeister, 2000; Muraven, Tice, & Baumeister, 1998; Vohs, Baumeister, & Ciarocco, 2005). If you make an effort to control one thing, then there's not as much left to control something else.

Given a limited energy supply at any given time, how energy is distributed becomes an important issue. The three aspects of personality—id, ego, and superego—compete for it. Each gains power only at the expense of the other two.

Early in life, of course, the id has all the energy. The energy is used to satisfy the id's needs and to operate the primary process. Investing energy in an activity or image is called forming a **cathexis.** The more important an object or activity, the more energy invested (cathected) in it. As we said earlier, the id doesn't distinguish reality from unreality. As far as the id is concerned, cathecting an image is as good as cathecting the object. This limitation lets the ego capture part of the id's energy for its own use.

The ego uses secondary process thought to find objects in the world that match the id's images. Because real objects satisfy needs better than images do, the ego gradually comes to control more and more of the id's energy. Over time and experience, the ego controls enough energy that a surplus is available for uses beyond gratifying the id's urges. The ego uses this surplus to bring intellectual functioning to a higher level and to form cathexes of its own. These **ego cathexes** form with objects and activities *associated with* satisfying needs. Regarding hunger, for example, ego might form cathexes with reading restaurant reviews, shopping for food, or watching cooking shows on TV.

The ego also has to use energy to restrain the id from acting irrationally or immorally. The restraining forces are called **anticathexes,** because they prevent cathexes from being expressed. The clearest illustration of an anticathexis is **repression.** Repression is investing energy to keep an upsetting idea or impulse in the unconscious. This keeps the cathexis from being expressed. The harder it pushes to emerge, the more energy must be used to keep it hidden.

In the short run, anticathexes are useful because they keep troubling urges from being expressed. They create problems in the long run, though, because they drain energy from the ego that could be used in other ways. Remember, there's only so much energy to go around at any given time (Baumeister, 2002; Muraven & Baumeister, 2000). If too much of it is tied up in anticathexes, the ego has little left for anything else. When resources are lacking, behavior becomes less flexible and accommodating (Finkel & Campbell, 2001).

The superego also gathers energy from the id, through a process of *identification.* It goes like this: Young children depend on parents for need satisfaction. This leads the child into id-based cathexes toward the parents. As parents impose rules—punishing bad behavior and rewarding good behavior—the child determines which behaviors maximize need satisfaction. The child's affection for the parents (its cathexis to them) leads the child to act in ways the parents value and to *hold* those values. Cathected parental ideals thereby become part of the ego ideal, and cathected prohibitions become part of the conscience.

The competition for energy among the three aspects of personality is never ending. It's yet one more way the aspects conflict with one another. Energy, after all, is the power to control. As one aspect of personality gains control, the influence of the others diminishes.

Two Classes of Drives: Life and Death Instincts

As with many aspects of Freud's work, his ideas about drives changed over time. Ultimately, he contended that all the basic instincts form two classes (Freud, 1933). The first class is termed **life** or **sexual instincts** (collectively called **Eros**). Eros is a set of drives that deal with survival, reproduction, and pleasure. Despite the label *Eros,* not all life instincts deal with erotic urges per se. Hunger and pain avoidance, as well as sex, are life instincts. Collectively, the energy of the life instincts is known as **libido.**

Although not all life instincts are explicitly sexual, sexuality plays an important role in psychoanalytic theory (Freud, 1953a/1905). According to Freud, there's not one sex drive but many. Each is associated with a different area of the body called an **erogenous zone**. The erogenous zones are the mouth, anus, and genitals. Erogenous zones are sources of tension. Manipulating them relieves tension and produces pleasure. Thus, sucking or smoking produces oral pleasure, emptying the bowels produces anal pleasure, and rubbing the vagina or penis produces genital pleasure.

A second set of drives is **death instincts** (also termed **Thanatos**). Freud's view of them is reflected in his statement that "the goal of all life is death" (Freud, 1955/1920). He believed that life leads naturally to death and that people desire (unconsciously) to return to nothingness. The expression of death instincts is usually held back by the life instincts, however. Thus, the effects of the death instincts aren't always visible.

Freud never coined a term for the energy of death instincts, and Thanatos has received less attention than Eros. Today's biology, however, holds that a death instinct does exist in human physiology. That is, there is an active gene-directed suicide process that occurs in human cells in certain circumstances. This process, termed **apoptosis,** is a critical element in development (e.g., W. R. Clark, 1996). It also seems to be involved in the body's defense against cancer (Tyner et al., 2002). The cell death machinery is coded in your cells (Hopkin, 1995). This fact suggests that death is an ultimate goal for parts of the body. Perhaps the principle also extends more broadly into the personality.

An aspect of the death instinct that *has* received attention from psychologists concerns aggression. In Freud's view, aggression isn't a basic drive but stems from the thwarting of the death drive. That is, if Eros blocks expression of the death drive, tension remains. Energy is unspent. It can be used in aggressive or destructive actions against others. In this view, acts of aggression express *self*-destructive urges but turned outward onto others.

Coming Together of Libidinal and Aggressive Energies

Usually sexual and aggressive energies are released in separate activities. Sometimes, however, they exist side by side, with one expressed and then the other. This pattern is termed *ambivalence*. Sometimes the two even fuse and jointly energize a single activity (Freud, 1933). This merging of sex and aggression is termed *sadism*.

Several research areas bear on the interplay between sexual and aggressive energies. One of the more interesting ones sought to examine effects of pornography on aggression, rather than test psychoanalytic theory per se (for reviews, see Donnerstein, 1983, or Malamuth & Donnerstein, 1984). Nevertheless, some of the findings are instructive regarding the competition between these energies and their possible blending.

The major point in this literature is that sexual arousal can facilitate or inhibit aggression, depending on other factors. When a person is angry, exposure to *mild* sexual stimuli typically reduces aggression (e.g., Baron, 1974a, 1974b, 1979; Baron & Bell, 1977; Donnerstein, Donnerstein, & Evans, 1975; Frodi, 1977). In one study (Baron, 1974a), men were angered (or not) and later retaliated. Before retaliation, half viewed pictures of nude women, and the rest saw pictures of scenery, furniture, and abstract art. Exposure to erotica significantly reduced aggression among the angry subjects.

In contrast to this, creation of *intense* sexual arousal *increases* aggression among angry persons. In one study (Zillmann, 1971), male subjects were angered (or not) and later retaliated. Just beforehand, they viewed either a neutral film or a highly erotic, explicitly sexual film. The highly erotic film increased the aggression of angry subjects to a level even higher than was created by watching a violent fight film. Others have found that highly erotic material increases aggression toward women (Donnerstein & Hallam, 1978), especially when the erotic stimuli are themselves aggressive (Donnerstein, 1980). In sum, the evidence suggests that sexual and aggressive urges are sometimes antagonistic to each other but sometimes combine with each other (for broader discussion, see Zillmann, 1998).

CATHARSIS

We said earlier that if a drive's tension isn't released, the pressure remains and even grows. At some point, the buildup of energy may be so great that it can't be restrained any longer. At this point, the impulse is unleashed. The term **catharsis** is used to refer to the release of emotional tension in such an experience. (The term also has a second use that's discussed in Chapter 9.)

This view of catharsis has been studied mostly with respect to aggression. The principle of catharsis leads to two predictions. First, engaging in aggression should reduce tension, because the aggressive drive is no longer being stifled. Second, because this act dissipates the drive's energy, the person should be less likely to be aggressive again in the near future.

This view of aggressive energy and its release is echoed in the ideas of other theorists. Megargee (1966, 1971; Megargee, Cook, & Mendelsohn, 1967) argued that people with strong inhibitions against aggression rarely blow off steam, even when provoked. Over time, though, their feelings build until their restraints can no longer hold. Because so much energy has built up, the aggression released may be quite brutal. Ironically, the final provocation is often trivial (see also N. Miller, Pederson, Earleywine, & Pollock, 2003). Once the episode is over, these people (whom Megargee terms *overcontrolled aggressors*) revert to their overcontrolled, passive ways.

This portrayal is consistent with the psychoanalytic view of aggression, if one assumes the id impulses of these people are overcontrolled by ego and superego processes. The dynamics of overcontrolled aggression have also received a fair amount of verification (see, e.g., Blackburn, 1968a, 1968b; Megargee, 1966). Note, though, that overcontrolled aggressors are a rather select group of people.

How accurate is the catharsis hypothesis for aggression in *most* people? People seem to *think* aggression will make them feel better (Bushman, Baumeister, & Phillips, 2001), but the evidence is mixed (Baron & Richardson, 1994). Aggression can help dissipate arousal (Geen, Stonner, & Shope, 1975; Hokanson & Burgess, 1962a, 1962b; Hokanson, Burgess, & Cohen, 1963), but it's less clear why. For example, in one

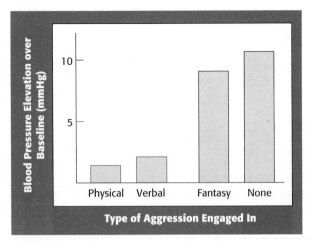

FIGURE 8.3
Tension-reducing effects of aggressive acts. This figure portrays elevations in systolic blood pressure after being provoked and then engaging in various kinds of aggression, in comparison with levels before provocation. Both physical and verbal aggression were relatively effective in returning participants to their initial levels, whereas fantasy aggression was not.

Source: Adapted from Hokanson & Burgess, 1962b.

study (Hokanson & Burgess, 1962b), subjects working on a task were harassed by the experimenter, which raised their blood pressure. Later, some could retaliate physically, others verbally, others in fantasy (writing an aggressive story in response to a TAT picture), and some not at all. As shown in Figure 8.3, the results supported the idea that true retaliation produces emotional catharsis. Subjects who retaliated physically or verbally showed decreases in blood pressure. In contrast, fantasy aggression had little effect.

Although this general pattern of effects has been obtained many times, there are important limiting conditions. The target of the aggression can't be high in status (Hokanson & Shetler, 1961) and must either be the instigator or linked to the instigator (Hokanson et al., 1963). Moreover, tension reduction doesn't require aggression per se. Virtually *any* response that stops a provocation can reduce arousal (e.g., Hokanson & Edelman, 1966; Hokanson, Willers, & Koropsak, 1968; Stone & Hokanson, 1969). There's even evidence that responding to provocation in a friendly fashion reduces arousal among women more than does responding aggressively (Hokanson & Edelman, 1966). This doesn't fit the catharsis hypothesis very well.

What about the other reflection of catharsis? Does aggression make the person less aggressive in the near future? The findings here are even more mixed. Baron and Richardson (1994) concluded that this happens only under very specific conditions. Aggression reduces later aggression only if it's a response to an instigation (e.g., Bramel, Taub, & Blum, 1968; Doob, 1970; Konecni, 1975) and the retaliation is toward the instigator and about equivalent to the instigation (e.g., Berkowitz & Alioto, 1973; Ebbesen, Duncan, & Konecni, 1975; Goldstein & Arms, 1971; Goranson, 1970; Mallick & McCandless, 1966). Interestingly enough, the retaliation may be done by someone else and still reduce aggression (E. J. Murray, 1985). On the other hand, sometimes engaging in aggression actually *increases* later aggression (Geen et al., 1975), contradicting the catharsis hypothesis. Fantasy aggression can also increase later aggression (Bartholow & Anderson, 2001; Bushman, 2002).

In sum, although some evidence suggests catharsis effects, the effects occur only under very specific circumstances. Moreover, other evidence seems to contradict catharsis. Taken together, the evidence doesn't support this aspect of psychoanalytic theory very well.

DISPLACEMENT AND SUBLIMATION OF MOTIVE FORCES

The life and death instincts provide for a wide range of behavior. Behavior is rendered even more diverse by two processes that influence how these drives are expressed. **Displacement** is a change in how energy is used or the object toward which it's used. Displacement lets blocked energy be released in another way or toward another object. For example, a hostile impulse toward your boss might be displaced and vented toward your apartment mate.

Strictly speaking, the word *displacement* applies to any shift in object choice. There's a special kind of displacement, however, that's important enough that it has a special name: **sublimation.** In sublimation, a shift occurs from a socially unacceptable form of action to an acceptable or even praiseworthy form of action.

Consider two students who are angry over criticisms a professor wrote on their term papers. Both want to hit the professor with a baseball bat. Neither does, though. One goes home, kicks his dog, and yells at his roommates. The other writes a letter to the school newspaper, criticizing a policy of the university. In both cases, aggressive energy is released in actions that substitute for the desired act (hitting the professor). Writing the letter, however, is more acceptable than taking out anger on the dog and roommates. The one who kicked the dog was displacing. The one who wrote the letter was both displacing and sublimating.

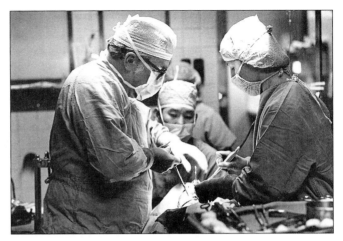

One view of surgery is that it allows unacceptable aggressive energy to be sublimated and released through a more socially acceptable form of activity.

As another example, consider two women who are experiencing sexual urges toward their best friend's boyfriend. One of them displaces this impulse by acting out the sexual impulses toward the person she happens to be dating. The other one sublimates the sexual energy by composing a poem.

Although displacement presumably occurs for both sexual and aggressive energy, most research on displacement looks at aggression. It's absolutely clear that displacement happens (e.g., Holmes, 1972; Marcus-Newhall, Pedersen, Carlson, & Miller, 2000; N. Miller et al., 2003; Twenge, Baumeister, Tice, & Stucke, 2001). As an example, Fenigstein and Buss (1974) found that people who'd been provoked were more aggressive in the context of a task even when the person on the receiving end was just an innocent bystander.

The concepts of displacement and sublimation are very important in psychoanalytic theory. They give it flexibility to account for the diversity of human behavior. From the psychoanalytic view, such wide-ranging phenomena as works of art and music, altruism, creativity, critical thinking, and excellence in sports can all be attributed to patterns of displaced and sublimated sexual and aggressive energy.

Indeed, the concept of sublimation is even more important than that. Sublimation permits humans to be civilized. Freud believed that without sublimation, people would act wholly from greed and their own desires. Thanks to sublimation, people are capable of acts of altruism and cooperation. Sublimation, then, is the path by which humans can transcend their animal nature and form societies.

Psychosexual Development

Freud derived his ideas primarily from a few case histories of adults in therapy. Despite this, he wrote a lot about how personality develops during childhood. He believed that early experiences are critical in determining a person's adult personality. Indeed, Freud thought that personality is largely determined by age 5. During later life, the expression of personality becomes more symbolic and less literal.

Freud viewed personality development as movement through a series of stages. Each stage reflects a body zone through which sexual energy is discharged in that period. For this reason, they're called *psychosexual stages.* In Freud's view, the child has conflicts at three stages. If the conflict isn't well resolved, too much energy gets permanently invested in that stage, a process called **fixation.** This means less energy is available to handle conflicts in later stages. As a result, it's harder to resolve later conflicts. In this sense, each stage builds on previous ones.

Fixation can occur for two reasons. A person who is overindulged in a stage may be reluctant to leave it and move on. One whose needs are deeply frustrated *can't* move on until the needs are met. In either case, personality gets partly stuck at this stage, as a portion of the libido becomes invested in the concerns of that stage. The stronger the fixation, the more the libido is invested in it. In a very strong fixation, the person is so preoccupied—unconsciously—that there is little energy left for anything else.

THE ORAL STAGE

The **oral stage** extends from birth to roughly 18 months. During this time, much of the infant's interaction with the world occurs through the mouth and lips, and gratification focuses in that area. The mouth is the source of tension reduction (eating) and pleasurable sensations (tasting, licking, and sucking). At the same time, infants are completely dependent on others for their survival. The conflict of this stage concerns the ending of this arrangement: the process of weaning—literal and figurative. That is, toward the end of this stage, children are under increasing pressure to let go of their mother and become less reliant on her.

This stage has two substages. During the first (lasting roughly 6 months), the baby is helpless and dependent. Because the baby is more or less limited to taking things in (food and other experiences), the first part of the oral stage is called the *oral incorporative phase.* Freud thought that several traits develop here, including a general sense of optimism versus pessimism, trust versus mistrust, and dependency on others. Recall Freud's fascination with symbolism and the transformation of the literal into the symbolic. This fascination extended to his ideas about traits. He believed that the trait of gullibility—the tendency to "swallow" everything you're told—arises from events during the oral incorporative phase.

The second part of the oral stage starts with teething. It's called the *oral sadistic phase.* Sexual pleasure now comes from biting and chewing (and even inflicting pain—thus sadistic). During this time, the infant is weaned from the bottle or breast and begins to bite and chew food. Traits arising during this phase trace to this newly acquired ability. This phase is thought to determine who is verbally aggressive later on and who uses "biting" sarcasm.

In general terms, oral characters should relate to the world orally. They should be more preoccupied than others with food and drink. When stressed, they should be more likely than others to engage in activities involving the mouth, such as smoking, drinking, and nailbiting. When angry, they should be verbally aggressive. Oral characters should be concerned with getting support from others, and should do things to ease interactions with people.

Although oral gratification may be most important during infancy, the pleasure of oral stimulation continues throughout life.

Is this characterization accurate? Perhaps. Joseph Masling and his colleagues found that tests of oral imagery relate to both obesity (Masling, Rabie, & Blondheim, 1967; Weiss & Masling, 1970) and alcoholism (Bertrand & Masling, 1969). Orality has also been related to measures of interpersonal interest and social skills. For example, oral imagery has been related to the need to nurture others (Holt, 1966) and to interpersonal effectiveness (Masling, Johnson, & Saturansky, 1974). Persons high in oral imagery also volunteer readily for interpersonal tasks (Bornstein & Masling, 1985; Masling, O'Neill, & Jayne, 1981) and rely on other people's judgments during ambiguous tasks (Masling, Weiss, & Rothschild, 1968).

More generally, people who display oral imagery seem to be highly motivated to gain closeness and support from others and are sensitive to how others react to them. They have greater physiological reactivity to social isolation (Masling, Price, Goldband, & Katkin, 1981) and to subtle cues of rejection (Masling, O'Neill, & Katkin, 1982) than people who display less oral imagery. They also use more physical contact during social interaction (Juni, Masling, & Brannon, 1979) and are more self-disclosing (Juni, 1981) than less oral people.

We should point out that you don't have to be extremely oral to seek oral gratification. Lots of people chew gum. Nor is the expression of sexual energy through oral contact limited to early childhood. Indeed, there's evidence all around you that seeking of oral pleasure continues into adulthood. After all, what is serious kissing but an oral expression of sexuality? Nor is that the only way sexuality is expressed orally among adults. In sum, the mouth seems to be an important part of the body through which the human's sexual nature is expressed.

THE ANAL STAGE

The **anal stage** of development begins at about 18 months and continues into the third year. During this period, the anus is the key erogenous zone, and pleasure comes from stimulation that occurs in defecation. The big event of this period is toilet training. For many children, toilet training is the first time that external constraints are systematically imposed on satisfaction of internal urges. When toilet training starts, children can't relieve themselves whenever and wherever they want. They must learn that there's an appropriate time and place for everything.

The personality characteristics said to arise from fixations during this period depend on how toilet training is approached by parents and caretakers. Two orientations are typical. One involves urging the child to eliminate at a desired time and place and praising the child lavishly for success. This places a lot of attention on the elimination process and reward for the child. This convinces the child of the value of producing things (in this case urine and feces) at the "right" time and place, by whatever means possible. To Freud, this provides a basis for adult productivity and creativity.

The second approach to toilet training is harsher. Rather than praise for a job well done, the emphasis is on punishment, ridicule, and shame for failures. This practice yields two patterns, depending on how the child reacts. If the child adopts an active pattern of rebellion, eliminating forcefully when the parents

An anal retentive personality might be displayed in an excessively neat and tidy workplace.

least want it, a set of *anal expulsive traits* develop. These are tendencies to be messy, cruel, destructive, and overtly hostile.

If the child tries to get even by withholding feces and urine, a set of *anal retentive traits* develops. The anal retentive personality is a rigid, obsessive style. The characteristics that form this pattern are sometimes called the *anal triad:* stinginess, obstinacy, and orderliness. *Stinginess* stems from the desire to retain feces. *Obstinacy* reflects the struggle of wills over toilet training. *Orderliness* is a reaction against the messiness of defecating. This pattern does seem to exist. In one study (Rosenwald, 1972), male students assessed as having the most anal anxiety were also the most compulsively neat (see also Juni & Fischer, 1985; Juni & Lo Cascio, 1985).

THE PHALLIC STAGE

The **phallic stage** begins during the third year and continues through the fifth year. During this period, the focus shifts to the genital organs. This is also the period when most children begin to masturbate, as they become aware of the pleasure that arises from genital manipulation.

At first, the awakening sexual desires are completely *autoerotic* in nature. That is, sexual pleasure is totally derived from self-stimulation. Gradually, however, libido shifts toward the opposite-sex parent, as boys develop an interest in their mothers and girls develop an interest in their fathers. At the same time, the child becomes hostile toward the same-sex parent, due to the perception of competition between them over the affection of the other parent.

Boys' desire to possess their mothers and replace their fathers is termed the **Oedipus complex** (after the character in the play *Oedipus Rex,* who unwittingly marries his mother after killing his father). Comparable feelings in girls are sometimes called an *Oedipus complex* and sometimes an *Electra complex* (after the Greek character Electra, who persuades her brother to kill both their mother and their mother's lover in revenge for the death of their father). These patterns reflect forces that are similar in many ways, but the forces are displayed differently for boys and girls. At this point, the developmental patterns for boys and girls diverge.

Let's consider first what happens to boys. Two changes take place: His love for his mother transforms into sexual desire, and his feelings for his father shift toward hostility and hatred, because his father is a rival for his mother's affection. Over time, the boy's jealousy and competitiveness toward his father may become extreme. Such thoughts may induce feelings of guilt. At the same time, the boy fears that his father will retaliate against him for his desire toward his mother. In traditional psychoanalytic theory, the boy's fear is quite specific: He fears that his father will castrate him to eliminate the source of his lust. Freud termed this **castration anxiety.**

Ultimately, castration anxiety causes the boy to push his desire for his mother into the unconscious. Castration anxiety also causes the boy to **identify** with his father, a term that has a somewhat different meaning here than earlier in the chapter. Here *identification* means to develop feelings of similarity to and connectedness with someone else. This does several things. First, it gives the boy a kind of "camouflage." Being like his father makes it seem less likely that his father will harm him. Second, by identifying with desirable aspects of the father, the boy reduces his ambivalence toward him. Identification thus paves the way for development of the superego, as the boy introjects his father's values.

Finally, by identifying with the father, the boy gains vicarious expression of his sexual urges toward his mother. That is, he gains symbolic access to his mother *through*

Box 8.5   Penis Envy or Vagina Envy?

As discussed elsewhere in the chapter, Freud assumed that developing girls eventually confront the fact that they don't have a penis. He believed this discovery has shattering impact. Girls feel castrated—betrayed—and they blame their mothers for it. This feeling of incompleteness and castration haunts them for the rest of their lives. In his view, the envy women develop for men—penis envy—motivates much of their later behavior, both directly and symbolically.

There are many examples. Women try to recover their lost penises symbolically by incorporating one into their bodies through sex and by giving birth to male children. In today's society, they also seek to obtain the power the penis confers by entering business, law, and other power-related pursuits. Penis envy can also be expressed by desiring others to share the same fate. Thus, some women try to reduce men to the same pitiful state, castrating men symbolically by being "sharp" and "cutting" in social interactions.

This description is entirely compatible with psychoanalytic thought. A case can be made that at least some girls experience a sense that they're missing something boys have, something that may be important. But the idea that penis envy is a prime source of women's motivation is not exactly calculated to win friends among women. Many see this position as condescending and demeaning toward women and a gross distortion (Horney, 1939, 1967).

To point out the arbitrariness of Freud's assumptions, Peterson (1980) proposed a different hypothesis. According to her, Freud got things backward (perhaps because the truth was too threatening to him). It's not women who are envious of men; it's men who are envious of women. Young boys, growing up, sooner or later confront the fact that they have no vagina. This shattering discovery leads to an envy from which they never recover. The resentment that stems from this envy influences all male behavior.

As did Freud, Peterson assumed that the manifestations of this envy are primarily symbolic. This, suggested Peterson, is why men insist on having pockets in their pants. Lots of pockets. Indeed, the three-piece suit (worn by businessmen and others making vain, pathetic attempts to convey an image of power) is a virtual orgy of symbolic wish fulfillment. It has pants pockets, vest pockets, jacket pockets, even an *internal* jacket pocket—symbolism on top of symbolism!

It should be obvious that Peterson's argument was made tongue in cheek. However, she also was making a more serious point about psychoanalytic theory and about theory more generally. There are places in psychoanalytic theory (as in any theory) where assumptions are made that are arbitrary, seemingly based on societal preconceptions rather than theoretical necessity. It's always important to think about the basis for assumptions in order to decide for yourself whether they're sensible.

---

his father. The more the boy resembles the father, the more easily he can fantasize himself in his father's place.

For girls, the conflict of the phallic stage is more complicated. As we said earlier, girls abandon their love relationship with their mother for a new one with their father. This shift occurs when the girl realizes she has no penis. She withdraws love from her mother because she blames her mother for her castrated condition (after discovering that her mother has no penis either). At the same time, the girl's affection is drawn to her father, who does have a penis. Ultimately, the girl comes to wish that her father would share his penis with her through sex or that he would provide her with the symbolic equivalent of a penis—a baby.

Freud referred to these feelings as **penis envy** (though see Box 8.5). Penis envy is the female counterpart of castration anxiety in boys. As do boys, girls resolve the conflict through identification. By becoming more like her mother, the girl gains vicarious access to her father. She also increases the chances that she'll marry someone just like him.

Fixations that develop during the phallic stage result in personalities that, in effect, continue to wrestle with Oedipal conflicts. Men may go to great lengths to demonstrate that they haven't been castrated. The way to do that is to seduce as many

Box 8.6 The Theorist and the Theory

Freud's Own Oedipal Crisis

The idea that personal experiences of personality theorists influenced the very form taken by their theories is vividly illustrated by the life of Sigmund Freud. In fact, it's widely believed that several aspects of Freud's life had a direct impact on his theories.

Freud's father, Jakob, a merchant, was 40 years old at the time of Sigmund's birth (1856). By all accounts, he was a strict and authoritarian father. Given this, it would be no surprise that Freud's feelings about his father were ambivalent. Freud's memories were, in fact, of hating his father as well as loving him. A hint of scandal concerning Sigmund's birth may also have had a bearing on his relationship with his father. Two different dates are indicated in various places as his birthdate. This may have been a clerical error. Some believe, however, that the later date was

an effort to disguise the fact that Freud's mother was pregnant when she and his father married (Balmary, 1979).

Jakob Freud had had two sons in a prior marriage and was himself a grandfather when Sigmund was born. His wife, Amalie, on the other hand, was only 20. Sigmund was her first child and her favorite. Sigmund responded by developing a highly idealized image of his mother and a strong affection for her. By all accounts, they had a very close relationship.

In short, the relationships of Freud's childhood had all the elements of what he would later call the *Oedipal conflict.* There was a deep attachment to his mother, which some have said had sexual overtones. There was also a strong ambivalence toward his father. (Freud was even late for his father's funeral, an act he later saw as having been unconsciously motivated.) It seems hard to ignore the possibility that Freud used his own

experiences as a model for what he came to argue were universal aspects of development.

Nor was the Oedipal crisis the only aspect of Freud's thinking to be influenced by events in his own life. World War I, in which 10 million people died, deeply disillusioned Freud, along with many other Europeans. Newspapers were filled with accounts of the slaughter, which seemed truly purposeless. Two of Freud's sons fought in the war, and his fears for their safety must have been a great strain on him. Shortly after the end of the war, Freud wrote his view of the death instinct: that people have an unconscious wish to die, which they turn outward toward others in murderous actions such as war. It seems likely that this view was partly Freud's attempt to understand how the atrocities of that war could have come to happen. Thus, once again, the elements of the theory seem formed by the experiences of the theorist.

women as they can or father many children. The attempt to assert their masculinity may also be expressed symbolically by attaining great success in their career. Alternatively, they may fail sexually and professionally (purposely, but unconsciously) because of the guilt they feel over competing with their father for their mother's love.

Among women, the continuation of the Oedipal conflict is displayed by relating to men in a way that is excessively seductive and flirtatious, but with a denial of the sexuality. This style of relating first develops toward the father. She was attracted to him first, but by now has repressed the sexual desire that first drew her. The pattern then applies to her later social interactions. This is a woman who excites men with her seductive behavior and then is surprised when the men want sex with her.

Freud felt that identifying the Oedipus complex was one of his key theoretical contributions. This brief span involves considerable turmoil filled with love, hate, guilt, jealousy, and fear. He believed that how children negotiate the conflicts and difficulties of the phallic stage determines their attitudes toward sexuality, interpersonal competitiveness, and personal adequacy (see also Box 8.6).

Fixations that develop during these first three stages of development presumably form much of the basis of adult personality. Some of the traits said to derive from fixations during these stages are summarized in Table 8.1.

Table 8.1 Personality Qualities Believed to Follow from Fixations in the First Three Stages of Psychosexual Development.

Stage of Fixation	Personality Qualities
Oral	Incorporative: Dependent, gullible, jealous Sadistic: Sarcastic and verbally aggressive
Anal	Expulsive: messy, cruel, destructive Retentive: obstinate, neat and orderly, stingy
Phallic	Among males: macho aggressive sexuality, excessive striving for career power; alternatively, sexual and occupational impotence Among females: flirtatious, seductive behavior that doesn't lead to sexual interaction

THE LATENCY PERIOD

At the close of the phallic stage, the child enters a period of relative calm, termed the **latency period.** This period, from about age 6 to the early teens, is a time when sexual and aggressive drives are less active. The lessening of these urges results partly from the emergence of the ego and superego. During this period, children turn their attention to other pursuits, often intellectual or social in nature. Thus, the latency period is a time when the child's experiences broaden, rather than a time when new conflicts are confronted. As an example, parental identifications during the phallic stage may be supplemented in the latency period by identifications with other figures of authority, perhaps religious figures or teachers.

With the onset of puberty (toward the end of this period), sexual and aggressive urges again intensify. In addition, conflicts of previous periods may be re-encountered. This is a time when the coping skills of the ego are severely taxed. Although adolescents have adult sexual desires, the release of sexual energy through intercourse isn't socially sanctioned. As a result, sexual gratification is sought in other ways.

THE GENITAL STAGE

In later adolescence and adulthood, the person moves into the final stage of psychosexual development, the **genital stage.** If earlier psychosexual stages have been negotiated well, the person enters this stage with libido still organized around the genitals, and it remains focused there throughout life. The sexual gratification during this stage differs, however, from that of earlier stages. Earlier attachments were narcissistic. The child cared only about his or her own sexual pleasure. Others mattered only insofar as they furthered the child's own pleasure. In the genital stage, a desire develops to share mutual sexual gratification with someone. Thus, the person becomes capable of loving others not just for selfish reasons but also for altruistic ones.

Ideally, the person is able to achieve full and free orgasm on an equal basis. This ability to share with others in a warm and caring way and to be concerned with their welfare is the hallmark of the genital stage. Persons in this stage also have more control over impulses, both sexual and aggressive, and are able to release them in smaller amounts (but more frequently) in sublimated, socially acceptable ways. In this manner, the person becomes transformed from a self-centered, pleasure-seeking infant into a well-socialized, caring adult.

Freud believed that people don't enter the genital stage automatically and that this transition is rarely achieved in its entirety (see Fenichel, 1945). Most people have less control over their impulses than they should, and most have difficulty gratifying sexual desires in completely satisfying and acceptable ways. In this sense, the genital personality is an ideal to strive for, rather than an end point to be taken for granted. It is the perfect culmination of psychosexual development from the analytic point of view.

Psychoanalytic Structure and Process: Problems and Prospects

The psychoanalytic view on how personality is organized and functions has been influential since its development. It has also been controversial. From the start, people were reluctant to accept aspects of the theory. Many were incensed by the prominence of sexual themes. They were shocked that anyone would suggest that the behavior of young children is sexually motivated. It also was difficult for many to believe that behavior is determined largely by forces outside awareness.

The scientific community faulted psychodynamic theory on other grounds. The primary problem from a scientific standpoint is that the theory is very hard to test. One reason is that many psychoanalytic concepts are defined ambiguously. An example of this is provided by the term *libido*. Freud used this term to refer to sexual energy, a psychological quality that arises from physiological processes. We know little else about it. Where does it come from? What makes it sexual in nature? How do you measure it? Without some way to measure it, you can't study it. By implication, other ideas to which libido is linked (e.g., psychosexual development, fixation) are also hard to study. Indeed, many psychoanalytic concepts—cathexis, the death wish, id, ego— are also problematic from a research point of view. When a theory's concepts can't be pinned down, the theory can't be tested.

Part of the ambiguity of psychoanalytic concepts comes from Freud's tendency to describe concepts differently from one time to another. Even more ambiguity comes from the fact that Freud thought about personality in such a metaphorical way. This metaphorical approach is deeply embedded in descriptions of the theory. As a result, it's difficult to know when Freud should be read literally and when he should be read metaphorically.

Consider, for example, the Oedipal complex. Should we believe Freud meant literally that every boy comes to desire his mother sexually at around age 4? Or should we assume he was using the Oedipal theme as a metaphor to describe the conflict between young children and their parents? Freud wrote at one point that many of the specific explanatory devices he used could be replaced or discarded without damaging the theory (Silverman, 1976). Clearly, then, parts of what he wrote shouldn't be taken literally. Unfortunately, we don't know which parts.

As a metaphorical statement, the Oedipal theme makes a good deal of sense. As a literal statement, it doesn't hold up as well. As Sears (1943, p. 136) wrote, "Freud's notion of the universal Oedipus complex stands as a sharply etched grotesquerie against his otherwise informative description of sexual development."

Scientific psychologists also criticize the evidence on which psychoanalytic theory rests. One focus of this criticism is Freud's heavy reliance on case studies in developing his ideas, particularly ideas involving infantile sexuality. The case study has several problems. It's very subjective, influenced as much by what the researcher brings to the situation as by what the object of study brings. It's hard to be sure whether the insights gained by one observer would be gained by another, even looking at the same case.

The problem of reliability is even further compounded in this instance. Freud acted both as theorist–researcher and as therapist. Thus, he took an active role in the development of the case history, becoming involved in the interpretation of what was said and done. Freud's actions as a participant–observer may have biased the kinds of things his patients said even more than usual (Powell & Boer, 1994). For example, more sexually toned material emerged as therapy proceeded. Was this because repression was weakening or because patients learned over time that this was what Freud was interested in? Indeed, there is evidence that Freud was sometimes highly directive with patients (Esterton, 1998).

Freud allowed himself to be biased in another way, as well, by relying so much on patients. He carefully screened potential patients and allowed into therapy only those he thought were very good candidates. Thus, he developed his ideas from observations of a biased set of cases. We can't be sure how much or in what ways these people differed from the overall population, but they certainly weren't chosen randomly.

Moreover, the number of cases Freud relied on for a database was distressingly small. In fact, in all his writings and works, Freud described case histories of only a dozen or so people. Yet from this very narrow database—a dozen or so people, all of whom he had carefully chosen and all of whom were in therapy—he went on to formulate what he regarded as universal rules about personality functioning in general. Many researchers find this problematic.

Another criticism of psychoanalytic ideas is the tendency to confuse *facts* with *inferences*. For example, certain observations led Freud to infer the existence (and universality) of an Oedipal complex. He then went on to discuss the Oedipal complex as though its existence were a fact. A general tendency to mix fact with inference has contributed to an intellectual climate in psychoanalytic circles in which basic concepts have gone untested—because it apparently was thought they didn't *need* to be tested (Crews, 1996; Esterson, 1993).

Despite these problems, there's been a resurgence of interest in the ideas that make up both the topographic model of mind and the structural model of personality (Bargh, 1997). With respect to the topography of the mind, many people who start from different perspectives now argue that important aspects of memory cannot be brought to consciousness voluntarily. In some cases, this is because the elements are too small or too hard to locate. Sometimes it apparently is because the thing we're looking for (by its very nature) can be *used* but not *viewed*. Sometimes it's because the thing we might be looking for has become so automatic that, in effect, it's fallen out of our mental "address book" and become lost. Although these aren't quite the same as the unconscious phenomena Freud emphasized, they represent new interest in the idea that the mind has more than two regions.

With respect to the structural model, it is being re-emphasized that we shouldn't get distracted by the idea that the mind has three components. Think of them instead as three modes of functioning (Grigsby & Stevens, 2000). Take the descriptions less literally. The id is simply the psychological nature of the infant. Infantile qualities are overlaid in all of us by effects of socialization, but those infantile qualities remain in some sense the basic structure from which we grew. The id is the part that *wants*— wants as the 1-year-old wants, without regard to dangers or disapprovals. We all still have that part, and it still makes its presence known. The ego is the set of restraints we learn, restraints that diminish the pain we experience from grabbing too fast for what we want without looking for danger. The superego is the abstract rules we learn, to become part of a society in which we can't always have our way, even if we wait patiently.

The idea that humans begin life grabbing for what they want when they first want it, and only gradually learn to restrain themselves, makes a lot of sense. The idea that people later learn abstractions concerning morality also makes sense. So does the idea that the moral abstractions can conflict with the wants. In sum, the structural model expresses a fair amount of truth about the human experience.

What is the future of these ideas? Some see them as being of historical interest only. Others see them as valuable. They remain an important part of the course you're taking. We suspect they'll remain there for a long time.

· SUMMARY ·

Freud's topographical model assumes three regions of mind: the conscious, the pre-conscious (ordinary memory), and the unconscious (a part of mind that isn't accessible to consciousness). The unconscious holds threatening or unacceptable ideas and urges.

Freud's structural model assumes three facets of personality. The id (the original part) is the source of all energy. It follows the pleasure principle (that all needs should be immediately gratified), exists only in the unconscious, and uses primary process thinking (primitive and separate from reality). The ego eventually develops because the id ignores the demands of the external world, and they cannot be ignored. Ego follows the reality principle (that behavior must take into account external reality), operates in all three regions of the mind, and tries to see that the id's impulses are gratified in a realistic way. The ego uses secondary process (reality-based) thought. The third facet, superego, is a representation of rules by which parents reward and punish the child. It has two parts: Ego ideal is standards of moral perfection. Conscience is a representation of behaviors that are considered bad. Both function in all three regions of the mind. Once the superego develops, the ego must mediate among id, superego, and reality.

Investing energy in a need is called a *cathexis*. Restraining forces (from the ego) are called *anticathexes*. Id impulses form two categories: Life instincts aim for self-preservation and sexual pleasure. Death instincts are self-destructive and may turn outward as aggression. Catharsis in aggression is releasing an aggressive urge, which is thought to reduce tension and decrease the need to aggress. Displacement releases the impulse onto a different target from that initially intended. Impulses can also be sub-limated, or transformed into socially acceptable acts.

Freud argued that child development proceeds through psychosexual stages and that adult personality is influenced by how crises are resolved at each stage. In the oral stage, sexuality centers on the mouth, and the crisis involves being weaned. In the anal stage, sexuality centers on the anus, and the crisis involves toilet training. In the phal-lic stage, sexuality centers on the genitals, and the crisis (creating Oedipal and Electra complexes) involves lust for the opposite-sex parent and fear of and rivalry with the same-sex parent. The latency period is a calm interval with no serious conflict. The genital period is maturity, in which genital sexuality shifts from selfish narcissism to mutual sharing.

· GLOSSARY ·

Anal stage   The second stage of development, centered around issues in toilet training.

Anticathexis   The investment of energy in suppressing an impulse or image.

Apoptosis   Biologically programmed cell death.

Castration anxiety   A boy's fear (from the phallic stage) that his father will perceive him as a rival and castrate him.

Catharsis   The release of emotional tension.

Cathexis   The investment of psychic energy in a desired activity or image.

Conscience   The part of the superego that punishes violations of moral standards.

Conscious   The part of the mind that holds what one is currently aware of.

Death instincts (Thanatos)   Self-destructive instincts, often turned outward as aggression.

Displacement   The shifting of an impulse from its original target to a different target.

Ego   The rational part of the personality that deals pragmatically with reality.

Ego cathexis   Binding psychic energy in an ego-guided activity.

Ego ideal   The part of the superego that represents perfection and rewards for good behavior.

Ego strength   The ability of the ego to function despite the competing demands of the id, superego, and reality.

Erogenous zone   A sexually responsive area of the body.

Fixation   The condition of being partly stuck in a stage of psychosexual development.

Genital stage   The final stage of development, characterized by mature and mutual sexual involvement with another.

Id   The original, primitive component of personality; the source of all energy.

Identify   To develop feelings of similarity to and connectedness with another person.

Introjection   Absorbing the values of one's parents into one's superego.

Latency period   The period in which the crises of the phallic stage give way to a temporary calm.

Libido   The collective energy of the life instincts.

Life instincts or **sexual instincts (Eros)** Survival and sexual instincts.

Oedipus complex   The mix of desire for the opposite-sex parent and fear of or hatred for the same-sex parent.

Oral stage   The first stage of psychosexual development, in which oral needs create a crisis over weaning.

Penis envy   A girl's envy of males, from feelings of having been castrated.

Phallic stage   The third stage of development, in which a crisis occurs over sexual desire for the opposite-sex parent.

Pleasure principle   The idea that impulses should be gratified immediately.

Preconscious   The region of the mind that corresponds to ordinary memory.

Primary process   The id process that creates an unconscious image of a desired object.

Reality principle   The idea that actions must take into account the constraints of external reality.

Reality testing   The ego's checking to see whether plans will work before they are put into action.

Repression   Preventing an idea or impulse from becoming conscious.

Secondary process   The ego process of rationally seeking an object to satisfy a desire.

Structural model   Freud's model of three components of personality.

Sublimation   Altering an unacceptable id impulse to an activity that's more socially acceptable.

Superego   The component of personality that seeks moral perfection.

Topographical model   Freud's model of three regions, or areas, of the mind.

Unconscious   The region of the mind that's not accessible to consciousness.

Wish fulfillment   The creation of an unconscious image of a desired object.

CHAPTER 9

Anxiety, Defense, and Self-Protection

Dan and Jamie are talking about a club they went to last weekend, at which one of their friends got flagrantly, ostentatiously drunk—something she's done weekly for the past year.

"Man, I can't believe how much Robin *drinks*," says Jamie. "She soaks it up like a sponge."

At this moment, Robin rounds the corner, practically running into them.

"Hey Robin, are you still high from last weekend?" Jamie asks.

"What are you talking about?" replies Robin. "I didn't drink *that* much."

"Seriously, Robin," Dan throws in, "aren't you concerned about how much you've been drinking?"

Robin's face takes on an offended look. "Look, guys, I don't have a problem, so just stay off my back," she says, as she turns and walks away.

Dan and Jamie look at each other and shrug.

Roselyn and Roy, who have been dating for several months, are at a party. Also there is Tim, a very attractive guy they both know. At the end of the evening, after Tim and his date have left, Roselyn is talking with Roy and some friends. She says, "Didn't you see the way Tim was coming on to me? I wish he wouldn't do it, but he does it all the time."

Later, on the way home, Roy says to her, "Roselyn, you just made a fool of yourself—and me—in front of all those people. Tim didn't come on to you at all. I can't imagine where you got such an idea."

CHAPTER 8 described the psychoanalytic view of human nature. In this chapter, we consider more deeply some ways in which human nature is reflected in behavior, according to that view. In many respects, the points made here are extensions of the logic of Sigmund Freud's theory. Some of the ideas, however, came from other people. Most prominent among them was his daughter, Anna Freud (1966).

Anxiety

Much of the activity of personality—in people who are perfectly normal, as well as people with problems—concerns **anxiety.** Freud (1936/1926) saw anxiety as a warning signal to the ego that something bad is about to happen. Naturally, people seek to avoid or escape anxiety.

Freud (1959/1926) distinguished among three types of anxiety, which reflect three kinds of bad things. The simplest is **reality anxiety,** which arises from a threat or danger in the world. It's what you experience when you realize you're about to be bit by a dog, crash your car, be yelled at for a mistake at work, or fail an exam. As its name implies, reality anxiety is rooted in reality. We deal with it by fixing, avoiding, or escaping from the situation producing the feeling.

The second type is **neurotic anxiety.** This is unconscious fear that your id impulses will get out of control and have you do something that will get you punished. People with a lot of neurotic anxiety are constantly worried about the id's escaping from the ego's control (though the worry is unconscious). This isn't a fear of expressing id impulses per se. It's a fear of the punishment that will result from expressing them.

Because people are often punished for impulsive behavior, particularly if it's behavior that society disapproves of, this type of anxiety has a kind of basis in reality. In this case, however, the danger arises from within the person, from the urges of the id. For this reason, neurotic anxiety is harder to deal with than reality anxiety. You can drive carefully, prepare for exams, and avoid dangerous dogs, but you can't escape from your id. It always has the potential to get out of control.

The third type, called **moral anxiety,** is the fear people have when they've violated (or are about to violate) their moral codes. If your moral sense forbids cheating and you're tempted to cheat, you will feel moral anxiety. If your moral sense forbids sex before marriage and you're just about to have sex with someone, you will experience moral anxiety. Moral anxiety is felt as guilt or shame.

Moral anxiety arises from the conscience that's part of your superego. The stronger your superego, the more likely you'll have moral anxiety. Again, it's important to be clear about the difference between this and reality anxiety. People may be punished by society for moral lapses, but the threat of punishment from society isn't the basis of moral anxiety. Its source is internal, in your conscience. As with neurotic anxiety, it's hard to deal with. Just as you can't escape your id, you can't run away from your conscience.

Mechanisms of Defense

If your ego did its job perfectly, you'd never feel anxiety. External dangers would be avoided or dealt with, preventing reality anxiety. Id impulses would be released in degrees at appropriate times, preventing neurotic anxiety. And you'd never let yourself do anything (or even *want* to do anything) that your superego prohibits, preventing moral anxiety. No one's ego works this well, however. As a result, most people experience some anxiety, and many people experience a lot. This is part of normal life.

When anxiety arises, the ego responds in two ways. First, it increases rational problem-oriented coping efforts. It tries to deal (consciously) with the source of the threat. This works pretty well for reality anxiety. Second, it engages **defense mechanisms,** tactics the ego develops to help it avoid the other kinds of anxiety. When defenses work well, they keep anxiety away altogether. Defense mechanisms share two characteristics: First, they all can operate unconsciously. Second, they all distort or transform reality in one way or another.

Varying defense mechanisms have been proposed (A. Freud, 1966). The next sections outline several of them.

REPRESSION

The central mechanism of defense is called **repression.** Indeed, Sigmund Freud often used the terms *defense* and *repression* interchangeably. Repression can be done consciously (which Anna Freud called *suppression*), as the person tries to force something out of awareness (see also Box 9.1). Most discussions of repression, however, focus on it as an unconscious process.

Box 9.1   UNINTENDED EFFECTS OF THOUGHT SUPPRESSION

People sometimes consciously try to keep particular thoughts out of their minds. If you're trying to quit smoking, you want to avoid thinking about cigarettes. If you're trying to lose weight, you want not to think of food. If you've just broken up with someone, you don't want to think about the things you used to do together. In each case, you try to keep these ideas out of your consciousness.

Sometimes thought suppression works, but trying not to think of something can have unintended side effects. Dan Wegner and his colleagues conducted a program of studies on thought suppression (Wegner, 1989, 1994; Wenzlaff & Wegner, 2000), and their conclusions may surprise you. Trying not to think about something can actually make that thought become *more* likely later on, especially if the thought's an emotionally arousing one (Wegner, Shortt, Blake, & Page, 1990).

The idea of conscious thought suppression contains a paradox. Thought suppression involves two steps: deciding to suppress the thought and then getting rid of all evidence of the thought, including the plan to suppress it. This seems to require you to be

conscious of your intent and not conscious of it, all at once. (If repression occurs unconsciously, of course, this problem is avoided, because the plan to get rid of the thought is unconscious.)

So what happens when people try to suppress a thought? Initial research taught people a think-aloud technique in which they reported all thoughts that came to mind. They then did this for periods of five minutes under two different conditions. In one condition, they were to try not to think of a white bear. Every time a white bear came to mind, they were to ring a bell in front of them. In the other condition, they were to *think* of a white bear and to ring the bell when they did. For some, the suppression came first, then the thinking. For others, the order was reversed.

Two findings emerged. First, it was hard to avoid thinking of a white bear. (The most effective strategy was focusing on something else.) Interestingly, most intrusions of the unwanted thought occurred when the person had just finished another thought and was silent. It was as though the thought could be kept out as long as the mental machinery was fully occupied, but when an opening came up, the thought leaped in. Suppression is hard unless you have a distractor to think of

instead. To put this idea in psychoanalytic terms, it's apparently easier to form an alternative cathexis than to form an anticathexis.

The second finding was that people who suppressed showed a rebound effect. That is, when they were later asked to think of the bear, they did so more frequently and consistently than did the other people. Their reports of the white bear were stable over the five-minute period. In contrast, those who'd started by thinking of the bear wore out fairly quickly, and their reports fell off over the five-minute period. Rebound effects have been found repeatedly, even in dreams! (Wegner, Wenzlaff, & Kozak, 2004).

In practical terms, what are the implications of findings such as these? What should you do if you want *not* to think about something? Wegner (1989) argues that, as odd as it may sound, the best medicine is to let the thoughts in. Experience the feelings associated with the intrusion, and let the experience run its course. Only by relaxing mental control, he says, can we regain it. By lowering your defenses, you eventually reduce the pressure of the unwanted thought, and it will go away on its own (perhaps through the mechanisms of the unconscious).

We said in Chapter 8 that repression can mean forming an anticathexis with an id impulse. This restrains it from being expressed. If you have the impulse to fondle the person next to you in class, your ego (presumably) takes action to keep the impulse out of your awareness. But the idea also applies to information that's painful or upsetting. Sometimes such information is the memory of impulses you already expressed. If you did something last week you're ashamed of, you try not to think about it and eventually may be unable to recall doing it.

Painful and threatening thoughts have many sources, not all of them id impulses. Threat can come from personal lapses—for example, forgetting to lock your apartment, thus letting someone steal your TV. It can come from things about yourself that you see as failings—for example, the fact that you're unpopular or the fact you can't dance. It can come from being part of a group that others put down (Steele, 1997) or from the realization you will eventually die (Pyszczynski, Greenberg, & Solomon, 2000). Threat can come from situations that conflict with your superego's standards—for example, the fact that you're not doing anything about people in the world who are starving or the thought that your parents have an active sex life with certain preferred positions for intercourse.

It's important to realize that repression need not be total. It's easiest to talk about defenses in all-or-nothing terms, but this can be misleading. You can partly hide a moderately distressing memory, so you don't think about it often. In essence, you simply avoid retrieving it (Shane & Peterson, 2004). You haven't forgotten it. If reminded of it, you're still aware it's there. But you'd just as soon not be reminded of it. This would be a partial repression. (For more on repression see Box 9.2.)

DENIAL

Another simple defense occurs when people are overwhelmed by a threatening reality. This defense is **denial:** the refusal to believe an event took place or a condition exists. An example is the mother who refuses to believe the message that her son has been killed in combat. Another is a child abused by a parent who goes on as if nothing were wrong (Freyd, 1996). A less extreme case is a college student who refuses to believe the grade by her name and assumes there's been some sort of mistake. It may also be denial when a young boy plays a superhero, thereby hiding the reality of his weakness.

As people mature and the ego gets better at assessing reality, denial becomes harder. That is, the more you know, the more clearly reality stares you in the face. Denial remains possible at any age, though. It's common for people who have serious problems with alcohol or drugs to deny the problem (as in the opening of the chapter). It's common for someone whose lover is straying to deny it. Many victims of Nazi persecution failed to flee while there was still time, apparently because of denial. Indeed, it's been argued that self-report measures of well-being can be untrustworthy because some people deny to themselves the distress that they're experiencing (Shedler, Mayman, & Manis, 1993).

Denial prevents us from becoming aware of unpleasant things in our lives.

Denial resembles repression in many ways. Both keep from awareness what the person feels unable to cope with. They differ in the source of the threat. Repression deals with threats that originate within the dynamics of the mind. Denial deals with threats with other sources.

Box 9.2   Recall of Traumatic Childhood Memories

Breakdown of Repression, or Events That Never Happened?

Repression can keep memories of past trauma from reaching awareness. If the events can't be recalled, the person is spared any anxiety, anguish, or guilt associated with the experience. It's possible, however, for repression to break down. If that happens, people will recall episodes from their lives they might prefer not to recall. Sometimes, however, the memories that are "recalled" aren't real. This has created a huge controversy.

Consider, for example, a case reported by Elizabeth Loftus (1997). Nadean Cool sought psychiatric help to deal with her reactions to a trauma experienced by her daughter. Through hypnosis and other techniques, she recalled repressed memories of abuse she herself had endured. She became convinced she had repressed memories of having been in a satanic cult, eating babies, being raped, having sex with animals, and being forced to watch the murder of her 8-year-old

friend. In reality, none of these events had ever happened. The therapist's procedures induced her to think they had. When she realized this, she sued the psychiatrist for malpractice and eventually won a $2.4 million settlement. (See Loftus [1997] for other examples of memories being inadvertently planted by therapists.)

Indeed, false memories are surprisingly easy to induce. For instance, researchers had people recall childhood events that relatives recalled (e.g., Loftus, Coan, & Pickrell, 1996; Loftus & Pickrell, 1995). A few events that the relatives didn't mention (because they never happened) were embedded among the real ones. Not surprisingly, most people (80% or so) recalled something about the real events. More surprising was the percentage who reported memories about the events that never happened. Twenty to 30% of people typically report memories of nonexistent events, and the rate sometimes exceeds 60%!

False memories seem to depend partly on the event's being plausible. However, even events that are unusual or highly unlikely can produce false recall (Hyman, Husband, & Billings, 1995; Spanos, 1996). Another

important variable seems to be the extent to which the events are verifiable. False memories are more likely for events that can't be easily verified (Lynn, Myers, & Malinoski, 1997).

Interest in so-called recovered memories runs high today, partly because the memories often lead to accusations of terrible acts that had been repressed. Many persons have been accused of acts of physical and sexual abuse on the basis of such newly recovered memories. Some of them have been shown to be innocent. Yet they've undergone public humiliation in ways that permanently changed their lives.

It's very important to bear in mind that the occurrence of false memories doesn't mean that the spontaneous recall of traumatic events is never true. Children are sometimes the victims of sexual, physical, and emotional abuse. Sometimes those events are repressed to avoid distress. However, it does seem clear that not all cases of recalled trauma are real. Sometimes people are misled into remembering things that never happened. It can be very hard to tell whether a vivid memory is true or false. But a great deal can depend on deciding which it is.

Everyone uses repression and denial because they work (Erdelyi, in press). They save you from pain or anxiety. But too much repression or denial has a cost. These defenses take energy. Energy tied up this way can't be used for other things. If an act of repression continues, the energy is more or less permanently tied up. Thus, despite the fact that repression and denial are sometimes needed, they can eventually work against you.

Perhaps for that reason, other defenses also develop. These other mechanisms operate in combination with repression (and one another). They free some of the energy, while still keeping unacceptable impulses, thoughts, or feelings from registering on consciousness.

PROJECTION

In **projection**, anxiety is reduced by ascribing your own unacceptable qualities to someone else. You project traits, impulses, desires, or even goals (Kawada, Oettingen,

Gollwitzer, & Bargh, 2004). Projection provides a way to hide your knowledge of a disliked aspect of yourself while still expressing that quality, though in a highly distorted form (Mikulincer & Horesh, 1999).

For example, if you feel hostility toward others, you remove the feelings from awareness through repression. The feelings are still there, however. By projecting, you develop the perception that others hate you or are out to get you. In this way, your hostile impulse is expressed, but in a way that's not threatening to you (Schimel, Greenberg, & Martens, 2003). Another example is a woman who has sexual urges toward someone she shouldn't have and accuses him of being seductive toward her (the second example opening the chapter). The impulse gets out in a distorted form, while the woman remains unaware of her own desires.

Thus, projection serves two purposes. It helps to get the id's desires into the open in one form or other, releasing some of the energy required to repress them (Schimel et al., 2003). When you project, you're recognizing that the threatening quality *exists*, because you're seeing it. Just as important, though, the desire emerges in such a way that the ego and superego don't recognize it as belonging to you. Thus, the threat is sidestepped (see Figure 9.1).

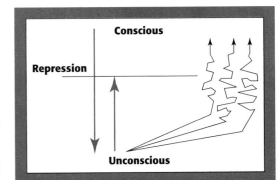

FIGURE 9.1

Defenses begin with repression, removing threatening material from the conscious region of the mind to the unconscious. What has been repressed cannot be brought out directly because it's too anxiety provoking. Repressed material can sneak around the barrier, however, by being transformed so as to make it less recognizable. Though these distortions permit the repressed urges to gain expression, the expression is weaker and less effective than the initial urge. Thus, pressure to express the urge remains.

RATIONALIZATION

Another important defense mechanism is **rationalization.** In rationalization, the person reduces anxiety by finding a rational explanation (or excuse) for a behavior that really was done for unacceptable reasons. For example, the man who cheats on his income tax may rationalize his behavior as reducing the amount of money spent on weapons in the world.

Rationalization also protects against other kinds of threats. For example, after a failure, rationalization maintains self-esteem. If you don't get into medical school, you may convince yourself that you really didn't want to be a doctor anyway. A man who's turned down for a date may convince himself that the woman really wasn't so great after all. Rationalization is very common in people's responses to success and failure. It's been shown repeatedly that people tend to take credit for good performances and blame bad performances on forces outside their control (e.g., Ross & Fletcher, 1985).

INTELLECTUALIZATION

Another defense is the tendency to think about threats in cold, analytical, and emotionally detached terms, which is called **intellectualization.** Thinking about events in a clinical fashion allows people to dissociate their thoughts from their feelings. This process separates and isolates the threatening event from the feeling that normally would accompany it—thus, no anxiety (Feldman, Barrett, Williams, & Fong, 2002).

For example, the woman who finds out her husband is dying of cancer may try to learn as much about cancer and its treatment as she can. By focusing on the disease intellectually and compartmentalizing that information, she shields herself from distress. A man who is sexually aroused by a co-worker may analyze in detail the qualities that make her attractive, considering her from the point of view of an uninvolved connoisseur of beauty. Doing this lets him distance himself from his desires.

Freud (1961/1915) made a more general point about this aspect of defense when discussing the separation of the unconscious from the conscious part of the mind. He suggested that an idea can exist in both parts of the mind at once, in different forms. The intellectual aspect of the idea can be in consciousness, even if it's a threatening idea, such as hating your father. This can be managed if the emotional quality attached to the idea—the deeply personal part that makes the idea psychologically meaningful—remains repressed. This sounds like a perfect description of intellectualization.

REACTION FORMATION

One way to guard against the release of an unacceptable impulse is to make a point of stressing its *opposite*. Doing this is called **reaction formation.** For example, a child may deal with hostile feelings toward a new baby in the family by repressing her hostile feelings and replacing them with effusive positive displays. Adults may react to uncertainty about some aspect of the self by asserting greater confidence in another aspect (McGregor & Marigold, 2003).

Freud believed that it's hard to tell whether an act stems from its apparent motivation or from the opposite impulse. Reaction formation is often inferred from the size of the response. If the person seems to "go overboard" or the response seems out of proportion to the context, you may be seeing reaction formation. Another clue is that the act may incorporate tinges of the impulse being defended against. For example, the child just described may try to "love her new brother to death" by hugging him so hard he begins to hurt. Another example of this is so-called friendly advice that is subtly disparaging.

Further examples are easy to suggest. A man who acts as a superstud, sleeping with one woman after another, may be trying to hide from himself fears about his sexual adequacy. Cases have been reported in which legislators who tried to pass laws against homosexual rights were rumored to be homosexual themselves. They may have been trying to prevent themselves from facing their true nature by behaving in a way that was its opposite.

You can also display reaction formation in interpreting the behaviors of people close to you. For example, people confronting evidence that their romantic partners have important faults may distort their perceptions of the evidence. The result is to turn the faults into virtues (Murray & Holmes, 1993).

REGRESSION

In Chapter 8, we described stages of psychosexual development and how people can become fixated in them. *Fixation* means that energy remains tied up in the cathexes of that stage. Anna Freud (1966) believed that stress causes people to abandon mature coping strategies and use patterns of the stages in which they are fixated. She called this **regression,** because it means giving up a more advanced form of coping in favor of one that's more primitive and infantile.

For example, an adult who's fixated at the oral stage might smoke more or eat or drink more when stressed at work. Someone with an anal fixation may respond to stress by becoming even more obstinate and compulsive than usual. The stronger the fixation, the more likely the person will regress under stress to that mode of functioning. Recall that fixations can arise when needs were well gratified in an early stage of development. Thus, regression often is a return to a way of relating to the world that used to be very effective (A. Freud, 1966).

Regression can occur at any point in development. An older child can regress to patterns of earlier childhood. Adults can also regress. In adult regression, people don't always act literally as they did during the earlier stage (although they may). Rather, the person's thoughts and actions become permeated with the concerns of the earlier stage. The manifestation of these concerns is often symbolic, rather than literal.

IDENTIFICATION

In Chapter 8, we also described how a person who lacks power (or some other desired quality) can acquire it symbolically through **identification.** Identification is linking oneself symbolically with some other person who has the missing quality. Thus, boys in the Oedipal crisis acquire strength and power symbolically through identification with their fathers. This identification also gives them symbolic possession of their mothers. There's evidence that this defense predicts better psychological well-being later on (Cramer & Tracy, 2005).

DISPLACEMENT AND SUBLIMATION

Two final defense mechanisms were introduced in Chapter 8: displacement and sublimation. These are generally considered less neurotic than the others we've described and more adaptive. **Displacement** is shifting an impulse from one target to another. This often happens when the intended target is threatening. Displacement is a defense in such cases because substituting a less threatening target for the original one reduces anxiety.

For example, the student who's angry with her professor and takes out her hostility on her very understanding boyfriend avoids the anxiety that would arise from attacking her professor. The person with an inappropriate lust who displaces that urge onto a permissible target avoids the anxiety that would arise from expressing the desires toward the true target.

Sublimation also lets impulses be expressed by transforming them to a more acceptable form. In this case, it's not something about the target that creates the threat, but something about the impulse. Sublimation is a defense because anxiety goes down when a transformed impulse is expressed instead of the initial one. Freud felt that sublimation, more than any other mechanism, reflects maturity. Sublimation is a process that keeps problems from occurring, rather than a tactic that people turn to after anxiety is aroused.

People often express impulses in symbolic form. Sometimes people live out their impulses through their children—or even their pets!

RESEARCH ON DEFENSES

What's the scientific status of defense mechanisms? A fair amount of research has been done on this topic; after a quiet period, interest is growing again (Cramer, 2000). Consider a study of projection by Halpern (1977). People who did or did not seem sexually defensive (by a self-report scale) either were or were not exposed to erotic photos before making ratings of someone else. Sexually defensive people rated the other person as more "lustful" if they'd seen erotic photos than if they hadn't. Those who weren't defensive about sexual issues didn't display this projection. This pattern makes sense from a psychody-namic perspective. You project only about things that threaten you.

Research has also tested the idea that projection occurs when people actively try to suppress thoughts about something they don't like about themselves (Newman, Duff, & Baumeister, 1997). This active effort to suppress seems to cause thoughts about the unwanted trait to push back and become even more accessible (recall Box 9.1). This in turn causes the thoughts to be ready to use when someone else's behavior even remotely fits the trait. On the other side, there's also evidence that when a stereotype involving that trait applies to someone else, it makes projection more likely (Govorum, Fuegen, & Payne, 2006).

These studies seem to support the idea of defense. But the literature as a whole is ambiguous, and it's often easy to find alternative interpretations. As a result, differ-ent readers draw different conclusions. To Sherwood (1981) there was substantial evidence of projection, whereas to Holmes (1981) there wasn't. Many people are con-vinced that repression occurs in the short term (e.g., Erdelyi, 1985, in press; Paulhus & Suedfeld, 1988), although in the longer term, there are more questions.

Recent research has begun to take a different angle on the study of repression. This work looks at individual differences in the tendency to repress and asks whether repressors differ in important ways from people who repress less. In one study, partic-ipants did a task that required them to make associations to phrases with sexual and aggressive content (Weinberger, Schwartz, & Davidson, 1979). Repressors reported the least distress during this task, but they also showed the most physical arousal. In other research, repressors were less able to recall emotional memories from childhood and from their day-to-day experiences than were other people (Davis, 1987; Davis & Schwartz, 1987). Repressors are also better at suppressing memories of embarrassment than other people (Barnier, Levin, & Maher, 2004). These findings suggest that the search for evidence of repression may be coming closer to fruition.

EVIDENCE OF UNCONSCIOUS CONFLICT

Much of this discussion of ego defenses assumes that conflicts are buried in the unconscious through repression to avoid neurotic or moral anxiety. Although unconscious, the conflicts presumably continue to affect behavior. That is, repressed desires leak out through such processes as projection, reaction formation, and sublimation.

Sometimes, though, the conflicts emerge through symptoms, such as depression. The idea that unconscious conflicts cause symptoms has been studied by Lloyd Silverman and his colleagues (Silverman, 1976, 1983; Weinberger & Silverman, 1987). This idea is hard to test, because it requires arousing the conflict in the unconscious but not letting it reach awareness. The solution was to present material subliminally, at exposures so brief people couldn't tell what they were seeing.

Subliminal stimuli apparently do register. When susceptible people were shown things designed to stir up their unconscious conflicts, their symptoms increased. One susceptible group is depression-prone people. In the psychoanalytic view, depression reflects unconscious death wishes. Such wishes can be stirred up by words (e.g., *cannibal eats person*) or pictures (e.g., one person stabbing another). In several studies, showing such material subliminally to people prone to depression caused them to have deeper feelings of depression (Silverman, 1976). This did *not* happen if the stimuli were allowed to enter consciousness by using longer exposures. This supports the idea that it's the unconscious producing the symptoms.

Other research in this series involved arousing or diminishing Oedipal feelings in men (Silverman, Ross, Adler, & Lustig, 1978). Participants first did a competitive dart-throwing task and then viewed subliminal stimuli. In one condition it said, "Beating Dad is wrong"; in another condition it said, "Beating Dad is OK"; in a third condition the stimuli weren't related to Oedipal issues. Then the men repeated the dart-throwing task. Stirring up Oedipal feelings ("Beating Dad is OK") led to better scores (see Figure 9.2). Presumably, Oedipal feelings translated into stronger competition. Pushing Oedipal desires down ("Beating Dad is wrong") led to worse scores.

In sum, there's evidence that behavior can be influenced by arousing a conflict at an unconscious level. There are limitations. Some effects occur reliably only among people in whom the conflict is already well established. In the last study described, in contrast, the effect was more general, presumably because *all men* have experienced the Oedipal conflict.

We should also note that Silverman's research has been controversial, partly because others have found it hard to obtain the same effects (e.g., Heilbrun, 1980). Another problem is a lack of evidence of processes assumed to underlie the effects (Weinberger & Hardaway, 1990). Despite the controversy—or perhaps even because of it—it seems likely that this technique will continue to be explored as a way to study unconscious conflict.

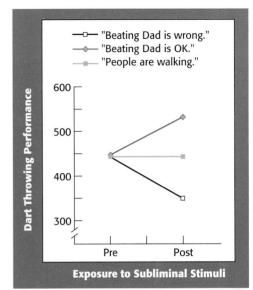

FIGURE 9.2
Effects of subliminal activation (or deactivation) of Oedipal feelings on competitive dart throwing. Participants threw darts for one score before exposure to the subliminal stimuli (pre) and threw again afterward (post). Subjects exposed to "Beating Dad is wrong" got lower scores the second time. Those exposed to "Beating Dad is OK" got higher scores the second time. Those exposed to "People are walking" were not affected. *Source: Adapted from Silverman et al., 1978.*

Exposing the Unconscious

We've been focusing on how the ego handles conflicts. To guard against neurotic and moral anxiety, the ego represses threatening desires. The desires, now unconscious, continue to influence behavior through further ego defenses.

Freud believed that the unconscious is where the vital forces of human life are at work, influencing people in complex ways. There is where the true motives lie. Gaining access to the conflicts and desires of the unconscious seems very hard. Freud believed, though, that it's not as hard as it seems. He thought unconscious impulses are revealed constantly in everyday events. You just have to look for them.

THE PSYCHOPATHOLOGY OF EVERYDAY LIFE

One way such motives are revealed is in people's mistakes. We all make mistakes from time to time. We forget things, get our words jumbled, and have accidents. Freud (1960b/1901) referred to such events as the *psychopathology of everyday life* (a phrase that also conveys his belief that all normal life contains a little of the abnormal). He believed such events, far from being random, stem from urges in the unconscious. The urges emerge in a distorted form, as mistakes. Thus, memory lapses, slips of speech, and accidents provide indirect insights into a person's true desires. (For a contrasting opinion, however, see Reason and Mycielska, [1982].)

Collectively, these events are termed **parapraxes.** (A literal translation from the German term is "faulty achievement" [Bettelheim, 1982].) Perhaps the simplest parapraxis is forgetting. From a psychoanalytic perspective, forgetting reflects repression, an attempt to keep something from consciousness. Sometimes it's easy to see why forgetting occurs (e.g., the student who forgets to return an important book to someone he doesn't like). At other times, it's harder to see the motive. Yet a motive can often be found, if enough is known about the situation.

A simple example comes from a psychology professor we know. He was heading off to a small conference of eminent psychologists, including some he had professional disagreements with. He arrived at the airport only to discover he'd left his wallet at home. As a result, he was unable to board the plane (and would have been unable to pick up his rental car at his destination). The delay caused him to miss the first half-day of the conference.

If forgetting is a successful act of repression, slips of the tongue are partially *un*successful acts of repression. That is, the person expresses all or part of the unconscious thought or wish, despite the effort to keep it hidden. As with forgetting, the hidden meaning may be obvious to observers. Consider the woman who reveals her ambivalent feelings toward her lover by telling him he's exactly the kind of person she'd like to *bury* (instead of *marry*).

There's evidence that these verbal slips are related to anxiety, although the evidence falls short of indicating that the anxiety is unconscious. Motley (1985) and his colleagues induced people to make a certain kind of slip. In this slip, a pair of words is read as a different word pair (for example, saying *flute fry* instead of *fruit fly*). The research requires creating specific pairs that are easy to misread into slips with particular overtones. The research involved creating specific anxieties and seeing whether those anxieties increase relevant slips.

For example, in one case, men were made to feel anxious about receiving electric shocks. In another, the session was run by a provocatively dressed woman to arouse anxiety over sexual issues. Both conditions included word pairs that could be misread as shock related (e.g., *damn shock* instead of *sham dock*) and pairs that could be misread as sex related (e.g., *happy sex* instead of *sappy hex*). As can be seen in Figure 9.3, men led to be nervous about shocks made more shock-related slips than anyone else; men led to think about sex made more slips with sexual connotations than anyone else. Sexual slips were also most frequent among men high on a measure of sex guilt (Motley, 1985).

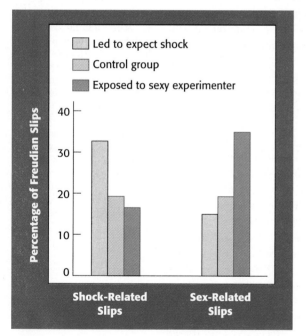

FIGURE 9.3
Freudian slips induced in the laboratory. When participants expected to receive electric shocks, they made more shock-related slips (left side). When participants had been exposed to a provocatively dressed experimenter, they made more sex-related slips (right side). *Source: Adapted from Motley, 1985.*

When accused of making a slip, most people blame fatigue, distraction, or being in a hurry. Freud held that such factors help but don't cause slips. The real cause always comes from the unconscious. A person is more likely to make a slip when tired or inattentive, but the form of the slip depends on unconscious forces.

Accidents, on the other hand, are more complicated. Accidents that are most interesting from a psychoanalytic point of view are those that stem from carelessness. To decide whether something is an accident, you must look at the circumstances. If you learn a man was struck by a motorboat while scuba diving, you might think it was an accident. But if you learn that the man, an experienced diver, failed to put out a diving marker and didn't pause to listen for motors before surfacing, you might be more inclined to conclude that (for whatever reason) he had an unconscious desire to do himself harm.

Accidents are complicated for another reason as well. Because they can involve injury, accidents can serve several functions at once. In harming yourself, you can also harm someone else—someone who cares for you. In this sense, an accident can serve both as crime (causing someone else to feel bad) and as punishment (causing you to suffer an injury).

DREAMS

Freud (1953b/1900) believed the unconscious also reveals itself through dreams, which he referred to as "the royal road to the unconscious." Freud began by distinguishing two kinds of dream content. **Manifest content** is the sensory images of the dreamer—what most of us think of as the

Freud believed that accidents often result from an unconscious desire to cause harm.

dream. More interesting, to Freud, was the **latent content**—the unconscious thoughts, feelings, and wishes behind the manifest content. Latent content tells why a dream takes the form it takes (see Box 9.3 for another view).

Freud believed that latent content derives from three sources. The first is the *sensory stimulation* that bombards us as we sleep: a thunderstorm, a passing siren, the barking of a dog. These sounds can prompt dreams and be absorbed into them. When this happens, the stimuli are part of the dream's latent content. Dreams are said to be "guardians of sleep," because absorbing an outside stimulus into a dream prevents it from awakening the sleeper.

The second source of latent dream content is thoughts, ideas, and feelings connected to the sleeper's waking life—**current concerns**—which remain active in the unconscious while you sleep. For example, during the day, you may have been thinking about an upcoming exam, an interesting person you'd just met, or a financial problem you have. Incorporating thoughts about that topic into dreams prevents them from waking you, just as with sensory stimuli.

The third source of latent dream content is unconscious *id impulses* that the ego has blocked from expression while you're awake. Often these impulses relate to childhood conflicts. For this reason, the impulse is often infantile in form and primitive in content. Freud believed that every dream incorporates some unconscious impulse or urge.

Manifest content consists of conscious sensory impressions (usually visual). Manifest content is a fantasy in which the latent wish or impulse is expressed. To use a term from Chapter 8, the dream is *wish fulfillment* on the part of the id.

During early childhood, the tie between latent and manifest content is quite transparent. Consider the dream of a 2-year-old boy a few days after his mother brought home a new baby (Brenner, 1957). The boy reported as manifest content "See baby go away." It takes little imagination to infer the latent content especially because the mother felt the boy had resented the new baby from the moment he learned it was coming. In this case, then, the manifest content was a direct translation of the latent content—the boy's wish to have the new baby no longer a part of his life. The manifest content simply fulfilled this wish in the form of visual images.

Box 9.3   Functions of Sleep and Dreams

Sleep has long been a source of wonder and mystery. Each of us spends a substantial part of each day in a state somewhere between life and death. And what are dreams? Fragmented recollections of journeys to other dimensions? Bits of truth whispered by gods (on the condition we not remember them for long)? Are dreams reflections of the primary process, visual echoes of the snarling and lurid passions of the id? Or are they just a jumble of nonsense, mutterings of a brain left to idle like a car at a red light?

In Freud's time, little was known about sleep and dreams. It seemed natural to him to think of dreams as the pathway to the unconscious, given their surreal and symbolic qualities. In later years, though, scientists have studied sleep and dreaming, and a little more is now known about them (e.g., Domhoff, 2003; Hobson, 1988; Walker, 2005; Winson, 1985, 1990).

For starters, everybody dreams, although many people don't remember the dreams. A sleep state was discovered decades ago, in which people's eyes move rapidly, breathing is irregular, heartrate increases, and movement is suppressed (Aserinsky & Kleitman, 1953). Because rapid eye movement (REM) is a key feature, it's known as *REM sleep*. Whatever's going on in that state apparently is necessary. When people are kept out of REM (by being awakened whenever it starts), they show an increased tendency to enter it. REM sleep occurs four or five times a night for adults; infants spend nearly eight hours a day in REM sleep.

People awakened from REM sleep almost always report they were dreaming. People awakened from non-REM sleep don't say that as often. It used to be thought that REM is synonymous with dreaming. It's now clear, though, that that's wrong (Nielsen, 2000; Solms, 2000). Nonetheless, because dreaming is more common in REM, most examinations of dreams focus on REM.

Why is REM sleep necessary? What's going on there? Winson (1985) argued that new experiences are integrated with old ones during REM sleep. If this were so, a single set of brain structures could guide action when you're awake and consolidate when you're asleep. This would let us get the most out of our nervous system, because it's being used around the clock, rather than just when we're awake. Others have also suggested that REM sleep is involved in memory consolidation, based on different evidence (Walker, 2005).

Others disagree with that idea (Vertes, 2004). One reason is that antidepressant medications greatly reduce REM sleep but don't negatively affect memory. Vertes (2004) says that REM sleep is the nervous system's way of throwing a little stimulation at the sleeping brain, to keep it from stopping altogether and to prepare it for eventual awakening. He thinks the content of the stimulation is random and the dreaming is without meaning.

Yet another view, with fascinating implications, is that dreaming is an "off-line" model of the world, in which the sleeping brain runs simulations (Revonsuo, 2000). More specifically, this idea is that dreaming is a mechanism for simulating and rehearsing threat perception and threat avoidance. This would account for why dreams are generally somewhat organized and why misfortunes and aggressive interactions are so common in dreams (McNamara, McLaren, Smith, Brown, & Stickgold, 2005). Revonsuo (2000) believes that your nightmares are working for your well-being, preparing you for hazards you may face in your waking life.

These views are extremely different from one another. Although we know more about sleep and dreams than was true in Freud's time, we obviously need to learn much more before we can say we really understand them.

During later childhood and adulthood, the relationship between latent and manifest content becomes less obvious. Indeed, dreams sometimes seem complete gibberish. How can such dreams relate to wish fulfillment? The answer is that, with age, it becomes more important to distort or disguise the dream's latent content. The ego and the superego must remain unaware that an unacceptable impulse is being expressed. Keeping them unaware gets harder as people grow. Thus, even in dreams, the defense mechanisms remain at work.

Two processes allow forbidden impulses to be represented in the manifest content of dreams. In **symbolization,** unacceptable latent content is expressed in manifest content directly but symbolically. The symbol is a form that's less recognizable to the ego and the superego and is thereby less threatening. Symbolization might be considered the dreaming equivalent of sublimation. In **dream work,** latent content is disguised ways other than symbols to make it more acceptable to the ego and the superego. This can be done by jumbling separate thoughts into a single thought. (When they're jumbled, it's harder to tell what's what, and the threat is reduced.) It can be done by the **mechanism of opposites,** in which an unacceptable element of latent content is expressed manifestly as its opposite (much like reaction formation, when awake).

Interpretation of dreams involves examining manifest content, seeking its unconscious meaning. Freud believed many symbols that appear in dreams are unique to the dreamer. He also believed, however, that there are certain categories of shared symbols that have shared meanings. The universality of some symbols makes dream analysis easier.

HUMOR

The unconscious also reveals itself through humor (Freud, 1960a/1905). Humor often rests on threatening desires that are transformed in amusing ways. Much humor reflects hostility, which is blunted by distorting it into something ludicrous. Many jokes depend on there being an underlying inhibited thought. The joke telling slips around the inhibition, diverts attention, and lets the internal censor of the ego relax. When the punchline comes, the forbidden thought is abruptly expressed, too fast for the censor to recover. The energy devoted to restraining the forbidden thought is released in laughter.

Humor is similar to dreams in some respects, but there are also differences. Dreams let the unconscious urges emerge only in a symbolic and unrecognizable form. Humor, in contrast, is communicated from one person to another. Whereas dreams conceal their latent content, humor exposes the underlying content more completely (Oring, 1984). The symbolism and the laughter protect us from the threat, but the latent content is far closer to the surface than in dreams.

Projective Techniques of Assessment

The preceding sections focused on ways in which the unconscious reveals itself in everyday life. We now turn to ways in which the unconscious reveals itself in formal assessment, as practiced from the psychoanalytic perspective.

Formal methods of assessing unconscious processes are called **projective techniques** (Frank, 1939). These tests confront people with ambiguous stimuli. Because there's no obvious response, people's responses are determined primarily by their own feelings, attitudes, desires, and needs. (Recall our discussion of the TAT as a projective technique in Chapter 5.) These tests let people apply the defense of projection to their hidden feelings and put the feelings into their interpretations of what they see. What's projected presumably is beyond the person's conscious control and thus reflects the unconscious.

Several projective techniques exist. In *associative techniques,* people respond to a stimulus with the first word or thought that comes to mind. In *constructive techniques,* they create stories. *Completion techniques* involve completing a thought begun in an incomplete stimulus, such as a sentence that begins, "I wish. . . ." Although the techniques differ in format, they share several features. They all use ambiguous stimuli. The test taker is never told the purpose of the test. Instructions stress that there are no right or wrong answers and that the test takers can respond in whatever way they

FIGURE 9.4
Example of inkblot similar to those used in the Rorschach test. *Source: Courtesy of Jeremy Matthews Scheier and Meredith Matthews Scheier.*

wish. Finally, because of the open-ended and ambiguous nature of the technique, scoring relies heavily on subjective clinical judgments.

We focus for the rest of this section on one device that's often used to assess unconscious processes: the **Rorschach inkblot test.**

RORSCHACH INKBLOT TEST

Swiss psychiatrist Hermann Rorschach is usually credited with formalizing the use of inkblots for assessment (Rorschach, 1942). He finally arrived at a set of ten blots, chosen for their ability to evoke different responses from different groups of psychiatric patients. (His strategy thus made use of the criterion-keying approach to test development, described in Chapter 3.)

The ten inkblots in the Rorschach set are all bilaterally symmetrical, meaning that they are approximately the same on both sides of an imaginary center line (see Figure 9.4). The ink on five of them is all black, but the intensity is uneven, ranging from solid black to light gray. Two have both black and red ink. Three have pastel colors, including blue, green, yellow, and orange.

The Rorschach usually is administered to one person at a time in a two-stage procedure. First the person views the inkblots in a predetermined order and indicates what he or she sees in them, or what the inkblot resembles or suggests, while the examiner records what's being said. Then the person views all 10 cards again. The examiner provides reminders of what was said earlier about the card and asks what it was about the card that made the person say that.

Several systems have been devised for scoring the Rorschach. The most popular is that of John Exner (1974, 1993). In Exner's system, the responses are first compared against those of people with known personality qualities. Then the responses are examined as a progression from one card to the next. Finally, content is analyzed in terms of location, determinants, and content. *Location* is where in the blot the response focuses (the whole blot, a commonly noted detail, an unusual detail, the space surrounding the blot). *Determinants* include form, color, shading, or perceived movement in the location that prompted the response. The *content* of the response is its subject. Table 9.1 has examples of common interpretations of specific responses. Be aware, however, that a given response is interpreted only in the context of the entire test profile.

Although it's interesting as a technique, the Rorschach has serious psychometric problems. Its internal consistency is low, its test–retest reliability and inter-rater reliability are low, and its validity has been hard to establish (Anastasi, 1988; Lilienfeld, Wood, & Garb, 2000). Exner and his collaborators have tried to improve these qualities, but their efforts have not been entirely well received. Wood, Nezworski, and Stejskal (1996a, 1996b) criticized Exner's work on methodological grounds, bearing on issues of reliability and validity (see also Lilienfeld et al., 2000). On the other side, Ganellen (1996a, 1996b) has reported that the Rorschach does better at identifying depressed and psychotic persons than does the MMPI-2. Some of the issues raised in

Table 9.1 Rorschach Inkblot Responses. Here are three categories in which responses to the Rorschach are placed. In the left column is the category name, followed by its definition in the second column. The third column gives examples of responses that would be placed into each category. The far-right (fourth) column gives an interpretation for each example and an indication of why this interpretation is made.

Name of Category	Nature of Category	Example Response	Possible Interpretation (with critical feature identified)
Location	Place on blot from which response arose	"Overall, it reminds me of a cornstalk."	Suggests ability to think conceptually (response is based on whole blot)
		"That thing there looks like a hammer."	Suggests need to be exact and precise (response is based on a commonly noted detail)
Determinant	Quality of blot that led to response	"It's a whale, that's bleeding."	Suggests high degree of emotionality (response is based on color)
		"It's a bat flying."	Suggests high degree of imagination (response is based on perceived movement)
Content	Subject matter of response	"It's a man about to be beaten up by other people."	Suggests anxiety over hostile feelings (response involves aggression)
		"It's a person diving into the ocean waves."	Suggests strong fantasy life (response involves *human* movement)

the critiques of Exner's scoring system are technical; some are not (for example, much of the relevant evidence is unpublished). Not surprisingly, Wood et al.'s conclusions have been disputed by Exner (1996).

Many who favor projective tests respond to criticisms by saying that psychometric criteria are irrelevant to the Rorschach's usefulness. In their view, its value is in the insights it gives the examiner. Perhaps psychologists should stop treating it as a *test* and think of it instead as a *tool*. From this perspective the Rorschach is a supplementary interview aid in the hands of a trained clinician, giving clues and suggesting hypotheses worth further investigation.

It's too early to say how the Rorschach (and instruments like it) will come to be viewed. Continued efforts to standardize scoring procedures may yield better psychometric properties. Even if the Rorschach is viewed only as a clinical aid, though, it is not likely to be discarded soon as part of the psychoanalytic assessment battery.

Problems in Behavior, and Behavior Change

This chapter has emphasized two ideas: First, people use ego defenses to protect themselves from anxiety. Second, repressed urges and memories continue to influence behavior via the defenses. Psychoanalytic theorists believe that everyone uses defense mechanisms. Merely using defense mechanisms is not a sign that the person has a problem.

On the other hand, this is a viewpoint on personality in which normalcy shades easily into abnormality, with no clear boundary. Psychoanalytic theorists tend to distinguish normal from abnormal functioning by how much defenses dominate the person's life. Too much use of defense mechanisms is a sign of problems. Heavy use of defenses can save the person from dealing with conflicts, but it ties up too much energy in anticathexes. This leaves little energy for the person to use in dealing with new challenges. As the person's level of functioning begins to deteriorate, it becomes clearer that he or she has a problem.

Our discussion of problems and how they can be dealt with emphasizes the themes stressed all along. Freud believed the unconscious holds the secrets of people's difficulties in life. Only by delving into the unconscious can those difficulties be identified and resolved. This section begins by considering the psychoanalytic perspective on ways in which problems arise.

ORIGINS OF PROBLEMS

Problems have several possible origins. One origin is childhood experiences. As stated in Chapter 8, Freud believed adult personality is determined by early psychosexual development. If the person handles early stages well, little residue is carried into adulthood. However, it's rare for a person to enter the later stages of development unmarked. Most persons are partly fixated at earlier stages. If fixations are strong, a lot of energy is invested in them. In a very strong fixation, the preoccupation—albeit unconscious—leaves the person with little energy for anything else. This is one source of problems: overinvestment of energy in a fixation. This prevents flexible adult functioning by depleting energy the ego requires (Baumeister, 2002).

Another source of problems is a broad repression of basic needs and urges. If an overly punitive superego or a harsh environment causes too many urges to be buried, the person's basic nature is distorted and denied. The person is cramped and can't function in the way he or she is supposed to function. The repressed needs can squeeze their way past the repression only in twisted forms. This isn't really effective in meeting the needs. Again, the repression required to keep the needs hidden is a constant drain on energy available to the ego.

A third source of problems is buried trauma. Although traumatic incidents can occur at any point in life, most discussion of trauma focuses on early childhood. Indeed, at one point early in the evolution of his thinking, Freud believed most of his patients had suffered childhood sexual abuse. The "seduction theory," as it came to be known, was later abandoned when Freud decided the seductions hadn't actually taken place.

It was this change in his thinking that led to Freud's theory of the Oedipal conflict (Chapter 8), in which children deal with a sexual attraction to their opposite-sex parent. The Oedipal theory accounted for sexual imagery among patients, and it did so in a way that didn't require Freud to believe that large numbers of parents had seduced their children (though see Box 9.4).

Box 9.4 Seduction Fantasies, Child Molestation, or Neither?

A controversy arose in the 1980s about Freud's abandonment of his seduction theory of the origin of psychological disorder. As indicated in the main text, Freud eventually realized that the accounts he heard from patients weren't true. The women hadn't been seduced as children. Rather, they had unconsciously distorted their own sexual desires for their parents into a symbolic form and projected it outward.

That's the way Freud put it: He'd realized the truth. In 1984, however, Jeffrey Masson challenged that statement. Drawing from previously unpublished letters, he said the seductions were in fact real, that Freud knew it, and that he'd chosen to back away from the reality. Masson said Freud lacked the courage to admit the truth: that child sexual abuse was widespread.

Why would Freud lack the courage to stand up for what he believed? Masson said Freud was concerned for his professional reputation. His first presentation of the seduction theory, in a speech to a professional society, was met with utter silence. Masson said Freud was later urged not to publish it (though others contradict this assertion; Ellenberger, 1970; Esterson, 2002; McCullough, 2001). Perhaps Freud needed a way out to salvage his career prospects.

Masson also argued that *seduction* is an extremely unfortunate label. He said the word is not at all typical of Freud's first statement of the theory, in which he also used the terms *rape, abuse, attack, assault, aggression,* and *trauma*. Even as the theory was being set aside, Masson held, using the term *seduction* made the theory's implications seem more benign. Perhaps the terminology was one last defense against the truth.

Not everyone found Masson's account convincing. Some criticisms of his view are even less flattering to Freud than Masson's own view. Esterson (1993, 2001) said the seduction theory was a sham from the start—that the alleged evidence of molestation in patient accounts simply did not exist. Esterson argued that Freud projected his own preconceived ideas onto what patients said. Freud himself even wrote that patients assured him they did not believe their memories were of sexual contact (Esterson, 2001). Thus, to Esterson, the issue is not whether patient reports were recollection or fantasy. The issue is that it wasn't the patients who generated the recollections but Freud himself (see also Schimek, 1987).

What really *is* the truth? We will probably never know. We can't return to Freud's era to study the rate of child abuse. If Freud was aware of frequent abuse, he might have interpreted any hint of sexual contact—even a symbolic hint—in such terms. But perhaps even more worrisome is the assertion that he let himself be guided by his preconceptions, letting them stand in place of patient reports, as Esterson argues. If so, there would be little reason to believe either the seduction theory *or* its successor.

Despite this change, Freud's theory clearly holds a place for traumas such as sexual and physical abuse. His altered view simply reflects his conclusion that abuse isn't common. Still, a child who experiences physical abuse, especially repeated abuse, has a deeply unpleasant part of reality to deal with. The same is true of a child who is sexually abused. Indeed, many events that objectively are far less traumatic can loom large in the experience of a child: rejection by a parent, death of a person (or a pet) close to the child, exposure to fighting parents. Children who experience traumas such as these have large threats to deal with. They're dealt with first and foremost by repression—always the first response to overwhelming anxiety. Once again, the energy invested in forgetting is a constant drain on resources.

These three points of origin for problems differ, and the problems that result may also differ. All three paths, however, share one mechanism: In each case, the original fixation, urge, or trauma is repressed. This repression may protect the person, but it does so at a cost.

BEHAVIOR CHANGE

What can be done about this situation? The therapeutic methods of psychoanalysis developed by trial and error in Freud's practice. His understanding of how to deal with problems evolved along with his views on the *reasons* for the problems. Early on, he found that symptoms could be reduced by hypnotically inducing the person to relive highly emotional (and thus repressed) events—relive them fully and emotionally. The release of energy seemed to free the person from the problem, by diminishing the energy investment in the repressed event. This experience is often referred to as a *catharsis* because of the release of emotional energy.

Two discoveries radically changed Freud's approach. First, he found it wasn't necessary to hypnotize people. If the person just said aloud whatever came to mind—a procedure called **free association**—what was hidden in the unconscious would gradually emerge. In free association, the person is not to censor any thoughts but to say immediately whatever thoughts arise, even if they seem trivial, illogical, or embarrassing. The therapist stays out of view to minimize the person's inhibitions against speaking.

Freud's second discovery was that what emerged often wasn't literally true. As noted earlier, he had initially believed patients had experienced childhood seductions. Eventually he decided those encounters had not taken place. This led to a reorganization in how Freud viewed both the content of free association and also childhood sexuality. Free association was producing something important, but it wasn't quite what it had seemed to be.

In Freud's newer view, unconscious material emerges through free association in *symbolic* form. The symbolism makes it less threatening to the person, thus letting it emerge. Images of seduction are less threatening than images of one's own carnal desires. Free association often creates a jumble of symbols that make no sense on the surface. Yet, as in a crossword puzzle, they provide a partial context from which missing elements may be inferred (Erdelyi, 1985).

As noted earlier, many problems serious enough to produce behavioral problems are thought to stem from repressed conflicts and urges and from suppressed libidinal energy. The goal of therapy is to uncover the conflicts and loose the restrained energy (see also Box 9.5). Free association is a first step, because it allows symbolic access to the problem. It rarely gets to the heart of the problem, though, because of the threat in the repressed material.

Indeed, people in therapy sometimes actively fight against becoming aware of repressed conflicts and impulses. This struggle is called **resistance**. Resistance may be conscious—for instance, when a person has an association that arouses anxiety but doesn't report it. Resistance also may be unconscious, an automatic use of ego defenses against the possibility of anxiety. Its occurrence is usually a sign that something important is nearby, that the person is close to revealing something sensitive.

Whether conscious or unconscious, resistance provides an illustration of how emotionally wrenching psychoanalytic therapy can be. The person in therapy is trying to uncover distressing truths—truths that have been buried in the unconscious precisely *because* they're too painful to admit. It's no wonder that the process of uncovering them is hard.

An important element in psychoanalytic therapy is **transference**. Transference is a set of *displacements*. Feelings toward other people in the patient's life are displaced (transferred) onto the therapist. The feelings can be love or hatred. Transference serves as another defense, in that the therapist provokes less anxiety than does the original object of the feelings.

Transference can interfere with therapy because the patient may become caught up in his or her feelings toward the therapist. These feelings don't reveal the real

Box 9.5 Repression, Disclosure, and Physical Health

Our main discussion focuses on the idea that repression has a psychological cost. Evidence is accumulating, however, that holding back thoughts and feelings can also have a *physical* cost. An example is a study of women undergoing breast biopsies (Greer & Morris, 1975). Women who reported suppressing their emotions (most notably anger) were more likely to have cancer than those who didn't (see also Jensen, 1987). Another study looked at atherosclerosis over a 10-year period (Matthews, Owens, Kuller, Sutton-Tyrrell, & Jansen-McWilliams, 1998). Women who said they suppressed their anger had more atherosclerosis 10 years later. Not all evidence supports the view that suppression relates to disease (O'Donnell, Fisher, Rickard, & McConaghy, 2000; Price et al., 2001), but enough support exists to make the idea worth further study.

The flip side of this idea is that releasing threatening thoughts and feelings can have physical benefits. James Pennebaker and his colleagues have been at the forefront of research on disclosure of suppressed thoughts and feelings (Pennebaker, 1989;

Pennebaker & Chung, 2007; see also Smyth, 1998). Participants in this research are asked to describe (with complete anonymity, in most studies) their deepest thoughts and feelings either about a specific nontraumatic event or about "the most upsetting or traumatic experience of your entire life." Ideally, the event the participant is to talk about (or write about) is one that he or she hasn't talked about much with others. Thus, it's more likely to be something that's been repressed, at least partially. The disclosure of thoughts and feelings typically takes place for about 20 minutes at a time on four successive days.

The short-term effect of disclosing trauma is that people feel more distress. In the longer term, however, self-disclosure seems to have health benefits. In one study, students who disclosed about traumatic events were less likely to visit the health center in the next six months than those not asked to disclose (Pennebaker & Beall, 1986). Results of another study suggest that disclosure has an influence on the functioning of the immune system (Pennebaker, Kiecolt-Glaser, & Glaser, 1988). In a study of Holocaust survivors, those who seemed to let go the most during disclosure were least

likely to visit their physicians later (Pennebaker, 1989).

Why might disclosure of painful memories and the thoughts and feelings that accompany them have health benefits? Pennebaker is pursuing the idea that the mechanism lies in the cognitive changes that occur during and after the disclosures. He's found evidence that people who come to organize their experiences into causal narratives benefit more than people who do not (Pennebaker & Graybeal, 2001). Interestingly enough, it apparently isn't *having* a coherent story that helps, but the process of *creating* the story.

Pennebaker (1993) argued that the body expresses itself linguistically and biologically at the same time. As we struggle to create meaning from trauma, we create beneficial changes in our biological functions as well. The result is better biological functioning and ultimately better health. This view of the effects of emotional expression surely will continue to evoke controversy and interest. It is a viewpoint with many important implications. If it continues to be supported by research evidence, it will change the way many people think about therapy and even about such activities as keeping a diary!

conflict, because the conflict pertains to someone else. On the other hand, transference can point out the significance of the feelings that are being displaced. When transference occurs, then, its interpretation is an important part of the therapy process.

The goal of psychoanalytic psychology is **insight.** Insight in therapy isn't an intellectual understanding. Rather, this term implies the re-experiencing of the emotional reality of repressed conflicts, memories, or urges, previously unconscious parts of one's personality (see Table 9.2). Intellectual understanding has no power to change the person. For a cognitive reorganization to be useful, it must come in the context of an emotional catharsis. On the other hand, emotional release does not help without reorganization (Kelly, Klusas, von Weiss, & Kenny, 2001).

The development of true insight allows people to see how the conflicts and urges have influenced their functioning for years. The insight provides a basis to

Table 9.2 Three Origins of Problems in Personality and the Goal of Psychoanalysis in Treating Each.

Origin	Goal
Fixation	Relive prior conflict to work through
Repressed trauma	Relive experience for catharsis of feelings
Repressed basic needs	Gain emotional insight into the needs and their acceptability

work from so that they can attain greater acceptance of these previously unacceptable parts of the self. One result is that people can get by with less defense in the future.

DOES PSYCHOANALYTIC THERAPY WORK?

Psychoanalytic therapy is long (literally years) and usually emotionally painful. Given the costs, financial and emotional, an important question is whether it's effective. Even Freud's view changed over the years. Initially, he was optimistic. He believed that patients, particularly those who were bright and well educated, could benefit from the insights they gained. He expected them to become better and ultimately happier people.

During the middle of his career, however, his thinking began to shift. He became more convinced that the real value of his work was in his theory of the mind, not the therapy. By the end of his career, he'd become pessimistic about the effectiveness of psychoanalysis. He'd come to believe that most of what happens to a person is due to biological factors that are beyond anyone's control.

How effective *is* psychoanalytic therapy? Early reviews concluded that therapy in general, including psychoanalysis, isn't much help (Eysenck, 1961; Feldman, 1968; Wolpe, 1981). Other reviews, however, found that therapy works and that analytic therapy does about as well as other techniques (M. L. Smith & Glass, 1977; M. L. Smith, Glass, & Miller, 1980).

A problem in interpreting the studies stems from the fact that there are several ways to define success. Whether therapy is successful depends on how success is defined. It could be defined by a therapist's judgment of improvement. It could be defined by the patient's reports of less distress (symptoms such as anxiety or depression). These are, in fact, the ways in which success is typically defined in outcome research.

Psychoanalysts, however, tend to use different criteria of success. Although it's hard to find complete consensus, success in psychoanalysis is often defined by how much insight patients gain into their conflicts and dynamics. This insight may or may not yield less distress. Some believe, however, that the goal of psychoanalysis should be insight, rather than reduced distress. Given this different goal, it's hard to be sure what negative findings say about the success of psychoanalytic therapy (for detail see Fisher & Greenberg, 1977).

This discussion also makes it more understandable why people continue to seek out and endure the painful effort of psychoanalysis. People who undergo this treatment presumably think that they're getting something out of it, or they wouldn't do it. It seems likely that people will find value in psychoanalysis if they believe the psychoanalytic perspective and believe insight is of value. Perhaps the hope of a better life that this conviction can bring is a sufficient benefit in itself to warrant undertaking the therapy process.

Psychoanalytic Defense: Problems and Prospects

The ideas presented in this chapter extend those in Chapter 8, thus adding complexity to the theory with respect to its problems and it prospects. These ideas also can be evaluated on their own merits. How do they fare in today's personality psychology? What are their implications for the broader usefulness of psychoanalytic theory?

We said at the end of Chapter 8 that one problem with psychoanalysis is that its concepts are hard to test. The ideas in this chapter create an even larger problem in that respect. Specifically, defense mechanisms provide limitless flexibility. They can be used to explain virtually anything that might occur. Flexibility is good, because it lets a theory account for a lot. However, it also makes prediction hard. If a theory is too flexible, you can reconcile *any* finding with it. To the extent that findings contrary to prediction can be explained away, the ideas being tested aren't tested at all.

Suppose, for example, you were interested in the idea that anal fixation relates to neatness. If the data show that neatness and anality relate positively, the idea is supported. But if the data show the opposite, you just add a twist. You assume that the messiness is a reaction formation, protecting these people against the anxiety that's created by their underlying need to be neat.

Given the defense mechanisms of psychoanalytic theory, such a twist can always occur. If a desire is too threatening, it's repressed. It emerges in a disguised or distorted form, even opposite to its original form. If this is too threatening (perhaps because a reversal doesn't hide the threat well enough because it's too obvious), then a different distortion occurs. Thus, the theory can explain any outcome. As a result, its predictions can never be disconfirmed. Unfortunately, if a theory can never be disconfirmed, it can never really be confirmed, either.

Despite these criticisms, the basic idea that humans have defenses and self-protective tendencies has been absorbed deeply into the fabric of today's understanding of personality. This principle has been widely accepted, even by people who accept nothing else of the psychodynamic viewpoint.

Other criticisms of the elements of psychoanalysis introduced in this chapter concern the techniques of assessment and therapy. Assessment in this approach relies largely on projective techniques. These techniques have received serious criticism. It's not clear whether projective tests will ever live up to the psychometric standards set by most personality psychologists.

Regarding psychoanalytic therapy, disagreement about its efficacy reflects disagreement on its goals. A further difficulty in evaluating psychoanalysis as therapy is that information isn't always available to verify insights that emerge during therapy. If someone experiences a sudden realization that she's always resented her mother, who died five years ago, is this a realization or a self-deception? If you free associate long enough, eventually you'll recall bad feelings about someone. But in many cases, it's hard to tell how important the bad feelings actually were.

Given the various problems associated with psychoanalytic theory, why has it been so popular? Indeed, there's been a resurgence of interest in psychoanalytic theory in recent years, after a fallow period. There seem to be at least three reasons for this enduring popularity. One is that Freud's was the first comprehensive theory of personality. Whenever something comes first, its influence persists for a long time. Second, Freud spoke to questions that lie at the heart of personality: How does childhood influence later life? What is mental health? To what extent are people's motives accessible to them? The questions he posed began to stake out the territory of what would become personality psychology.

A final reason for the theory's popularity concerns the intuitive appeal of its major themes. Any metaphor that's incorporated into a language is adopted because it captures an element of reality in a striking and vivid way. Psychoanalytic theory uses many images and metaphors. Apart from their scientific status, notions such as unconscious motivation, psychosexual development, and the intrapsychic tug-of-war of conflicting pressures from id, ego, and superego have an emotional appeal. The ideas are novel, exciting, and interesting. In a word, they are *seductive*. Freud's theory undoubtedly took root in part because it portrayed personality in a way that people found—and continue to find—interesting.

· SUMMARY ·

Anxiety is a warning signal to the ego. *Reality anxiety* is fear of a threat in the world. *Neurotic* anxiety is fear that id impulses will get out of control and get you in trouble. *Moral anxiety* is fear of violating the superego's moral code. The ego deals with anxiety (and sometimes prevents it from arising) by employing defense mechanisms.

The basic defense is *repression*—forcing id impulses and other threatening material out of consciousness. Repression is useful, but it ties up energy. *Denial* is a refusal to acknowledge the reality of something that lies outside the mind. Other defenses, which typically act along with repression, are projection (attributing an unacceptable impulse to someone else), rationalization (developing an acceptable but incorrect explanation for your action), intellectualization (separating your thoughts from your feelings and allowing the thoughts but not the feelings to be in awareness), reaction formation (acting in a way opposite to the initial impulse), regression (returning to a mode of behavior fitting an earlier stage of development), displacement (shifting an impulse from one target to another, usually a safer one), and sublimation (transforming an unacceptable impulse to an acceptable one).

The psychoanalytic orientation holds that the unconscious is the key to personality. Freud believed that the unconscious reveals itself in many ways in day-to-day life. *Parapraxes* are slips of the tongue and pen that occur when unconscious desires cause you to act in a way other than you consciously intend. Similar processes are believed to underlie many accidents. Unconscious processes are also revealed in humor and in dreams. Dreams have manifest content (what's in the dream) and latent content (the determinants of the dream, many of which are unconscious). Manifest content usually is symbolic of latent content, which also may be distorted through other mechanisms such as *dream work*.

The unconscious can also be revealed more formally, through projective assessment techniques such as the Rorschach inkblot test. Projective techniques allow the person's unconscious to release symbolic versions of threatening material while describing ambiguous stimuli. The Rorschach is somewhat controversial in that its reliability and validity have not been strongly supported by research evidence.

In the psychoanalytic view, behavioral problems reflect overuse of defenses. Problems may derive from fixations (unresolved conflicts during psychosexual development), from a general repression of libido, or from repressed traumas. In such cases, too much energy is spent in confining the threatening material in the unconscious. The goal of therapy is to release some of the repression, thereby freeing some of the energy.

Psychoanalytic therapy begins with *free association,* saying whatever comes to mind without censoring it in any way. This approach typically produces an incomplete matrix of symbolic meanings from which other elements can be inferred. People in therapy often display *resistance*, which implies that the ego is trying to defend itself against something the therapy is starting to touch on. Often the person in therapy displays *transference*, displacing onto the therapist the feelings related to the person about whom the conflicts exist. The goal of the therapy is *insight*, an emotional experiencing of previously unconscious parts of personality.

Freud came to believe that psychoanalysis was not as beneficial as he had first thought. This pessimistic view also emerged from early evaluation studies of therapy, although more recent studies have been more encouraging. Even in the absence of strong support for the usefulness of psychoanalytic therapy, many people continue to engage in it because they believe it provides benefits that are not adequately assessed by the measures used in outcome research.

· GLOSSARY ·

Anxiety   A feeling warning the ego that something bad is about to happen.

Current concerns   Preoccupations in one's current waking life.

Defense mechanism   An ego-protective strategy to hide threats from yourself and thereby reduce anxiety.

Denial   A refusal to believe that some real condition exists.

Displacement   The shifting of an impulse from its original target to a different one.

Dream work   Processes that distort latent dream content and transform it into manifest content.

Free association   A therapy procedure of saying without hesitation whatever comes to mind.

Identification   Linking oneself symbolically with someone who has a desired quality that is missing from the self.

Insight   An emotional re-experiencing of earlier conflicts in one's life that occurs during therapy.

Intellectualization   The process of thinking about something clinically and without emotion.

Latent content   The underlying sources of symbolic dream images.

Manifest content   The images that make up the dream experience as it is recalled.

Mechanism of opposites   A process in which an unacceptable element of latent content is expressed manifestly as its opposite.

Moral anxiety   The fear of behaving in conflict with the superego's moral code.

Neurotic anxiety   The fear that your id impulses will get out of control and get you into trouble.

Parapraxis   A slip of the tongue, behavior, or memory.

Projection   Ascribing a threatening urge or quality in yourself to someone else.

Projective techniques   An assessment in which you project from the unconscious onto ambiguous stimuli.

Rationalization   Finding a plausible but incorrect explanation for an unacceptable action or event.

Reaction formation   Doing the opposite of what your impulses are.

Reality anxiety   The fear of danger in the world.

Regression   A return to a mode of coping from an earlier developmental stage.

Repression   The process of keeping an idea or impulse in the unconscious.

Resistance   An attempt to avoid becoming conscious of threatening material in therapy.

Rorschach inkblot test   A projective test that uses inkblots as ambiguous stimuli.

Sublimation   The alteration of an id impulse into a socially acceptable act.

Symbolization   The transformation of unacceptable latent dream content into less threatening symbols.

Transference   The displacement onto your therapist of feelings that are tied to an object of conflict.

part 5

The Neoanalytic Perspective

The Neoanalytic Perspective: Major Themes and Underlying Assumptions

As the term *neoanalytic* implies, this perspective on personality derives in part from the psychoanalytic perspective. Sigmund Freud attracted many colleagues and followers. All of them adopted aspects of his viewpoint, but they also differed from him in important ways. They dealt with their ambivalence about psychoanalysis by recasting and extending Freud's ideas in their own terms. In doing so, they de-emphasized aspects of his theory they disliked and expanded those they liked. Their disagreements with Freud are basic enough that their views seem distinctly different from Freud's. For this reason, we've chosen to treat them as a distinct perspective on personality.

These so-called post-Freudian psychodynamic theorists were fairly diverse in their thinking. As a result, there are as many different post-Freudian theories as there were theorists. Treatment of each theory by itself can create a jumble of ideas that's hard to keep straight. On the other hand, there are at least two themes that many of these theories share. As a result, the two chapters on this perspective don't simply discuss each theory in isolation from the others. Rather, they focus on several of the theories that most clearly reflect the two themes that are most salient in post-Freudian psychodynamic thinking. Points made by other theorists that supplement these core ideas are introduced where they seem most relevant.

The theorists who form the neoanalytic group differed from Freud on several grounds. Some neoanalytic theorists were bothered by Freud's emphasis on the importance of sexuality and the idea that sexual issues are important even in infancy. Others took issue with Freud's strong emphasis on the importance of unconscious processes. Perhaps the most frequent criticism among Freud's followers, however, was that he didn't give enough attention to the ego. As a result, many neoanalytic theories focus on the ego and how it functions. As a group, these theories emphasize the existence of certain ego processes and how they come to be. This line of thinking is the focus of Chapter 10.

Theorists who emphasize ego functioning and ego development tend to focus more on how the ego works than on the content of the problems and situations it confronts. However, a second group of neoanalytic theories focuses on the question of what kinds of situations are central in the ego's transactions with the world. In general, the theorists of this second group have held that the ego's primary tasks revolve around the quality of the person's relationships. The theories deriving from this assumption focus on how the ego interacts with, and is affected by, other individuals and the broader social and cultural matrix. The theories with this emphasis on social interaction are described in Chapter 11.

Ego Psychology

Jeremy has an irresistible attraction to computer games. He will sit transfixed for hours at a time in front of any challenging game. When he isn't pumping quarters into an arcade machine, he's parked in front of his computer, trying out whatever new game has just come out. His scores are so high that most of his friends have stopped playing with him. It's just Jeremy and the machine, locked in combat. Why? It's obviously not that he wants to be best in his group or even the best in town (he's long since been that). When asked, Jeremy shrugs and replies, "It's hard to explain—I just want to be as good at it as I can be."

WHY DO people spend large amounts of time becoming good at things that have no practical value? Name an activity, and people somewhere spend countless hours perfecting their skills at it: bowling, golf, cow-chip tossing, ballet, hog calling, and, yes, computer games. Why? Psychoanalysis says there's an explanation for everything. You just need to find the symbolic meaning behind the activity. But how do you feel about the idea that getting good at computer games is, for example, a symbolic reflection of Oedipal urges?

This question raises a more general point. If you're like most people, you had a mixed reaction to psychoanalysis. Most people find aspects of the theory reasonable. For example, many agree that early experience has a big effect on personality. Many agree that conflict is inherent in personality functioning. Most agree that people usually try to gain pleasure and avoid pain. Probably, though, there were aspects of the theory you found less convincing. Maybe you don't agree with Freud's stress on the unconscious. Maybe you're put off by his insistence that so much of human behavior is sexually motivated.

Even Freud's close followers were ambivalent. There were several areas of disagreement, but perhaps the most frequent criticism was that Freud didn't give enough attention to the ego and what it does (see Box 10.1 for another disagreement). Interestingly enough, toward the end of his career, Freud felt the same way. He began to wonder whether the ego might have a more important and autonomous status than he'd earlier believed.

Freud died before he could openly indicate his shifting position on this matter. Even his last publication (Freud, 1949/1940) gives no hint of it. Others knew of his informal statements, though, and found his shifting

Box 10.1 Another Kind of Psychodynamics: Jung's Analytical Psychology

This chapter focuses on people who modified Freud's ideas by emphasizing the ego and de-emphasizing the unconscious. We should, however, note another theorist of the time whose ideas moved in the other direction: Carl Jung (e.g., 1960/1926, 1968). Jung was not a follower of Freud but a *contemporary* of Freud (though 20 years younger) who was influenced by many of the same currents of thought as molded Freud's work. Thus, similarities in some of the ideas they advanced seemed initially to give them common ground.

Freud and Jung associated professionally and personally for six years, during which Freud began to view Jung as his "crown prince" and eventual successor (McGuire, 1974). However, two factors drove a wedge between them. The first was a series of theoretical differences. The second was a growing interpersonal difficulty. Freud saw himself as a father figure to Jung, and he began to suspect that Jung wished to usurp his power and authority (note the Oedipal overtones). Jung found this attitude hard to tolerate, and he eventually broke away.

Jung's theory differs from Freud's in many ways. It's a theory of great complexity, and we can make only a couple of points about it here. Jung felt that Freud overemphasized sexuality as a motive but had too limited a view of spirituality. Unlike Freud, for whom spirituality reflected sublimation of sexual drives, Jung considered it a fundamental aspect of human existence.

Jung's thinking was also dominated by the **principle of opposites:** the idea that the human experience consists of polarities, qualities that oppose and tend to balance each other. He proposed a set of dichotomies in human functioning, each of which has some resemblance to what others would view as aspects of ego functioning. Jung believed that people are dominated by one of two attitudes: introversion or extraversion. People dominated by extraversion are absorbed by external experiences and spend their time engaged with the world around them. People dominated by introversion are preoccupied by their inner experiences and tend to be less outgoing. Both tendencies can facilitate adaptation. And even though you're dominated by one of them, the other remains inside you as well, opposing and balancing it.

Jung also assumed two more pairs of opposed functions. The functions in one pair, *thinking* and *feeling,* are both rational, in that each involves a kind of judgment. Thinking is a judgment of which ideas are true; feeling is a judgment about whether you like or dislike something. The functions in the other pair, *sensing* and *intuiting,* are nonrational, in that they don't rely on thought. Both are ways of perceiving—one using senses, the other using the unconscious. Each of these pairs also forms a polarity, with one of each pair tending to dominate the other. Indeed, a further polarization exists between the rational and irrational. Jung believed that combinations of dominance of these functions (plus introversion–extraversion) produce the range of individual differences in personality. Today, these tendencies are measured by an instrument called the Myers-Briggs Type Indicator (Myers & McCaulley, 1985), which is widely used for assessment in settings such as businesses and career counseling (DeVito, 1985).

Although Jung's theory has certain similarities to ego psychology, there are also great differences. For example, instead of de-emphasizing the unconscious, Jung emphasized it even more. Jung believed human beings share a **collective unconscious,** or "racial memory," a set of memories from our human and even prehuman ancestors. He believed that these memories, which aren't recalled consciously, go back for countless generations. They provide the basis for images called **archetypes,** aspects of the world that people have an inherited tendency to notice. Jung described many archetypes, including birth, death, power, magic, unity, God, and the self, which he believed are experienced by everyone. Each of these, in Jung's view, exists in the person because it's been part of the experience of human and prehuman life for millennia.

views more compatible with their own thinking. Encouraged by his change, they began to develop a set of ideas that collectively came to be called **ego psychology.** As the name implies, ego psychology is a psychodynamic framework in which ego functioning has more status than Freud gave it.

The emergence of ego psychology was a subtle and gradual process that began well before Freud's death. Indeed, many would say that some of the ideas in Chapter 9 are just as relevant to ego psychology as to psychoanalysis. It was Anna Freud (1966) who analyzed defenses so carefully, and her ideas weren't identical to those of her father. Recall that the defenses are used *by the ego* to protect itself. Thus, they're easily seen as ego functions and a part of ego psychology.

Principles of Ego Psychology

Anna Freud's analysis of defense mechanisms is a transitional statement. That is, it can be applied either to traditional psychoanalysis or to ego psychology. But other aspects of ego psychology depart more clearly from psychoanalysis. Sigmund Freud emphasized that the ego's primary task was to mediate among the id, the superego, and external reality. From the vantage point of ego psychology, the ego does far more than that. It's involved in the process of *adaptation,* of fitting better into the world. This view holds that adaptation and the conscious processes by which it occurs are more important than is unconscious behavior (Wolberg, 1967).

This isn't the only break from Freud. Ego psychologists widely assumed that the ego exists at birth and has its own energy source. One ego psychologist (Fairbairn, 1952) even went so far as to suggest that there is no id—only ego—and that what were seen as id functions are simply reflections of an ego at a primitive stage of development. All these ideas follow from the core assumption of the ego psychologists: that ego processes are important in their own right.

SHIFTING THE EMPHASIS FROM THE ID TO THE EGO

Because many of the people who became known as ego psychologists began as followers of Freud, they faced a dilemma. They wanted to emphasize the ego, but many also wanted to avoid undermining the core ideas of psychoanalysis. This was a hard problem, because psychoanalysis had given the ego a specific role: to help the impulses of the id gain expression.

Heinz Hartmann (1958/1939, 1964) had a creative and simple solution to this dilemma: He ignored it. He proposed that the ego does two things at once. On the one hand, it reduces conflict between the id and superego and between the id and external reality, just as Freud had said. On the other hand, it acts through its cognitive processes to adapt the person better to the world.

Hartmann held that the ego acts in two different modes to handle these different functions (see Figure 10.1). When it acts to reduce conflict, it's operating in what he called the *conflict sphere* of personality. When it acts to promote adaptation, it's operating in the *conflict-free sphere.* Thus, said Hartmann, Freud's view of the ego was right and so was the emerging view of ego psychology. Each view simply emphasizes different aspects of what the ego does.

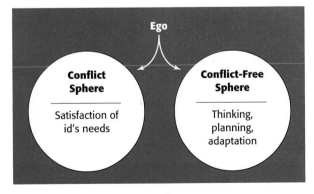

FIGURE 10.1
Hartmann assumed that the ego can operate in either of two modes. In the conflict sphere, it acts to see that the id's impulses are satisfied. In the conflict-free sphere, it engages in activities for its own purposes, aimed at better adaptation.

How can the ego function in two spheres? Hartmann assumed that the ego and the id have the same biological source. Thus, part of the ego stays in contact with the id throughout life. This part of the ego operates in the conflict sphere and tries to satisfy the id's needs. The rest develops more independently and operates in the conflict-free sphere, working for its own purposes. The latter aspect of the ego is what Hartmann and (other ego psychologists) were interested in.

Having said that Freud was partly right (that the ego functions in the conflict sphere), Hartmann then proceeded to ignore that aspect of the ego almost entirely. In that way, he managed to remain connected to psychoanalysis while heading off in a new direction.

ADAPTATION AND AUTONOMY

In Hartmann's view, adaptation to the environment is the ultimate goal of behavior. This became an important theme throughout ego psychology. Adaptation occurs on several levels. *Physically,* people must learn to move their bodies to get where they want to go and do what they want to do. *Psychologically,* people must learn to gain control over their impulses, modifying them and channeling them into appropriate actions.

Hartmann agreed with Freud that sexual and aggressive energies provide the foundation of much of human behavior. He differed, however, in how he viewed people's attempts to deal with their impulses. Freud saw the struggle to inhibit impulses in terms of avoiding anxiety (by avoiding punishment or danger). Hartmann (and others) saw the effort to inhibit impulses as part of a broader process of adaptation. The difference isn't so much in *what* happens as in *why* it happens. To Hartmann, impulse control is rooted in the ego's own goals.

In describing the ego, Hartmann talked about two kinds of autonomy. First, he said that ego processes exist from birth and can function apart from the id; this principle is called **primary ego autonomy.** Thus, people can get satisfaction from using ego processes to think, plan, imagine, integrate information, and so on (see also Box 10.2).

BOX 10.2 THE JOY OF THINKING

Explorations in the Need for Cognition

The idea that ego processes are gratifying in their own right is consistent with a literature on a topic called the **need for cognition.** This is the need to think about and impose meaningful structure on experiences (Cohen, 1957; Cohen, Stotland, & Wolfe, 1955). People high in the need for cognition are likely to evaluate, organize, and elaborate spontaneously on information to which they're exposed. They're less easily bored than people lower in the need (Watt & Blanchard, 1994). They attend more to the details of others' behavior (Lassiter, Briggs, & Bowman, 1991) and think more about its meaning (Lassiter, Briggs, & Slaw, 1991). People high in this need also are flexible and tend to explain events in complex ways (Fletcher, Danilovics, Fernandez, Peterson, & Reeder, 1986). They aren't

necessarily smarter—they just like to think things over (Cacioppo, Petty, Kao, & Rodriguez, 1986; Cacioppo, Petty, & Morris, 1983).

This ego function is reflected in several ways (for a review see Cacioppo, Petty, Feinstein, & Jarvis, 1996). For example, it's known that persuasion affects people in two different ways. When people get a persuasive message, some evaluate it and even *elaborate* on it in their minds. Others just take it at face value. Cacioppo and Petty (1982, 1984) argued that this difference in response rests on the need for cognition. People high in the need for cognition evaluate and elaborate; people low in the need for cognition accept what they're given.

Cacioppo and associates examined this idea by finding people who held the same attitudes on a target issue but differed in their need for cognition (Cacioppo et al., 1983; Cacioppo et al., 1986, Experiment 1). They received an essay trying to persuade them to change

their opinion. Either the essay was full of weak arguments (which people resist), or it was full of strong arguments (which are more persuasive). As you might expect, people with a high cognition need reported thinking harder about the message than those with a lower cognition need. They also remembered more of the arguments in it.

Does thinking harder and remembering more create more persuasion? Not necessarily. Thinking about strong arguments produced more persuasion. Thinking about weak arguments, however, caused people to be more resistant to persuasion. In sum, people high in the need for cognition thought more about the value of what they'd read and used the value as a guide for deciding whether to change their attitudes. This pattern seems much in line with the functions the ego psychologists emphasized as people try to deal effectively and adaptively with external reality.

In this view, being effective is pleasurable in itself. As you exercise your ego, you become more adept, and more efficient (better adapted) in dealing with the world.

The phrase **secondary ego autonomy** refers to the idea that an ego function that was originally done for one purpose may continue to be done long after that purpose has been satisfied. The original purpose may have been to fill another need (even an id need), but the ego function is now gratifying itself. This idea is similar to Allport's (1961) concept of **functional autonomy.** When a behavior that was originally done for one reason continues to occur after that reason no longer applies, the behavior is said to have acquired functional autonomy. It's as though the behavior has now become an end in itself. As an example, think of a person who began an exercise program to lose weight. Even after she's lost the weight, she continues to exercise, because she now finds the exercise itself satisfying.

The idea of an autonomous ego that has the goal of adaptation was widely adopted by other theorists, who extended it in a variety of ways. Among others, Rapaport (1960), Gill (1959), G. S. Klein (1970), and White (1959, 1963) were interested in how the ego goes about fitting itself better to the world.

THE EGO, ADAPTATION, AND COMPETENCE MOTIVATION

Although many ego psychologists view the exercise of ego processes as a source of pleasure and satisfaction, this idea was perhaps elaborated most compellingly by Robert White (1959, 1963). White used two motivational concepts. **Effectance motivation** is the motive *to have an effect* or an impact on one's surroundings. White believed effectance is a basic human motive. During early childhood, it's the major outlet for the ego's energies.

This motive gradually evolves into the more complex **competence motivation.** This is a motive *to be effective* in dealing with the environment. Thus, this motive underlies adaptive ego functioning. Competence motivation can be exercised endlessly. There are always new competencies (and higher levels of competence) to attain. The competence motive thus moves the person toward ever-new masteries (recall Jeremy and his games from the chapter opening).

There are important differences between merely attaining goals and satisfying the competence motive. Attaining a goal satisfies the desire to reach that goal, but the goal itself may or may not pertain to your sense of competence. For instance, if you get a perfect exam score in a course you think is too easy, it won't enhance your sense of competence.

Consider an example of how effectance and competence motives are expressed in behavior and differ from each other. Imagine an infant, surrounded by toys in her crib, who lunges at a dangling mobile and gives it a good whack with her fist. As the mobile jangles and bounces, the child has visible evidence of her impact on the world. This gratifies her desire for effectance. Knocking things over, moving toys around, spreading stewed carrots all over her table tray—each of these actions has an effect on the world around her. Each satisfies the effectance motive. Infants clearly do these things, and they do seem to enjoy them.

Children often seem driven to figure things out on their own. Successful mastery of the environment is important in developing feelings of competence.

Feelings of inferiority can produce strivings for superiority.

But competence motivation is different. Suppose the child is just learning how to stand up. She struggles over and over to pull herself up against the wall of her crib. She does it even though every effort meets with failure. When success finally comes, she giggles and shrieks with pleasure. She has exercised a mastery over the environment, a new competence in dealing with it.

In White's view, effectance and competence motives reflect the way the brain is organized. He held that people inherently seek stimulation from exploring. This urge can be shown in many ways, but its most advanced form is the desire to be competent and feel competent in dealing with the world. This is an adaptive urge. It causes people to engage in effective commerce with their environment to the greatest extent possible.

This theme has had reverberations in other perspectives on personality, not just ego psychology. As you'll see in Chapter 13, some learning theorists came to believe that the sense of personal efficacy is a major determinant of people's actions. It can easily be argued that that line of thought traces to White's emphasis on an intrinsic desire to master the environment. Another theoretical similarity will emerge when you read about humanistic views in Chapter 14.

IS COMPETENCE STRIVING AUTOMATIC, OR IS IT DONE TO REMEDY INFERIORITY?

White considered the desire for greater competence to be the major force behind people's attempts to be effective. Alfred Adler (1927, 1929, 1931), another ego psychologist, also believed that people strive for greater competence, but for different reasons.

Adler began with an interest in a medical question: Why does one person develop heart trouble, a second respiratory problems, and a third ulcers? Adler proposed that people have an inferiority in some part of the body that makes them vulnerable to illness at that site. He called this weakness an **organ inferiority** (Adler, 1917). He also argued that people try to *compensate* by strengthening the weak organ through exercise and training. He termed this effort a *striving for superiority*. Adler's belief in this principle of compensatory striving was doubtlessly influenced by his own life. He was a sickly child who nearly died in childhood. Through considerable effort, however, he overcame his health problems.

Support for the idea of compensatory striving comes from a study of undersea divers engaged in a demanding task (Helmreich, LeFan, Bakeman, Wilhelm, & Radloff, 1972). This study found that the divers who performed best had had a serious illness during childhood. From Adler's perspective, they were compensating behaviorally for their earlier body inferiority.

Adler went on to expand his thinking to include *all* kinds of inferiority and to extend the principle to personality. He proposed that whenever a person has **feelings of inferiority** (any sense of inadequacy), a compensatory process is activated and the person strives for superiority (Adler, 1927, 1929, 1931). For example, think of a sprinter who feels inferior because she can't run 100 yards in 10 seconds. Because she feels inferior, she trains until she breaks the 10-second barrier. Her satisfaction, however, is relatively short lived. Feelings of inferiority set in again, as she realizes she could be even faster, and the struggle to improve begins anew.

As another example, think of a college freshman who arrives for his first semester knowing no one. He's a little shy, and in a few minutes, he feels a sense of inferiority because people all around him are engaged in conversations. What does he do? He grits his teeth and approaches a group of three people to introduce himself. Within a month, new friendships are sprouting like summer weeds. By now, though, just having friends isn't enough. He feels inferior because the friendships are a little superficial. He thinks he should know some people better than he does. To overcome that, he gets involved in a church group that meets once a week to talk with others about personal reactions to the experience of college life.

There are many ways to respond to a feeling of inferiority. Adler coined the term **lifestyle** to refer both to a person's concerns over inferiority and his or her preferred way of striving for superiority. Having a healthy lifestyle moves the person forward in an adaptive path of development. It allows the person to attain meaningful goals and to get along well with others.

But there are also what Adler called **mistaken lifestyles.** Some people respond to feelings of inferiority by trying to dominate others, or becoming dependent and taking things from others instead of attaining them on their own. Other people respond to feelings of inferiority by trying to avoid situations in which such feelings can arise. They avoid a sense of inferiority by never trying. Other people respond to such feelings by being as useful as they can to others, thereby drawing their own attention away from their inferiorities. These people almost deny the validity of their own ego and their own feelings. Consistent with this view, people who are *excessively* concerned with the needs of others are lower in self-esteem and more likely to neglect their own needs than people whose concern with others is more moderate (Fritz & Helgeson, 1998; Helgeson & Fritz, 1998, 1999).

Adler believed that inferiority feelings and superiority strivings continue to cycle with each other constantly. The result (unless the person has a mistaken lifestyle) is that people keep working to get better, more proficient at what they do. Adler thus viewed the struggle for increased competence to be an important part of healthy ego functioning. He called it the "great upward drive." He believed that healthy people continue to work this way throughout life toward ever-greater integration and perfection.

To Adler, effort toward improvement begins with and stems from feelings of inferiority. He believed everyone has these feelings periodically. These feelings are part of being human. Because the major result of inferiority feelings is an effort to better oneself, the behavior that emerges is exactly the same as the pattern White described. But the two theorists proposed very different mechanisms for it. To White, competence strivings are an intrinsic part of the ego's activity. To Adler, they're a reaction to, and an attempt to replace, feelings of inferiority.

EGO CONTROL AND EGO RESILIENCY

The theorists named thus far all emphasized that the primary goal of the ego is better adaptation to the world. Let's consider this idea a little more closely. *Adaptation* can be seen as having two aspects. One part is learning to *restrain impulses*. This lets you gain better command of your transactions with the world. It prevents mistakes that would arise from acting impulsively. Part of successful adaptation, though, is being *flexible* in dealing with the world. This is knowing when to restrain yourself and when to behave more freely. These issues surrounding restraint of impulses in the service of better adaptation lie at the heart of the work of contemporary ego psychologists Jeanne H. and Jack Block (1980; J. Block, 2002; J. Block & Block, 2006). They and their colleagues examined both aspects of ego functioning.

Block and Block called one aspect **ego control.** This is the extent to which the person tends to inhibit the expression of impulses. At one extreme are people who undercontrol—people who can't delay gratification, who express their feelings and desires immediately. Block and Block described these impulsive people as having many but brief enthusiasms and interests, as being distractible and exploratory. They are nonconforming and unconventional and comfortable with ambiguity and inconsistency. They live impromptu lives.

At the other end are people who overcontrol—people who delay gratification endlessly, who inhibit their actions and feelings, and who insulate themselves from outside distractions. Block and Block describe them as conforming rather than exploratory, as planful and organized. They are uneasy in ambiguous or inconsistent situations, and have narrow and unchanging interests. From their description of what these people are like, it's clear that the Blocks believe great restraint doesn't necessarily mean better adaptation (see Block & Block, 2006).

In the middle of the dimension are people who inhibit and control impulses to a degree but don't overdo it. These people are less organized than those high in ego control, but they're less impromptu and chaotic than those low in ego control. The people in the middle seem better adapted than are those at either extreme.

The other aspect of ego functioning that Block and Block focused on is called **ego resiliency.** This is flexibility. It's the capacity to modify your usual level of ego control—*in either direction*—to adapt to the demands of a given situation. People low in ego resilience can't break out of their usual way of relating to the world, even when it's temporarily good to do so. People who are ego resilient are resourceful and adapt well to changing circumstances. If there's a situational reason to be organized, they can do it without trouble. If there's a reason to be crazy and impulsive, they can be that way too. As Block and Kremen (1996) put it, the ego-resilient person is "as undercontrolled as possible and as overcontrolled as necessary" (p. 351). This means being responsive to what's possible and what's necessary in a given situation.

Not surprisingly, there's evidence that people who are high in ego resilience are better adjusted than people who are low (Klohnen, 1996). For example, in two samples of women, those higher in ego resiliency did better at negotiating menopause than those who were ego brittle. They were more likely to continue their education or career building and had fewer health problems (Klohnen, Vandewater, & Young, 1996). Another project found that children high in ego resilience were faster to develop in their understanding of friendships and moral reasoning than children lower in ego resilience (Hart, Keller, Edelstein, & Hofmann, 1998).

It might be tempting to conclude that people with high ego resilience are just smarter than people with less ego resilience. Thus, they're quicker to recognize what a situation calls for. Although these variables are related, it's not all about intelligence (Block & Kremen, 1996). Pure ego resilience—controlling for effects of IQ—relates to competence in the world of interpersonal interaction.

Ego control and ego resilience have both been related to restraint, in the form of delay of gratification. Funder and Block (1989) conducted a study in which the participants were 14-year-olds being paid four dollars for each of six sessions. After each session, they were given the choice of being paid then or deferring payment until the end. Each time they deferred payment, they'd get a small bonus in "interest." The

Table 10.1 Observer-Rating Items That Distinguished among Three Groups of 18-Year-Olds. Those of one group were total abstainers from drug use, those of the second group were occasional experimenters, and those of the third group were frequent users. *Source*: Adapted from Shedler & Block, 1990.

Items Distinguishing Frequent Users from Occasional Experimenters	Items Distinguishing Total Abstainers from Occasional Experimenters
Is self-indulgent	Is moralistic
Gives up and withdraws in the face of frustration, adversity	Favors conservative values in a variety of areas
Thinks and associates to ideas in unusual ways	Prides self on being objective, rational
Is unpredictable and changeable in behavior, attitudes	Overcontrols needs and impulses; delays gratification unnecessarily
Undercontrols needs and impulses; unable to delay gratification	Is facially and/or gesturally expressive (lower score)
Tends to be rebellious and nonconforming	Is unpredictable and changeable in behavior, attitudes (lower score)
Characteristically pushes and tries to stretch limits	Enjoys sensuous experience (touch, taste, smell, physical contact) (lower score)

question was how often (from five opportunities) they chose to delay. Decisions to delay related to ego control, as expected (controlling for ego resiliency and intelligence). Ego resiliency also played a role. Recall that delay is sometimes a good policy, sometimes not. This situation was set up so that delay produced extra payoff, so delay was good. Flexible people pick up on this and choose to delay, even if that's not their usual style. Thus, ego resiliency related to delay choices (controlling for ego control and intelligence).

These ego qualities have also been related to other kinds of behavior. One program of research found that greater ego control related to longer delays before sexual intercourse (Jessor & Jessor, 1975; Jessor, Costa, Jessor, & Donovan, 1983). Other studies found that ego control has a similar relation to drinking: Undercontrol relates to problem drinking and overcontrol relates to total abstinence (M. C. Jones, 1968, 1971). Shedler and Block (1990) reported similar results with respect to drug use (see Table 10.1).

In theory, ego control and ego resilience are distinct. However, there's evidence that the situation is more complex than that (Eisenberg, Fabes, Guthrie, & Reiser, 2000). It probably is intrinsically harder for someone who's at an extreme in ego control to be resilient, compared with someone with moderate ego control. If so, there would be low ego resilience at both extremes of the ego control dimension.

Several recent studies (Asendorpf & van Aken, 1999; Robins, John, Caspi, Moffitt, & Stouthamer-Loeber, 1996) have found exactly that. These studies found three clusters of people (see Figure 10.2). Overcontrolled people are high in ego control and low in ego resilience. Undercontrolled people are low in ego control and low in ego resilience. Resilient people are moderate in ego control and high in ego resilience. The overcontrolled and undercontrolled groups have the characteristics just described for highs and lows in ego control. The resilient group has the characteristics just described for highs in ego resilience. Future research on this topic may focus more on these three patterns.

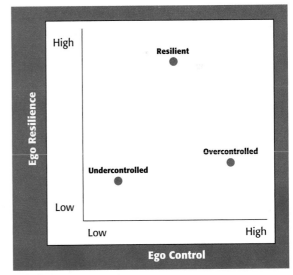

FIGURE 10.2
Approximate locations in two-dimensional space of three clusters of persons. Two clusters are at the extremes in ego control. The third cluster is identified by being high in ego resilience. *Source: Based on information from Robins et al., 1996; Asendorpf & van Aken, 1999.*

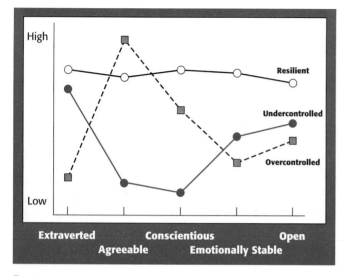

FIGURE 10.3
Idealized five-factor profiles of people who are resilient, undercontrolled, and over-controlled. *Source: Based on information from Robins et al., 1996; Asendorpf & van Aken, 1999.*

EGO CONTROL, EGO RESILIENCE, AND THE FIVE-FACTOR MODEL

We've noted in earlier chapters that widespread interest in the five-factor model of trait structure (Chapter 4) has led people to ask how other views of personality fit with that model. Several studies have looked at this question regarding ego control and ego resilience (Asendorpf & van Aken, 1999; Robins et al., 1996). The results are very similar across studies. Idealized profiles of three groups of people are shown in Figure 10.3.

The easiest to characterize is the resilient group: They're at the "good" ends of all the scales. The undercontrolled group is as extraverted as the resilients, but they're low in agreeableness and conscientiousness and moderately low in emotional stability and openness. This suggests someone who's impulsive and cares little about other people's opinions, which fits with other descriptions of these people. In contrast to both of these, the overcontrolled group is introverted, but they are as agreeable as the resilient group. They're also the lowest in emotional stability (i.e., highest in neuroticism) and only moderately open and conscientious. Consistent with the Blocks' portrayal, they seem withdrawn, conforming, and anxious. It seems, then, that there's a fairly easy integration between qualities in the Blocks' model and the five-factor model.

Ego Development

Thus far, we've emphasized the idea that a primary function of the ego is to establish better adaptation to the world. Now we turn to a slightly different viewpoint on this function. Though different, it's fully compatible with the themes emphasized thus far.

Jane Loevinger (1969, 1976) has argued that the ego is primarily a synthesizer and integrator of experience. This function certainly fits the overall goal of enhancing adaptation. In her view, the ego adapts to the world by making sense of the experiences the world presents. She argues that this synthesizing function isn't just one of many things the ego *does*. Rather, this is what the ego *is*. To Loevinger, the process of synthesis and integration is the essence of the ego.

Loevinger has proposed a detailed account of the ego's development (Loevinger, 1966, 1976, 1987; Loevinger & Knoll, 1983). By ego development, she doesn't mean a process by which the ego comes to *exist*. Rather, she means how this synthesizing function evolves across life. Her theory rests on ideas about cognitive development from theorists such as Piaget. A core idea is that as cognitive capabilities grow, people organize and structure their experience in more elaborate ways. As a result, the integrating function that comprises the ego must also act in more elaborate ways.

Loevinger's is a *stage theory*. She believes each shift in the nature of ego functioning derives from, and thus depends on, the nature of ego functioning in the preceding stage. Thus, the person moves through the stages in a particular order. As the person moves to each higher stage, the ego's syntheses become more differentiated and complex but also more integrated.

Why do people move forward into the next stage? It's generally assumed that cognitive development and ego development both emerge because existing functions don't quite fit reality. That is, if an ego function works perfectly, there's no reason to change it. If it doesn't work perfectly, though, there's pressure for it to evolve in ways that work better (Baumeister, 1994; J. Block, 1982). Thus, ego development depends partly on having challenge in one's life (see also Helson & Roberts, 1994).

According to Loevinger, people move through the stages until they can go no further. How far you go is influenced by heredity and by life circumstances (Newman, Tellegen, & Bouchard, 1998). Loevinger does *not* assume that everyone goes through all the stages. It's possible for a person to remain fixed in even a fairly early stage. Such an adult would not be well adapted to certain complexities in life, but would get along adequately in many contexts. Your adult level of ego development is the highest stage you're able to attain as you grow to adulthood.

We should note two differences between this view and Freud's. First, Freud saw personality development as occurring early in life. Loevinger sees ego development as continuing well into adulthood. Second, in Freud's psychoanalytic theory, the ego's basic functioning remains much the same, though the issues it deals with change over the years. Loevinger, however, argues that the nature of the synthesizing process that *defines* the ego actually changes over the course of life.

Early Ego Development

The stages Loevinger identified are summarized in Table 10.2. At first, the ego is primitive. Its major task is to acquire the ability to distinguish self from nonself. This ability emerges during the first stage of ego development, called the *symbiotic* stage.

Table 10.2 Summary of Loevinger's Portrayal of the Stages of Ego Development.
Source: Adapted from Loevinger, 1987.

Stage Name	Behavioral Manifestations
Symbiotic	Working to acquire sense of separation between self and nonself
Impulsive	Assertion of self through impulse expression; relationships with others are exploitive, for own needs
Self-protective	Begins to grasp rules but only as guides to avoid punishment; no moral sense; personal expediency, opportunism
Conformist	Rules adopted because they are accepted by group; concerned with appearing properly to the social group
Self-aware	Realization that rules have exceptions; increased introspection with increased awareness that own behavior isn't perfect
Conscientious	Use of self-evaluated standards rather than group's norm; realization that events have multiple meanings
Individualistic	Clearer sense of individuality; greater tolerance for individual differences
Autonomous	Realization of interdependency among people; awareness of conflicts among one's own needs; recognition of others' need for autonomy
Integrated	Conflicting demands have been resolved; not just tolerance but intense appreciation of others' viewpoints

This name comes from the fact that a young child's tie to the mother is so strong that the child has trouble distinguishing itself from the mother. The process of consolidating a sense of being a separate person is assisted greatly by the emergence of language.

The next period of ego development is the *impulsive* stage. Loevinger says that children of this stage release impulses purposely, as a way to affirm their existence. In effect, the ego is acting to have an impact on the world (note the similarity to effectance motivation). This is a time when phrases such as "by *myself*" emerge often (and often loudly) from the child. The child orients to the present, with little consideration of the future or broad implications of behavior. Children's need for other people is high, because they can't do many things for themselves. But the relationships are exploitive: Others are valued only for what they can give the child.

It's of interest that the behaviors of this period are things that a traditional psychoanalytic view would see as caused by the id. Behavior is impulsive and demanding, and the child doesn't *relate* to other people so much as *use* them. Loevinger argues, though, that the actions reflect not an id, but a poorly developed ego struggling to assert itself. These very different views of the same qualities of behavior illustrate a way in which the ego psychologists' perspective differs from the psychoanalytic perspective.

MIDDLE STAGES OF EGO DEVELOPMENT: CONTROL OF IMPULSES

The intentional releasing of impulses eventually gives way to a different way of relating to the world. The *self-protective* stage marks the first step toward self-control of impulses. During this stage, children start to grasp the idea that there are rules about how to act and that breaking the rules leads to punishment. Children still lack full appreciation of the meaning of rules, however. At this stage, rules simply give information about how the world works—what you have to do to avoid punishment. As Loevinger (1976) put it, the main rule is "Don't get caught." The child's only morality at this stage is expediency.

The self-protective quality of this stage comes from the fact that children use whatever rules they learn mostly for their own advantage. Behavior thus remains exploitive. On the other hand, Loevinger (1987) says this isn't calculated opportunism. It's just an open expression of self-interest. In Loevinger's view, the best indicator of the self-protective mode isn't exploitive behavior but the absence of long-term goals and purposes.

Once again, it seems useful to point to the relation between this theory and Freud's theory. This stage is where the theories bear the greatest resemblance in their views of the ego. Recall that to Freud, the ego is amoral; it acts to satisfy the desires of the id expeditiously, without concern about right or wrong. The behavioral result looks much like what Loevinger describes as happening at the self-protective stage. Yet there's a difference. Loevinger doesn't see this as reflecting the emergence of a new structure in personality. Rather, it reflects a change in how the ego synthesizes and integrates in its efforts to adapt to the world.

The next stage of ego development is called the *conformist* stage. Children attain it by starting to link their own welfare and security to that of a group (family or peers). This is when rules start to be truly internalized. This change requires developing a sense of trust in the group. Rules no longer are seen as ways to avoid punishment. They're used because they reflect social consensus about how to act. Conformists obey rules precisely because the group has them. Little distinction is made between rules that matter and those that don't. Rules are rules. The power of rules comes from their social basis. Thus, the punishments that are most effective during this stage involve social disapproval ("You let us down" or "We don't like what you did").

At this stage, the ego is preoccupied with issues of reputation and social appearance. The appearances are one dimensional, though. Life is seen in stereotypes. People at the conformist level often seem very conventional, but that's not a reliable clue to being at the conformist level. Indeed, real conformists often appear radically different from "most" people. At the same time, though, they're conforming closely to the norms of their own social group. Many adolescents display this pattern, and some people never outgrow it. Control of impulses is regulated by more shame (from looking bad to the group) than in previous stages (Einstein & Lanning, 1998).

The next stage (Loevinger, 1987) seems to be the most common level of ego development among Americans between ages 16 and 26 (Holt, 1980). It's called the *self-aware* level. The name reflects the fact that the person in this stage is seeing—for the first time—multiple possibilities for the self.

Loevinger describes this stage by asking what pressures might move a person beyond conformity. She says that people move on when they come to see they don't fit the "perfect person" stereotype held out to them by conformist thinking. Such a perception seems to depend on developing a greater capacity for (or tendency toward) introspection. During this stage, the person begins to differentiate "what I am" from "what I ought to be." People at this level realize that rules of conduct often have qualifications or exceptions. You can do this "if you're old enough." You can't do this "until you're married." Despite a developing inner complexity, however, people at this stage are still basically conformists in their actions.

One more cognitive change seems to be needed for movement into the *conscientious* stage: an awareness of the fact that events have multiple meanings. This awareness makes it possible to understand and assimilate abstract moral rules. Abstract rules eventually matter more than group-consensus rules. The weakening influence of consensus means that morality now is truly internalized. During this stage and from now on, shame becomes less important in keeping people from breaking moral codes. Loevinger (1987) holds that the distinctive mark of this stage is self-evaluated standards. That is, you approve or disapprove of your conduct because of what you personally believe, not because of the wishes of some social group.

The life of the person at the conscientious stage is richer and more complex than was possible at earlier stages. Instead of seeing other people as just good or bad, you see them as complicated, with good and bad qualities. Achievement is valued for its own sake, rather than as a way to gain advantage over someone else (as in the self-protective stage) or as a way to gain social recognition (as in the conformist stage). Fitting this, there's evidence that women who reach the conscientious stage by middle age also increase in the qualities of *achievement via independence* and *tolerance* during that period (Helson & Roberts, 1994).

ADVANCED STAGES OF EGO DEVELOPMENT: TAKING EVEN MORE INTO ACCOUNT

A transitional level comes between the conscientious stage and the next full stage of development. This transition is called the *individualistic* level. The person at this level has a heightened sense of individuality and lifestyle. There's an emerging tolerance for differences among people concerning these matters. People at the individualistic level also have more appreciation of the fact that a given person is different when in different roles (e.g., wife, mother, daughter, lover, career woman, tennis partner).

These themes are elaborated even more fully as the person moves into the *autonomous* stage. Now the ego is preoccupied with the interdependency among people and the search for self-fulfillment (as opposed to achievement). The person has the capacity to recognize and cope with conflicts among differing needs, differing duties, and combinations of needs and duties. For example, you may need to study all evening for an exam tomorrow, but you also have the duty to "be there" for a friend who's taking the recent death of her father very hard. At the individualist stage, you'd view this conflict as being between your own need and an unyielding environment. In the autonomous stage, you accept the fact that many such conflicts occur intrinsically, even among your own wishes and needs.

The term *autonomous* can be a confusing label for this stage, because the key isn't a desire for one's own autonomy. It's an awareness of *others'* need for autonomy. Along with the ability to deal effectively with your own turmoil comes a greater tolerance for others dealing with their conflicts. Parents who recognize their children's need to learn from their own mistakes display this quality when they let the children make mistakes without stopping them. Loevinger believes that full attainment of this level of ego development (i.e., the ability to use this mode of relating to the world in all of one's interactions) is relatively rare.

The final stage of ego development, which is even more rare (1% of the population), is called *integrated*. Entry into this stage means the person has come to grips with internal conflict and has found a way to satisfy conflicting demands. If necessary, goals that are unattainable or unrealistic are abandoned. In the integrated stage, tolerance for others' viewpoints goes beyond mere tolerance to an intense appreciation of those viewpoints. A conscious attempt is made in this stage to weave the threads of previous stages into an integrated whole.

In summary, Loevinger holds that as the ego passes through these stages of evolution, it acquires greater complexity in its functioning and in its ability to relate and adapt to the world around it. Loevinger also argues that the ego plays the major role in acquiring moral character, impulse control, and internalization of rules of conduct. The ego gradually develops these capabilities over time and experience.

It seems useful to make one last comparison between Loevinger's theory and Freud's. Many qualities that the ego displays in later stages of Loevinger's theory resemble the functions of the superego in Freud's theory. Recall that Loevinger attributes the *lack* of impulse control at an early age to the ego, rather than the id. Similarly, she attributes a moral sense to the ego, rather than superego. From theories such as this, it's clear that ego psychologists elevated the status of the ego partly by ascribing functions to it that Freud had assigned to the id and superego.

RESEARCH ON EGO DEVELOPMENT

Loevinger's analysis of ego development has been studied empirically, but the work is hard to do. One reason is that her model doesn't predict many clear relationships between ego development and overt behavior (Hauser, 1976). Its predictions are more about the mental dynamics that underlie a given behavior. Consequently, much of the research on this theory has been descriptive.

It's known, for example, that older adolescents score higher on a measure of ego development than younger adolescents and that adults score higher than adolescents (Avery & Ryan, 1988). This fits the idea that the characteristics have a developmental progression. Girls seem to develop faster during middle and late childhood, though boys catch up by adulthood (Cohn, 1991). Ego development also relates to development of moral-reasoning capabilities (Lee & Snarey, 1988). This finding establishes convergent validity for both concepts, because there are certain logical similarities between changes in moral reasoning and changes in how the ego deals with reality. In a similar way, ego development has been related to increasing maturity in thinking about interpersonal intimacy (White, Houlihan, Costos, & Speisman, 1990).

Another study obtained evidence on other psychological qualities that should be tied to variations in ego development. Rozsnafszky (1981) studied hospitalized veterans, collecting both self-ratings and observer ratings (made by nurses and therapists) of the participants' traits. These ratings then were related to participants' levels of ego development (Table 10.3). Those at the impulsive or self-protective level showed poor socialization and limited self-awareness. Those at the conformist and self-aware levels were seen as valuing rules, possessions, physical appearance, and social conventions. Those at higher levels displayed greater insight into their own personality and motives. All of these findings are just as would be expected theoretically.

Although studies of behavioral reflections of ego development are somewhat rare, they aren't entirely lacking. There's evidence, for example, that social conformity is greatest among people who are at the conformist and self-aware stage of development. It falls off among people whose development attains higher stages (Hoppe, 1972; Westenberg & Block, 1993). Research has also found that higher ego development relates to higher peer ratings of mature functioning in careers and community involvement (Adams & Shea, 1979). Finally, there's evidence that adolescent inner-city delinquents have lower levels of ego development than nondelinquents (Frank & Quinlan, 1976).

Table 10.3 Observer-Rating Items That Were Found to Distinguish among Three Groups of Male Research Participants. People of one group were at the impulsive or self-protective level of ego development, those of the second group were at the conformist or self-aware level, and those of the third group were at higher levels. *Source:* Adapted from Rozsnafszky, 1981.

Impulsive/Self-Protective
- Exploitive; sees people as sources of supply; *good* seems to mean "good for me"
- Sees what he can get away with; follows rules only to avoid punishment
- Is self-defensive, manipulative, and opportunistic
- Impulsive; when he doesn't get what he wants, he may be self-destructive in an impulsive way

Self-Aware
- Tends to feel guilty if he has not done his duty
- Behaves in a sympathetic, considerate, and helpful manner
- Is concerned with the impression he makes on others
- Compares self to others; wants to be like others (i.e., normal)

More Advanced Stages
- Has insight into own motives and behavior
- Behaves in an ethically consistent manner; is consistent with own behavior
- Is comfortable with uncertainty and complexities; resists seeing the world as black and white
- Values his own and others' individuality and uniqueness

Other research has examined variables that may influence advancement through the stages. It's been found that progress is tied to having a clearer sense of identity (Adams & Shea, 1979) and to being psychologically minded (Helson & Roberts, 1994; Westenberg & Block, 1993). Ego development has also been related to autobiographical memories that emphasize integrating new meanings in life (Bauer, McAdams, & Sakaeda, 2005). Ego development is related to general intelligence, but they are not the same (Cohn & Westenberg, 2004).

Life challenge (in the form of having a successful career) has predicted progression to higher levels of ego development in adult women (Helson & Roberts, 1994). Indeed, even the successful handling of marital separation and divorce seems to promote ego development (Bursik, 1991). It's also of interest that ego resiliency (flexibility in degree of ego control), discussed earlier in the chapter, relates to attaining higher ego development (Westenberg & Block, 1993).

EGO DEVELOPMENT AND THE FIVE-FACTOR MODEL

Does this view of ego development relate in any way to the five-factor model? The available information suggests that the two do not have a lot in common. Einstein and Lanning (1998) found higher ego development related to greater conscientiousness in men but not women. Higher ego development related to greater openness in women but not men. The authors concluded that the two models are best thought of as complementary, as was also suggested by Loevinger (1993).

However, issues of measurement may play a role. Any of the five traits is likely to be manifested differently at different stages of ego development (Hogansen & Lanning, 2001). The five traits are measured by self-reports that don't permit that diversity to emerge. That is, you get to answer only the items you're given, and the items may or may not relate well to how that trait is reflected at your stage of ego development. Hogansen and Lanning (2001) figured out a way to measure the five factors from the sentence completions used to assess ego development. With the five factors scored this way, level of ego development related strongly to openness ($r = .59$) and more modestly to introversion and emotional stability. Whatever constitutes openness to experience seems to go along well with ego development. For the rest of the traits, the earlier conclusion may be right: These are better thought of as complementary models.

Assessment

Throughout this chapter, we've pointed to ways in which ego psychology differs from Freudian psychoanalysis. It's also useful to consider that issue with respect to assessment. Assessment in ego psychology differs from psychoanalytic assessment in two ways. First, ego psychologists are interested more in the ego than in unconscious conflict. As a result, the techniques they've developed focus on assessing qualities of the ego.

A second difference (which goes hand in hand with the first) is a general difference in technique. Given the de-emphasis on the role of the unconscious, it didn't seem so important to try to ease information from the unconscious by projective techniques. Thus, ego psychology shifted away somewhat from projective tests. Some ego psychologists moved all the way to self-report instruments, although most blend projective and self-report methods.

One similarity does remain, however. Ego psychologists are willing (as was Freud) to draw on a wide range of formal and informal sources to obtain clues about personality.

ASSESSMENT OF LIFESTYLES

Some assessment in ego psychology is highly informal. Recall Adler's belief that people form lifestyles. Your lifestyle leads you to be especially attuned to certain kinds of inferiorities and to deal with them in a characteristic way.

How do you identify a person's lifestyle? Adler believed a lifestyle can be identified by asking the person about his or her earliest memories from childhood or infancy. Adler thought the nature of these memories gives a clue to the themes playing themselves out in the person's life, an idea that has been borne out in research (Bruhn & Schiffman, 1982). In this research, people who saw themselves as having control over events in their lives reported early memories of mastery over the environment. People who saw themselves as having little control tended to recall experiences in which they were passive and events were beyond their control.

Interestingly enough, Adler didn't think it was important that the memories be accurate. What's important is how people view the experiences they recall. It's *how the person looks at the event* that identifies the person's concerns, the inferiority feelings, and the domains in which the person is striving for superiority. Adler believed, in fact, that memories are likely to be distorted by lifestyle (cf. Ross, 1989). For example, if your lifestyle is organized around the idea that others don't give you enough credit, then your memories will tend to reflect that idea. Although any memories can be revealing, Adler felt that a person's earliest memories reveal the most, because they reflect the person's fundamental view of life. "It offers us an opportunity to see at one glance what he has taken as the starting point for his development" (Adler, 1956, p. 351).

Adler collected interesting illustrations of links between early memories and lifestyle. An example is a man whose life was filled with anxiety and jealousy over the possibility that others would be preferred to him. His earliest memory was of being held by his mother and then being put down so she could pick up his younger brother. Adler's own first memories were of illness and death, and his lifestyle oriented around pursuit of a career in medicine (see also Box 10.3). Indeed, Adler found that among a group of medical doctors, memories of serious illness or a death in the family were frequently reported as first memories.

ASSESSMENT OF LEVEL OF EGO DEVELOPMENT

Another aspect of ego functioning that can be useful to assess is level of ego development. Loevinger's analysis of the stages of ego development has been used to create a systematic measure called the Sentence Completion Test for Ego Development (Loevinger & Wessler, 1970; for a more recent manual, see Hy & Loevinger, 1996). It consists of a series of partial sentences to which the person writes an ending. Thus, its format is projective. Unlike most projective tests, though, it has good reliability and validity (Lilienfeld, Wood, & Garb, 2000).

Each response is classified as reflecting one of the stages in Loevinger's model, from the impulsive stage onward (primitive earlier stages can't be measured with this test). Examples of responses reflecting various stages are in Table 10.4. The codings given to each response are entered into a formula, yielding an index of the person's overall ego development. Scorers who've been trained carefully show high interjudge reliability, and there's evidence of high internal consistency and test–retest reliability as well (Redmore & Waldman, 1975). This test was used to assess stage of ego development in the research done on Loevinger's theory discussed earlier in the chapter.

Table 10.4 Examples of Responses to a Sentence-Completion Item and the Stages They Reflect. The item stem, "The thing I like about myself is–," is from the Washington University Sentence Completion Test. *Source:* Adapted from Hy & Loevinger, 1996.

Stage Name	Response	Theme
Presocial	[Not assessed]	
Symbiotic	[Not assessed]	
Impulsive	. . . that I'm nice	Self-gratification
Self-protective	. . . that people like me	Exploitiveness
	. . . my grade in math	
Conformist	. . . that I'm athletic	Stereotypic thinking
	. . . that I don't hate other people	
Self-aware	. . . I'm very considerate of others	Modified stereotype
	. . . that I'm a straightforward person	
Conscientious	. . . that I can forgive and maintain caring feelings	Events in social context
	. . . my ability to look for the good in most things	
Individualistic	. . . that I'm different, but that's OK—I don't want to be like everyone else	Multiple viewpoints
	. . . that I'm really aware of others and how they relate to me	
Autonomous	. . . my personality, my constant striving to become more competent, and yet my ability to be patient	Recognition of mutual autonomy needs
	. . . my outlook on life, the fact that I can take people for who they are, and that I can stand by them while they deal with their problems	
Integrated	. . . the fact that I try to be honest with myself, even though I'm aware that that perception may be delusional	Fully integrated
	. . . that I can think independently and creatively, that I don't judge people I meet, and that I can still be a child when I feel like it	

Problems in Behavior, and Behavior Change

Different ego psychologists have emphasized different aspects of ego functioning, but one theme runs through them all: the key role of the ego's ability to adapt itself to the world. In line with this theme, problems in behavior are seen as reflecting deficiencies in this adaptation.

Ego psychologists view the process of adaptation as never ending. In a sense, then, problems are part of life. People struggle to make themselves better, and difficulties in that struggle are inevitable. Problems become serious only if deficiencies are extreme. Thus, well-being is defined not by whether you confront difficulties but by how well you cope.

INFERIORITY AND SUPERIORITY COMPLEXES

Adler exemplified this view. Recall his belief that inferiority feelings and superiority strivings cycle throughout life. The result usually is that people continue trying to get more proficient at what they do. The issue of inferiority is confronted repeatedly. Problems arise only if feelings of inferiority are so strong as to be overwhelming, preventing you from striving. When feelings of inferiority are that strong, the person is said to have an **inferiority complex**.

BOX 10.3   THE THEORIST AND THE THEORY

Adler's Lifestyle and the Ideas to Which It Led

The work of Alfred Adler provides an excellent illustration of how the elements of a theory often stem from the life experiences of the theorist (see Hoffman, 1994). Several themes that Adler contributed to ego psychology drew directly from his own life, as he was well aware (Bottome, 1939). Let's consider a couple of them.

Perhaps the easiest point to make pertains to what we've just said in the main text about early memories. Adler's lifestyle was organized partly around his interest in medicine and the body. His earliest memories were of illness. Adler's lifestyle also reflected personal anxiety and fear of inferiority, and for good reason. As noted, he was seriously ill as a child, and his parents were once told it was futile to try to educate him. Yet he struggled against these obstacles.

This aspect of his lifestyle is deeply symbolized in another of his early memories. He recalled being about 5 years old and being frightened over the fact that the path to school led through a cemetery (Adler, 1927). The other children weren't afraid, which only exaggerated his feelings of inferiority. One day, in an effort to rid himself of his fear, he ran back and forth through the cemetery, over and over. From then on, he was able to walk through it on his way to school without difficulty.

This memory neatly captures Adler's lifelong tendency to combat his fears by deliberately forcing himself to stand up to them. There's something else, though, that makes this example even more interesting. Many years later, Adler met a former schoolmate and asked him something about the cemetery. The man was bewildered by the question, replying that there hadn't *been* a cemetery. After seeking out other former schoolmates and getting the same reply, Adler finally realized that his memory was wrong. This experience doubtlessly played a role in his view that it doesn't matter whether memories are accurate or not—they're still revealing.

As another illustration of how personal experience influenced Adler's views, consider his analysis of birth order. Adler saw the second born as someone who has a constant sense of inferiority by virtue of being developmentally behind the first born. This can work in the second born's favor, because it serves as a constant spur to strivings. But it can also lead to lifelong competitiveness and jealousy. Of considerable interest is the fact that Adler was second born (1870) and throughout his life felt overshadowed by his older brother, who was a wealthy businessman. (His name, ironically, was Sigmund.) It seems likely that this experience led Adler to argue more generally for the impact of birth order on personality.

Finally, and most generally, recall how Adler's theory focuses on how people experience repeated feelings of inferiority and engage in compensatory strivings for superiority. This pervasive theme reflects virtually all of the experiences of Adler's life. His feelings of inferiority in several domains—physical and psychological—led to a great upward drive in his own behavior. This experience, in turn, helped lead Adler to believe that these same processes characterize everyone.

Adler believed an inferiority complex can have either of two sources. One source is neglect or rejection during development. Being neglected may cause a person to feel unworthy and inferior in ways too large to overcome. This person may develop a lifestyle involving dependency or avoidance. Another source is pampering during childhood. Spoiling can undermine the child's desire to strive for superiority, again producing a mistaken lifestyle.

Sometimes an inferiority complex leads to passivity or avoidance. Sometimes, though, strong feelings of inferiority lead a person to *over*compensate, strive for superiority to an exaggerated degree or in inappropriate ways. Inappropriate striving is seen in a lifestyle that involves efforts to dominate others. Sometimes a lifestyle involves a driven way of striving in which the person has to excel at all costs. Such exaggerated striving is sometimes called a **superiority complex.**

Adler also believed that people with problems tend to use certain strategies to protect whatever small sense of superiority they're able to hold onto. These strategies are aimed at diminishing the sense of inferiority. One strategy is to blame others for your shortcomings or failures. People using this strategy may spend all their time seeking revenge instead of making up the failure. Another strategy is to deprecate the accomplishments or qualities of other people. This implies that your own qualities are better than they actually are. This strategy obviously can be applied when competing with others, but it can also apply elsewhere. For example, having very high standards for a mate (you wouldn't consider someone who's not good looking, intelligent, a successful professional, and rich) may mean you're just trying to ease your own sense of inferiority. If no one out there is good enough for you, you must be *really* good.

Overcontrol and Undercontrol

Another way of thinking about problems returns us to the concept of ego control (Eisenberg et al., 2000). Specifically, being extreme on that dimension (and thus having low ego resilience) can create problems (Block, 2002). Both overcontrollers and undercontrollers lack the flexibility that would help them adapt to the world. Overcontrollers are prone to problems such as anxiety and depression (Eisenberg et al., 2004; Robins et al., 1996).

Undercontrollers, as their label suggests, are out of control. They are more likely to have school problems as adolescents and to have symptoms of conduct disorders (Eisenberg et al., 2004; Robins et al., 1996). As noted earlier in the chapter, they are also more prone to socially problematic behavior such as drug use, aggression, and sexual impulsiveness. Other research has similarly found that people with low self-control get worse grades, abuse alcohol, and have impaired social relationships (Tangney, Baumeister, & Boone, 2004).

Behavior Change

The process of therapeutic change from the viewpoint of ego psychology reflects the overall themes of this line of thought. Therapies practiced by ego psychologists place more emphasis on current problems than on factors in the past that might have led to the problems. The emphasis on current problems fits with a point about assessment in ego psychology. Ego psychologists are more likely than Freudian psychoanalysts to take the person's behavior at face value and not look for symbols and hidden meaning.

The therapist who operates from this viewpoint is more supportive than one who operates from the psychoanalytic viewpoint. On the other hand, the ego psychologist is also clear about where the source of change must lie. That is, problems are viewed as something patients have let emerge in their own lives. The patient thus must take responsibility for dealing with the problems. This tendency to be direct with the patient is another way in which the therapeutic approaches differ.

One consequence of this shift in emphasis is to draw the patient into the therapeutic process as a *collaborator*. This increased emphasis on patient involvement evolves directly from the core idea of ego psychology. That is, the major task of the ego is to promote adaptation to the world. If behavioral problems arise, it's because the ego isn't doing its job. For the ego to alter what it's doing, the patient has to become involved.

Ego Psychology: Problems and Prospects

The group of neoanalysts who came to be known as ego psychologists includes a large number of people. As a group, they proposed a fairly diverse set of ideas. In all cases, however, the ideas reflect the theme that the ego is the most important aspect of personality. This theme is one of two that stand at the forefront of neoanalytic thinking.

Although ego psychology has had its adherents, it's fair to stand back and ask some questions about it. One reasonable question is whether these ideas really have anything at all to do with the psychoanalytic theory from which they evolved. Are these neoanalytic ideas really "analytic"? Or despite the absorption with psychoanalytic traditions, do these ideas actually have more in common with concepts from other areas of personality psychology?

Keep in mind the angle from which the neoanalysts proceeded. Most of them wanted to develop their own ideas, but at the same time, they wanted not to stray too far from Freud. After all, these people were *analysts*. That was their professional identity— to themselves, to one another, and to the world at large. As analysts, they thought of their ideas as amendments to Freud's theory, rather than as separate and distinct theories.

All this orienting toward Freud, however, produced what was in some respects a very narrow view. As a result, the ideas can seem more revolutionary (to analysts) than they are. For example, it's widely believed that Freud created the concept of ego. Ego psychologists certainly saw themselves as building on a Freudian idea. But according to Loevinger (1976), Freud's theory was itself partly a reaction *against an already existing nineteenth-century ego psychology*. She also notes that her own theory of ego development was strongly foreshadowed in the writings of people who came before Freud (e.g., Bain, 1859; Mill, 1962/1859; A. Smith, 1969/1759).

Another comparison is also instructive. Aspects of ego psychology resemble ideas from a group of theorists (discussed later in the book) called *humanistic*. Though the latter group had a starting point very different from that of the neoanalysts, many of their themes resemble themes of ego psychology. Despite this, analytically oriented people tend to ignore humanists. Again, the analytically oriented tend to view their ideas in relation to Freud's theory, rather than in relation to the broader spectrum of ideas in personality psychology.

It's easy to understand why the writings of the ego psychologists disregard nineteenth-century ideas. *Most* psychologists don't know much about nineteenth-century ideas. However, the failure to note other literatures may say something more about ego psychology per se. In particular, psychoanalysis in the United States has long been identified with medicine. Nearly all psychoanalysts begin their training with an MD degree followed by a psychoanalytic specialization. This also was true for early ego psychologists. (Adler and Hartmann, for example, were MDs.) There's a natural tendency to use ideas that are discussed within one's professional circle and to disregard ideas from outside. Because analytically oriented theorists were mostly medical people, they took the ideas of other medical people most seriously.

To some extent, ego psychology began relatively apart from the rest of psychology. It was a branch of psychoanalysis that was growing in the direction of psychology. This changed over the years, as psychologists became more prominent in this group. Theorists such as the Blocks and Jane Loevinger have helped pull ego psychology toward academic personality psychology. This shift has served to integrate neoanalytic ideas more into the mainstream of academic thought. This integration has also yielded an increase in the tolerance and regard that academic psychologists in general have had for psychodynamic conceptualizations.

The evolution of ego psychology appears, however, to carry with it the seeds of a more complete break with traditional psychoanalytic theory. What's unique about psychoanalysis is its emphasis on the dynamics of the unconscious and on the importance of powerful primitive impulses. In large part, ego psychologists have abandoned this conceptual heritage. Although the theories are often still called *psychodynamic,* the dynamics that remain are very, very different from those that Freud asserted. In moving toward greater harmony with the rest of psychology, ego psychology is at the same time leaving Freud behind.

What are the prospects, then, for this view of human behavior? Some of the ideas of this group already have a permanent place in personality psychology—for example, White's ideas about effectance and competence. We are also certain that Loevinger's theory and that of the Blocks will continue to stand as influential views of human development and behavior. If these two theories in particular continue to inspire active research activities, as they do now, ego psychology will continue to remain an essential part of personality psychology.

· SUMMARY ·

Neoanalytic theorists differed from Freud on several points. Many shared a feeling that Freud hadn't given enough emphasis to the ego and its functions. Accordingly, they devised ideas in which the ego plays a more central role. For this reason, they are termed *ego psychologists.*

Hartmann argued that the ego can function to facilitate the id's impulses but can also function autonomously in the service of better adaptation to the environment. He believed that the ego has a separate existence at birth (primary ego autonomy) and that ego functions often continue long after their initial purposes are served (secondary ego autonomy). Others, such as White, emphasized that the ego strives for competence and mastery over the environment. The motive to become more competent serves the goal of better adaptation.

Adler also proposed that people strive for better adaptations, but he assumed a different underlying reason. Adler argued that people repeatedly experience feelings of inferiority in one or another aspect of life and that they respond to those feelings with a compensatory striving for superiority—that is, movement toward greater perfection. Adler used the term *lifestyle* to refer to the person's characteristic constellation of inferiority feelings and preferred way of dealing with them. Some lifestyles are effective, but others (called *mistaken lifestyles*) are not.

Block and Block examined the effects of two other kinds of individual differences: differences in ego control (impulse control) and ego resiliency (flexibility in ego control). Too much ego control is bad; so is too little. Ego resiliency fosters better adaptation. Both qualities relate to behaviors that reflect restraint or impulsiveness, and ego resilience relates to better social development. Evidence suggests that ego control and ego resiliency may combine to form three clusters of persons—overcontrolled, undercontrolled, and resilient. The nature of these clusters converges in an interesting way with the five-factor model from Chapter 4.

Loevinger has examined how the ego's abilities grow and become more complex through a series of stages that extend into adulthood. In early stages, the ego is focused on differentiating itself from others and on affirming its separate existence through expression of impulses. Later, the person begins to learn rules of conduct and to follow them to avoid group censure. Still later, the person begins to appreciate the diversity of viewpoints on existence and experience. People develop through these stages until they exhaust their ability to move further; not everyone goes through all stages. This approach to personality does not connect well at all to the five-factor model, except that ego development seems related to openness to experience.

Assessment in ego psychology partly shifts away from projective techniques toward more objective techniques (though Loevinger's test of ego development is projective). The content of assessment from this viewpoint focuses on the ego and how it's functioning.

From the viewpoint of ego psychology, problems in behavior always are a matter of degree, because no one is perfectly adapted to the world. Struggle is an intrinsic part of life, but serious feelings of inferiority can produce an *inferiority complex* (paralyzing inability to strive) or a *superiority complex* (overcompensatory strivings), either of which is disruptive. Another view of problems is that they derive from being either too high or too low in ego control, both of which represent patterns that are too rigid for successful adaptation.

The approach that ego psychologists take to therapy is similar in some ways to the psychoanalytic approach, but it also differs in important ways. For one, it focuses on the here-and-now problems that the person has, rather than on buried fixations. There is much less of an attempt to probe for deep meanings and a stronger tendency to accept statements at face value. The person seeking treatment is also brought more into the treatment process as a collaborator in the attempt to produce behavior change.

· GLOSSARY ·

Archetypes   Aspects of the world that people have an inherited tendency to notice or perceive.

Collective unconscious   Memories everyone has from human and even prehuman ancestors.

Competence motivation   The motive to be effective or adept in dealing with the environment.

Effectance motivation   The need to have an impact on the environment.

Ego control   The extent to which a person modifies or inhibits impulse expression.

Ego psychology   The neoanalytic theories that give ego functions central importance.

Ego resiliency   The capacity to modify one's usual level of ego control to adapt to new situations.

Feelings of inferiority   The realization that one is deficient in some way, minor or major.

Functional autonomy   The continuance of an act even after its initial purpose no longer exists.

Inferiority complex   Feelings of inferiority bad enough to suggest an inability to solve life's problems.

Lifestyle   A person's pattern of inferiority feelings and manner of striving for superiority.

Mistaken lifestyle   A lifestyle that isn't effective in adapting or attaining superiority.

Need for cognition   A need to think about and impose meaningful structure on experiences.

Organ inferiority   A weakness in an area of the body, making one vulnerable to illness there.

Primary ego autonomy   The idea that the ego exists independently from the id from birth on.

Principle of opposites   The idea that life consists of polarities that oppose and balance each other.

Secondary ego autonomy   The idea that an ego function can become satisfying in its own right.

Superiority complex   Exaggerated striving to excel to compensate for deep inferiority feelings.

Psychosocial Theories

Ever since she was in high school, Christina has had a particular pattern in her love relationships with men. She is close and clingy as the relationship is first being established, wanting almost to be joined to him. Later on, an ambivalent quality emerges. She wants closeness, but at the same time, she does things that drive her lover away: She gets upset with him, gets into arguments over nothing, and isn't satisfied by anything he does to calm her. As he gets more and more irritated by this and their relationship becomes more and more strained, she makes her final move—she breaks up. Even afterward, there's ambivalence. Sometimes she recalls a former lover as being too good for her. Sometimes she thinks of them as no good at all. "Why can't I ever find the right kind of man?" she wonders.

A S THE ego became more prominent in neoanalytic theories and as its functions were examined in more detail, another change was also taking place. There was an increasing emphasis on the idea that personality is inherently social. Theorists began to stress that many issues in personality concern one's relationships with other people.

This is a considerable change of direction. As described in Chapters 8 and 9, Freud's ideas focused within the person. To him, people deal with outside reality only to satisfy impulses better. Even many ego psychologists tended to focus on the internal. They were more interested in how the ego works than in the interplay between it and the social world. This wasn't true of all ego psychologists. For example, though Adler (1930) stressed striving for superiority, he also noted the importance of caring for others, which he saw as necessary to a complete person.

Adler's ideas about the social nature of personality were fairly simple, but others developed more complex ideas on this theme. Those ideas form the basis of this chapter.

Object Relations Theories

We begin with a group of theories that have diverse origins and terminologies but are strikingly similar to one another. This group is referred to by the phrase **object relations** (for overviews, see J. Klein, 1987; Masling & Bornstein, 1994; St. Clair, 1986). In the phrase *object relations,* the object is another *person*. Thus, these theories focus on the individual's relations to others.

The concept of object relations derives from an idea of Freud's (Eagle, 1984). Freud saw an ego cathexis as a bond from the ego to an external object. It forms in order to release id energies effectively. Object relations theories focus on these bonds, but only for people as objects. Here, the point isn't to satisfy the id. Instead, the bond is a *basic ego function*. It's personality's main focus. As in other neoanalytic theories, the emphasis is on the ego (e.g., Fairbairn, 1954).

Object relations theories were developed by several people. They differ in many ways but share two broad themes (J. Klein, 1987; St. Clair, 1986). First, they all emphasize that a person's pattern of relating to others is laid down in early childhood. Second, they all assume that the patterns formed then tend to recur over and over throughout life.

One influential object relations theorist was Margaret Mahler (1968; Mahler, Pine, & Bergman, 1975; see also Blanck & Blanck, 1986). She believed that newborns begin life in a state of psychological fusion with others. In her view, personality development is a process of breaking down this fusion, of becoming an individual who's separate and distinct.

The period when the infant is fused with its mother is called **symbiosis.** Boundaries between mother and self haven't arisen yet (e.g., the infant doesn't distinguish its mother's nipple from its own thumb). At around 6 months of age, the child starts to become aware of its separate existence. Mahler termed this process **separation–individuation.** It involves gradual exploration away from the mother.

The child experiences a built-in conflict between two pressures during this time. The first is a wish to be taken care of by and united with the mother. The second is a fear of being overwhelmed in a merger with her and a desire to establish one's own selfhood. Thus, the child strives for individuation and separation but also wants the earlier sense of union. This conflict is important in adult behavior, as well.

The mother's behavior during this period is important to the child's later adjustment. She should combine emotional availability with a gentle nudge toward independence. If the mother is too present in the child's experience, the child can't establish a separate existence. If the mother pushes too much toward individuation, the child will experience a sense of rejection and loss called *separation anxiety*.

Eventually (at about age 3), the child develops a stable mental representation of its mother. Now, she will be with the child all the time symbolically. The *object relation* is internalized. In the future, the child will use this image in two ways. First, it will be a lens through which the child will view its mother in the future. Second, this internal image will be generalized to other people. In many respects, the child will act toward other people as though they were its mother (and father).

Often, the early years include some stresses—a sense of rejection from a parent or too much smothering fusion. If so, the stresses are carried by your internal object representations into your later life. Because this internalization derives from infant experiences, there can be a lot of distortion. Object representations don't always reflect experiences accurately. What matters, though, isn't what *happens* in childhood but what the child *experiences* as happening.

You may not be very persuaded by the idea that you relate to others as though they were your mother and father. You may think you treat everyone uniquely. An object relations theorist would reply that you think this because you're looking at yourself from *inside* your patterns (Andersen & Chen, 2002). Being inside them, you don't notice them. You notice only variations *within* the patterns. You think the variations are big, but in some ways they're really quite minor.

In this view, the pattern of relating to others that you develop in early childhood forms the core of your way of relating to others for the rest of your life. Indeed, this pattern forms the very core of your personality. You take it for granted, as much as any other aspect of your personality. It's the lens through which you view not just your parents but the entire world.

Self Psychology

Another important neoanalyst was Heinz Kohut. Because Kohut felt that relationships form the structure of the self, his theory is called **self psychology** (A. Goldberg, 1985). Despite this different label, his theory focuses on experiences that others termed object relations.

Kohut began with the idea that people have narcissistic (self-centered) needs that have to be satisfied through others. He used the term **selfobject** to refer to someone who helps satisfy your needs. In early childhood, selfobjects (parents) are experienced as extensions of the self. Later, the term *selfobject* means any person *as he or she is experienced within the structure of the self*. Even then, selfobjects (other people) exist from the self's point of view and to serve the self's needs.

Kohut thought the child acquires a self through interaction with parents. Parents engage in **mirroring:** responding to the child in an empathic, accepting way. Mirroring gratifies the child's narcissistic needs, because it makes the child temporarily the center of the universe. The child's sense of self is grandiose at first. The illusion of all importance must be sustained to some degree throughout development to create a sense of self-importance to be carried into adulthood. It also must be tempered, though, so the child can deal with difficulties and frustrations later in life.

In a healthy personality, the grandiosity is modified and channeled into realistic activities. It turns into ambition and self-esteem. If there are severe failures of mirroring, though, the child never develops an adequate sense of self. This child will have deeper narcissistic needs than other people later in life, because the needs have been unmet. As a result, he will continue relating to other people immaturely. A delicate balance is required here: The parents must give the child enough mirroring to nurture development but not too much. This is similar in some ways to the balance between forces in Mahler's theory regarding separation–individuation and fusion with the other.

Mirroring continues to be important in relationships throughout life (Tesser, 1991). Later mirroring involves **transference** from parents to other selfobjects. This use of that term means that you *transfer* the orientation you've developed to your parents to other people, using it as a frame of reference for them (Andersen & Chen, 2002). In effect, other people become parent substitutes, and you expect them to mirror you as your parents did. This parallels Mahler's idea that the internal object relation pertaining to a parent is used in forming later relationships.

Kohut's conception of love illustrates adult mirroring. He thought of a love relationship as one in which two people are selfobjects for each other. They mirror each other and enhance each other's self-esteem (Kohut, 1977). Thus, a healthy narcissism in normal adults, which Kohut saw as part of life, is satisfied and nurtured properly through mutual mirroring.

Attachment Theory and Personality

The ideas discussed thus far fit in many ways with ideas proposed by theorists interested in the infant's **attachment** to its mother (e.g., Ainsworth, Blehar, Waters, & Wall, 1978; Bowlby, 1969, 1988; Sroufe & Fleeson, 1986). Attachment is an emotional connection. The need for such a connection is a basic element of the human experience (see Baumeister & Leary, 1995).

The first attachment theorist was John Bowlby. He believed the clinging and following of the infant serve an important biological purpose. They keep the infant close to the mother. That, in turn, increases the infant's chances of survival.

A basic theme in attachment theory is that mothers (and others) who are responsive to the infant create a secure base for the child. The infant needs to know that the major person in his or her life is *dependable*—is there whenever needed. This sense of security gives the child a base from which to explore the world. It also provides a place of comfort (a safe haven) when the child is threatened (see Figure 11.1).

Attachment theorists also believe that the child builds implicit mental "working models" of the self, others, and the nature of relationships. These working models are later used to relate to the world (Bowlby, 1969). This idea resembles both Mahler's beliefs about internalized object representations and Kohut's beliefs about selfobjects.

To assess infant attachment, Mary Ainsworth and her colleagues devised a procedure called the **strange situation** (Ainsworth et al., 1978). This is a series of events involving the infant's mother and a stranger. Of special relevance are two times when the infant is left alone with the stranger and then the mother returns. Assessors observe the infant throughout, paying special attention to its responses to the mother's return.

This procedure has identified several patterns. *Secure attachment* is shown by normal distress when the mother leaves and happy enthusiasm when she returns. There are also two main types of *insecure attachment*. An *ambivalent* (or *resistant*) baby is clingy and becomes very upset when mother leaves. The response to the mother's return mixes approach with rejection and anger. The infant seeks contact with the mother but then angrily resists all efforts to be soothed. In the *avoidant* pattern, the infant stays calm when the mother leaves and responds to her return by ignoring her. It's as though this infant expects to be abandoned and is retaliating in kind.

Observations made in the home suggest a basis for variations in attachment (Ainsworth, 1983; Ainsworth et al., 1978). Mothers of securely attached infants respond quickly to their infants' crying and return their smiles. They also show *synchronous* behavior—making appropriate replies to a variety of infant

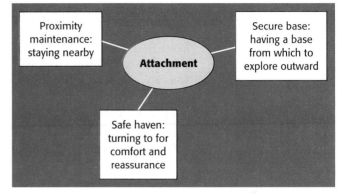

FIGURE 11.1
Three defining features of attachment and three functions of attachment. Attachment provides a secure base for exploration, keeps the infant nearby and safe, and provides a source of comfort. *Source: Adapted from Hazan & Shaver, 1994.*

Early attachment patterns can influence the quality of later social relationships.

actions (Isabella, Belsky, & von Eye, 1989). Mothers of ambivalent babies are inconsistent: sometimes responsive and sometimes not. Mothers of avoidant babies are distant, radiating a kind of emotional unavailability and sometimes being outright rejecting or neglectful. Not surprisingly, the personality of the mother relates to how she interacts with the infant (Kochanska, Friesenborg, Lange, & Martel, 2004).

Interestingly enough, it's not always the actions themselves that differ between groups but rather the timing. For example, mothers of secure and avoidant infants don't differ in how much total time they spend holding their babies. Mothers of avoidant babies, however, are less likely to hold their babies *when the babies signal they want to be held*. Timing apparently can be very important.

On the basis of findings such as these, Hazan and Shaver (1994) characterized the secure, ambivalent, and avoidant attachment patterns as reflecting three possible answers to the question, Can I count on my attachment figure to be available and responsive when needed? The possible answers—yes, no, and maybe—correspond to the secure, avoidant, and ambivalent patterns.

In theory, it's possible to get past an insecure attachment by forming a better one with someone later on. This is hard, however, because insecure attachment leads to actions that alienate others. This interferes with creating a new attachment. The clinginess mixed with rejection in the ambivalent pattern can be hard to deal with. (Recall Christina in the chapter opening, who displays an adult version of this.) So can the aloofness and distance of the avoidant pattern. Each of these patterns causes others to react negatively. That, in turn, reconfirms the perceptions that led to the patterns in the first place. Indeed, people with an insecure attachment pattern appear to distort their memory of interactions over time to make them more consistent with their working models (Feeney & Cassidy, 2003). An insecure pattern thus has a self-perpetuating quality.

At the very least, the patterns do seem fairly stable early in life, though they take slightly different form (see Table 11.1). In one study, infant attachment coded at age 1 could be identified by responses to parents at age 6 for 84% of the children (Main & Cassidy, 1988, Study 1). Secure children were still acting secure, avoidant ones were still withdrawn, and ambivalent ones were still being both dependent and sullen.

Table 11.1 Three Forms of Attachment-Related Behavior, Viewed at 1 Year and 6 Years of Age. *Source:* Adapted from Main & Cassidy, 1988.

Name of Pattern at 1 Year	Behavior at 1 Year	Behavior at 6 Years
Secure	Seeks interaction, closeness, contact with returning parent. Readily soothed by parent and returns to play.	Initiates conversation with returning parent or responds to parent's overture. Remains calm throughout.
Avoidant	Actively avoids and ignores returning parent, looks away, remains occupied with toys.	Minimizes opportunity for interaction with returning parent, looking and speaking only briefly, returns to toys.
Ambivalent	Distress over separation isn't soothed by parent. Child wants contact but shows subtle to overt signs of anger.	Posture and voice exaggerate sense of intimacy and dependency. Shows some resistance, subtle signs of hostility.

ATTACHMENT PATTERNS IN ADULTS

Attachment behavior in childhood is interesting, but more relevant to our goals here is how these ideas relate to adult personality. Research on this question began with the idea that the working models of relationships developed in childhood are carried into adulthood (with modifications along the way). These working models influence the adult's social relationships. In that way, they represent the core of personality.

During the past two decades, research on adult attachment patterns has exploded (see Cassidy & Shaver, 1999; Feeney, 2006; Mikulincer & Goodman, 2006; Mikulincer & Shaver, 2007; Rholes & Simpson, 2004). The first study was done by Cindy Hazan and Phillip Shaver (1987). Participants classified themselves from descriptions as being secure, ambivalent, or avoidant. They then described the most important romance of their life (past or current) on several scales (see Figure 11.2).

Secure adults described their most important love relationship as more happy, friendly, and trusting, compared with adults in the other two groups. Their relationships also had lasted longer. Avoidant adults were less likely than the others to report accepting their lovers' imperfections. Ambivalents experienced love as an obsessive preoccupation, with a desire for reciprocation and union, extreme emotional highs and lows, and extremes of both sexual attraction and jealousy. These people were also more likely than others to report that a relationship had been "love at first sight."

Hazan and Shaver also investigated the mental models these people held on the nature of relationships (see Table 11.2). Secure adults said, in effect, that love is real and when it comes, it stays. Avoidants were more cynical, saying that love doesn't last. Ambivalent subjects showed their ambivalence. They said falling in love is easy and happens often to them, but they also agreed that love doesn't last.

Other research suggests that ambivalent college students are most likely to have obsessive and dependent love relationships (Collins & Read, 1990) and also to be most obsessive about lost loves (Davis, Shaver, & Vernon, 2003). Avoidants are the least likely to report being in love either in the present or in the past (Feeney &

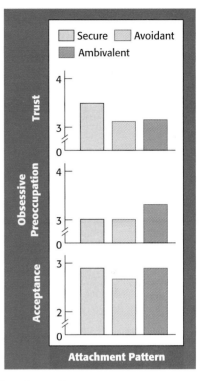

FIGURE 11.2

Adults with a secure attachment pattern report higher levels of trust in their romantic partner than do adults, those with an ambivalent pattern report greater obsessive preoccupation, and those with an avoidant pattern report lower levels of acceptance of their partners' imperfections. *Source: Adapted from Hazan & Shaver, 1987.*

Table 11.2 Mental Models of Love Held by Adults of Three Attachment Groups.
Source: Adapted from Hazan & Shaver, 1987.

Endorsed *more* often by secure adults than others:
   In some relationships, romantic love really lasts; it doesn't fade with time.

Endorsed *less* often by secure adults than others:
   The kind of head-over-heels romantic love depicted in novels and movies doesn't exist in real life.

Endorsed *more* often by avoidant adults than others:
   Intense romantic love is common at the beginning of a relationship, but it rarely lasts forever.
   It's rare to find someone you can really fall in love with.

Endorsed *more* often by ambivalent adults than others:
   It's easy to fall in love.
   I feel myself beginning to fall in love often.

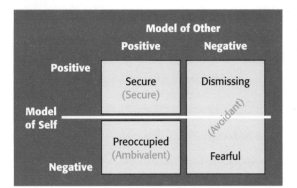

	Model of Other	
	Positive	**Negative**
Positive	Secure (Secure)	Dismissing
Model of Self		*(Avoidant)*
Negative	Preoccupied (Ambivalent)	Fearful

FIGURE 11.3
Combinations of positive and negative views of self and other, yielding four types of attachment patterns. In color are shown the names of the comparable patterns from the three-category model.
Source: Adapted from Bartholomew & Horowitz, 1991.

Noller, 1990), and are the most likely to cope in self-reliant ways after a breakup (Davis et al., 2003). Secures show the most interdependence, commitment, and trust (Mikulincer, 1998; Simpson, 1990). If they experience a breakup, they turn to family and friends as safe havens (Davis et al., 2003). The many ways in which adult attachment affects the course of romantic relationships have become the focus of a great deal of additional research in the past few years (Mikulincer & Goodman, 2006).

HOW MANY PATTERNS?

The proliferation of work on adult attachment has raised many issues, complicating the picture. Early studies used the three main categories from the infancy work, but another approach has also emerged. Bartholomew and Horowitz (1991) started with Bowlby's notion of working models, but focused on models of self and other, rather than models of the relationship. They argued for two dimensions. One is a positive-versus-negative model of self (the self is lovable or not). The other is a positive-versus-negative model of others (others are trustworthy or not). The dimensions are often termed *anxiety* and *avoidance,* respectively (Brennan, Clark, & Shaver, 1998). With this approach, hypotheses often are tested using the two dimensions. Sometimes instead, groups are formed by combining extremes on models of self and other (see Figure 11.3). Two of the groups that result are equivalent to the secures and ambivalents from the three-group approach. However, avoidants from that approach split into two separate groups here, which are called *dismissive* and *fearful,* depending on whether attachment anxiety is also involved.

Each approach has a conceptual strength. The three-category approach nicely conveys the sense that a significant other can be either available, unpredictable, or unavailable. The two-dimensional approach nicely conveys the sense that two separate issues are involved in the attachment response. However, the literature appears to be gradually moving toward the two-dimensional approach.

STABILITY AND SPECIFICITY

Two more questions about this view of personality concern its stability and its generality. If the attachment pattern is part of personality, it should remain fairly stable. Does it? If attachment concerns key figures in one's life, are the same patterns used in casual interactions or groups?

First, let's consider stability. Although findings are mixed, attachment seems moderately stable over fairly long periods of time. Fraley (2002) concluded from a review of studies that a prototype for close relations arises in infancy and doesn't go away, despite new experiences. On the other hand, moderate stability is not total stability. Some people change more than others. Evidence suggests that people who vary in self-portrayal over time are insecure at the core but periodically feel more secure (Davila, Burge, & Hammen, 1997). Research on stability over more extended periods is continuing (Grossmann, Grossmann, & Waters, 2005; Mikulincer & Shaver, 2007).

What about specificity? Does each person have one pattern of relating to others? Or do people have many patterns for different relationships? The answer seems to be many patterns. Even infants sometimes display one pattern to one parent and a different pattern to the other parent. This diversity in relational behavior also appears in adults (Baldwin, Keelan, Fehr, Enns, & Koh-Rangarajoo, 1996; Bartholomew & Horowitz, 1991; Cook,

2000; La Guardia, Ryan, Couchman, & Deci, 2000; Overall, Fletcher, & Friesen, 2003; Pierce & Lydon, 2001). For example, one study had participants define each of their 10 closest relationships in terms of the three categories. Across the 10 descriptions, almost everyone used at least two patterns and nearly half used all three (Baldwin et al., 1996). There's also evidence that people have patterns of attachment to groups, distinct from their patterns for close relationships (Smith, Murphy, & Coats, 1999). There's even evidence that religious beliefs involve yet another pattern of attachment (Kirkpatrick, 1998).

Thus, the ways people relate to others in their lives—even significant others—do seem to have variability. There may be a general orientation for starting new relationships, or a central tendency among the various orientations that a person takes (Crittenden, 1990; Pierce & Lydon, 2001), and it may well derive from early childhood experiences. But adult behavior definitely is more complex than would be the case if each person had just a single way of relating to others.

OTHER REFLECTIONS OF ADULT ATTACHMENT

A surprising range of behaviors has been tied to the attachment patterns that people report for close relationships. Hazan and Shaver (1990) studied relations between attachment and people's orientations to work. Recall that ambivalence involves a sense of insecurity. Consistent with this, ambivalents report unhappiness with the recognition they get at work and their degree of job security. They're also most likely to say their work is motivated by a desire for others' approval. Avoidants report a desire to keep busy with work, and they socialize less during leisure time. Hazan and Shaver suggested that avoidants use work as a way to escape from their lack of relationships.

A good deal of research has looked at how attachment patterns relate to comfort seeking and caregiving in stressful situations (Collins, Ford, Guichard, & Feeney, 2006). In one study (Simpson, Rholes, & Nelligan, 1992), women were told they were going to do a task that creates anxiety. They then waited for five minutes with their boyfriends, who were to do a different task. As anxiety increased, secure women sought support from their partners, talked about being nervous, and so on. Avoidant women did the opposite: The more anxious they got, the *less* they sought support. The men also varied. Among secure men, the more anxiety their partners showed, the more reassuring they were. Among avoidant men, the more anxiety their partners showed, the *less* reassuring they were (see also Kobak & Hazan, 1991). Others have found avoidant men even getting angry when their partners show signs of distress (Rholes, Simpson, & Oriña, 1999). It's interesting in this regard that avoidance predicts greater stress reactivity during discussion of a relationship conflict (Powers, Pietromonaco, Gunlicks, & Sayer, 2006).

This pattern of results has been confirmed and extended in several ways. The tendency to give less support to stressed partners has been shown among avoidant women as well as men (Simpson, Rholes, Oriña, & Grich, 2002). These patterns have also been confirmed by Feeney and Collins (2001) using different methods. They found that avoidance related inversely to a measure of responsive caregiving; avoidance also related inversely to reports of prosocial orientation, trust, and interdependence. Anxiety related to compulsive caregiving and also to higher levels of egoistic motivation and lower levels of trust.

Seeking and supplying support have been looked at in other situations as well. For example, Fraley and Shaver (1998) observed couples at an airport, where one person was leaving on a flight. They found that avoidant women sought contact less, did less caregiving, and displayed more behavioral avoidance than more secure women. Westmaas and Silver (2001) looked at how students reacted to a stranger they thought was being treated for cancer. Avoidants were less supportive in interacting with her than were others. Another study looked at the experience of becoming a new parent (Rholes, Simpson, & Friedman, 2006). Avoidants experienced more stress and found parenting less satisfying compared to people with other attachment patterns.

Additional research suggests that the sense of attachment security makes people more compassionate and responsive to the needs of others in general (Mikulincer & Shaver, 2005). This is true even if the sense of security is increased experimentally, rather than varying naturally (Mikulincer, Shaver, Gillath, & Nitzberg, 2005). The result is that the sense of attachment security promotes altruism for others in need.

Not surprisingly, the motivation for helping others depends on the person's attachment style. Avoidants are more likely to report helping for egotistical reasons (e.g., because they want something in return or because they feel obligated and want to avoid the negative consequences of not helping) and are less likely to report helping because they enjoy helping or have a genuine concern over their partner's well-being (Feeney & Collins, 2003). On the other side, secure persons explain away their partner's unsupportive behavior, whereas insecure persons exaggerate the negative implications of the partner's failure to offer help.

Other research has looked at variation in people's coping responses to stress. One study concerned threats of missile attacks in Israel (Mikulincer, Florian, & Weller, 1993). Avoidants used more "distancing" coping (trying not to think about the situation) than did other people. Ambivalents had higher levels of ineffective emotion-focused reactions (self-criticism, wishing they could change how they felt). Secure people used their social support more than did the other groups.

Recall that one aspect of secure infant attachment is the sense of a secure base. This aspect of attachment has also been examined among adults in several studies. Security relates to an exploratory orientation (Feeney, 2004; Green & Campbell, 2000), perhaps because the sense of security causes people to react more positively to stimuli (Mikulincer, Hirschberger, Nachmias, & Gillath, 2001). Security also reduces the typical negative reactions to outgroups (Mikulincer & Shaver, 2001), suggesting willingness to explore. On the other side of the coin, there's evidence that the avoidant pattern leads people to perceive hostile intent underlying others' behavior (Mikulincer, 1998).

Also of interest is how people with various attachment patterns relate to one another. Not surprisingly, secures are most desired as partners, and they tend to wind up with each other (Collins & Read, 1990). Relationships where the man is avoidant and relationships where the woman is ambivalent are unsatisfying to both partners. On the other hand, there's evidence that avoidant men with ambivalent women tend to be stable pairings (Kirkpatrick & Davis, 1994), despite the dissatisfactions. Why? Avoidant men avoid conflict, which may help the relationship run smoothly. Ambivalent women may work harder at holding things together.

Pairings of avoidants with avoidants and of ambivalents with ambivalents are rare (Kirkpatrick & Davis, 1994). This fits with the idea that people with insecure attachment patterns steer away from partners who would treat them as they were treated in infancy. Avoidants avoid partners who will be emotionally inaccessible, and ambivalents avoid partners who will be inconsistent (Collins & Read, 1990; Kirkpatrick & Davis, 1994; Pietromonaco & Carnelley, 1994; Simpson, 1990).

This pattern of findings also suggests more generally that people are sensitive to the issue that was critical to them earlier. Perhaps in holding the mental model that people will let them down, avoidants consider as partners only people who display more closeness than they'd had earlier. Perhaps in holding the mental model that people are inconsistent, ambivalents consider only people who provide consistency—even if the consistency is consistent distance.

ATTACHMENT PATTERNS AND THE FIVE-FACTOR MODEL

Recall that many people are interested in how various views of personality relate to the five-factor model of trait structure. This has also been examined with attachment patterns in adults. At least two groups have found substantial correlations between measures of adult attachment and two traits from the five-factor model (Carver, 1997a; Shaver & Brennan, 1992). These studies used the three-category view of attachment. They found that avoidants are introverted, secures are extraverted, and ambivalents are high in neuroticism or anxiety proneness.

An even stronger correspondence seems implied by the alternate approach to attachment. As noted earlier, it rests on two dimensions, which are sometimes termed *attachment avoidance* and *attachment anxiety.* Although the focus in each case is on relationships as a context, the dimensions strongly resemble introversion–extraversion and neuroticism. Maybe avoidants are simply not that interested in social connections because they're introverts. That would be consistent with the finding that avoidants encode less when listening to a tape about relationships than do secures (Fraley, Garner, & Shaver, 2000). If we add the twist of viewing extraversion as a desire for social incentives (from Chapter 7) and the idea that neuroticism is essentially anxiety proneness, the fit is even closer. It might even be argued that the attachment patterns represent relationship-focused versions of extraversion and neuroticism.

Do these patterns in personality arise from patterns of parenting (as held by psychosocial theorists)? Or are they manifestations of genetically determined traits, manifestations that simply happen to be social (as held by others)? One study of a very large national adult sample found that reports of interpersonal trauma (e.g., abuse, threat with a weapon, parental violence) related to insecure adult attachment (Mickelson, Kessler, & Shaver, 1997). So did a history of parental depression and anxiety. These findings suggest a social origin to the patterns. Simpson et al. (2002) reported that measures of extraversion and neuroticism did not duplicate the effects of attachment patterns. So even though there is overlap, the attachment dimensions don't seem identical with the "big five" traits.

Erikson's Theory of Psychosocial Development

We turn now to what is probably the most elaborate of psychosocial theories, that of Erik Erikson (1950, 1963, 1968). Erikson adopted Freud's view that personality develops in a series of stages. However, whereas Freud's is a theory of psycho*sexual* development, Erikson's is a theory of psycho*social* development. It describes the impact of social phenomena across life.

Another difference pertains to the age span involved. The stages that Freud described unfold in the first few years of life. In contrast, Erikson believed that personality evolves throughout life, from birth through maturity to death. He also

According to the principle of life-span development, all periods of a person's life are important, infancy through adulthood—even old age.

believed no part of life is more important than any other. Erikson was thus one of the first to propose the idea of **life-span development.** Many consider this to be one of his most important contributions to psychology.

EGO IDENTITY, COMPETENCE, AND THE EXPERIENCE OF CRISIS

The central theme of Erikson's theory is **ego identity** and its development (Erikson, 1968, 1974). *Ego identity* is the consciously experienced sense of self. It derives from transactions with social reality. A person's ego identity changes constantly in response to events in the social world. To Erikson, forming and maintaining a strong sense of ego identity is critical.

A second major theme in Erikson's theory concerns competence and personal adequacy. His stages focus on aspects of mastery. If a stage is managed well, the person emerges with a sense of competence. If not, the person has feelings of inadequacy. This theme in Erikson's theory—that a desire for competence is a motivating force behind people's actions—is similar in many ways to White's ideas about competence, discussed in Chapter 10. One difference is that Erikson's theory was more focused on competence in the social environment.

Erikson viewed development as a series of periods in which some issue is prominent. In his view, people experience a **psychosocial crisis,** or **conflict,** during each stage. The terms *crisis* and *conflict* are interchangeable here. They have a special meaning, though, that differs from the use of either word in day-to-day speech. Here, a crisis is a *turning point:* a period when potential for growth is high but the person is also quite vulnerable. Each crisis is fairly long (none is shorter than about a year), and some are quite long (perhaps 30 years). Thus, Erikson's use of the word conveys the sense of crucial importance more than the sense of time pressure.

The "conflict" in each crisis isn't a confrontation between persons, nor is it a conflict within personality. Rather, it's a struggle between attaining some psychological quality versus failing to attain it. To Erikson, the conflict never ends. Even handling it in the period when it's most intense doesn't mean you've mastered it once and for all. The conflict is always there to some degree, and you confront it repeatedly in different forms throughout life.

Erikson identified eight psychosocial stages. Each focuses on some aspect of transactions with social reality. Each has a conflict, or crisis. Each conflict pits two possibilities against each other, as a pair of opposed psychological qualities. One of the pair is obviously adaptive; the other appears less so. The labels that Erikson gave to the two qualities indicate the nature of the crisis.

People negotiate each stage by developing a balance between the qualities for which the stage is named. The point isn't just to acquire the good quality. In fact, it's important that the ego incorporate *both* sides of the conflict, at least a little. Having too much of the quality that seems good can create problems. For example, if you had only *basic trust* and absolutely no sense of *basic mistrust,* you'd be unable to deal effectively with a world that's sometimes *not* trustworthy.

Nonetheless, successful negotiation of a stage does imply that the balance is weighted more toward the positive value than the negative one. If this occurs, the person emerges from the crisis with a positive orientation toward future events concerning that conflict. Erikson used several terms to refer to this positive orientation: **ego quality, ego strength,** and **virtue** (Erikson, 1964; Stevens, 1983). Once established, these qualities remain a part of your personality.

Erikson was very reluctant to specify age norms for stages. He believed that each person has a unique timetable. Thus, it's hard to say when each stage will begin and end for a person. The ages given here are only rough approximations.

INFANCY

The first four stages parallel stages of psychosexual development outlined by Freud. The first stage

Old Age	Ego integrity vs. despair
Adulthood (to 60s)	Generativity vs. stagnation
Young Adulthood (mid-20s)	Intimacy vs. isolation
Adolescence (12–20)	Identity vs. role confusion
School Age (6–11)	Industry vs. inferiority
Preschool (3–5)	Initiative vs. guilt
Early Childhood (2–3)	Autonomy vs. shame and doubt
Infancy (first year)	Trust vs. mistrust

FIGURE 11.4
Erikson's eight psychosocial stages, the approximate age range in which each occurs, and the crisis that dominates each stage.

(see Figure 11.4) is infancy, roughly the first year. The conflict at this stage—the most fundamental crisis of life—is between a sense of *basic trust versus basic mistrust.* In this stage, the infant is totally dependent on others to meet its most basic needs. If the needs are met, the infant develops a sense of security and trust. This is reflected by the infant's feeding easily, sleeping well, and eliminating regularly. Caretakers can leave the infant alone for short periods without causing too much distress, because the infant has learned to trust that they'll return. Mistrust is reflected by fitful sleep, fussiness in feeding, constipation, and greater distress when the infant is left alone.

The sense of trust is extremely important. It provides a basis for believing that the world is predictable, especially relationships. Trust is enhanced by interactions in which caregivers are attentive, affectionate, and responsive. A sense of mistrust is created by inconsistent treatment, emotional unavailability, or rejection. This portrayal closely resembles ideas concerning object relations, basic anxiety, and attachment patterns earlier in this chapter. A predominance of trust over mistrust gives rise to the ego strength of *hope.* Hope is an enduring belief that wishes are attainable. It's a kind of optimism about life.

EARLY CHILDHOOD

The second stage is early childhood (the second and third years of life). Children begin to focus on gaining control over their actions. The crisis of this stage concerns these efforts. It's about creating a sense of *autonomy in actions versus shame and doubt* about being able to act independently.

Erikson followed Freud in assuming that toilet training was an important event here but for different reasons. To Erikson, acquiring control over bladder and bowels is a way to gain feelings of autonomy (self-direction). Achieving control over these functions means you're not at the mercy of your body's impulses. But this is just one way to gain these feelings. When children interact effectively with people and objects, feelings of autonomy and competence emerge. If the efforts lead to failure, ridicule, or criticism—or if parents don't let the children act on their own—the result is feelings of shame and self-doubt. Management of this conflict properly leads to the

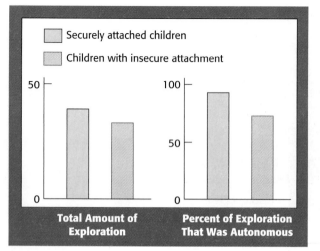

FIGURE 11.5
Children with a greater sense of basic trust and security at 1 year explore more at 2½ years of age than do less securely attached children, and a higher proportion of their exploration is self-initiated, or autonomous. This finding suggests that successful management of the first crisis prepares the child to do better with the second crisis.

Source: Adapted from Hazen & Durrett, 1982.

ego quality of *will:* a determination to exercise free choice.

Much of the research bearing on Erikson's theory focuses on the idea that successful management of one crisis prepares you to deal with the next one. Let's consider how this idea applies to the first two stages. The sense of basic trust is reflected in secure attachment. In one study, attachment was assessed at 1 year; then at 2½ years the children and their mothers came to a laboratory where they could explore a play area (Hazen & Durrett, 1982). Observers coded how many times the child went alone (or led the mother) to a new part of the area—action that reflects autonomy and self-initiation of behavior. They also coded how often the child *was led by* the mother into new parts of the area—action that's *not* autonomous.

As can be seen in Figure 11.5, children who'd been securely attached a year and a half earlier explored more than those who'd been less securely attached. Further, more of the exploration was self-initiated (autonomous) among the securely attached. Conceptually similar results have been reported by several others (e.g., Matas, Arend, & Sroufe, 1978). Thus, a sense of basic trust seems to promote more autonomy later on.

PRESCHOOL

The next period is preschool (from about 3 to 5). Being autonomous and capable of controlling your actions is an important start, but it's only a start. An ability to manipulate objects in the world leads to an increasing desire to exert influence, to make things happen—in short, a desire for *power* (McAdams, 1985). This period corresponds to the stage where Freud saw Oedipal conflicts emerging. As we said earlier, people who are skeptical about the Oedipal conflict tend to treat Freud's depiction as a metaphor for a more extensive power struggle between parents and child, who by now has become willful. Erikson focused on this power struggle.

The conflict at this stage concerns *initiative versus guilt.* Children who take the initiative are seeking to impose their newly developed sense of will on their surroundings. They express and act on their curiosity as they explore and manipulate their world and ask about things going on around them. (This pattern resembles the impulsive stage in Loevinger's theory, described in Chapter 10.)

Acts and words can also be perilous, however. Action that's too powerful can cause others pain. (Grabbing a toy you want can distress another child.) Asking too many questions can become tiresome to adults. If taking the initiative too often leads to disapproval, feelings of guilt will result. Because constantly exerting power does tend to produce some disapproval, initiative eventually must be tempered by restraint. If this crisis is managed well, the child emerges with the ego quality of *purpose:* the courage to pursue valued goals without fear of punishment.

Research has asked whether attaining a sense of basic trust during the first year fosters later initiative. In one study (Lütkenhaus, Grossmann, & Grossmann, 1985), attachment was assessed at age 1 and the children were studied again (at home) at age 3. Those who'd been securely attached were quicker to show initiative in interacting with a stranger than those who'd been insecurely attached. During a game involving a failure, securely attached children responded by increasing their efforts, but the other children decreased their efforts. Thus, the sense of basic trust seems to provide groundwork for the sense of initiative and purpose.

SCHOOL AGE

The next stage corresponds to Freud's latency period (from about 5 to 11). Unlike Freud, Erikson held that this period also has a conflict. He called it *industry versus inferiority*. The term *industry* reflects the fact that the child's life remains focused on doing things that have an impact. But now the nature of those efforts acquires a different shade of meaning. In particular, it's no longer enough just to take the initiative and assert power. Now there's pressure to do things that others judge to be *good,* in two senses. Industriousness isn't just *doing* things; it's doing things that others *value*. It's also doing things in ways that others regard as *appropriate* and *commendable*.

The crisis over this sense of industry begins about when the child enters elementary school. School is aimed at teaching children to become productive and responsible members of society. The school years are also the period when intellectual skills are first tested. Children are urged to do well in school, and the adequacy of their performance is explicitly evaluated.

The school experience also involves learning social roles. Children are beginning to learn about the nature of adult work. They're also being exposed to some of the tools of adult work. In former times, these were tools of farming, carpentry, and homemaking; today, it's more likely to be computers. Another role children are acquiring is that of citizenship. Thus, the child's sense of industry is being judged partly by the acceptability of his or her behavior to the social group.

Children with a strong sense of industry differ in several ways from children with less industry (Kowaz & Marcia, 1991). They tend to prefer reality-based activities over fantasy. They're more able to distinguish the role of effort from that of ability in producing outcomes. They get better grades. And they agree more with statements that are socially desirable.

To emerge from this stage successfully, children must feel they're mastering the tasks set for them in a fashion that's acceptable to those around them. The danger at this stage is developing feelings of inferiority. Such feelings can arise when children are led by others to view their performance as inadequate or morally wrong. Managing the conflict between industry and inferiority results in the ego quality termed *competence:* the sense that one can do things that are valued by others.

ADOLESCENCE

Next comes adolescence, a period that begins with the physical changes of puberty and lasts until roughly age 20. This stage is a larger break with the past than any stage up to this point. Part of the sense of separation comes from the physical changes of puberty. Your body doesn't just get larger during this period but also changes in other ways. You have desires you never had before. You're not quite the same person you used to be. But who *are* you?

Part of the break with the past reflects the fact that you're now beginning to think explicitly about yourself and your life in relation to the adult world. You'll have to find your place in that world, and doing so requires you to decide what roles fit your identity. This, in turn, means knowing who you are.

The crisis of this stage is *identity versus role confusion. Identity* reflects an integrated sense of self. It's the answer to the question, Who am I? The phrase *role confusion* reflects the fact that every self has many facets that sometimes seem incompatible. The greater the incompatibility, the harder it is to pull the facets together, and the more confused you are. Worse yet, you can even be in a position where *no* role seems to fit your identity.

To emerge from adolescence with a strong sense of identity requires the person to evolve in two ways. First, you must consolidate the self-conceptions from the previous stages, merging them in a way that's sensible. Second, this integrated self-view must be integrated with the view of you that others hold. This reflects the fact that identity is something you develop in a consensus with the people you relate to. Only by considering both views does a full sense of identity emerge.

Thus, from Erikson's perspective, identity derives from a blending of private and social self-conceptions. The result is a sense of personal continuity or inner congruence. Erikson placed great emphasis on the importance of developing a sense of identity. In many ways, he saw this as each person's major life task (see also Box 11.1).

If the person fails to form a consolidated identity, the result is *role confusion*, an absence of direction in the sense of self. Role confusion is reflected in an inability to select a career (or a college major that will take you toward a career). Role confusion can also lead people to identify with popular heroes or groups (or even antiheroes) to try to fill the void. The virtue associated with successful identity formation is *fidelity*. Fidelity means truthfulness. It's the ability to live up to who you are, despite the contradictions that inevitably occur among the values you hold.

Box 11.1 The Theorist and the Theory

Erikson's Lifelong Search for Identity

Erikson's life had a distinct impact on the form of his theory, particularly his emphasis on the importance of attaining a sense of identity (see Friedman, 1999). Erikson was born in Germany in 1902 to Danish parents. His father abandoned his mother before he was born, and three years later she married Theodor Homburger, a Jewish physician. Erik wasn't told for years that Homburger wasn't his real father. He later referred to that as an act of "loving deceit."

He grew up as Erik Homburger, a Jew with the appearance of a Scandinavian. Jews saw him as a gentile; gentiles saw him as a Jew. For this reason, he wasn't accepted by either group and he began to form an image of himself as an outsider. By adolescence, he'd been told of his adoption, and his identity confusion was further complicated by the realization that his

ancestry was Danish, rather than German.

As he wandered Europe during his early twenties, his feelings of a lack of identity deepened. He worked as a portrait painter but never developed a clear sense of identity as an artist. Eventually, he took a teaching job in Vienna, at a school created for children of Freud's patients and friends. There he became familiar with a number of psychoanalysts, including Anna Freud, with whom he went on to train as an analyst. In 1933, he moved to the United States, where he established a practice as a child analyst. As Erik Homburger, he was also in the research team that Henry Murray brought together, which led to development of the motive approach to personality described in Chapter 5.

In 1939, Homburger became a U.S. citizen. At that time, he took the name *Erikson*. This was an event—and a choice of name—that unquestionably had much personal meaning, symbolizing his full attainment of the sense of identity.

In later years, Erikson spent time studying methods of childrearing and other aspects of cultural life among the Sioux of South Dakota and the Yurok of northern California. These studies were important for two reasons. First, they led to themes that would permeate Erikson's thinking concerning the importance of culture and society in identity. Second, they revealed to him symptoms of dislocation, feelings of having been uprooted and separated from cultural traditions. The members of these tribes appeared to have lost their sense of identity, much as Erikson himself had done earlier in his life. Erikson also saw similar qualities in the lives of veterans of World War II who returned with emotional difficulties.

From all these experiences, Erikson came to believe that the attainment and preservation of a sense of identity—not wholly separate from but rather embedded in one's own society—was the critical task of growing up. This idea was to stand as one of the major themes of his viewpoint on personality.

A good deal of research has evolved from Erikson's ideas about the development of identity during adolescence, much of it by James Marcia (1966, 1976, 1980) and his colleagues. Marcia argued that two things are important in the formation of an identity. The first is the occurrence of an an **identity crisis.** Marcia's use of the word *crisis* here is similar to Erikson's use. An identity crisis is actively exploring different ways of viewing oneself and giving serious thought to the implications of those views. The second is making an **identity commitment.**

Marcia (1966) distinguished four **identity statuses,** each of which is defined by whether a crisis was experienced and whether a commitment was made. *Identity achievement* is the status of a person who's experienced a period of crisis and then made a commitment. *Moratorium* applies to a person who's now in crisis (exploring alternatives) but has no commitment. *Foreclosure* is the status of a person who's made a commitment but with no crisis—for example, a young man planning to be a surgeon because his father and grandfather were surgeons. In *identity diffusion,* there's no crisis and no commitment. Not surprisingly, either achieving or foreclosing on an identity has a benefit. People in these two groups feel better about themselves than people who haven't made commitments (Prager, 1982).

YOUNG ADULTHOOD

The next stage in Erikson's theory is young adulthood (through the mid-20s). The conflict here concerns the desire for *intimacy versus isolation. Intimacy* is a close, warm relationship with someone, with a sense of commitment to that person. Erikson saw intimacy as an issue in relationships of all kinds, nonsexual as well as sexual.

True intimacy requires you to approach relationships in a caring and open way and to be willing to share the most personal aspects of yourself with others. You also must be open and receptive to others' disclosures. Intimacy requires the moral strength to live up to a commitment, even when it requires sacrifice. Erikson believed people are capable of intimacy only if they have a strong sense of identity.

The opposite pole at this stage is *isolation,* feeling apart from others and being unable to make commitments to them. A person can drift into isolation if conditions aren't right for intimacy—if no one's there who fills his or her needs. Sometimes, though, people withdraw into isolation on their own—for instance, if they feel a relationship threatens their sense of separate identity. Withdrawing can have other consequences, however. People can become self-absorbed to the point that they aren't able to establish intimate relationships in the future (Erikson, 1982). The ego quality associated with the ability to be intimate is *love.* This is a mutuality that subdues the antagonisms of separate identities.

The theme that handling one crisis prepares you for the next one continues here. Erikson said people need a strong sense of identity to be able to attain intimacy. Is this true? One study looked at identity strength in college and intimacy in middle age (Kahn, Zimmerman, Csikszentmihalyi, & Getzels, 1985). Intimacy was assessed in terms of whether subjects had married and, if so, whether the marriage had been disrupted by divorce. There was a clear link between a strong identity and a later capacity for intimacy. The effect differed slightly, however, between men and women (see Figure 11.6). Men with stronger identities were more likely to have married

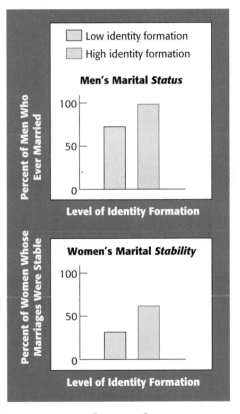

FIGURE 11.6
Percentage of men who had ever been married during the 18-year period after art school and percentage of women who had married and whose marriages remained intact during the same period, as a function of pre-assessed identity formation.
Source: Adapted from Kahn et al., 1985.

One way in which feelings of generativity are displayed is by helping the next generation learn about life.

during the 18 years. Identity didn't predict whether the women married, but among those who *had* married, those with a strong identity were less likely to divorce. Conceptually similar findings have been reported by others (e.g., Orlofsky, Marcia, & Lesser, 1973; Schiedel & Marcia, 1985; Tesch & Whitbourne, 1982).

The other pole of the conflict of this stage—isolation—has drawn interest in its own right (e.g., Peplau & Perlman, 1982; Shaver & Rubenstein, 1980; Weiss, 1973). Two aspects of it are distinguishable from each other. *Social isolation* is a failure to be integrated into a society. People who stand apart from social groups fail to develop a sense of belonging. In contrast, the failure to have intimacy in your life is termed *emotional isolation*—more simply, loneliness.

Emotional isolation feeds on itself. Recall that to experience intimacy requires self-disclosing, opening oneself to others. Lonely people don't do this (W. H. Jones, Hobbs, & Hockenberg, 1982; Mikulincer & Nachshon, 1991). They're also less responsive, ask fewer questions, and seem less interested in what the other person is saying. As a result, they're hard to get to know and are likely to remain lonely.

ADULTHOOD

Young adulthood is followed by adulthood, the longest of the psychosocial stages, typically lasting into the mid-60s. The crisis of adulthood centers around being able to generate or nurture. For this reason, the central conflict in this stage is termed *generativity versus stagnation*.

The desire for generativity is the desire to create things in the world that will outlive you (Kotre, 1984)—children, for example. By creating a new life tied to yours, you symbolically ensure your continuation into the future. Consistent with this idea, McAdams and de St. Aubin (1992) found that men who'd had children scored higher on a self-report measure of generativity than did childless men. Generativity has also been found to relate to a view of the self as a role model and source of wisdom for one's children (Hart, McAdams, Hirsch, & Bauer, 2001) and to a parenting style that fosters autonomy (Pratt, Danso, Arnold, Norris, & Filyer, 2001).

Although generativity is partly a matter of creating and guiding the growth of the next generation, the concept is broader than that. It includes creating ideas or objects, teaching young people who aren't your own children, and anything that influences the future in a positive way (see Table 11.3). Erikson believed that the desire for

Table 11.3 Aspects of Generativity. *Source:* Adapted from Kotre, 1984, p. 12.

Aspect	Description
Biological	Creating, bearing, and nursing an infant
Parental	Raising, nurturing, shaping, and socializing children, providing them with family traditions
Technical	Teaching the skills that make up the *body* of a culture, training a new generation in techniques for doing things
Cultural	Creating, changing, and maintaining a symbol system that represents the *mind* of a culture, passing it on to the next generation

generativity reflects a shift in focus from one close relationship (intimacy) to a broader concern with society as a whole.

Consistent with this idea, highly generative persons express high levels of commitment to assisting the next generation; they also show an integration between that commitment and a sense of agency (Mansfield & McAdams, 1996; see also de St. Aubin, McAdams, & Kim, 2004; McAdams, Diamond, de St. Aubin, & Mansfield, 1997). Once the quality of generativity emerges, it may continue through the rest of one's life (Zucker, Ostrove, & Stewart, 2002).

Adults who fail to develop this sense of generativity drift into stagnation. *Stagnation* is an inability or unwillingness to give of oneself to the future. These people are preoccupied with their own concerns. They have a self-centered or self-indulgent quality that keeps them from deeper involvement in the world around them. There's also evidence that an absence of generativity is related to poorer psychological well-being (Vandewater, Ostrove, & Stewart, 1997).

If there's a positive balance of generativity, the ego quality that emerges is care. *Care* is a widening concern for whatever you've generated in your life, be it children, something in your work, or something that emerged from your involvement with other people.

Old Age

The final stage is maturity, or old age. This is the closing chapter of people's lives. It's a time when people look back and review the choices they made and reflect on their accomplishments (and failures) and on the turns their lives have taken (see also Box 11.2). The crisis here is termed *ego integrity versus despair*. If you emerge from this review feeling that your life has had order and meaning, accepting the choices you made and the things you did, a sense of ego integrity emerges. This is a sense of satisfaction, a feeling that you wouldn't change much about your life.

The opposite pole of this conflict is despair: the feeling that your life was wasted. It's a sense of wishing you'd done things differently but knowing that it's too late. Instead of accepting your life's story as a valuable gift, there's bitterness that things turned out as they did.

Emerging from this life review with a sense of integrity creates the ego quality of *wisdom*. Wisdom involves meaning making and benevolence (Helson & Srivastava, 2002). It is an active concern with life and continued personal growth, even as one confronts the impending reality of death (see also Baltes & Staudinger, 1993; Kunzmann & Baltes, 2003).

The Epigenetic Principle

One more issue to address about Erikson's theory is that a given conflict is presumed to exist outside the stage in which it's focal. In the science of embryology, **epigenesis** is the process by which a single cell turns into a complex organism. For this process to occur requires a "blueprint" at the beginning, with instructions for all the changes and their sequencing. Erikson applied this idea to his theory, saying that there's a readiness for each crisis at birth. The core issue of each crisis is especially focal during a particular stage, but all of the issues are always there.

The principle of epigenesis has several implications. For one, as already indicated, it means your orientation to a particular crisis is influenced by the outcomes of earlier ones. It also means that in resolving the core crisis of any stage, you're preparing solutions (in simple form) for the ones coming later. As you deal in adolescence with the conflict between ego identity and role confusion, you're also

BOX 11.2   IS THERE A MIDLIFE CRISIS?

From Erikson's point of view, the last years of life are spent in review, examining choices that were made, values that were pursued, and passions that were abandoned. Erikson saw this review as coming late in life, after the opportunity to make changes has passed.

Others have also talked about a life review (Gould, 1980; Levinson, 1978; Stewart & Vandewater, 1999; Vaillant, 1977) but one that occurs earlier, around age 40 or so. Given its timing, the phenomenon is popularly referred to as the *midlife crisis*. It's a questioning of the decisions you've made over your adult years, the validity and worth of your goals, the adequacy of your life situation—nearly everything about your existence. It's a time of re-evaluation, but it's also a chance to change the way things are before it's too late. If you don't like your life, change it: remake decisions, rearrange your priorities, change careers, change your marriage (or leave it).

The notion of a midlife crisis rests partly on the typical course of life's major events in Western culture. It's common in the United States to finish college and take a job in one's early

20s and to marry and start raising a family in one's 20s and 30s. Depending on when the children are born, they're growing up and leaving home when the parents are in their 40s or early 50s. Around that time, it's also common to experience the death of one or both of one's own parents. Many changes of midlife are profound ones. Is it any wonder that they seem to cry out for a re-evaluation of life?

Another contributor to a crisis is cultural assumptions about the timing of these events. As a result, people do a certain amount of checking to see whether their lives are "on schedule." If you're in your mid-30s, are you making as much money as you're supposed to be? Are you in line for the career advancement you planned on? If you're nearing 40 with no children, you may hear the so-called biological clock ticking, telling you that you'll never have that experience if you don't hurry. Comparing your life against these markers of a "normal" life can produce a lot of soul searching.

Is there a midlife crisis? We're inclined to feel there's some truth to the idea. We know the feelings we've just written about. (We also know why one of us bought a motorcycle some years ago.) People do experience

regrets at midlife, and that does cause some people (though not all) to make life changes (Stewart & Vandewater, 1999).

Yet the evidence doesn't indicate that a real midlife crisis is all that common. Two longitudinal studies found little support for the idea in fairly large samples (Clausen, 1981; Haan, 1981). On the other hand, the participants in those studies lived through some very hard times—the Great Depression and World War II—and it's possible that having survived those experiences made them less likely to re-evaluate their choices and goals at midlife. Perhaps the midlife crisis is actually a baby-boomer phenomenon.

Alternatively, it may be that the midlife crisis isn't so much a matter of midlife as it is a reflection of a more consistent tendency to worry. This conclusion would fit with findings obtained by Costa and McCrae (1980) concerning life satisfaction over time. They found that satisfaction was relatively stable across a period of 10 years and that dissatisfaction related to the broad trait of neuroticism. Maybe, then, people who are inclined to worry do so throughout life, and it just happens to be more obvious at midlife.

moving toward handling the crisis of intimacy versus isolation. Finally, this principle means that crises aren't resolved once and for all. Your resolutions of previous conflicts are revisited and reshaped at each new stage of life (Whitbourne, Zuschlag, Elliot, & Waterman, 1992).

IDENTITY AS LIFE STORY

The sense of the epigenetic principle is well conveyed in some of the work of Dan McAdams. His work focuses partly on motivations that underlie personality (discussed in Chapter 5) and partly on the idea that people construct their identities as narratives, or life stories (McAdams, 1985, 1993, 2001). In his view, your story is never completed until the end of your life. It is constantly being written. Indeed, it's constantly under revision, just as your identity is constantly evolving.

As in any good book, the opening chapters of your narrative begin setting the stage for things that happen much later. Sometimes future events are foreshadowed; sometimes things that happen in early chapters create conditions that have to be reacted to later on. As chapters pile up, characters reinterpret events they experienced earlier or understand them in different ways. All the pieces eventually come together into a full and integrated picture, and the picture that results has qualities from everything that's happened throughout the story. McAdams thus sees the broad crisis of identity as one that continues to occupy each person throughout life (McAdams, 2001).

Of interest is how categories of narrative themes show up in many people's lives. McAdams and his colleagues have found that highly generative midlife adults often report life stories in which they had early advantages, became aware of the suffering of others, established a personal belief system that involved prosocial values, and committed themselves to benefiting society. McAdams calls these *commitment stories.* Often these commitment stories also contain *redemption themes,* in which a bad situation somehow is transformed into something good (McAdams, 2006; McAdams, Reynolds, Lewis, Patten, & Bowman, 2001). Indeed, the link from the sense of redemption to the quality of generativity appears quite strong (McAdams, 2006). Adults who are low in generativity sometimes have stories involving *contamination themes,* in which a good situation somehow turns bad.

LINKING ERIKSON'S THEORY TO OTHER PSYCHOSOCIAL THEORIES

Let's look back to the theories discussed earlier in this chapter to make a final point. Those theories represent contributions of their own. Yet in a sense, the fundamental theme of each is the same as that of the first crisis in Erikson's theory: basic trust versus basic mistrust. That's a big part of what security in attachment is about. It seems implicit in object relations theories. This issue is also the core of Erikson's own theory, providing the critical foundation on which the rest of personality is built.

Humans seem to need to be able to trust in the relationships that sustain our lives. In the minds of many theorists, that trust is necessary for adequate functioning. People who are deeply mistrustful of relationships or are constantly frightened about possibly losing relationships have lives that are damaged and distorted. The damage may be slight, or it may be significant. Avoiding such mistrust and doubt (or recognizing and overcoming it, if it's already there) seems a central task in human existence.

Assessment

Let's turn now to assessment from the psychosocial viewpoint. In general, assessment here is similar to that of the ego psychologists. There are two aspects of assessment, however, that are specific to this view.

OBJECT RELATIONS, ATTACHMENT, AND THE FOCUS OF ASSESSMENT

One difference concerns what's being assessed. The psychosocial approach places a greater emphasis than other approaches on assessing the person orientation to relationships.

There are several ways in which a person's mental model of relationships might be assessed. Relevant measures range from some that are open ended in nature (e.g., Blatt, Wein, Chevron, & Quinlan, 1979) to structured self-reports (e.g., Bell, Billington, & Becker, 1986). Some measures assess a range of issues pertaining to relationships (Bell et al., 1986). Others focus specifically on the attachments you have to other people in close relationships (e.g., Bartholomew & Horowitz, 1991; Carver, 1997a; Collins & Read, 1990; Griffin & Bartholomew, 1994; Simpson, 1990).

The object-relations measure of Bell et al. (1986) is a good illustration of content assessed from this viewpoint. It has four scales. The *alienation* scale measures a lack of basic trust and an inability to be close. People high on this scale are suspicious, guarded, and isolated, convinced that others will fail them. This resembles avoidant attachment. Another scale measures *insecure attachment,* which resembles the ambivalent pattern, a sensitivity to rejection and concern about being liked and accepted. The third scale, *egocentricity,* assesses narcissism, a self-protective and exploitive attitude toward relationships and a tendency to view others only in relation to one's own needs and aims. The final scale measures *social incompetence,* shyness and uncertainty about how to engage in even simple social interactions.

A different approach to assessment is the open-ended measure of Blatt et al. (1979). It has a coding system to assess the maturity of people's perceptions of social relations. This measure asks you to describe your mother and father. If you're at a low level of maturity, you tend to focus on how parents acted to satisfy your needs. Higher-level descriptions focus more on parents' values, thoughts, and feelings apart from your needs. At a very high level, the description takes into account internal contradictions in the parent and changes over time. This measure reflects a person's level of separation and individuation from the parent.

Play in Assessment

Another facet of the psychosocial view on assessment reflects the emphasis on experiences of childhood as determinants of personality. As a result, this view deals with child assessment more than others. The assessment of children tends to emphasize the use of play as a tool. It's often said that children's play reveals their preoccupations (e.g., Axline, 1947, 1964; Erikson, 1963; M. Klein, 1935, 1955a, 1955b). Play lets them express their concerns in ways they can't do in words. Erikson (1963) devised a play situation using a specific set of toys on a table. The child is to imagine that the table is a movie studio and the toys are actors and sets. The child is to create a scene and describe what's happening. Other techniques use less structured settings, but elements almost always include a variety of dolls (e.g., mother, father, older person, children, baby). This permits children to choose characters that relate to their own concerns or preoccupations.

The play situation is projective, because the child imposes a story on ambiguous stimuli. It often has two objective characteristics, however. First is a *behavioral record*. This includes what the child says about the scene and a description of the scene and the sequence of steps taken to create it. Second, the face value of the child's behavior receives more attention than is usual in projectives. It isn't automatically assumed that the child's behavior has deeply hidden meanings.

Children often reveal their feelings through play.